Guide for Translating Husserl

PHAENOMENOLOGICA

COLLECTION PUBLIÉE SOUS LE PATRONAGE DES CENTRES
D'ARCHIVES-HUSSERL

55

DORION CAIRNS

Guide for
Translating Husserl

DORION CAIRNS

Guide for
Translating Husserl

MARTINUS NIJHOFF / THE HAGUE / 1973

ISBN 90 247 1452 4

PRINTED IN THE NETHERLANDS

PREFACE

This multilingual glossary is a guide for translating writings by Edmund Husserl into English. It has been compiled and improved in the course of about thirty years for my own guidance. Its initial purpose and the tests it has undergone in use have determined its contents. The translations I have made are far from being limited to those I have published or intend to publish. As I read and translate more, occasions will doubtless arise to include more expressions in the glossary and to improve the lists of English renderings I shall thenceforth use. The glossary is given the present title and submitted now for publication because numerous experts have said it would be useful not only to other translators of Husserl but also to his readers generally.

For a translation of such writings as Husserl's the guidance offered by ordinary bilingual dictionaries is inadequate in opposite respects. On the one hand, there are easily translatable expressions for which numerous such dictionaries offer too many equivalent renderings. On the other hand, there are difficultly translatable expressions that any such dictionary either fails to translate at all or else translates by expressions none of which fit the sense. In following such dictionaries a translator must therefore practise consistency on the one hand and ingenuity on the other. Hence the need for a written glossary such as this one.

So far as possible someone who translates such writings as Husserl's into another language should always render the same German expression by the same expression in the other language, and different German expressions by different expressions in the other language. In many cases he must choose among a number of obvious legitimate renderings and, to insure consistency, record his choice. Accordingly this glossary includes German expressions concerning which the only important problem has been that of ascertaining and sticking to the best uniform rendering. For this reason not all the renderings rejected in this glossary are, in my opinion, "wrong."

When collating my English translations with French translations of some of Husserl's writings, I have recorded in this glossary many French renderings of German expressions. Because, as stated at the outset, the glossary is a guide for translating writings by Edmund Husserl into English, I have however recorded no preference in cases where the same German expression is rendered by two or more French ones.

There follow three separate remarks on this glossary and an explanation of abbreviations used in it.

1. *Catchwords* in parentheses I have not yet found in Husserl's writings. They are included because they may nevertheless occur there.

2. *English words* in square brackets or in parentheses are either translations not to be used ordinarily or else parts that may be omitted from a translation.

3. *English translations* separated by commas (not by semicolons) are usually listed in order of preference.

Urbana (Illinois), october 1972

Dorion Cairns

With deep regret we announce the death of Dorion Cairns, the author of this Guide, before printing had been completed. He passed away suddenly in New York on 4th. January 1973.

H. L. van Breda,
President, "Phaenomenologica" Editorial Committee.
Leuven (Louvain), March 1973

ABBREVIATIONS

adj.	adjective.
adv.	adverb.
ant.	antonym.
Arith	Husserl, Edmund: *Philosophie der Arithmetik. Psychologische und logische Untersuchungen. Erster Band*, Halle-Saale, 1891.
B	Husserl, Edmund: *Logique formelle et logique transcendentale*. Traduit par Suzanne Bachelard, Paris, 1957.
BG	Husserl, Edmund: *Ideas: General Introduction to Pure Phenomenology*. Translated by W. R. Boyce Gibson, London and New York, 1931.
Bn	Baldwin, S. Mark, editor: *The Dictionary of Philosophy and Psychology*. Vol. I, 1901; vol. II, 1902.
Boring 1942	Boring, Edwin G.: *Sensation and Perception in the History of Experimental Psychology*, New York, 1942.
Boring 1950	Boring, Edwin G.: *A History of Experimental Psychology*. Second Edition, New York, 1950.
Br	Brentano, Franz.
CM	Husserl, Edmund: *Cartesianische Meditationen und Pariser Vorträge*. Herausgegeben und eingeleitet von Prof. Dr. S. Strasser (Husserliana, Band I), Haag, 1950.
de M	de Muralt, André: *L'idée de la phénoménologie. L'exemplarisme husserlien*, Paris, 1958.
E.u.U.	Husserl, Edmund: *Erfahrung und Urteil. Untersuchungen zur Genealogie der Logik*. Redigiert und herausgegeben von Ludwig Landgrebe, zweite unveränderte Auflage, Hamburg, 1954.
f.	feminine.
F	Farber, Marvin.
Fr.	French.
Idee d. Phän.	Husserl, Edmund: *Die Idee der Phänomenologie*.

Fünf Vorlesungen. Herausgegeben und eingeleitet von Walter Biemel (Husserliana, Band II), Haag, 1958.

Ideen I   Husserl, Edmund: *Ideen zu einer reinen Phänomenologie und phänomenologischen Philosophie. Erstes Buch: Allgemeine Einführung in die reine Phänomenologie.* Herausgegeben von Walter Biemel (Husserliana, Band III), Haag, 1950.

K   Kant, Immanuel.

Krisis   Husserl, Edmund: *Die Krisis der europäischen Wissenschaften und die transzendentale Phänomenologie. Eine Einleitung in die phänomenologische Philosophie.* Herausgegeben von Walter Biemel (Husserliana, Band VI), Haag, 1954.

l.   line.

L   Lauer, Quentin.

Lat.   Latin.

Logik   Husserl, Edmund: *Formale und transzendentale Logik. Versuch einer Kritik der logischen Vernunft,* Halle, 1929.

LU II/1, Einl. *and*
LU, I. ... V. Unters. Husserl, Edmund: *Logische Untersuchungen. Zweiter Band: Untersuchungen zur Phänomenologie der Erkenntnis. I. Teil,* fünfte Auflage, Tübingen, 1968.

LU, VI. Unters.   Husserl, Edmund: *Logische Untersuchungen. Zweiter Band: Elemente einer phänomenologischen Aufklärung der Erkenntnis. II. Teil,* vierte Auflage, Tübingen, 1968.

m. *or* masc.   masculine.

MEU   Fowler, H. W.: *A Dictionary of Modern English Usage,* Oxford and London, 1927.

MS   *Muret-Sanders enzyklopädisches englisch-deutsches und deutsch-englisches Wörterbuch, Hand- und Schulausgabe.* Teil I, Berlin-Schöneberg, 1909; Teil II, ebenda, 1910.

MS 1, 2 ...   first, second ... sense listed in MS.

n.   note.

neut.   neuter.

obs.   obsolete sense or word.

OED   Onions, C. T., editor: *The Shorter English Dictionary on Historical Principles.* 2 vols., Oxford, 1933.

Pf	Pfänder, Alexander: *Logik*. Jahrbuch für Philosophie und phänomenologische Forschung, IV. Bd., Halle a.d.S., 1921, pp. 139–494.
pl.	plural.
PL	Husserl, Edmond: *Méditations Cartésiennes*. Traduit par Gabrielle Pfeiffer et Emmanuel Levinas, Paris, 1931.
q.v.	*quod vide*, which see.
R	Husserl, Edmund: *Idées directrices pour une phénoménologie et une philosophie phénoménologique pures*. Tome premier. Traduit par Paul Ricoeur, Paris, 1950.
RBF	Farell, R. B.: *Dictionary of German Synonyms*. Cambridge, 1961.
Sch	Schutz, Alfred.
sing.	singular.
trln	translation
WH	Wildhagen, Karl, and Héraucourt, Will: *English-German, German-English Dictionary*. Vol. II, Wiesbaden and London, 1958.
WH 1, 2 ...	first, second ... sense listed in WH.
Zeitv.	Husserl, Edmund: *Vorlesungen zur Phänomenologie des inneren Zeitbewusstseins*. Herausgegeben von Martin Heidegger. Jahrbuch für Philosophie und phänomenologische Forschung, IX. Bd., Halle a.d.S., 1928, pp. 367–498.
Ziehen	Ziehen, Th.: *Lehrbuch der Logik ... mit Berücksichtigung der Geschichte der Logik*. Bonn, 1920.

A

Abänderung, (great:) alteration ⟨WH 1, MS 1⟩, (slight:) modification ⟨Bn, WH, MS⟩. Cf. **Abwandlung, Veränderung, Wechsel.**

Abbau, unbuilding, (removal ⟨WH 2⟩). Cf. **Aufbau, Bau.**

Abbild, depiction, (depictive) image, (*copie* ⟨R⟩). So far as possible, save "copy" ⟨WH 1, MS 2⟩ for "Nachbild". Cf. **Abbildung, Bild.**

abbilden, to depicture, to depict, (*dépeindre* ⟨R⟩), (*copier* ⟨R⟩). So far as possible save "to copy" ⟨MS 1, WH, BG⟩ for "nachbilden".

abbildlich, depictive.

Abbildung, depiction, depicturing, (*copie* ⟨R⟩), (math:) representation ⟨Bn, WH 1⟩. Cf. **Abbild, Vorstellung 5.**

Abbildungsbewusstsein, consciousness of a depicturing, (*conscience de copie* ⟨R⟩).

Abbildungsfunktion, depictional functioning, (*fonction de copie* ⟨R⟩). Cf. **Funktion.**

Abblendung, screening off.

abgehoben ⟨adj.⟩, (made) outstanding, (made) prominent, (made) salient, (*mis en relief* ⟨B⟩), (made) conspicuous; differentiated. Cf. **abheben.**

abgehoben ⟨adv.⟩, outstandingly, (*en se détachant* ⟨B⟩).

Abgehobenheit, outstandingness, prominentness, prominency, prominence, saliency, salience, salient, (*relief* ⟨R⟩), (*ce qui se détache* ⟨B⟩); differentiatedness, contrast, conspicuousness. Cf. **abheben, Abhebung, Unabgehobenheit.**

abgelaufen, that has run its course, (of a temporal object:) receded. Cf. **Ablauf, Ablaufen.**

(Abgemessenheit), (*praecisio* ⟨K⟩).

abgeschlossen, self-contained, (*autonome* ⟨B⟩), (*délimité* ⟨B⟩), exclusive ⟨WH, MS⟩, separate; complete ⟨MS⟩. Cf. **geschlossen, vollständig.** | ∼e **Evidenz,** complete evidence, (*évidence se suffisant à elle-même* ⟨B⟩). | **in sich** —, self-contained ⟨WH⟩, (*clos* ⟨B⟩), (*autonome* ⟨B⟩), (*qui a* (ou *ayant*) *son autonomie* ⟨B⟩). Cf. **in sich geschlossen** (*sub* **geschlossen**). | **selbständig** —, self-sufficiently complete, (*autonome* ⟨B⟩). Cf. **selbständig.**

Abgeschlossenheit, self-containedness, (*autonomie* ⟨B⟩).

abgestuft, at different levels, (*de degré en degré* ⟨B⟩). Cf. **Abstufung, Stufe.** | ∼er **Wert,** degree of value.

abgezogen, abstract ⟨MS⟩.

abgliedern, Cf. **gliedern.** | **sich** —, to stand out as a member. Cf. **sich abheben (von)** (*sub* **abheben**).

Abgliederung, disarticulation. Cf. **Gliederung.**

Abgrenzung, delimitation ⟨WH, MS⟩, (*délimitation* ⟨R⟩). Cf. **abschliessen, Begrenzung, Grenze, Umgrenzung, Umschreibung.**

abhebbar, distinguishable, (*que l'on peut détacher* ⟨B⟩).

abheben, to make stand out, to make prominent, (*mettre en relief* ⟨B⟩), to make conspicuous; to remove, (*détacher* ⟨B⟩), to abstract; to distinguish; (to block out). Cf. **abgehoben, kennzeichnen, unterscheiden.** | **abstraktiv** —, to disengage abstractively, (*détacher abstractivement* ⟨B⟩). | **sich** — (**von**), to stand out ⟨WH, MS⟩ (from *or* against ⟨MS⟩), (*se détacher* ⟨R, B⟩), to become (*or* be) prominent; to become (*or* be) distinguished, distinguishable). Cf. **sich abgliedern** (*sub* **abgliedern**), **hervortreten.**

Abhebung, standing out, salience, protrusion; distinguishing. Cf. **Abgehobenheit.** | **zur — kommen,** to become outstanding, to become prominent, etc. Cf. **abgehoben** ⟨adj.⟩.

Ablauf, (of a temporal object:) recession; (of time:) elapse, flow; (of a process;) course. Cf. **Belauf, Fluss, Fortgang, Verlauf.**

Ablaufen, initiation ⟨?⟩, (*développement* ⟨B⟩); (into the past:) receding. Cf: **abgelaufen.**

Ablaufscharakter, recession-characteristic. Cf. **Charakter.**

Ablaufsmodus, recession-mode.

Ablaufsphänomen, recession-phenomenon.

Ablaufsphase, recession-phase.

ablehnen, to reject ⟨WH, MS, RBF⟩, (*récuser* ⟨B⟩), (*écarter* ⟨R⟩), Cf. **abweisen.**

Ablehnung, refusal ⟨MS 1, WH 2⟩; (*refus* ⟨R⟩), rejection ⟨?⟩ ⟨MS 1, WH 3, BG⟩, (*rejet* ⟨B⟩).

ableitbar, deducible ⟨WH⟩. Cf. **deduktiv.**

ableiten, to derive ⟨WH, MS⟩, (*dériver* ⟨B⟩), (*derivare* ⟨K⟩), to deduce ⟨WH⟩; to divert ⟨WH⟩. Cf. **erschliessen 1, folgern, herleiten, schliessen.**

Ableitung, derivation ⟨WH, MS⟩, (*dérivation* ⟨R, B, de M⟩), derivative; (*deductio* ⟨K⟩). Cf. **Abwandlung.**

Ableitungsform, derivative form, (*forme dérivée* ⟨B⟩).

Ableitungsgestalt, derivative formation, (*forme dérivée* ⟨B⟩). Cf. **Gestalt.**

ablösen, to detach ⟨WH⟩, (*détacher* ⟨B⟩), (*dissocier* ⟨B⟩), to sever. | **für sich abgelöst,** detached as (something) selfsufficient, (*détaché d'une manière indépendante* ⟨B⟩). Cf. **für sich.**

abschatten, to adumbrate ⟨WH 1, MS 1⟩, to shadow forth ⟨in OED⟩, (*s'esquisser* ⟨R⟩). | **sich —,** to be adumbrated, to be shadowed forth, (*s'esquisser* ⟨R⟩).

Abschattung, 1. (technical sense:) adumbration ⟨MS 1, WH⟩, forthshadowing (not in OED, but "shadow forth" is), (*esquisse* ⟨R, de M⟩. Not "perspective shading" ⟨F⟩. 2. (of a color, non-technical sense only:) shade ⟨WH, MS⟩, nuance ⟨F⟩.

abschätzig, depreciatory ⟨WH⟩. Not "disdainful" ⟨L⟩. Cf. **Schätzung.**

abscheiden, to separate ⟨WH 1, MS 1⟩, (*séparer* ⟨B⟩). Cf. **scheiden.** | **sich —,** to be isolated, (*se circonscrire* ⟨B⟩).

Abscheidung, separation ⟨WH 1, MS 1⟩, (*séparation* ⟨B⟩), isolation, (*mise à part* (*comme quelque chose séparée*) ⟨B⟩); discrimination, (*considération à part* ⟨B⟩). Cf. **Scheidung.**

abschliessen, to conclude; to delimit, (*délimiter* ⟨B⟩); to shut off ⟨WH⟩. Cf. **Abgrenzung, schliessen, Umgrenzung, umschreiben.**

Abschnitt, (Teilstück): part ⟨WH, MS⟩, (*section* ⟨R⟩). Not "section" ⟨BG⟩.

absehen, 1. to purpose, to aim at ⟨MS⟩, (*avoir en vue* ⟨B⟩). Cf. **beabsichtigen, hinauswollen auf, hinmeinen auf.** 2. to see ⟨RBF⟩. Cf. **einsehen, erschauen, schauen, sehen.** | **es ist nicht abzusehen,** it is impossible to see.

Absehen, purpose, (*dessein* ⟨B⟩), aiming, aim ⟨MS⟩, (*visée* ⟨B⟩), intention ⟨WH, MS⟩, what one has in mind, (intent). So far as possible save "intention" for "Intention." Cf. **Absicht, Abzielung, Strebung, Vorhaben, Ziel, Zielstellung, Zielung, Zweck, Zwecksetzen, Zwecksetzung.** | **im — auf Entdeckung lebend,** living with a view to discovering, (*vivant dans le but de découvrir* ⟨B⟩) | **sein — auf etwas haben,** to have something in view ⟨WH 1, MS 1⟩ | **unser — geht auf etwas,** we are intent on something.

Absicht, purpose ⟨WH 2, MS 2⟩, aim, intention ⟨WH 1, MS 1⟩, (*intentio*

(Baumgarten)), intent. So far as possible save "intention" for "Intention." Cf. **Absehen, Vorhaben, Ziel, Zweck.** | **die — haben,** to purpose, to aim, (to intend ⟨WH, MS⟩) | **in dieser —,** with a view to this. | **mit —,** on purpose ⟨WH⟩, with an aim, (with an end in view).

absichtlich ⟨adv.⟩, purposely ⟨WH 1⟩.

absprechen, to deny ⟨WH 1⟩ (a predicate). Cf. **zusprechen.**

Abstand von, distance from ⟨WH 1, MS 1⟩. Cf. **Ferne.**

abstandslos ⟨adj.⟩, without discrepancy.

abstrakt ⟨adj.⟩, | ∼e **Vorstellung,** objectivation of an abstraction. Cf. **Vorstellung 1.**

Abstraktion, abstraction, ((rarely:) abstracting).

Abstraktum, abstractum, (*abstrait* ⟨R⟩).

Abstückung, division into pieces (*décomposition en éléments* ⟨B⟩), breaking off. Cf. **Stück, Zerstückung.**

Abstufung, number of levels; different levels, (*niveaux différents* ⟨B⟩); (*gradation* ⟨R⟩). Cf. **abgestuft, Stufe.**

abwandelbar, variable, modifiable, changeable; (grammar:) capable of inflexion. Cf. **Veränderlichkeit, verwandelbar.**

Abwandeln, varying, modifying; (grammar:) inflecting. Cf. **Sichabwandeln.**

abwandelnd, | **kontinuierlich sich —,** undergoing continuous modifications.

Abwandlung, 1. variant, (*variante* ⟨B⟩), variation ⟨Sch⟩, (*variation* ⟨B⟩), modification ⟨MS⟩, (*modification* ⟨B⟩), modifying, changing, (change), (*mutation* ⟨R⟩), (derivative ⟨?⟩), (*dérivation* ⟨de M⟩). Cf. **Abänderung, Ableitung, Formenabwandlung, Möglichkeitsabwandlung, Selbstabwandlung, Umwandlung, Urabwandlung, Verwandlung, Wandel, Wandlung, Wechsel, Wendung, Wesensabwandlung.** 2. (grammar:) inflexion ⟨WH⟩, conjugation ⟨WH⟩, declension ⟨WH⟩. | **katego-**riale —, categorial variant, (*variante catégoriale* ⟨B⟩). | **logische —,** logical variant, (process:) logical variation. | **modale —,** modal variant, (*variante modale* ⟨B⟩), (process:) modal variation, (*variation modale* ⟨B⟩). | **retentionale —,** retentional modification, (*variation rétentionelle* ⟨B⟩). | **syntaktische —,** syntactical variant.

Abwandlungsbegriff, variational concept, (*concept qui est une variante* ⟨B⟩), (modificational concept).

Abwandlungsgestalt, variant formation, (*variante* ⟨B⟩). Cf. **Gestalt.**

Abwandlungsmodus, variant mode, (*mode dérivé* ⟨B⟩), (*mode de variation* ⟨B⟩).

abweisen, to reject ⟨RBF⟩, (*repousser* ⟨B⟩), (*démentir* ⟨R⟩). Cf. **ablehnen.** | **sich —,** (*se démentir* ⟨R⟩).

Abwendung, turning away from. Cf. **Wendung, Zuwendung.**

Abziehen, Cf. **abgezogen.**

Abzielen (auf), aiming (at) ⟨F⟩, (*visée* ⟨B⟩). Cf. **Absehen, Abzielung.**

Abzielung, aiming. Cf. **Absehen, Abzielen, Strebung.**

achten auf, to heed ⟨BG⟩, to take heed (that), (*porter attention sur* ⟨B⟩), (to pay attention to ⟨MS 1, WH, BG⟩), (*prêter attention à* ⟨R, B⟩), (*considérer* ⟨B⟩), (*observer* ⟨R⟩). Cf. **aufmerken, beachten, bemerken, beobachten.** | **darauf —, dass,** to see to it that ⟨WH 1⟩, (*veiller à* ⟨R⟩).

Achten auf, heeding of, (paying attention to). Cf. **Achtsamkeit auf.**

achtend, heeding, heedful, (*de l'attention* ⟨R⟩).

achtsam, heedful ⟨WH 1⟩.

Achtsamkeit auf, heedfulness ⟨WH 2⟩ of, attention ⟨MS 1, WH⟩ to, (*observation* ⟨R⟩). Save "heeding" ⟨BG⟩ for "Achten". So far as possible save "attention" for "Attention" and "Aufmerksamkeit".

Achtung, (*observation* ⟨R⟩); respect ⟨WH, L⟩.

Adäquatheit, adequateness, (*adéquation* ⟨R⟩). Cf. **Adäquation** (an), **Inadäquatheit.**

Adäquation (an), adequation (to),

(*adéquation* (*à*) ⟨B⟩), adequacy (to); comparison (with *or* to). Cf. **Adäquatheit, Angemessenheit.** | in — an, as standing in a relationship of adequation to, (*dans une adéquation à* ⟨B⟩). | zur — bringen, to bring to an adequation, (*amener à l'adéquation* ⟨B⟩), to make adequate (to).

Adjektivität, adjectivity ⟨not in OED⟩, (*adjectivité* ⟨B, de M⟩); adjective.

Affektion, affecting, (*affection* ⟨B⟩).

Affirmat, affirmation, (*affirmation* ⟨R⟩). Not "what is affirmed" ⟨BG⟩.

ähnlich ⟨adj.⟩, similar ⟨Lipps trln of Hume, quoted in LU, II. Unters.; Bn; WH; MS; BG⟩, (*semblable* ⟨B⟩), (resembling ⟨Gomperz trln of Mill, quoted in LU, II. Unters.; WH 1, MS 1⟩). Save "alike" ⟨MS⟩ and "like" ⟨WH, MS⟩ for "gleich", q.v.

ähnlich ⟨adv.⟩, similarly ⟨WH 1⟩, (*d'une manière analogue* ⟨B⟩).

Ähnlichkeit, similarity ⟨Gomperz trln of Mill, quoted in LU, II. Unters.; WH 3; MS⟩, (resemblance ⟨Schultze trln of Hume, quoted; Gomperz trln of Mill, quoted in LU, II. Unters.; Bn; MS 1; WH 2⟩), (*ressemblance* ⟨B⟩). Save "likeness" ⟨WH 1, MS⟩ for "Gleichheit", q.v.

Ähnlichkeitsüberschiebung, overlapping (*or* partial coincidence) of similars. Cf. **Überschiebung.**

Aktbegriff, concept of an act. Cf. **Begriff.**

Aktbewusstsein, act-consciousness, (*conscience de l'acte* ⟨B⟩), (*acte de conscience* ⟨R⟩). Not "consciousness as act" ⟨BG⟩. Cf. **Bewusstsein.**

Aktcharakter, act-characteristic, act-character ⟨?⟩. Cf. **Charakter.**

Aktimpression, act-impression, (*impression d'acte* ⟨R⟩). Not "acts of perception" ⟨BG⟩.

aktiv ⟨adj.⟩, active. Cf. **aktuell.** | ~es Gebilde, formation produced actively, (*formation active* ⟨B⟩). Cf. **Gebilde.**

Aktleistung, act-productivity. Cf. **Leistung.**

Aktmaterie, act-material. Cf. **Materie.**

Aktmodus, act-mode, (act-modus ⟨BG⟩), (*mode d'acte* ⟨R⟩).

Aktregung, act-impulse ⟨?⟩, (*amorce d'acte* ⟨R⟩). Cf. **Erregung, Regung.**

Aktsphäre, | ausserdoxische —, sphere comprising extradoxic acts.

aktualisiert, actualized, (*actualisé* ⟨B⟩), actionalized.

Aktualisierung, actualization, (*actualisation* ⟨B⟩); actionalization. Cf. **aktuell** ⟨adj.⟩ 3, **Verwirklichung.**

Aktualität, 1. (temporal): (actual) presentness.
2. (ant. Inaktualität 2, Potentialität:) actuality ⟨MS 1⟩. Cf. **Inaktualität 2, Wirklichkeit.**
3. (ant. Inaktualität 1, Habitualität:) actionality ⟨not in OED⟩. Cf. **Ichaktualität, Inaktualität 1.**
4. activeness ⟨?⟩.
5. (without distinction ⟨?⟩:) (*actualité* ⟨R, B⟩).

Aktualitätsmodus, actionality mode, (*mode d'actualité* ⟨R⟩). Not "actuality mode" ⟨BG⟩. Cf. **Modus der Inaktualität** (*sub* **Inaktualität**).

aktuell ⟨adj.⟩, 1. (temporal:) actual present, (actually) present, (*actuel* ⟨B⟩), existent at the time. Cf. **gegenwärtig, jetzig, vorliegend.**
2. (wirklich, ant. potenziell:) actual ⟨MS 1, BG⟩, (*actuel* ⟨R, B⟩), (actually) occurring. Cf. **daseiend, faktisch, vorhanden, wirklich.**
3. (ant. inaktuell, habituell:) actional ⟨not in OED⟩, actively engaged in (or performed), (active). Not "wakeful" ⟨BG⟩. Cf. **inaktuell.**
4. active ⟨MS⟩. Cf. **aktiv, handelnd, tätig.**
5. (without distinction ⟨?⟩:) (*actuel* ⟨R, B⟩). | — werden, to become actional; to come into (active) play. | ~ e Stellungnahme, active taking of a position, (*prise de position actuelle* ⟨R⟩). Not "actual position assumed" ⟨BG⟩. Cf. **Stellungnahme.**

aktuell ⟨adv.⟩, 1. (temporal:) (actually) at present, (now).
2. (wirklich, ant. potenziell:) (now) actually, (*effectivement* ⟨R⟩). Cf. **wirklich.**
3. (ant. habituell:) actionally.
4. actively.

5. (without distinction ⟨?⟩:) (*d'une manière actuelle* ⟨B⟩). Not "in present experience" ⟨BG⟩.

Aktuntergrund, act-substratum. Cf. **Untergrund.**

Aktvollzug, performing of an (*or* the) act, (*opération d'acte* ⟨R⟩). Not "enacted act" ⟨BG⟩. Cf. **Urteilsvollzug, Vollzug.**

All, All (noun signifying universe since 1593, not obs. in this sense), universe ⟨WH 1, MS 1⟩. Cf. **Ich-all, Seinsall, Weltall.**

Alleinheit, all-inclusive unity. (*totalité une* ⟨B⟩). Cf. **Einheit.**

allgemein ⟨adj.⟩, universal ⟨WH 1, RBF 1, MS 2, BG⟩, (*universel* ⟨B⟩), (*universalis* ⟨K⟩), of something (*or* the *or* a) universal, (*de caractère universel* ⟨R⟩), common ⟨WH 3, MS⟩ (to all), (rarely:) general ⟨Gomperz trln of Mill, Lipps trln of Hume, Ueberweg trln of Berkeley, all quoted in LU, II. Unters.; MS 1; WH 2; BG⟩, (*général* ⟨R, B⟩), (inclusive). So far as possible save "general" for "general" and "generell". Cf. **formal-allgemein, überhaupt, universal, universell. | ~e Anschauung,** universal intuition. **| ~e Bedeutung,** signification of a universal. **| ~er Name,** common name ⟨Bn⟩, general name ⟨trln of Mill in Arith⟩. **| ~e Vorstellung,** objectivation of a (*or* the) universal, (universal-objectivation). Cf. **Vorstellung 1. | ~erer Gesichtspunkt,** more inclusive point of view. **| Allgemeines,** something universal, (*l'universel* ⟨B⟩). **| ~es Urteil,** universal judgment, (*jugement universel* ⟨B⟩). Cf. **Überhaupt-Urteil. | ~es Vorstellen,** objectivating of something (*or* the) universal. Cf. **Vorstellen 1. | das ~e,** the universal ⟨WH 1⟩, (*l'universel* ⟨B⟩). **| im ~en,** in general, (*en général* ⟨R⟩). Not "speaking generally" ⟨BG⟩.

allgemein ⟨adv.⟩, universally ⟨MS⟩, generally, in a universal (*or* general) manner, (*d'une façon générale* ⟨B⟩). Cf. **generell** ⟨adv.⟩.

allgemeiner ⟨adv.⟩, with greater universality, (*d'une manière plus générale* ⟨B⟩).

Allgemeinheit, universality ⟨WH 1, MS 1⟩, (*universalitas* ⟨K⟩), commonness ⟨MS 2⟩ (to all), (rarely:) generality ⟨Ueberweg trln of Berkeley, quoted in LU, II. Unters.; WH 2; MS 3⟩, (*généralité* ⟨R, B⟩), (*général* ⟨B⟩). Cf. **Generalität, Umfangsallgemeinheit, Wesensallgemeinheit. | prinzipielle —,** absolute universality; universality (of something) as concerned with principles. Cf. **prinzipiell** ⟨adj.⟩. **| prinzipielle ~en,** the universality of principles. Cf. **prinzipiell** ⟨adj.⟩.

Allgemeinheitsbewusstsein, universality-consciousness, consciousness of a universality (*or* of universals).

Allgemeinheitsbeziehung, reference with universality. Cf. **Beziehung.**

All(-)gemeinschaft, universal community, (*communauté totale* ⟨B⟩). Cf. **All, Gemeinschaft.**

Allgemeinvorstellung, (with reference to Twardowski:) universal objectivations. Cf. **allgemein (adj.), allgemeine Vorstellung** (*sub* **Vorstellung**).

Allheit, allness ⟨in OED⟩, universality ⟨Bn, WH 2, MS 2⟩, (*universitas* ⟨K⟩), universal totality, totality ⟨WH 1, MS 1⟩, (*totalité*), (*Totalität* ⟨K⟩). Cf. **Gesamtheit.**

allheitlich, integral ⟨?⟩, (*totalitaire* ⟨B⟩).

Allheitsform, allness-form, (*forme de totalité* ⟨B⟩).

Allmenschheit, total humanity. Cf. **Menschheit 2.**

Allnatur, totality of Nature, (*totalité de la nature* ⟨R⟩), universal Nature. Not "universe" ⟨BG⟩. Cf. **Natur.**

allseitig, all-round, on every side, (*omnilateral* ⟨B⟩). Save "universal" ⟨WH 1, MS 1⟩ for "allgemein" ⟨q.v.⟩ and "universal" ⟨q.v.⟩.

Alterego, other ego, (*alter ego* ⟨B⟩). Cf. **ego.**

an, | — sich, in itself ⟨WH 1, MS 1⟩, (*en soi* ⟨B, de M⟩), intrinsical-

ly. Not "per se". Cf. **für sich, in sich.**
| — **sich seiend,** existing in itself,
(*existant en soi* ⟨B⟩), self-existent.
Cf. **An-sich-sein, seiend.** | — **und für
sich,** in and of itself, (*pris en soi*
(*-même*) ⟨B⟩). Not "in itself and by
itself" ⟨L⟩. Cf. **für sich.**
Analogie, analogue, (rarely:) analogy
⟨WH 1, MS 1⟩, (*analogie* ⟨B⟩).
analytisch ⟨adj.⟩, analytic, of ana-
lytics.
analytisch ⟨adv.⟩, analytically, by
analysis.
analytisch-formal, analytico-formal,
(*analytico-formel* ⟨B⟩).
analytisch-logisch, of (*or* in) analytic
logic, (*de la logique analytique* ⟨B⟩),
(*de l'analytique logique* ⟨B⟩). Cf.
**apophantisch-logisch, formal-lo-
gisch, logisch, rein-logisch.**
andere, | **A~,** others, other egos. |**An-
derer,** someone else, someone other. |
der A~, someone else. | **eines ~n
willen,** for the sake of something
else (*en raison d'un autre* ⟨R⟩). |
jeder A~, everyone else.
ändern, to alter ⟨WH 1, MS 2⟩, (*faire
subir une altération* ⟨R⟩), to change
⟨MS 1, WH⟩, (*changer* ⟨R, B⟩),
(*modifier* ⟨B⟩). Save "to modify"
⟨WH, BG⟩ for "modifizieren". Cf.
**Auffassungsänderung, Einstellungs-
änderung, variieren, Veränderung,
verwandeln, Vorzeichenänderung,
wandeln, Wechsel.**
andeuten, indicate ⟨WH 1, MS 1, RBF,
L⟩, (*indiquer* ⟨R, B⟩), to suggest
⟨WH, RBF⟩. Cf. **anzeigen, bedeuten,
deuten, hindeuten, hinweisen auf,
hinzeigen, vordeuten, zeigen.**
Andeutung, indication ⟨WH 1, MS 1,
L⟩, (*indication* ⟨B⟩), indicating,
foreshadowing. Cf. **Deutung.**
andichten, to attribute fancifully.
Aneinanderreihung, falling into sequence with one another.
anerkannt, acknowledged ⟨WH 1, MS
1⟩, recognized ⟨WH 3, MS 5⟩, ad-
mitted ⟨WH 2, MS 2⟩, (accepted
⟨WH 4⟩). So far as possible save
"accepted" for "geltend" ⟨q.v.⟩.
anerkennen, to acknowledge⟨Ueberweg

trln of Berkeley, quoted in LU, II.
Unters.; WH 1; MS 1⟩, to recognize
⟨WH 2, MS 2, L⟩, to admit ⟨WH,
MS⟩, (*admettre* ⟨B⟩), (to accept
⟨WH⟩). So far as possible save "to
accept" for "hinnehmen", "in Gel-
tung haben (*or* halten)" (*q.v. sub*
Geltung) and "gelten lassen" (*q.v.
sub* gelten). Cf. **annehmen, erkennen.**
Anerkennung, acknowledgment ⟨WH
1⟩, recognition ⟨MS 1, WH 3⟩, (acceptance ⟨WH 2, Br⟩). So far as
possible save "acceptance" for "Geltung" ⟨q.v.⟩. Cf. **Erkenntnis, Erkennung.**
An-etwas-Gefallen-haben, liking. Cf.
Gefallen, Gefallenhaben.
Anfangsphase, beginning-phase.
Anfangspunkt, beginning-point, point
of beginning, starting-point ⟨WH 1,
MS 1⟩.
angeboren, innate ⟨Bn, MS 2, WH 3⟩
inborn ⟨MS 1, WH 2⟩. Not "con-
genital" ⟨Bn⟩.
angelegt sein auf, to be aimed at, to
point toward; to have a tendency
toward.
Angelegtsein auf, pointedness toward
(*disposition à* ⟨B⟩). Cf. **Anlage.**
angemessen, fit ⟨WH, MS⟩, fitting
(*approprié* ⟨B⟩). Cf. **anmessen**
Angemessenheit, fitness ⟨Bn, MS 1
WH⟩, suitableness ⟨MS 2, WH⟩
(adequacy). Cf. **Adäquation, anmessen, Zweckmässigkeit.**
angenehm, agreeable ⟨WH 1, MS 2⟩
(*agréable* ⟨R⟩). Save "pleasant"
⟨MS 3, WH, BG⟩ for "gefällig". Cf
unangenehm.
Angeschautes, the intuited, what i
intuited, what one intuits. Cf. **an
schauen, anschaulich bewusst (***su***
anschaulich** ⟨adv.⟩**), Anschauung.**
angezeigt, indicated. Cf. **anzeigen.**
anhaften, to inhere in, to cling to ⟨WH
1, MS 2⟩, to stick to ⟨MS 1⟩, t
pertain to.
anhaftend, inherent ⟨WH 1⟩ (in), be
longing to (Gomperz trln of Mill
quoted in LU,I. Unters.). Cf. **ge
hörig, zugehörig.**

anheben, to commence ⟨WH⟩, (*commencer* ⟨R⟩).

anhebend, commencing.

Anhieb, commencement.

Animalia, -en, animate beings, (*êtres animés* ⟨R⟩), (*animalia*). Not "animals". Cf. **Tier.**

animalisch, animate, (*animé* ⟨R⟩), of men and other animals, (psychophysical). Not "animal" ⟨WH 1, MS 1, BG⟩. Cf. **beseelt.**

Animalität, the psychophysical, psychophysical being, (*animalité* ⟨B⟩).

anknüpfen an, to relate to, (*rattacher à* ⟨B⟩); to begin with, to start with ⟨BG⟩ (*or* from), (*partir de* ⟨R, B⟩). Cf. **beziehen.**

anknüpfend, related, (*qui s'y rattachent* ⟨B⟩); connective.

Anknüpfung, annexation, connexion ⟨WH 1, MS⟩, (*liaison* ⟨R, B⟩), (literary:) reference. Cf. **Verbindung, Verknüpfung, Zusammenhang.**

Anlage, rudiment ⟨Bn⟩, germ ⟨WH, MS⟩, (disposition ⟨Bn; Kemp Smith trln of K; Buchenau trln of Descartes' "*dispositio*"; WH; MS⟩), (pathological:) *predisposition* ⟨Bn, WH⟩, (attitude ⟨Boring 1950⟩). But consult WH and RBF. Cf. **angelegt sein auf, Angelegt sein.**

anmessen, to fit, (*approprier* ⟨B⟩). Cf. **angemessen, Angemessenheit.**

anmuten, to deem possible, (*supputer* ⟨R⟩). | **sich — als etwas,** to suggest itself as possibly something, (*laisser supputer quelque chose* ⟨R⟩).

Anmutung, deeming possible, (*supputation* ⟨R⟩), (*supposition* ⟨B⟩), Not "suggestion" ⟨BG⟩.

Annahme, assumption ⟨WH⟩, (*supposition* ⟨B⟩), acceptance.

annehmen, to assume ⟨WH, MS, BG⟩, (*supposer* ⟨R⟩), to take on ⟨WH 3⟩, to adopt ⟨WH, MS⟩, (*adopter* ⟨R⟩), *prendre* ⟨B⟩), to accept ⟨WH 1, MS 1, RBF⟩, (*admettre* ⟨R, B⟩). Cf. **anerkennen, hinnehmen, in Geltung haben** *and* **in Geltung halten (***sub* **Geltung), gelten lassen (***sub* **gelten).**

Annex, (logic or grammar:) adjunct, (*annexe* ⟨B⟩).

Anordnung, ordering. Not "disposition" ⟨WH, L⟩. Cf. **Ordnung.**

Anpassung, fitting, adaptation ⟨Bn, WH 1, MS 3⟩, accomodation ⟨Bn, MS 1, WH 2⟩, conformity ⟨WH 3⟩.

anregen, to evoke, to suggest (Ueberweg trln. of Berkeley quoted in LU, II. Unters.), (to raise), (*stimuler* ⟨B⟩). Not "to occasion" ⟨L⟩. | **eine Frage —,** to raise a question ⟨Gomperz trln of Mill, quoted in LU, II. Unters.; WH 1⟩. | **Phänomene —,** to evoke phenomena.

Ansatz, account, supposed ⟨WH, MS⟩; starting, (statement ⟨WH⟩), rudiment ⟨WH⟩, (*supposition* ⟨R⟩). | **— des Problems,** statement of the problem. | **ausser — bleiben,** to remain (*or* be) let out of account.

anschaubar ⟨adj.⟩, intuitable. Cf. **anschaulich** ⟨adj.⟩.

anschauen, to intuit, (*voir* ⟨R⟩). Cf. **Angeschautes, schauen.**

anschauend ⟨adv.⟩, in an intuiting, (*dans une intuition* ⟨R⟩).

anschaulich ⟨adj.⟩, 1. (broad sense:) intuitional ⟨L⟩, of intuition, to intuition, (*intuitif* ⟨B⟩).
2. (noetic:) intuitive ⟨MS 1⟩, of the intuiting.
3. (noematic or objective:) intuited, as intuited; intuitable ⟨BG⟩. Cf. **anschaubar** ⟨adj.⟩, **intuitiv** ⟨adj.⟩, **unanschaulich** ⟨adj.⟩, **veranschaulichen.** | **— machend,** making (*or* that makes) intuited, (*rendant intuitif* ⟨B⟩). Cf. **veranschaulichen.**

anschaulich ⟨adv.⟩, intuitionally, intuitively, (*intuitivement* ⟨B⟩), (*de façon intuitive* ⟨B⟩), in intuition, for intuition, (*par intuition* ⟨B⟩). | **— bewusst,** of which there is intuitive consciousness, intuited. Cf. **Angeschautes, bewusst.** | **— gegenwärtig,** intuitionally present, (*présent de façon intuitive* ⟨B⟩). Not "intuitively present" ⟨BG⟩.

Anschaulichkeit, 1. (broad sense:) (*intuitivité* ⟨R, B⟩).
2. (noetic:) intuitiveness.

3. (noematic or objective:) intuitability; intuitedness. Cf. **Unanschaulichkeit.** | **in** —, with intuitiveness, (*avec intuitivité* ⟨B⟩).

Anschauung, intuition ⟨Bn, WH, MS, RBF, F, BG⟩, (*intuition* ⟨R, B, de M⟩), (*intuitus* ⟨K⟩), intuiting; (loose sense:) view ⟨RBF⟩. Cf. **Blick, Einsicht, Einzelanschauung, Partialanschauung, Raumanschauung, Schauung, Sonderanschauung, Totalanschauung, Weltanschauung, Wesensanschauung, Zeitanschauung.** | **zur** — **bringen,** to make intuited, (*faire accéder à l'intuition* ⟨R⟩). Not "to bring into my intentional grasp" ⟨BG⟩.

Anschauungsgrundlage, intuitional basis. Cf. **Grundlage.**

anschauungsleer, devoid of intuition.

Anschauungsrichtung, direction of intuition. Cf. **Richtung.**

Anschauungsweise, mode of intuition. Not "mode of direct vision" ⟨BG⟩. Cf. **Weise.**

anschliessend, following, ensuing, (*qui s'y rattache* ⟨B⟩).

ansehen, (sometimes:) to note (something in something), (*voir quelque chose sur quelque chose* ⟨B⟩). Cf. **merken.**

ansetzen, to put down ⟨MS⟩, to posit, to suppose, (*supposer* ⟨R⟩), to start in, (*tenter,* ⟨R⟩). Cf. **setzen.**

Ansetzung, positings trial, (*supposition* ⟨R⟩). Not "application" ⟨WH, L⟩. Cf. **Setzung.**

An-sich-sein, being-in-itself (or-themselves). Cf. **an sich seiend, Sein.**

Anspruch, claim ⟨WH 1, MS 1, L⟩, (*prétention* ⟨B⟩); something that claims. Cf. **Prätention, Rechtsanspruch, Seinsanspruch, Zumutung.** | — **auf,** claim to ⟨WH 1, MS, L⟩, (*prétention à* ⟨B⟩); demand for ⟨MS 2⟩, title to ⟨WH 2, MS 3⟩. | **Aufmerksamkeit in** — **nehmen,** to engage attention ⟨WH 1, MS⟩, to engross attention ⟨MS⟩. | **den** — **erheben,** to claim, (*élever la prétention* ⟨B⟩). | **Dienste in** — **nehmen,** to have recourse to services ⟨MS⟩. | **ein Werk**

in — **nehmen,** to draw upon a work ⟨WH 1⟩. | **etwas in** — **nehmen,** (usually:) to lay claim to something ⟨WH 1⟩; (*revendiquer quelque chose* ⟨B⟩); to rely on something. Cf. **Inanspruchnahme.** | **Hilfe in** — **nehmen,** to call in help ⟨WH 1, MS⟩. | **in** — **zu nehmen,** reliable, (*qu'il faut revendiquer* ⟨B⟩). Cf. **Inanspruchnahme.** | **Jahre in** — **nehmen,** to require years. | **Kräfte in** — **nehmen,** to tax powers ⟨WH 1, MS⟩. | **Rechte in** — **nehmen,** to vindicate (or assert) rights ⟨MS⟩. | **Zeit in** — **nehmen,** to take up (or encroach on) time ⟨MS⟩.

Anweisung auf, reference to, (*référence à* ⟨B⟩). Cf. **Beziehung, Bezug.**

Anzahl, cardinal number (Arith), (*nombre cardinal* ⟨B⟩); (loosely:) number ⟨WH 1, MS 1⟩, (*nombre* ⟨B⟩); (strictly:) finite cardinal number.

Anzeichen, indicative sign, (indication ⟨WH 1, MS 4⟩), (*indication* ⟨R⟩), (index ⟨F⟩), (symptom ⟨MS 3⟩), (mark ⟨MS 1, F⟩), (token). Not "sign and symbol" ⟨BG⟩. Cf. **Anzeige, Anzeiger, Hinweis, Kennzeichen, Zeichen.**

Anzeichensein, being an indicative sign, indicativeness. Cf. **Zeichensein.**

anzeichnen, to mark ⟨WH 1, MS 1⟩. Cf. **bezeichnen, kennzeichnen, zeichnen.**

Anzeichnen, marking. Cf. **Bezeichnen, Bezeichnung.**

Anzeige, indication ⟨WH, F⟩, indicative relation (LU, I. Unters.). Cf. **Anzeichen, Anzeigen, Hinweis.**

anzeigen, to indicate ⟨WH 1, MS 1, L, BG⟩, (*indiquer* ⟨R⟩), (to indicate or imply ⟨Gomperz trln of Mill, quoted in LU, I. Unters.⟩); (to notify ⟨WH, MS⟩). Cf. **andeuten, bedeuten, hindeuten, hinweisen auf, vordeuten, zeigen.** | **sich** —, to be indicated, (*se signaler* ⟨R⟩), (*se traduire* ⟨R⟩). Not "to be revealed" ⟨BG⟩. Cf. **sich bekunden** (*sub* **bekunden**), **sich zeigen** (*sub* **zeigen**).

Anzeigen, indicating. Cf. Anzeige, Hindeutung.

anzeigend, indicative (of).

Anzeiger, indicator ⟨WH 1, MS 1⟩, pointer, (index). Cf. Anzeichen, Weiser, Zeiger.

anzuzeigend, to be indicated.

apodiktisch, apodictic ⟨WH 1, MS 1, this spelling preferred by OED⟩, (apodictique ⟨R⟩).

Apodiktizität, apodicticity ⟨not in OED⟩, (apodicticité ⟨R⟩), (apodictic character ⟨?⟩ ⟨BG⟩).

Apophansis, apophansis ⟨not in OED⟩, (Apophansis ⟨R⟩).

Apophantik, apophantics ⟨not in OED⟩, (apophantique ⟨R, B⟩).

apophantisch, apophantic ⟨not in OED⟩, (apophantique ⟨B⟩) | ~e Einstellung, focusing on the apophansis, (apophantic focusing), (attitude (ou position) apophantique ⟨B⟩). Cf. Einstellung.

apophantisch-logisch, of apophantic logic, (de la logique apophantique ⟨B⟩). Cf. analytisch-logisch, formallogisch, logisch, rein-logisch.

Apparenz, apparency (obs. in this sense ⟨OED⟩ but needed to reproduce the distinction between "Apparenz" and "Erscheinung" ⟨q.v.⟩).

Apperzeption, apperception ⟨WH 1⟩, (aperception ⟨R⟩).

apperzeptiv ⟨adj.⟩, (noetic:) apperceptive; (noematic:) apperceptional. | ~er Einfall, something coming to mind apperceptionally. Cf. Einfall.

apperzeptiv ⟨adv.⟩, (noematic:) apperceptionally, (de façon aperceptive ⟨B⟩).

a priori, a priori (two words). | — haben müssen, to have by apriori necessity, (devoir avoir a priori ⟨B⟩).

Apriori, Apriori (capitalized), (a priori (italiques) ⟨B⟩), apriority. Cf. das Formal-apriorische (sub formalapriorisch).

apriorisch ⟨adj.⟩, apriori (one word), (a priori ⟨R⟩), (apriorique ⟨B⟩).

apriorisch ⟨adv.⟩, a priori (two words).

Apriorismus, apriori-ism.

Apriorität, aprioriness.

Äquivokation, 1. (a quality:) equivocalness, ambiguity ⟨BG⟩, equivocality, (équivoque ⟨R⟩). Cf. Vieldeutigkeit.
2. (an expression:) equivocality, (équivoque ⟨B, de M⟩).
3. (a fallacy:) equivocation. | ~en, (sometimes:) various significations.

Arbeit, work ⟨MS 1, WH⟩, (travail ⟨B⟩), labor ⟨WH 2, MS⟩, effort ⟨MS⟩, efforts, (investigation). Cf. Erkenntnisarbeit, Leistung, Untersuchung, Urteilsarbeit. | in — nehmen, to take in hand ⟨MS 1, WH 2⟩. | Ordnung der ~en, order in which tasks are undertaken.

Arbeitsmaterial, material to work with, (stock-in-trade ⟨WH 1⟩).

Arithmetisierung, arithmeticizing ⟨not in OED⟩.

Art, 1. sort ⟨Ueberweg trln of Berkeley, quoted in LU, II. Unters.; WH; MS⟩, (sorte ⟨B⟩), (kind ⟨WH, MS, BG⟩), (genre ⟨R⟩), (type ⟨R, B⟩). Not "variety" ⟨WH, BG⟩.
2. (contrasted with Gattung:) species ⟨WH, MS⟩, (espèce ⟨R, B⟩).
3. manner ⟨MS 1, WH⟩, (manière ⟨B⟩), fashion, (façon ⟨R⟩), (specific) way, mode ⟨trln of Mill in LU II/1, Einl.; MS 2⟩.
4. (of an individual:) (specific) character.
Cf. Artung, Beschaffenheit, Bewusstseinsart, Differenz, Eigenart, Erlebnisart, Gattung, geartet, Grundart, Modus, Natur, Schlussart, Seinsart, Sosein, Spezies, Typus, Weise, Wesen, Wesensart. | — und Weise, manner ⟨MS 1⟩, (manière ⟨B⟩), (mode ⟨Gomperz trln of Mill, quoted in LU, II. Unters.; MS 2⟩). | immanenter —, of the immanental sort. Cf. immanent ⟨adj.⟩.

-artig, Cf. ichartig.

Artikulation, see Gliederung.

Artung, 1. sort, species, (espèce ⟨B⟩), kind ⟨L, BG⟩, (type ⟨R⟩); 2. (specific) character, (spécification ⟨R⟩). Not "class" ⟨BG⟩. Cf. Art, Beschaffenheit, Gattung, Natur, Sosein, Spezies, Typus, Weise.

Assoziation, | **Intentionalität der** —, associative intentionality, (*intentionalité de l'association* ⟨B⟩).
Assoziationsverflechtung, associational combination. Cf. **Verflechtung.**
assoziativ, associative, (*associatif* ⟨B⟩), associational, (*formé par association* ⟨B⟩). | **aus ~en Gründen,** because of associations, (*de l'association* ⟨B⟩).
assoziativ-apperzeptiv, because of associational apperception, (*aperceptif et associatif* ⟨B⟩).
Attribution, attributive.
Aufbau, (particularly when contrasted with Abbau ⟨q.v.⟩:) building up ⟨WH 2⟩, (*édification* ⟨B⟩), building ⟨WH 4⟩, (particularly when contrasted with Bau ⟨q.v.⟩:) construction ⟨WH 3⟩, (*construction* ⟨B⟩),'structure ⟨CM *164, l. 19f.*; Bn; WH⟩, (of a structure:) composition ⟨MS 2, WH⟩. Cf. **Bildung, Gebilde, Konstruktion, Struktur.**
Aufbauen, to build up ⟨MS 1, WH 3⟩, (*édifier* ⟨R, B⟩), to build ⟨WH⟩, to construct ⟨WH 2⟩, (*construire* ⟨B⟩). Cf. **bauen, bilden.**
aufbauend, up-building, (*édifiant* ⟨B⟩), building, that builds, constituent, constitutive ⟨WH 1⟩, constructive. Cf. **bildend, formbildend, konstruktiv.** | **sich —,** building up, (*s'édifiant* ⟨B⟩); being built. | **sich — auf,** basing itself on. | **vorgangsmässig sich —,** in process of construction, (*en se construisant à la manière d'événements* ⟨B⟩).
Auf-Begriffe-bringen, conceptualizing ⟨not in OED⟩, (*élaboration des concepts* ⟨R⟩).
Aufbewahrung, keeping ⟨MS 1⟩, preservation ⟨WH 1, MS 2⟩. Save "retention" ⟨Bn⟩ for "Retention".
aufdrängen, | **sich —,** to thrust itself to the fore, (*s'imposer* ⟨R, B⟩), to emerge. Cf. **auftreten.**
auffassen, to take ⟨WH⟩, to construe, to view ⟨WH 3⟩, to apprehend ⟨MS, BG⟩; (*considérer* ⟨R⟩), (*concevoir* ⟨R⟩), (a text:) to interpret ⟨WH⟩, (*interpréter* ⟨B⟩); to formulate. Despite LU, I. Unters. *34* and II.

Unters. *194*, save "to apperceive' for "apperzipieren". Not "to grasp" not "to conceive" ⟨Gomperz trln of Mill, quoted in LU, II. Unters. WH 2; MS⟩; not "to comprehend' ⟨WH 1⟩. Cf. **ausdeuten, auslegen, befassen, begreifen, betrachten, deuten, erfassen, erschauen, fassen Griff, mitaufgefasst, schauen.**
Auffassung, apprehension ⟨Bn, WH 2 MS 2⟩, (*appréhension* ⟨R, de M⟩) (apprehending), construing; (textual:) interpretation ⟨WH, MS, L⟩, conception ⟨WH 1, MS 1⟩, (*conception* ⟨B⟩), (view), (*hypothèse* ⟨B⟩) formulation. Cf. **Ausdeutung, Begriff, Deutung, Dingauffassung, Erinnerungsauffassung, Fassung, Konstruktion, Leerauffassung, Realitätsauffassung, Urauffassung, Vorstellung 7, Wahrnehmungsauffassung.** | **gegenständliche** —, objectival construing. Cf. **gegenständlich** ⟨adj.⟩.
Auffassungsänderung, alteration of construing, (*altération des appréhensions* ⟨R⟩). Cf. **ändern.**
Auffassungsdatum, apprehension-Datum. Cf. **Datum.**
Auffassungsgehalt, apprehensional constituent. Cf. **Gehalt.**
Auffassungsgrundlage, apprehensional basis. Cf. **Grundlage.**
Auffassungsinhalt, apprehension-content. Cf. **Inhalt.**
Auffassungsintention, apprehension-intention.
Auffassungskontinuität, apprehensional continuum. Cf. **Kontinuität.**
Auffassungssinn, apprehensional sense apprehension-sense ⟨F⟩, construing sense.
Auffassungsweise, manner (*or* mode), of apprehension (*or* construing), (*mode d'appréhension* ⟨R⟩), manner of conception, (*mode d'interprétation* ⟨R⟩). Cf. **Weise.**
Aufgabe, (to be done:) task ⟨MS, WH⟩, (*tâche* ⟨PL, B⟩); (to be solved:) problem ⟨WH, MS⟩. Cf. **Frage.**
aufhebbar, Cf. **unaufhebbar.**
aufheben, to annul ⟨WH, MS⟩, to

nullify, to rescind, to abrogate ⟨WH, MS⟩, (*supprimer* ⟨B⟩), to revoke, to do away with ⟨WH, MS⟩, to destroy, to abolish ⟨WH⟩, (of a deed:) to repudiate (*or* reject), (to remove), (to dispel). Cf. **durchstreichen, negieren, unaufhebbar.** | **die Einheit** —, to destroy the unity, (*supprimer l'unité* ⟨B⟩).

Aufhebung, annulment ⟨WH, MS⟩, nullification, rescindment, abrogation ⟨WH⟩, (*suppression* ⟨B⟩), abolition, (removal), (*suspension* ⟨R⟩), (*epochè* ⟨de M⟩). Cf. **Durchstreichung, Nichtigkeit, Selbstaufhebung, Vernichtung, Zunichtemachung.**

aufklären, to clear up ⟨WH 1, MS⟩, to clarify ⟨MS 1, WH⟩, (to elucidate ⟨WH, MS⟩), (to explain ⟨WH⟩). Cf. **erklären, klarlegen, klarstellen.**

aufklärend, | ~e **physiologische Psychologie,** explanatory physiological psychology.

Aufklärung, clarification, (elucidation ⟨WH⟩), (*élucidation* ⟨B⟩). Cf. **Erklärung, Klarlegung, Klärung.**

aufmerken, to pay attention to, to mark ⟨MS 1, WH⟩, (*remarquer* ⟨R⟩). Cf. **beachten, bemerken, gewahren, merken.** | — **auf,** to pay attention to, (to attend to ⟨MS⟩). Cf. **achten auf, beachten, bemerken, gewahren.** | **das Aufgemerkte,** the object of attention, (*ce que l'on remarque* ⟨R⟩).

aufmerkend, | ~er **Strahl,** ray of attention, (*rayon de l'attention* ⟨B⟩).

Aufmerksamkeit, attention ⟨WH 1, MS 1, BG⟩, (*attention* ⟨R⟩). Cf. **Achtsamkeit, Unaufmerksamkeit.**

aufnehmen, to take up ⟨WH⟩, to receive ⟨WH, MS⟩, (*recevoir* ⟨B⟩), to include ⟨WH⟩; (*apprehendieren* ⟨K⟩). | **in sich** —, to take up into itself, (*accueillir* ⟨B⟩ *en soi-même* ⟨R⟩), (*s'approprier* ⟨B⟩), to absorb ⟨WH 1, MS 2⟩.

aufschliessen, to unlock ⟨WH 1, MS 1⟩, to open ⟨WH, MS⟩ up, to disclose ⟨WH⟩.

Aufstufung, cumulation, build-up, climax ⟨MS⟩, (*organisation hiérarchi-*

que ⟨B⟩); increment; (superaddition). Cf. **Sinnesaufstufung.** | **In einer** —, to higher and higher levels, (*dans une succession de niveaux* ⟨B⟩).

auftreten, to make an (*or* its *or* one's ⟨WH⟩) appearance, (*faire son apparition* ⟨B⟩), (to appear ⟨WH⟩), (*apparaître* ⟨B⟩), to occur ⟨WH⟩, (*intervenir* ⟨B⟩), to emerge ⟨WH, BG⟩, to enter on the scene ⟨WH⟩, (to enter ⟨WH⟩), (*s'introduire* ⟨R⟩), (*s'insérer* ⟨R⟩), to present itself *or* oneself ⟨MS⟩, (*se présenter* ⟨R, B⟩), to become presented. So far as possible save "to present itself (*or* oneself)" for "sich darstellen", "sich geben" ⟨q.v.⟩ and "vorliegen"; and "to appear" ⟨BG⟩ for "erscheinen". Not "to figure" ⟨BG⟩. Cf. **sich aufdrängen,** (*sub* **aufdrängen**), **sich zeigen** (*sub* **zeigen**), **zur Erscheinung kommen** (*sub* **Erscheinung**).

Auftreten, making of one's appearance, making-one's-appearance, occurring, (*intervenir* ⟨B⟩), emerging, entering on the scene, (presenting itself), (*se présenter* ⟨B⟩), (appearing), (*apparaître* ⟨B⟩), (*apparition* ⟨B⟩). So far as possible save "appearing" for "Erscheinen". Cf. **Selbstdarstellung, Sich-selbst-darstellen, Sich-selbst-geben.**

aufweisbar, which can be brought to light, (*susceptible d'être exhibé* ⟨R⟩), (*que l'on peut apercevoir* ⟨B⟩). Cf. **ausweisbar, nachweisbar, nachweislich.**

aufweisen, to exhibit ⟨MS 1, WH 2⟩, to show ⟨WH 1⟩, (*montrer* ⟨B⟩), (*présenter* ⟨B⟩), to bring to light, (*expliciter* ⟨B⟩). Cf. **ausweisen, beweisen, erweisen, nachweisen, weisen.** | **sich** — **als,** to prove to be ⟨MS 1⟩.

Aufweisung, exhibition ⟨MS 1⟩, show ⟨MS⟩, (*exposition* ⟨B⟩), discovery, (*explicitation* ⟨B⟩). Cf. **Weisung.**

Aufwickelung, unravelling, (*déroulement* ⟨B⟩).

Auge, | **ins** — **fassen,** see *sub* **fassen.** | **vor** ~n **stehen,** to lie within view. Cf. **vorschweben haben** (*sub* **vorschweben**).

aus ⟨prep.⟩, from ⟨WH, MS, L⟩, (as) coming (*or* arising, *or* springing, *or* deriving, *or* starting, *or* issuing) from, (*à partir de* ⟨B⟩), (*précédant de* ⟨B⟩), (*constitué dans* ⟨B⟩), that comes (*or* arises, *or* springs, etc.) from, (*qui a sa source dans* ⟨B⟩), by virtue of, because of, thanks to, in consequence of, (*du fait de* ⟨B⟩), on the basis of, prompted by. | — **Quellen der,** by virtue of sources belonging to, (*aux sources de* ⟨B⟩). | — **Wesensgesetzen,** on the basis of eidetic laws, (*en vertu de lois d'essence* ⟨B⟩).

ausbreiten, | **sich** —, to spread ⟨WH⟩.
Ausbreitung, spread ⟨WH⟩.
ausdenkbar, conceivable ⟨WH⟩, (*imaginable* ⟨B⟩). Cf. **denkbar, erdenkbar.**
ausdeuten, to interpret ⟨WH 1, MS⟩. Cf. **auffassen, deuten, erklären.**
Ausdeutung, interpretation ⟨WH 1, MS⟩. Cf. **Auffassung, Deutung, Erklärung.**
Ausdruck, expression ⟨WH 1, MS 1, BG⟩, (*expression* ⟨R, B⟩). Cf. **Ausprägung, Urteilsausdruck, Wunschausdruck.** | ~**e,** expressions, (language ⟨Gomperz trln of Mill, quoted in LU, II. Unters.⟩). | **zum — bringen,** to give expression to, (*amener à l'expression* ⟨B⟩).
ausdrücken, to express ⟨WH 1, MS 1, BG⟩. | **mit** —, to connote. Cf. **(mitbegreifen), mitbezeichnen, (miteinbegreifen).**
ausdrückend, expressive ⟨MS 1⟩, expressing.
ausdrücklich ⟨adj.⟩, express ⟨MS 1, WH⟩, expressed, (*expressif* ⟨R⟩); explicit ⟨WH, BG⟩, (*explicitus* ⟨K⟩).
ausdrücklich ⟨adv.⟩, expressly ⟨WH 1, MS 1, BG⟩, (*expressément* ⟨B⟩).
Ausdrucksbewegung, expressive movement ⟨WH 1, MS 1⟩.
Ausdruck-sein, expressionhood.
Ausdruckserscheinung, expression-appearance, appearance (*or* appearing) of an expression. Cf. **Erscheinung.** | **physische** —, appearance of the physical expression.

Ausdrucksfunktion, expressional function, (*fonction expressive* ⟨B⟩) Cf. **Funktion.**
auseinanderlegen, to spread out ⟨WH 1, MS⟩, to explicate, to dissect. Cf **auslegen, entfalten, explizieren.**
Auseinanderlegung, explication. Cf **Auslegung, Entfaltung, Explikation, Explizierung.**
ausführen, (in words:) to point out ⟨WH⟩.
Ausführlichkeit, (*completudo* ⟨K⟩). Cf **Vollständigkeit.**
Ausführung, carrying-out ⟨WH 2⟩, execution ⟨WH, MS⟩, (*exécution* ⟨B⟩), working out, (*développement* ⟨R, B⟩), (*étude détaillée* ⟨B⟩); (in words:) explanation ⟨WH⟩, (*explication* ⟨R⟩), (*analyse* ⟨R⟩), exposition ⟨WH⟩, statement ⟨WH⟩ argument ⟨WH, L⟩. Not "development" ⟨BG⟩ and not "discussion" ⟨BG⟩. Cf. **Aussage, Darstellung, Vollziehung, Vollzug.**
ausfüllen, to fill out ⟨WH 1, MS⟩, to fill in ⟨WH⟩, to fill ⟨WH 2, MS⟩, (*satisfaire* ⟨B⟩). Cf. **erfüllen.**
Ausfüllung, filling out ⟨WH 2, MS 2⟩ filling in ⟨WH 3⟩; filling ⟨WH 1⟩, (*remplissement* ⟨R⟩), (*remplissage* ⟨R, B⟩). Cf. **Erfüllung, Füllung.**
Ausgangsakt, act that is the starting point. Not "point of departure" ⟨L⟩.
ausgeprägt, (sometimes:) expressed. Cf. **Ausprägung.**
Ausgeschlossensein, excludedness, (*être-exclu* ⟨B⟩). Cf. **ausschliessen, Beschlossensein.**
ausgestalten, to shape ⟨MS 1⟩, (*donner une forme à* ⟨B⟩), to fashion, (*organiser* ⟨B⟩); to develop ⟨MS 2⟩. Cf. **bilden, herausarbeiten, gestalten.**
Ausgestaltung, (further) forming, (*organisation* ⟨B⟩), particular formation, development ⟨MS⟩, (*élaboration* ⟨B⟩). Cf. **Bildung, Formung, Gestalt, Gestaltung.**
ausgezeichnet, signal, (*insigne* ⟨B⟩), conspicuous, (*remarquable* ⟨R⟩), pre-eminent, distinctive ⟨F⟩, (*distinctif* ⟨R⟩), distinguishing, distin-

guished ⟨WH, MS⟩. Not "select" ⟨F⟩. Cf. **unterscheidend.** | **das A ~e,** distinguishing characteristic, (*le caractère insigne* ⟨B⟩).

auslegen, to explicate, (*expliciter* ⟨B⟩), to lay out ⟨WH 1, MS 2⟩, (*exposer* ⟨B⟩), to spread out ⟨MS 1⟩, to display ⟨WH⟩; to explain ⟨WH, MS⟩; to construe ⟨WH, MS⟩. Cf. **auffassen, auseinanderlegen, entfalten, erklären, explizieren.** | **sich —,** to display itself, (*s'exposer* ⟨B⟩).

Auslegung, explication, (*explicitation* ⟨B⟩), display ⟨MS⟩, (*exposition* ⟨B⟩), (textual:) exegesis ⟨MS⟩, (*élucidation* ⟨B⟩). Cf. **Auseinanderlegung, Entfaltung, Erklärung, Explikation, Explizierung, Sinnesauslegung.** | **besinnliche —,** reflective sense-explication, (*explicitation effectuée par la prise de conscience* ⟨B⟩). Cf. **besinnlich, Sinnesauslegung.**

ausmachen, to make up ⟨WH⟩, (*former* ⟨B⟩), ((*se*) *constituer* ⟨R, B⟩), to be an integral part of, to be the sense of, to amount to ⟨WH⟩, to determine, to be. Save "to constitute" ⟨WH, MS, L, BG⟩ for "konstituieren". Cf. **bestehen (aus), bestimmen.** | **ein Bestandstück —,** (with sing. subject.:) to be a component (part).

Ausprägung, expression. Cf. **Ausdruck.**

Aussage, statement ⟨Bn, WH 3, MS 3, L, BG⟩, declaration ⟨WH 2, MS 2⟩, (*énoncé* ⟨R, B⟩), predication ⟨Bn, WH⟩, (assertion ⟨WH 1, MS 1, BG⟩). So far as possible save "assertion" for "Behauptung" and "predication" for "Prädikation". Not "enunciation" ⟨L⟩. Save "expression" ⟨L⟩ for "Ausdruck". Cf. **Ausführung, Äusserung, Feststellung, Urteilsaussage, Wahrnehmungsaussage, Wesensaussage, Wirklichkeitsaussage, Wunschaussage.**

Aussagebedeutung, statement-signification. Cf. **Bedeutung.**

Aussagegebilde, statement-formation, (*formation en tant qu'énoncé* ⟨B⟩).

aussagen, to state ⟨WH 2, MS⟩, to declare ⟨WH 1, MS⟩ (*énoncer* ⟨B⟩), to predicate ⟨MS⟩, to assert ⟨Gom-

perz trln of Mill, quoted in LU, II. Unters.; BG⟩. Save "to enounce" ⟨L⟩ for "aussprechen" ⟨q.v.⟩. Cf. **behaupten, feststellen, hinstellen, meinen, prädizieren.** | **etwas — von,** to predicate something of ⟨Gomperz trln of Mill, quoted in LU, I. Unters.; WH 1⟩, (*énoncer de* ⟨B⟩).

Aussagen, stating, declaring, (*acte d'énonciation* ⟨B⟩); predicating. Cf. **Tatsachen-aussagen.**

Aussagesatz, statement, (*énoncé* ⟨B⟩); predicative sentence, declarative sentence; predicative proposition, (*proposition énonciative* ⟨R, B⟩), stated proposition; (stated position), (*phrase* ⟨B⟩). Cf. **Satz 1 & 2.** | **einen — vollziehen,** to frame a statement, (*effectuer un énoncé* ⟨B⟩). Cf. **vollziehen.**

Aussageurteil, predicative judgment. Cf. **Urteil.**

ausschalten, to suspend ("ausgeschaltet d.h. suspendiert" — Idee d. Phän., *45;* ⟨WH⟩); to disconnect ("Sie ist weiter noch da, ... wie das Ausgeschaltete ausserhalb der Schaltung" — Ideen I, *65;* ⟨WH; MS⟩), (*mettre hors circuit* ⟨R⟩); to exclude ("aus unserem Urteilsfeld ausgeschaltet" — Ideen I, *136;* L), (*exclure* ⟨R, B⟩), to make inoperative; to eliminate ⟨Bn, WH 1, MS 1, F⟩. Cf. **ausschliessen.**

Ausschaltung, suspension ⟨WH⟩, suspending ⟨BG⟩; disconnexion ⟨WH, MS, BG⟩, (*mise hors circuit* ⟨R, B⟩), disconnecting; (ant. Einschaltung:) exclusion ⟨WH⟩; (*exclusion* ⟨B⟩); elimination ⟨WH 1, MS 1⟩. Cf. **Aufhebung, Einschaltung.**

ausschliessen, to shut out ⟨WH 1, MS⟩, to exclude ⟨WH, MS, BG⟩, (*exclure* ⟨B⟩); to preclude ⟨WH, MS⟩, (*interdire* ⟨R⟩). Cf. **ausschalten.**

aussen ⟨adv.⟩, (ant. innen:) outside ⟨WH 1, MS⟩, (*extérieurement* ⟨B⟩). | **von — her,** from outside, (*de l'extérieur* ⟨B⟩).

Aussenbetrachtung, external point of view. Cf. **Betrachtung.**

Aussenhorizont, outside horizon.

(Aussensein), outness ⟨used by Berkeley, Hume, Reid *et al.*⟩.

Aussenwelt, outside world, (external world ⟨Bn, WH 1, MS 1⟩), (*monde extérieur* ⟨R, B⟩), (outer world ⟨WH 2, MS 2, L, BG⟩).

äussere, (ant. innere:) external ⟨Gomperz trln of Mill, quoted in LU, II. Unters.; WH; MS; L⟩, (*externe* ⟨R, B⟩), (*externus* ⟨K⟩), (*extérieur* ⟨B⟩); outer ⟨WH, MS, F, BG⟩, (outward ⟨Gomperz trln of Mill, quoted in LU, II. Unters.⟩). | ∼s **Weltliches,** what belongs to the external world. Cf. **weltlich.** | **das Ä—,** (ant. das Innere:) the external, (the outside ⟨MS 1, WH 2⟩), (the exterior ⟨WH 1, MS 2⟩). | **ein Ä∼s,** something external; an externality, (*une extériorité* ⟨B⟩).

Aussereinander, entities (*or* phases *or* objects) outside one another; mutual externality.

Aussergeltungsetzung, depriving of acceptance, (rendering inoperative). Cf. **Geltung.**

äusserlich ⟨adv.⟩, outwardly.

Äusserlichkeit, outwardness ⟨MS 1, WH⟩, externality ⟨WH⟩, (*extériorité* ⟨PL⟩). Cf. **Innerlichkeit.**

äussern, 1. to manifest ⟨MS 1⟩. 2. to utter ⟨WH 1, MS⟩. Cf. **aussprechen.** | **sich —,** to utter ⟨MS 1⟩ (*or* declare ⟨MS 2⟩) oneself.

ausserthematisch, outside the theme. Cf. **thematisch.**

Äusserung, 1. (external) manifestation ⟨MS 1, WH⟩, (outward indication), (*extériorité* ⟨B⟩). 2. utterance ⟨WH, MS⟩, (loosely:) statement, (*assertion* ⟨B⟩). Cf. **Aussage, Behauptung.**

aussprechen, to enounce ⟨WH 2⟩, (*énoncer* ⟨R, B⟩), to utter ⟨WH, MS⟩, to state, (to pronounce ⟨WH 1, MS 1⟩), (*prononcer* ⟨B⟩), (*exprimer* ⟨R, B⟩), (*formuler* ⟨B⟩). Save "to express" ⟨WH, BG⟩ for "ausdrücken". Cf. **aussagen, äussern, unausgesprochen.** | **eine Bemerkung —,** to enounce an observation.

ausstatten mit, to furnish with ⟨WH,

BG⟩, (*pourvoir de* ⟨R⟩), (*douer de* ⟨B⟩).

Ausstattung, outfitting.

ausstellen, to put out ⟨MS 1⟩, to expose to view ⟨MS⟩, to exhibit ⟨WH, MS⟩. Cf. **darstellen, herausstellen, vorweisen.**

Ausweis, legitimation, (proof ⟨MS⟩). Cf. **Ausweisung, Begründung, Beweis, Erweis, Nachweis, Rechtgebung, Rechtsprechung.**

ausweisbar, that can be legitimated, that can be shown, demonstrable. Cf. **aufweisbar, nachweisbar, nachweislich.**

ausweisen, to legitimate, (*légitimer* ⟨R⟩), (to legitimize), to show ⟨WH, MS⟩, to demonstrate ⟨WH⟩, (to prove ⟨WH, MS⟩), (*prouver* ⟨B⟩). Cf. **aufweisen, beweisen, nachweisen, rechtausweisend, rechtgebend, weisen.** | **sich —,** to be legitimated, to be shown, to show itself, (*se démontrer* ⟨PL⟩), to give an account of oneself ⟨MS⟩, to prove oneself ⟨?⟩. Save "to manifest itself" ⟨L⟩ for "sich bekunden" (q.v. *sub* **bekunden**).

Ausweisung, legitimation, (*légitimation* ⟨R⟩), (*justification* ⟨B⟩), showing, demonstration ⟨BG⟩, proof, discovery, (*explicitation* ⟨B⟩). Save "setting forth" ⟨BG⟩ for "Darstellung" ⟨q.v.⟩. Cf. **Ausweis, Beweisung, Herausstellung, Nachweisung, Rechtgebung, Rechtsausweisung, Richtigkeitsausweisung, Wahrnehmungsausweisung, Weisung.**

auswirken, Cf. **wirken.** | **sich —,** to effectuate itself (*s'établir* ⟨B⟩), to operate ⟨WH⟩, to work out ⟨WH⟩, to result in, to develop as, (*se développer* ⟨B⟩).

Auswirkung, effectuation, (*effectuation* ⟨B⟩), effective development, effect ⟨WH⟩, (*manifestation* ⟨B⟩), operation, result ⟨WH⟩, outcome ⟨WH⟩, work. Cf. **Ergebnis, Folge 4, Leistung, Wirkung.** | **in aller — eines Interesses,** whenever we are actuated by an interest. | **zur — ge-**

kommen, developed, (*arrivé à se manifester* ⟨B⟩).
auszeichnen, see ausgezeichnet.
auszeichnend, distinguishing.

auszeigen, | sich —, Cf. sich bekunden.
Axiomenform, form of axioms, (*forme des axiomes* ⟨B⟩), (*forme axiomatique* ⟨B⟩).

B

Bau, structure ⟨Bn, WH, MS, BG⟩, (*structure* ⟨R⟩), edifice ⟨WH, MS⟩; build ⟨WH⟩, (*organisation* ⟨B⟩); building ⟨WH 1⟩, construction ⟨WH, MS⟩, (*construction* ⟨B⟩). Cf. Aufbau, Gebäude, Gebilde, Konstruktion, so gebaut (*sub* gebaut), Struktur, Stufenbau.
bauen, to build ⟨Gomperz trln of Mill, quoted in LU, I. Unters.; WH 1; MS 1⟩, (*édifier* ⟨B⟩); (*construire* ⟨B⟩). Cf. aufbauen, bilden, gebaut, übereinanderbauen. | sich auf etwas —, to base itself on something, to be based on something.
Bauglied, structural member, (*partie intégrante* ⟨B⟩). Cf. Glied.
Baumwahrgenommenes, tree-percept, (*perçu d'arbre* ⟨R⟩). Cf. Wahrgenommenes (*sub* wahrgenommen).
beabsichtigen, | etwas —, to purpose to do something, to have something in view ⟨MS⟩, to contemplate ⟨doing WH, MS⟩ something, to aim at something, (to intend something ⟨Gomperz trln of Mill, quoted in LU, II. Unters.; WH 1⟩). Cf. absehen, hinmeinen auf.
beabsichtigt, | das B~e, the object in view ⟨MS 1⟩. Cf. Absicht.
beachten, to heed ⟨WH⟩, to notice ⟨WH, MS, BG⟩, (*remarquer* ⟨R, B⟩), to note ⟨WH, L⟩, (*noter* ⟨R⟩), to pay attention to ⟨WH 1, MS⟩, (*faire (ou prêter) attention à* ⟨B⟩), (*considérer* ⟨R, B⟩). Not "to remember" ⟨BG⟩. Cf. aufmerken, gewahren, merken.
Beachten, heeding, (noticing ⟨BG⟩).
bedenken, to take into consideration.
Bedenken, doubt ⟨WH, MS⟩; objection ⟨WH⟩.
bedenklich, Cf. unbedenklich. | ~e Geistesart, a mind whose specific character is in doubt.

bedeuten, to signify ⟨MS 1, WH 2, F⟩, (*signifier* ⟨R, B⟩; *désigner* ⟨R⟩); to involve, (*impliquer* ⟨B⟩); to indicate, (*représenter* ⟨R⟩); to consist in; (*avoir* ⟨B⟩). Save "to mean" ⟨WH 1, MS⟩ for "meinen" ⟨q.v.⟩ and "vermeinen" ⟨q.v.⟩. Cf. andeuten, anzeigen, besagen, hindeuten, hinweisen auf, zeigen.
Bedeuten, signifying. Cf. Signifikation.
bedeutend, 1. signifying. Cf. bedeutungsmässig, gleichbedeutend, signifikativ, signitiv.
2. (wichtig:) significant ⟨WH 2, MS⟩. | ~e Funktion, signifying function, function of signifying.
bedeutsam ⟨adj.⟩, significant ⟨WH 2, MS 1⟩, (*significatif* ⟨B⟩), (*fort important* ⟨R⟩). Save "important" ⟨WH 1, BG⟩ for "wichtig". Cf. von Bedeutung (*sub* Bedeutung).
Bedeutsamkeit, significancy, (significance⟨WH 1, MS 1⟩). Cf. Bedeutung 2.
Bedeutung, 1. (Wortsinn:) signification ⟨LU, VI. Unters., *33 n.*; Gomperz trln of Mill, quoted in LU, I. and II. Unters.; Lipps trln of Hume, quoted in LU, II. Unters.; MS 1, WH⟩, (*signification* ⟨B⟩), (sense ⟨WH⟩), (import ⟨trln of Mill, quoted in LU II/1, Einl.; WH; MS⟩). So far as possible save "sense" for "Sinn". Save "meaning" ⟨WH 1, F, BG⟩ for "Meinen" and "Meinung". Not "significance" ⟨Gomperz trln of Mill, quoted in LU, I. Unters.; WH⟩ in this sense. Cf. Aussagebedeutung, Mitbedeutung. Signifikation, Teilbedeutung, Urteilsbedeutung, Verstand 2, Wortbedeutung 1.
2. (Relevanz oder Wichtigkeit:) significance, (*signification* ⟨B⟩), (*importance* ⟨B⟩). Cf. Bedeutsamkeit, Bedeutungsprädikat.

3. (noetic:) signification, mental signifying. Cf. **noetischer Bedeutungsbegriff** (*sub* **Bedeutungsbegriff**), **Signifikation, Wortbedeutung 2.**
4. (ohne Unterscheidung?:) (*signification* ⟨R, de M⟩). | **intendierende** —, intentive signification. | **von** —, of significance, significant ⟨Gomperz trln of Mill, quoted in LU, I. Unters.⟩. Cf. **bedeutsam.**

bedeutungerfüllend, signification-fulfiling. Cf. **erfüllen.**

bedeutunggebend, signification-bestowing, (*donateur de signification* ⟨B⟩). Not "signification-giving". Cf. **bedeutungsverleihend, gebend, sinngebend.**

Bedeutungsbegriff, concept of signification. Cf. **Bedeutungskategorie, Begriff.** | **noetischer** —, concept of noetic signification. Cf. **Bedeutung 3.**

Bedeutungsbewusstsein, significational consciousness. | — **des Ausdrucks,** significational consciousness pertaining to the expression.

Bedeutungsbeziehung, significational relation, (*relation* (ou *rapport*) *de signification* ⟨B⟩). Cf. **Beziehung.**

Bedeutungseinheit, significational unity, signification-unity, (*unité de* (*la*) *signification* ⟨B⟩). Cf. **Einheit.**

Bedeutungserfüllung, (process:) significational fulfilling; (result:) signification-fulfilment. Cf. **Erfüllung.**

Bedeutungserlebnis, mental signification-process, mental signifying process. Cf. **Erlebnis.**

Bedeutungsform, signification-form, (*forme de signification* ⟨B⟩), significational form, form of the signification, (pl.:) forms of the significations. Cf. **Gegenstandsform.** | ∼**en der Aussagen,** forms of the significations of statements, (*formes de la signification des énoncés* ⟨B⟩). Cf. **Aussage.**

Bedeutungsfunktion, significational function, (*fonction de la signification* ⟨B⟩). Cf. **Funktion.**

Bedeutungsgebilde, significational formation, signification-formation, (*formation de la signification* ⟨B⟩). Cf. **Gebilde.**

Bedeutungsgehalt, significational content(s), (*contenu signifiant* ⟨B⟩). Cf. **Gehalt.**

Bedeutungsinhalt, significational content. Cf. **Inhalt.**

Bedeutungsintention, (mere) significational intention. Cf. **Intention.**

Bedeutungskategorie, signification-category, (*catégorie de signification* ⟨B⟩). Cf. **Bedeutungsbegriff, gegenständliche Kategorie** (*sub* **Kategorie**).

bedeutungsleer, empty of signification.

bedeutungslos, without (a) signification, significationless. Not "unmeaning" ⟨Gomperz trln of Mill, quoted in LU, I. Unters.; WH⟩.

Bedeutungslosigkeit, lack of signification.

bedeutungsmässig ⟨adj.⟩, significational, (*significatif* ⟨R⟩), (*dans le plan de signification* ⟨B⟩), (in accordance with signification). Not "significant" ⟨BG⟩. Cf. **bedeutend, signifikativ, signitiv.** | ∼**es,** significational moment (cf. LU, V.Unters., *421, l. 1-9*), what is significational; signification-fitting sense. | ∼**es Wesen,** significational essence, (*essence significative* ⟨R⟩). Not "essence in the mode of meaning" ⟨BG⟩. Cf. **Wesen.**

bedeutungsmässig ⟨adv.⟩, significationally, signifyingly. Cf. **signitiv, signifikativ.** | — **gemeint,** signifyingly meant. Cf. **gemeint.**

Bedeutungsprädikat, significance-predicate. Cf. **Bedeutung 2.**

bedeutungstheoretisch, pertaining to theory of signification, (*emprunté à la théorie de la signification* ⟨R⟩).

Bedeutungsvorstellung, signification-objectivation. Cf. **Bedeutung 2.**

"Bedeutungsvorstellungen", "meaning imagery". Cf. **Vorstellung 7.**

bedeutungverleihend, signification-conferring. Not "meaning-conferring" ⟨F⟩. Cf. **bedeutunggebend, sinnverleihend, verleihend.**

bedingt (durch), conditioned ⟨BG⟩

(by) ⟨WH 1⟩, (*conditionné* ⟨B⟩); contingent (upon) ⟨WH⟩.

befangen, entangled ⟨MS 1⟩, (*engagé* ⟨R⟩), biased ⟨WH⟩, prepossessed, (*gêné* ⟨B⟩).

befassen, to lay hold of, (*saisir* ⟨B⟩), to apprehend, to comprehend, (*comprendre* ⟨B⟩), (by an expression:) to understand, to include ⟨WH 1, obs., L⟩, (*englober* ⟨R⟩), to extend to, (*comporter* ⟨B⟩), (*convenir à* ⟨B⟩). Cf. **auffassen, begreifen, erfassen, fassen, umgreifen, Unverständnis, verstehen.**

Befehlssatz, command positum. Cf. **Satz.**

befragen, to consult ⟨WH, MS⟩, to inquire of ⟨MS⟩, to interrogate ⟨WH 1, MS⟩, (*interroger* ⟨R⟩), to address inquiry to, to examine, (*mettre en question* ⟨B⟩), (*s'enquérir* ⟨B⟩). Cf. **fragen.**

begehren, to desire ⟨Bn, WH 1, MS, BG⟩, (*désirer* ⟨R⟩).

Begehren, (ant. Fliehen:) desiring ⟨WH 1⟩, (*désir* ⟨R⟩).

Begehrung, desire, (*désir* ⟨R⟩).

begreifen, to comprehend ⟨Bn, WH, MS, RBF⟩, (*comprehendere* ⟨K⟩), to grasp ⟨WH⟩, (*concevoir* ⟨B⟩), (*entendre* ⟨B⟩), (*assumer* ⟨B⟩). Cf. **auffassen, befassen, erfassen, fassen, greifen, mitbegreifen, umgreifen.**

begreiflich, | **das B~e,** (what we can conceive ⟨Ueberweg trln of Berkeley, quoted in LU, II. Unters.⟩).

begrenzt, limited ⟨WH⟩, bounded ⟨WH 1⟩, delimited. Save "finite" ⟨Bn, Br⟩ for "endlich" (q.v.). Cf. **abschliessen, beschränken, Grenze, unbegrenzt.**

Begrenzung, limitation ⟨WH⟩, delimitation ⟨MS 1⟩, (*délimitation* ⟨B⟩). Not "definition" ⟨BG⟩. Cf. **Abgrenzung, abschliessen, Grenze, Umgrenzung, Umschreibung.**

Begriff, concept ⟨WH⟩, (*concept* ⟨R, B⟩), (*conceptus* ⟨K⟩), (with reference to Berkeley:) notion ⟨Ueberweg trln, quoted; Br; WH; MS⟩; conception ⟨WH 1, MS, BG⟩. Cf. **Aktbegriff, Auffassung, Erfahrungsbegriff, Formbegriff, Gebietsbegriff,**

(Oberbegriff), Grenzbegriff, **Hauptbegriff, Teilbegriff, Totalbegriff,** (Unterbegriff), **Urbegriff, Urteilsbegriff, Wesensbegriff, Wortbegriff.**

begrifflich, conceptual ⟨WH⟩, (*conceptuel* ⟨R, B⟩). Not "conceptional" ⟨L⟩.

Begrifflichkeit, (set of) concepts. Cf. **Grundbegrifflichkeit.**

Begriffsbildung, concept-forming, concept-formation, (*formation des concepts* ⟨B⟩), (*formation du concept* ⟨B⟩). Cf. **Bildung.**

Begriffsgegenstand, object pertaining to the (*or* a) concept (cf. E.u.U., *396*).

Begründbarkeit, groundableness. Not "foundation-possibility" ⟨L⟩.

begründen, 1. to ground, to establish ⟨WH, BG⟩, to lay a solid foundation for, to base ⟨MS 2⟩, (to substantiate ⟨WH, MS⟩), to establish the legitimacy of, (to legitimate), to found ⟨WH 1⟩, (*fonder* ⟨R, B⟩). 2. to be the ground (*or* basis) for. Save "to justify" ⟨L⟩ for "rechtfertigen". So far as possible save "to found" ⟨WH 1, MS 1⟩ for "fundieren". Cf. **feststellen, gründen, stiften, zugrunde liegen.**

begründet, grounded, established ⟨MS 3⟩, (substantiated ⟨WH 1, MS 1⟩), well-founded ⟨WH 2, MS 2⟩, (*fondé* ⟨B⟩), (legitimated); rooted, (*enraciné* ⟨B⟩). Cf. **Triftigkeit.** | — **in,** having its basis in, (*fondé dans* ⟨B⟩). | **einsichtig** —, established by insight, (*fondé avec une évidence absolue* ⟨B⟩). Cf. **einsichtig** ⟨adv.⟩. | **prinzipiell** —, grounded on radical principles. Cf. **prinzipiell** ⟨adv.⟩.

Begründung, (rational) grounding, establishment ⟨WH, MS⟩, establishing, (substantiation), (*fondation* R, B⟩), (*acte de fondation* ⟨B⟩), (*fondement* ⟨PL, B⟩, (*justification* ⟨B⟩), (legitimation). So far as possible save: "foundation" ⟨WH, MS, L⟩ for "Fundament" (q.v.) and "Fundierung" (q.v.); "legitimation" for "Rechtgebung". Cf. **Ausweis, Ausweisung. Erkenntnisbegründung, Grund, Grundlegung.** | aus absoluter

—, grounded on an absolute foundation, (*à fondements absolus* ⟨PL⟩), (*issue d'une activité fondatrice absolue* ⟨B⟩). | **aus letzter** —, grounded on an ultimate foundation. | **zu näherer** —, to ground (something) more strictly, (*pour arriver à une justification plus précise* ⟨B⟩).

Begründungszusammenhang, (logical) grounding connexion, (rational connexion ⟨?⟩). Cf. **Zusammenhang.**

behandeln, to treat ⟨MS 1, WH 2⟩, (*traiter* ⟨R, B⟩), to deal with ⟨WH 1, MS⟩, (*manier* ⟨B⟩).

behaupten, to assert ⟨Lipps trln of Hume, quoted in LU, II. Unters.; WH; MS⟩. Cf. **aussagen, feststellen, meinen, prädizieren.**

behauptend, assertive, that asserts, assertoric, (*qui est une assertion* ⟨B⟩), (*qui affirme* ⟨B⟩). Save "affirmative" for "bejahend".

Behauptung, assertion ⟨WH, MS⟩, (*assertion* ⟨R, B⟩), *assertio* ⟨K⟩), (*thesis* ⟨K⟩). Save "affirmation" ⟨L⟩ for "Bejahung". Cf. **Aussage, Äusserung, Bejahung, Feststellung.**

Behauptungsgehalt, assertoric content.

Behauptungssatz, assertoric sentence, (*proposition qui forme l'assertion* ⟨B⟩). Cf. **Satz 2.** | **sprachlicher** —, assertoric sentence, (*assertion verbale* ⟨B⟩).

beherrschen, to govern ⟨WH, MS⟩, (*dominer* ⟨B⟩), to control ⟨WH⟩. Cf. **regeln, schalten, walten.**

Beherrschung, control ⟨WH 1⟩, (*domination* ⟨B⟩).

Bei-ihm-selbst-sein, being with it itself, (*être-près-de-cet-objet-lui-même* ⟨B⟩). Cf. **Dabei-sein.**

Beilage, supplement ⟨WH⟩.

beilegen, to attribute. Not "to give" ⟨L⟩.

beimessen, to attribute ⟨WH 2, L⟩.

Beisatz, (grammar:) adjunct, (*complément* ⟨R⟩), (addition ⟨BG⟩).

Beispielspaar, exemplary pair.

bejahend, affirmative ⟨WH 1, MS 1⟩, (*affirmans* ⟨K⟩). Cf. **behauptend.**

Bejahung, affirmation ⟨WH, BG⟩, (*affirmation* ⟨R, de M⟩). Save

"assertion" for "Behauptung". Cf. **zusprechen.**

bekannt, acquainted ⟨WH, MS⟩, known ⟨WH 1, MS, BG⟩ (by acquaintance), (*connu* ⟨R⟩), well-known ⟨WH 2, MS⟩. Save "familiar" ⟨WH, MS, BG⟩ for "vertraut". Cf. **unbekannt.**

Bekanntheit, acquaintedness. Save "familiarity" ⟨WH⟩ for "Vertrautheit".

bekräftigen, to confirm ⟨WH 1, MS 1⟩, (*confirmer* ⟨R⟩). Cf. **bestätigen, bewähren, Kraft.**

(Bekräftigung), confirmation ⟨Bn, WH 1, MS 1⟩. Cf. **Bestätigung, Bewährung, Entkräftigung.**

bekunden, to make known, to evince ⟨WH, MS⟩, to be indicative of, (*annoncer* ⟨R, B⟩). Cf. **kenntlich machen, kundgeben, kundtun.** | **einem etwas** —, to make something known to someone, (*faire part de quelque chose à quelqu'un* ⟨B⟩). | **sich** —, to make itself known, (*s'annoncer* ⟨R, B⟩), (*se déclarer* ⟨R⟩), to manifest itself ⟨BG⟩, (*se manifester* ⟨B⟩), to be evinced, to be indicated, (*se révéler* ⟨B⟩). Cf. **sich anzeigen** (*sub* **anzeigen**), **sich auszeigen.**

Belauf, (von Erlebnissen:) flow. Cf. **Ablauf, Fluss, Verlauf.**

Beleuchtungswechsel, changes in (something's) illumination, (*variation dans l'éclairage* ⟨R⟩). Cf. **Wechsel.**

Belieben, optionalness. Cf. **Beliebigkeit, Willkür.** | **nach** —, at will ⟨WH MS⟩, (*à volonté* ⟨B⟩).

beliebig ⟨adj.⟩, optional ⟨MS 1⟩, chosen (at will), no matter what, (*n'importe quel* ⟨R⟩), any (... whatever) ⟨WH⟩, just any, (*quelconque* ⟨B⟩), variable without restriction, (arbitrary ⟨L⟩), (*arbitraire* ⟨R, B⟩), (random); any number of. Not "any and all" ⟨BG⟩. Cf. **offen-beliebig, unbestimmt-beliebig.** | **eine** ∼**e**, just any. | **eine** ∼**en**, any number of. | ∼**es Etwas,** anything you please, (*un quelque chose arbitraire* ⟨B⟩). Cf. **Etwas überhaupt.**

beliebig ⟨adv.⟩, at pleasure, *ad libitum,* somehow, (*d'une manière arbitraire* ⟨B⟩).

Beliebigkeit, optional character, optionalness, (*arbitraire* ⟨B⟩); option, optional affair, (*élément arbitraire* ⟨B⟩). Cf. **Belieben, Willkür.**

bemerken, to notice ⟨WH, MS⟩, to remark ⟨WH, MS⟩, (*remarquer* ⟨R, B⟩, (to observe ⟨MS⟩), (*animadverto* ⟨K⟩). Cf. **achten auf, aufmerken, beachten, beobachten, merken.**

Bemerkung, remark ⟨WH 2, MS⟩, (*remarque* ⟨R⟩), observation ⟨WH 1, MS 1⟩. Cf. **Beobachtung, Betrachtung.** | **eine — aussprechen,** to enounce an observation.

(Benennung), denomination ⟨Bn, WH, MS⟩.

beobachten, to observe ⟨WH 1, MS 1, BG⟩, (*observer* ⟨R⟩). Cf. **achten auf, bemerken.**

Beobachtung, observation ⟨WH 1, MS 1, Bn⟩. Cf. **Bemerkung, Betrachtung, Selbstbeobachtung.**

berechtigen, | **sich —,** to become warranted, (*fonder son droit* ⟨B⟩).

berechtigt, legitimate ⟨WH, MS⟩, warranted, justified ⟨WH, MS, L⟩, (qualified). Cf. **echt, gesetzmässig, rechtmässig, unberechtigt, vollberechtigt.**

Berechtigung, warrant ⟨WH 2⟩, justification ⟨WH 1⟩. Cf. **Eigenberechtigung, Gerechtigkeit, Rechtfertigung, Rechtgebung.** | **— haben,** to be warranted.

Bereich, domain ⟨WH, MS⟩, (*domaine* ⟨B⟩), scope ⟨WH⟩, reach ⟨MS 1, WH, BG⟩, (sphere ⟨WH, MS⟩), (*champ* ⟨B⟩), (*ensemble* ⟨R⟩). Cf. **Bewusstseinsbereich, Geltungsbereich, Herrschaftsbereich, Kreis, Rahmen, Sinn, Sphäre, Tragweite, Umfang.**

berichtigen, | **sich —,** to become rectified, (*se rectifier* ⟨B⟩).

Berichtigung, correction ⟨WH 1, MS⟩, (*rectification* ⟨B⟩). Cf. **richtig.**

Beruf, vocation ⟨WH, MS⟩, (*vocation* ⟨B⟩), (rarely:) function ⟨WH⟩, (*mission* ⟨B⟩). Not "profession" ⟨WH, MS⟩, not "mission" ⟨WH⟩. Cf. **Funktion.** | **den — haben,** to be called on, (*avoir la mission* ⟨B⟩).

berufsmässig, vocational. Not "professional" ⟨WH 1, MS 1⟩.

besagen, to signify ⟨WH, MS⟩, (*signifier* ⟨B⟩), to say ⟨WH 1, MS⟩ (*vouloir dire* ⟨B⟩), to indicate, (*désigner* ⟨R⟩), to imply ⟨WH, MS⟩, to connote, to involve, (rarely:) to be, (*s'énoncer* ⟨B⟩). Save "to mean" ⟨WH, L, BG⟩ for "meinen" and "vermeinen". Not "to amount to" ⟨BG⟩. Cf. **bedeuten.**

beschaffen ⟨adj.⟩, (at least sometimes:) qualitied, (*constitué* ⟨B⟩).

Beschaffenheit, determination ⟨cf. Logik, *45, l. 10f.,* with Logik, *46, l. 13-15*⟩, attribute ⟨cf. LU, II. Unters., *224*⟩, (*propriété* ⟨R⟩), condition or quality, condition ⟨WH 1, MS⟩ (of something), (narrow sense:) quality ⟨WH, MS, BG⟩, (*qualité* ⟨R, B⟩), character ⟨WH, MS⟩, disposition ⟨WH, MS⟩, nature ⟨WH, MS⟩, (state ⟨MS 1, WH⟩), (mark). Save "property" for "Eigenschaft" (q.v.). So far as possible save: "quality" for "Qualität", "character" for "Charakter" (q.v.), "state" for "Zustand" (q.v.). Cf. **Art, Artung, Bestimmtheit, Bestimmung, Habitualität, Habitus, Merkmal, Sachbeschaffenheit, Zeichen.** | **charakteristische —,** characteristic mark. Cf. **charakteristisches Merkmal** (*sub* **Merkmal).**

beschliessen, to include, to comprise ⟨WH 1⟩, (*comprendre* ⟨B⟩), (*renfermer en soi* ⟨B⟩), (*receler* ⟨R⟩), to enclose, to imply, (*impliquer* ⟨PL⟩), to involve; to infer; to decree ⟨MS⟩, (*décréter* ⟨B⟩). Cf. **einbeziehen in, einlegen, einschliessen, erschliessen, folgern, schliessen, nach sich ziehen** (*sub* **ziehen).**

beschlossen in, included in, (*inclus dans* ⟨R, B⟩), comprised in, enclosed within, (*enfermé dans* ⟨B⟩), (*enveloppé dans* ⟨R⟩), (*impliqué dans* ⟨B⟩), (*entrant dans* ⟨B⟩). Not "involved in" ⟨BG⟩, not "present in" ⟨BG⟩.

Cf. **mitbeschlossen in.** | **deduktiv** —, deducibly included in, (*impliqué déductivement dans* ⟨B⟩). Cf. **deduktiv.**

Beschlossensein, includedness, being included, (*inclusion* ⟨R, de M⟩), impliedness, (*être-impliqué* ⟨B⟩), decidedness, concludedness. Not "self-containedness" ⟨BG⟩. Cf. **Ausgeschlossensein.** | **irreelles** —, being non-really included, (*inclusion intentionelle* ⟨de M⟩). Cf. **irreel.**

beschränken, to restrict ⟨WH⟩. So far as possible save "to limit" ⟨MS 1, WH⟩ for "begrenzen". Cf. **begrenzt, einschränken, binden.**

beseelen, to animate ⟨WH 1⟩, (*animer* ⟨R, B⟩).

beseelt, animated, (figurative, sometimes:) quickened. Cf. **animalisch.**

Beseelung, animation ⟨Bn, WH 1, MS 1⟩.

besinnen, | **sich** —, to investigate sense, to carry on sense-investigation, (to meditate (on the sense of)), (to reflect ⟨WH⟩), (to bethink oneself ⟨WH, MS⟩), (to bethink), (*prendre conscience* ⟨B⟩). Cf. **forschen, nachgehen, untersuchen.**

besinnlich, sense-investigative, (meditative ⟨WH⟩), reflective ⟨WH⟩, (*opéré par la prise de conscience* ⟨B⟩). | ~e **Auslegung,** reflective sense-explication, (*explicitation effectuée par la prise de conscience* ⟨B⟩). Cf. **Auslegung.** | ~e **Erfüllung,** clear sense-fulfilment, (*remplissement effectué par la prise de conscience* ⟨B⟩). Cf. **Erfüllung.**

Besinnung, sense-investigation, investigation of sense, meditation (on the sense of), meditating (on the sense of), reflection ⟨Bn, WH, L⟩, (sense-clarification), clarification; (loose sense:) deliberation; (*prise de conscience* ⟨B, de M⟩), (*prendre conscience* ⟨B⟩). So far as possible save "reflection" for "Reflexion" ⟨q.v.⟩. Cf. **Betrachtung, Rückbesinnung, Selbstbesinnung, Überlegung, Untersuchung.** | **prinzipielle** —, in-

vestigation of (the) essential sense. Cf. **prinzipiell** ⟨adj.⟩.

besondere, particular ⟨MS 1, WH⟩, (*particulier* ⟨R, B⟩), (*particularis* ⟨K⟩), (peculiar ⟨WH, MS⟩), (proper) (*propria* ⟨Br⟩), (*strict* ⟨B⟩). Not "special" ⟨MS, BG⟩. Cf. **eigen, eigentlich, einzeln, Eigentümlichkeit.**

Besonderheit, particularity ⟨MS 1, WH⟩, (*particularité* ⟨B⟩), (*particularisation* ⟨B⟩), peculiarity ⟨WH, MS⟩. Cf. **Eigenheit, Eigentümlichkeit.**

Besonderung, particularity ⟨L⟩, particularization, (*particularisation* ⟨R, B⟩), particular difference, particular species, particular example. Not "division" ⟨BG⟩. Save: "individuation" for "Individuation", "singularization" for "Vereinzelung" ⟨q.v.⟩, "specialization" for "Spezialisierung" ⟨q.v.⟩. Cf. **Differenz, Einzelheit, Singularität. Vereinzelung.** | — **eines Gesetzes,** particularity subsummed under a law, (*particularisation d'une loi* ⟨R⟩).

Bestand, composition, make-up (*ensemble* ⟨PL, B⟩), (*faisceau permanent* ⟨R⟩), stock ⟨WH, MS⟩, (*fonds* ⟨R⟩), store ⟨WH, MS⟩; (set); (Bestandteil:) component, (*composante* ⟨R⟩), (*caractère* ⟨B⟩); (*état* ⟨B⟩); existence ⟨MS 1⟩, (*permanence* ⟨R⟩). Save "constitution" ⟨BG⟩ for "Konstitution". Cf. **bestehen, Dasein, Erkenntnisbestand, Existenz, Gehalt, Kernbestand, Menge, Sein, Sinnesbestand, Sprachbestand, Wesensbestand.** | **inhaltlicher** —, stock of content(s), (*contenu* ⟨R⟩). Cf. **Inhaltlich, Inhaltsbestand.**

Bestände, components, (*composantes* ⟨R⟩), stock, (*fonds d'éléments constitutifs* ⟨B⟩), (constituents), (*états* ⟨B⟩). Cf. **Bestandstück, Bestandteil.**

beständig ⟨adj.⟩, continual, (*constant* ⟨B⟩), (perpetual ⟨Bn, WH, MS⟩). Save: "constant" ⟨WH 1, MS⟩ for "ständig" and "stet" ⟨q.v.⟩, "continuous" ⟨WH, MS, BG⟩ for "kontinuierlich", "stet", and "stetig". |

(~e Bewegung), perpetual motion ⟨Bn⟩.

beständig ⟨adv.⟩, continually ⟨BG⟩, (constantly ⟨L, BG⟩), (*constamment* ⟨R, B⟩), (*sans cesse* ⟨R⟩), (always). Cf. stets.

Bestandstück, (concrete) component, (*composante* ⟨R⟩), component part, (*partie intégrante* ⟨B⟩), (constituent ⟨BG⟩), (*élément constituant* (ou *constitutif*) ⟨B⟩). Not "constitutive portion" ⟨BG⟩. Cf. Stück, Urteilsbestandstück.

Bestandteil, component ⟨WH, MS⟩, (*composante* ⟨R⟩), component part ⟨WH⟩.

bestätigen, to corroborate ⟨MS 1, WH 2⟩, to confirm ⟨WH 1, MS 2, Br⟩, (*confirmer* ⟨R⟩). Cf. bekräftigen, Bewährung.

Bestätigung, corroboration ⟨WH 2, MS 2⟩, confirmation ⟨WH 1, MS 1⟩, (*confirmation* ⟨R⟩). Cf. Bekräftigung, Bewährung.

bestehen, to exist ⟨WH, MS⟩, (*exister* ⟨B⟩), to be ⟨WH⟩, to obtain, (*valoir* ⟨R⟩), (*subsister* ⟨B⟩); to last ⟨WH, MS⟩, (*persister* ⟨R⟩). Cf. ausmachen, sein. | — aus, to consist of ⟨WH 1, MS 2, BG⟩, (*consister en* ⟨B⟩), (*être constitué de* ⟨R⟩). | — in, to consist in ⟨WH 1⟩, (*consister en* ⟨B⟩).

Bestehen, existence, (*subsistance* ⟨R⟩). Cf. Dasein, Existenz, Sein.

bestehend, | — sein, to obtain. | das B ~e, that which obtains, (*ce qui demeure permanent* ⟨R⟩).

bestimmen, to determine ⟨WH, MS⟩, (*déterminer* ⟨R, B⟩), to induce ⟨WH⟩; to define ⟨MS⟩, to describe. Cf. ausmachen, unbestimmbar.

bestimmt, determinate ⟨Bn, WH, BG⟩, (*avec une détermination* ⟨B⟩), (*porteur de déterminations* ⟨R⟩), determined ⟨WH, MS⟩, (*déterminé* ⟨R, B⟩), definite ⟨WH, MS, BG⟩; (defined ⟨BG⟩); destined ⟨WH 1⟩, (*destiné* ⟨B⟩), designed ⟨WH⟩. Not "certain" ⟨Lipps trln of Hume, quoted in LU, II. Unters.; MS⟩. Cf. definit, soseiend, unbestimmt-beliebig.

Bestimmtheit, determination ⟨WH⟩, (*détermination* ⟨R⟩), determinateness, determinate property, determinancy ⟨BG⟩, definiteness ⟨WH 1⟩, (definition ⟨BG⟩). Cf. Definitheit, Eigenbestimmtheit, Erscheinungsbestimmtheit, Gattungsbestimmtheit, Unbestimmtheit.

Bestimmung, determination ⟨WH⟩, (*détermination* ⟨B⟩), (*determinatio* ⟨K⟩), determining; definition ⟨WH⟩ (decision ⟨WH⟩). Cf. Beschaffenheit, Dingbestimmung.

Bestimmungsgehalt, determination = content, (*statut de détermination* ⟨R⟩). Not "determining content" ⟨BG⟩.

Bestimmungsstück, (concrete) determining part. Save "component part" ⟨L⟩ for "Bestandstück" ⟨q.v.⟩ and "Bestandteil" ⟨q.v.⟩. Cf. Stück.

Bestimmungssubstrat, determinable substrate, (*substrat de (la) détermination* ⟨B⟩).

betätigen, to practise ⟨WH⟩, (*pratiquer* ⟨B⟩), to exercise, to activate ⟨WH⟩, to employ, (*se manifester* ⟨B⟩). ⟨Consult WH⟩. Cf. tätig, verwirklichen. | sich —, to busy oneself ⟨WH⟩.

Betätigung, activity ⟨F, WH, MS⟩, (*activité* ⟨R, B⟩), (*acte* ⟨B⟩), practice ⟨WH⟩; (*manifestation* ⟨B⟩). Cf. Aktualität 3, Handlung, Tätigkeit.

Betonung, emphasis ⟨MS⟩, stressing, accentuation ⟨Bn, MS⟩.

betrachtbar, viewable, (*se prêtant à l'examen* ⟨B⟩).

betrachten, to consider ⟨MS 1, WH, BG⟩, (*considérer* ⟨R, B⟩), to look at ⟨WH 1⟩, to regard ⟨MS 2, WH⟩, to view ⟨WH⟩, to inspect ⟨WH, MS⟩, to contemplate ⟨WH 2, MS⟩, (*contempler* ⟨R⟩). ⟨Consult WH⟩. Save "to observe" ⟨MS, BG⟩ for "beobachten". Cf. auffassen, erblicken, erschauen, ins Auge fassen (*sub* Auge), schauen. | thematisch —, to regard thematically, (*considérer thématiquement* ⟨B⟩).

betrachtend, considering, in (my)

considering, (*en considérant* ⟨R⟩), inspective.

Betrachtung, consideration(s) ⟨Br, MS 1, WH, BG⟩, (*considération(s)* ⟨B⟩), inspection ⟨MS 1, WH⟩, (*examen* ⟨B⟩), (*analyse* ⟨R⟩), contemplation ⟨MS 3, WH⟩, (meditation ⟨WH, MS 4⟩), (*réflexion* ⟨B⟩), (observation(s) ⟨MS⟩); point of view. Save "reflection" ⟨WH, MS⟩ for "Reflexion". Cf. **Aussenbetrachtung, Beobachtung, Besinnung, Erwägung, Fundamentalbetrachtung, Überlegung.**

Betrachtungsweise, mode of observation. Cf. **Weise.**

betreffen, to touch, to concern.

betroffen, (vom Ichstrahl betroffen:) struck (by), (*atteint* ⟨R⟩). Cf. **treffen.**

Betrübtsein, (ant. Sichfreuen:) being sorry, (sorrow ⟨BG⟩), (*tristesse* ⟨R⟩).

beurteilen, to judge of ⟨WH, MS⟩ (or about). Cf. **urteilen.**

bevorzugen, to prefer ⟨WH 1, MS 1⟩.

bevorzugend, preferential, (*privilégiant* ⟨B⟩).

bevorzugt ⟨adj.⟩, predominant, that predominates, important; (*préféré* ⟨R⟩), (*privilégié* ⟨B⟩).

Bevorzugung, pre-eminence, primacy; preference ⟨WH 1, MS 1⟩. | **unter —,** primarily in the case of, (*en donnant un privilège à* ⟨R⟩).

bewahren, to preserve ⟨WH 2⟩. Cf. **erhalten.**

bewähren, (normally:) to verify ⟨Bn, WH, MS⟩, (*vérifier* ⟨R⟩), (sometimes:) to confirm ⟨MS 1⟩, (*confirmer* ⟨B⟩); (of a method:) to prove ⟨WH 1⟩. Cf. **ausweisen, bekräftigen, bestätigen, erfüllend-bewährend, erkennend-bewährend.**

Bewährung, verification ⟨WH, MS⟩, (*vérification* ⟨B, de M⟩), confirmation ⟨WH 1, MS 1⟩. Cf. **Bestätigung, Entwährung, Erfahrungsbewährung, Rechtfertigung.** | **in —,** as undergoing verification, (*dans une vérification* ⟨B⟩). | **negative —,** negative verification, (*vérification négative* ⟨B⟩), verification of the negative.

Bewegung, (physical:) motion ⟨WH 1⟩. Cf. **Fortbewegung.**

Beweis, proof (of) ⟨MS 1, WH 2⟩, (particularly with reference to Berkeley:) demonstration ⟨WH⟩, (*démonstration* ⟨B⟩), argument ⟨Bn, WH, MS⟩. Cf. **Ausweis, Erweis, Nachweis, Nachweisung, Schluss 1.** | (teleologischer **—**), teleological argument ⟨Bn⟩.

beweisen, to prove ⟨MS 1, WH 2⟩, (*prouver* ⟨B⟩), to demonstrate ⟨Ueberweg trln of Berkeley, quoted in LU, II. Unters.; WH; MS⟩ (logically), (*démontrer* ⟨B⟩). Cf. **aufweisen, ausweisen, erweisen, nachweisen.**

beweisend, probative, proving.

(Beweisfehler), fallacy ⟨Bn⟩.

Beweisform, proof-form, (*forme de démonstration* ⟨B⟩). Cf. **Schlussform**

Beweisführung, proving.

bewerten, to value ⟨WH, MS, BG⟩ (*évaluer* ⟨R⟩); to determine. Cf **werten.**

Bewertung, valuation ⟨WH, MS⟩. Not "appreciation" ⟨Bn⟩. Cf. **Entwertung, Wertung, Wertschätzung.**

bewusst ⟨adj.⟩, conscious ⟨WH 1, MS 1⟩, (*conscient* ⟨R⟩), of which there is (or I have) consciousness, (*dont on a conscience* ⟨R⟩), given in (a) consciousness, (of which I am conscious), (*présent à la conscience* ⟨B⟩) (*qui accède à la conscience* ⟨R⟩), in tentional ⟨WH⟩, intended to, (*conne* ⟨B⟩); aware. Cf. **bewusstseinsmässig mitbewusst, intentional.** | A ist **—** (A is conscious), there is consciousness of A, A is an object of consciousness, A is given in a consciousness, A is intentional, A is intended to. | **A ist mir —,** I am conscious (or aware ⟨BG⟩) of A, (*j'ai conscience de l'A* ⟨R⟩). | **anschaulich —,** of which there is intuitive consciousness, intuited. Cf. **anschaulich** ⟨adj. and adv.⟩. | **B ~es,** an object of consciousness, something intentional, something intended to. | **— haben,** see **bewussthaben.** | **ich bin eines A —,** I am conscious (or aware) of an

A ⟨WH 1, MS 1⟩, (*j'ai conscience d'un A* ⟨R⟩).

bewusst ⟨adv.⟩, consciously ⟨WH 1⟩, (*consciemment* ⟨B⟩), intentionally ⟨WH⟩. Cf. **bewusstseinsmässig, intentional.**

bewusthaben, to be conscious ⟨L⟩ (*or* aware ⟨BG⟩) of, (*avoir présent à la conscience* ⟨B⟩), (*prendre conscience de* ⟨R⟩), to have as an object of consciousness, (to have consciousness of), (to have consciously), (to have consciously before one ⟨BG⟩).

Bewusst(-)haben, consciousness-of, consciousness of something, (*conscience* ⟨R⟩), (*avoir conscience de* ⟨B⟩), (awareness of), (*avoir-présent-à-la-conscience* ⟨B⟩). Not "having-consciousness" ⟨L⟩. Cf. **Hintergrundbewusthaben, Vordergrundbewusthaben.**

Bewusstheit, awareness (Boring 1950), (*pleine conscience* ⟨B⟩). | ~en, awarenesses, (*aspects conscientiels* ⟨R⟩).

bewusstlos, without consciousness, (*sans conscience* ⟨R⟩), non-conscious. Save "unconscious" ⟨WH 1, MS⟩ for "unbewusst".

Bewusstsein, 1. (noetic:) consciousness ⟨WH 1, MS, BG⟩, (*conscience* ⟨R, B, de M⟩); being conscious; (pl.:) intendings. 2. (noematic or objective:) being an object of consciousness, being intended. Cf. **Aktbewusstsein, bewusst, Denkbewusstsein, Erfahrungsbewusstsein, Erleben, Gegebenheitsbewusstsein, Gemeinschaftsbewusstsein, Nochbewusstsein, Sachbewusstsein.** | **es kommt uns zum —,** we become (*or* we are) conscious of it. | **reines — der Beliebigkeit,** consciousness of its purely optional character.

bewusstseinsabsolut, | das B~e, the absolute of consciousness, (*l'absolu de la conscience* ⟨R⟩), (consciousness in its absoluteness ⟨BG⟩).

Bewusstseinsaffiziertes, affected subject of consciousness. Cf. **Bewusstseinstätiges.**

Bewusstseinsart, mode of consciousness, (*type de conscience* ⟨R⟩). Cf. **Art.**

Bewusstseinsbereich, domain of consciousness, (*domaine de la connaissance* ⟨B⟩). Cf. **Bereich.**

Bewusstseinscharakter, consciousness-characteristic. Cf. **Charakter.**

Bewusstseinsdifferenz, different species of consciousness. Not "consciousness-differences" ⟨L⟩. Cf. **Differenz.**

Bewusstseinserlebnis, process of consciousness, process or state of consciousness, (*vécu de conscience* ⟨R, B⟩), consciousness-process, conscious process. Not "conscious experience" ⟨BG⟩. Cf. **Erlebnis.**

Bewusstseinsferne, distance for consciousness. Cf. **Ferne, Ichferne.**

Bewusstseinsfluss, flow of consciousness. Cf. **Bewusstseinslauf, Fluss.**

Bewusstseinsforschung, investigation of consciousness. Cf. **Forschung.** | **reine —,** investigation of pure consciousness, (*étude de la conscience pure* ⟨R⟩). Not "inquiry into the nature of pure consciousness ⟨BG⟩.

Bewusstseinsgegenwart, present of consciousness. Not "presence of consciousness" ⟨L⟩. Cf. **Bewusstseinspräsenz.**

Bewusstseins-Gemeintes, | alles —, everything that is a meant of consciousness.

Bewusstseinsgenesis, genesis in consciousness, (*genèse de la conscience* ⟨B⟩). Cf. **Genesis.**

Bewusstseinsgesetzmässigkeit, Cf. **Gesetzmässigkeit.** | **zeitkonstituierende —,** regularity of time-constituting consciousness, (*légalité de la conscience constitutive temporellement* ⟨B⟩).

Bewusstseinslauf, course of consciousness. Cf. **Ablauf, Bewusstseinsfluss, Verlauf.**

Bewusstseinsleben, conscious life, (*vie de la conscience* ⟨B⟩). Cf. **Leben.**

Bewusstseinsleistung, performance of consciousness; productivity of consciousness, (*effectuation de conscience* ⟨B⟩). Cf. **Leistung.**

bewusstseinsmässig, in the manner peculiar to consciousness, according to consciousness, conscious(ly), relative to consciousness, *(en rapport avec la conscience* ⟨R⟩), in consciousness, *(dans la conscience* ⟨R, B⟩), for consciousness, *(pour la conscience* ⟨R⟩), in conscious fashion, *(de façon consciente* ⟨R, B⟩), *(d'une manière consciente* ⟨B⟩), *(sous forme de la conscience* ⟨B⟩), intentional(ly). Not "in accordance with the requirements of consciousness" ⟨BG⟩, not "in some conscious measure" ⟨BG⟩. Cf. **bewusst** ⟨adj. and adv.⟩, **intentional.**

Bewusstseinspräsenz, presence for consciousness, *(présence à la conscience* ⟨B⟩). Cf. **Bewusstseinsgegenwart, Präsenz.**

Bewusstseinssphäre, | eigentliche —, sphere of consciousness proper. Not "proper sphere of consciousness" ⟨L⟩.

Bewusstseinsstrom, stream of consciousness. Cf. **Bewusstseinslauf.**

Bewusstseinstätiges, active subject of consciousness. Cf. **Bewusstseinsaffiziertes, tätig.**

Bewusstseinstätigkeit, activity *(or* operation) of consciousness, *(activité de la conscience* ⟨B⟩).

Bewusstseinssubjekt, subject of the consciousness, *(sujet qui a un tel mode de conscience* ⟨B⟩).

Bewusstseinsunterschied, difference partaining to consciousness, *(distinction sur le plan de la conscience* ⟨R⟩).

Bewusstseinsvorkommnis, event of consciousness ⟨L⟩. Cf. **vorkommen.**

Bewusstseinswandlung, change in consciousness, *(mutation qui affecte la conscience* ⟨R⟩). Cf. **Wandlung.**

Bewusstseinsweise, mode of consciousness, *(mode de conscience* ⟨R, B⟩). Cf. **Weise.**

Bewusstseinszusammenhang, nexus of consciousness, *(ensemble de la conscience* ⟨B⟩), *(flux conscientiel* ⟨B⟩). Cf. **Zusammenhang.**

bezeichnen, 1. to designate ⟨WH, MS, BG⟩, *(désigner* ⟨R, B⟩), (to refer to ⟨?⟩ ⟨BG⟩).
2. to put a sign on, to mark ⟨MS 1, WH⟩; to characterize ⟨WH, MS⟩, *(caractériser* ⟨R, B⟩), *(qualifier* ⟨B⟩); to point out ⟨WH⟩.
3. (with reference to Berkeley:) to signify ⟨Ueberweg trln, quoted in LU, II. Unters.⟩.
4. (with reference to Mill:) to denote ⟨Gomperz trln, cited in LU, I. Unters.⟩; to indicate ⟨MS⟩, (to signify ⟨?⟩ ⟨ibid.⟩). Not "to connote" ⟨Gomperz trln, cited in LU, I. and II. Unters.⟩.
5. (logic generally:) to denote ⟨WH, MS⟩.
6. to betoken.
7. to be.
Save "to describe" ⟨WH, BG⟩ for "beschreiben". Cf. **anzeichnen, hindeuten, hinweisen auf, kennzeichnen, mitbezeichnen, zeichnen. | scharf —,** to accentuate.

Bezeichnen, designating; marking. Cf. **Anzeichnen, Zeichen.**

bezeichnend ⟨adj.⟩, designative; characteristic ⟨WH 1, MS⟩, *(caractéristique* ⟨B⟩); apposite; *(significatif* ⟨B⟩). Cf. **mitbezeichnend.**

bezeichnet, designated, *(désigné* ⟨R⟩); characterized, *(caractérisé* ⟨R, B⟩); marked, indicated ⟨BG⟩. Save "signified" ⟨BG⟩ for "bedeutet".

Bezeichnung, designation ⟨WH 2, MS 2, L⟩, *(désignation* ⟨R⟩), (logical:) denotation ⟨Bn, WH⟩, characterization ⟨WH, L⟩, marking ⟨WH 1, MS 1⟩. Cf. **Anzeichnung, Bezeichnen, Mitbezeichnung, Zeichen.**

beziehbar, referable ⟨?⟩, *(pouvant être rapporté* ⟨B⟩).

beziehen, *(mettre en relation* ⟨R⟩). Cf. **anknüpfen an, bezogen. | eine Gattung auf etwas —,** to extend a genus to something, *(rapporter un genre à quelque chose* ⟨B⟩). | **etwas auf etwas —,** (usually:) to relate something to something. | **sich auf etwas —,** 1. to relate to something ⟨MS 2, WH⟩, *(se rapporter à quelque chose* ⟨R, B⟩), *(se

réferer à quelque chose ⟨R, B⟩), to have relation to something.
2. (particularly of persons and expressions:) to refer to something ⟨MS 1, WH⟩, (to have (*or* make ⟨MS⟩) reference to something ⟨WH⟩).
3. to concern something, (to bear on something ⟨WH⟩).
So far as possible save "to refer" for "verweisen" ⟨q.v.⟩.
beziehend ⟨adj.⟩, (*relationnel* ⟨R⟩). | **sich — auf,** relating to, (referential ⟨MS⟩).
beziehend ⟨adv.⟩, relatingly, (*d'une manière référentielle* ⟨B⟩).
Beziehung, (wherever possible:) relation ⟨Gomperz trln of Mill, quoted in LU, II. Unters.; WH; MS; BG⟩, (*relation* ⟨R, B⟩), (*rapport* ⟨B⟩), interrelation, relationship ⟨WH⟩, respect ⟨WH, BG⟩, connexion ⟨WH, MS⟩; (esp. literary:) reference ⟨WH, MS⟩, (*réference* ⟨B⟩); relating. Cf. **Allgemeinheitsbeziehung, Anweisung auf, Bedeutungsbeziehung, Bezug, Bezugnahme, Mitbeziehung, Relation, Rückbeziehung, Rückbezogenheit, Sinnbeziehung, Verhältnis, Verknüpfung, Wesensbeziehung, Zeitbeziehung, Zusammenhang.** | **auf etwas — haben,** to have (a) relation to something, to be relative to something, (of expressions or concepts, sometimes:) to refer to something ⟨MS 2⟩, (to bear upon something ⟨MS 1⟩. | **dingliche Ordnung und —,** physical order and connexion. Cf. **dinglich, Ordnung.** | **gegenständliche —,** see entry under **gegenständlich.** | **in — auf,** in relation to ⟨WH 1, MS 3, BG⟩, (*en relation avec* ⟨R⟩), relating to, relatively to, (*par rapport à* ⟨R, B⟩), in its relationship to, in respect of, respecting, concerning, with reference to ⟨MS 2⟩, (*en se référant à* ⟨R⟩), with regard to ⟨MS 1⟩. Cf. **bezogen auf, in Hinblick auf** (*sub* **Hinblick**), **mit Beziehung auf.** | **in — bringen,** to bring into relation, to relate. | **in — setzen,** to inter-

relate, (*mettre en relation* ⟨B⟩). | **in — setzen zu,** to relate (something) to (something); to put (something) into a relation to (something), (*poser* (*quelque chose*) *en relation à* (*quelque chose*) ⟨R⟩). | **in — stehen zu,** to relate to, to have (a) relation to. | **in — stehend,** related. | **in — stehend zu,** relative to. | **in dieser —,** in this connexion ⟨WH 1, MS 1⟩; in this respect ⟨WH 2, MS 2⟩. | **in jeder —,** in every respect ⟨MS 1⟩, from every point of view ⟨MS 2⟩, to all intents. | **in seiner — zu,** in its relation to, (*dans sa relation à* ⟨B⟩). | **mit — auf,** relating to, (*en rapport avec* ⟨R⟩), with reference to ⟨BG⟩; with respect to, in view of. Cf. **in Beziehung auf, bezogen auf.**
Beziehungsgesetze zwischen, laws that state the relation between, (*lois de la relation entre* ⟨B⟩).
bezogen, Cf. **beziehen, weltbezogen, zurückbezogen.** | **— auf,** relating to, (*relatif à* ⟨R⟩), (*rapporté à* ⟨B⟩). Cf. **in Beziehung auf, mit Beziehung auf.** | **— sein auf,** to be related to ⟨BG⟩, (*être rapporté à* ⟨B⟩), to relate to, (*se rapporter à* ⟨R⟩), to be relative to, to be connected with, (*se rattacher à* ⟨R⟩), to be concerned with, (to be extended to), (to have a reference to), (*renvoyer à* ⟨B⟩). | **immanent —,** relating to something immanent, (*rapporté de façon immanente* ⟨R⟩). Not "immanently related" ⟨BG⟩.
Bezogenheit (**auf** *oder* **zu**), relatedness (to), (reference (to)), (*réference* ⟨R, B⟩, (bearing ⟨WH⟩ (upon)). Cf. **Rückbezogenheit, Zeitbezogenheit, Zurückbezogenheit.**
Bezug, relation ⟨MS 3⟩ (to), (connexion ⟨MS 1⟩ (with)), (reference ⟨MS 2⟩ (to)). Cf. **Anweisung auf, Beziehung, Bezugnahme, Naturbezug, Verhältnis, Verknüpfung, Zusammenhang.** | **— haben auf,** to relate to ⟨MS 1⟩, (to refer to ⟨MS 2⟩). | **— habend (auf),** relative (to). | **— nehmen,** to refer. | **in — auf,** in relation to ⟨MS 3⟩, (*par rapport à*

⟨B⟩), with relation to, relative to, (*se rapportant à* ⟨B⟩), (literary:) with reference to ⟨MS 2, WH 2⟩, (with regard to ⟨MS 1, WH⟩), (concerning), (*en ce qui concerne* ⟨B⟩). | mit — auf, with relation to, in relation to ⟨MS 3⟩, (literary:) with reference to ⟨MS 2, WH⟩, (with regard to ⟨MS 1, WH⟩).

bezüglich ⟨adj.⟩, relative ⟨WH 1, MS 1, L⟩, (*relatif* ⟨B⟩), relational, relating, (*se rapportant* ⟨B⟩), (*qui se rapporte* ⟨B⟩), related, (*rapporté* ⟨B⟩); respective; in question. Cf. **Sachbezüglich.**

Bezüglichkeit, relativeness, relatedness, (reference). Cf. **Identitätsbezüglichkeit, Sachbezüglichkeit.**

Bezugnahme (auf), reference (to) ⟨WH 1, MS 1⟩, (*référence (à)* ⟨R⟩). Cf. **Beziehung, Bezug.** | mit — auf, with reference to ⟨MS 1, WH 2⟩, referring to, (respecting ⟨WH, MS⟩), (with regard to ⟨MS 2, WH⟩).

Bild, image ⟨Bn, MS 1; WH; Schultze trln of Hume, quoted; BG⟩, (*image* ⟨R, B⟩); picture ⟨WH, MS, BG⟩, (*image-portrait* ⟨R⟩), (*portrait* ⟨R⟩), metaphor. Save "copy" ⟨BG⟩ for "Abbild" ⟨q.v.⟩ and "Nachbild". Cf. **Abbildung, Bildobjekt, Gemeinbild, Phantasiebild, Urbild, Vorbild, Vor-Bild.** | inneres —, internal image, (*portrait interne* ⟨R⟩). Cf. **innere.**

Bildbewusstsein, image-consciousness, (picture consciousness), (*conscience de portrait* ⟨R⟩). Cf. **Abbildungsbewusstsein.**

bilden, to form ⟨WH 1, MS 1⟩, (*former* ⟨R, B⟩), to fashion ⟨WH 3, MS 4⟩, to shape ⟨WH 2, MS 2⟩, to frame, to cultivate ⟨WH, MS⟩, (to produce), to construct ⟨MS⟩, (*construire* ⟨R, B⟩); to make up, to be ⟨WH⟩. So far as possible save: "to constitute" ⟨WH⟩ for "konstituieren", "to shape" for "gestalten", "to build up" ⟨BG⟩ for "aufbauen" (q.v.). Cf. **einbilden, Gebilde, gestalten, herausarbeiten.**

Bilden, forming.

bildend, formative ⟨MS 1, WH⟩, (*formateur* ⟨B⟩), forming, (productive), (constructive). Cf. **aufbauend, formbildend, gestaltend, konstruktiv, leistend.**

Bildertheorie, image-theory, picture-theory, (*théorie des images* ⟨R⟩). Not "copy-theory" ⟨BG⟩.

bildlich ⟨adj.⟩, pictorial, as something depicted, (*du type portrait* ⟨R⟩). Cf. **verbildlichen.** | ∼e Vergegenwärtigung, making present as something depicted, (*présentification du type portrait* ⟨R⟩). Cf. **Vergegenwärtigung.**

bildlich ⟨adv.⟩, pictorially ⟨L⟩, (*en portrait* ⟨R⟩), as what is depicted. | — gemeint, meant as what is depicted. | — vorgestellt, objectivated pictorially. Cf. **Bildvorstellung, vorgestellt.**

bildmässig ⟨adv.⟩, pictorially. Not "imaginatively" ⟨BG⟩.

Bildobjekt für, picture-Object representing, (*objet-portrait à l'égard de* ⟨R⟩). Cf. **Objekt.**

Bildung, formation ⟨MS 1, WH, BG⟩, (*formation* ⟨R, B⟩), forming ⟨WH 1⟩, shaping ⟨WH 2⟩, fashioning, culture ⟨Bn, WH, MS⟩; (product), (construction), (*construction* ⟨R, B⟩), constructing. Cf. **Abbildung, Aufbau, Ausgestaltung, Bau, Begriffsbildung, Einbildung, Einheitsbildung, Formenbildung, Formbildung, Formung, Fortbildung, Gebilde, Gegenstandsbildung, Gestalt, Gestaltung, Konstruktion, Leistung, Selbstbildung, Sinnbildung, Stufenbildung, Umbildung, Urteilsbildung, Zahlbildung.**

Bildungsform, formation-form, form of a formation, (*forme de construction* ⟨B⟩). Cf. **Formenbildung, Formbildung.**

Bildungsmethode, method of formation, (*méthode qui forme* ⟨B⟩).

Bildvorstellung, image-objectivation, picture-objectivation. Save "image" ⟨BG⟩ for "Bild" ⟨q.v.⟩. Cf. **bildlich vorgestellt** (*sub* **vorgestellt**), **Vorstellung 1, Zeichenvorstellung.**

Billigung, approbation ⟨Bn, WH 1, MS 2⟩, (*approbation* ⟨R⟩), approval ⟨MS 1, WH 2, BG⟩; consent ⟨MS 3, WH 4⟩, agreement ⟨WH 3, MS 4⟩. Cf. **Missbilligung.**

binden, Cf. **beschränken, einschränken, gebunden an.** | — **an,** to restrict to, (*offrir une liaison avec* ⟨B⟩). | **sich** — **an,** to restrict oneself to, (*s'attacher à* ⟨B⟩).

Bindung an, restriction to, (*attaché avec* ⟨B⟩), (*liaison avec* ⟨B⟩). Cf. **gebunden an, Gebundenheit.** | **in** —, by obeying, (*en liaison avec* ⟨B⟩).

Blick, (wherever possible:) regard ⟨Bn⟩, (*regard* ⟨R, B⟩), look ⟨WH 1, MS 1, BG⟩, eye ⟨WH⟩, glance ⟨MS 2, WH, BG⟩, (*coup d'oeil* ⟨B⟩), (gaze ⟨WH, BG⟩), (*attention* ⟨B⟩); vision ⟨WH, BG⟩, (*vue* ⟨B⟩), sight ⟨WH⟩, view ⟨WH, MS⟩, (viewing ⟨?⟩). Not "scrutiny" ⟨BG⟩. Cf. **Anschauung, erblicken, Gesicht, Hinblick, Ichblick, Schau, Sehen.** | — **auf,** regard to; regarding (*or* viewing ⟨?⟩) of. Cf.**Blick-auf.**| **gegenständlich vor dem logischen** — **haben,** to have before one logically as one's object. | **im** — **haben,** to have one's eye on, (*avoir en vue* ⟨B⟩). Cf. **Im-geistigen-Blick-haben.** | **im thematischen** —, as an object of thematizing regard, (as a theme within one's field of regard (*or* vision)). Cf. **thematisch.** | **in einen** — **treten,** to become the object of a regard. | **thematischer** —, thematizing regard, (*regard* (ou *vue*) *thématique* ⟨B⟩). Cf. **thematisch.**

Blick-auf, regard-to, (*regard sur* ⟨R⟩). Not "glancing towards" ⟨BG⟩. Cf. **Blick auf** (*sub* **Blick**).

Blickfeld, field of regard ⟨Bn⟩, field of possible regard (cf. Ideen I, *105*, *n.*); (field of vision ⟨WH⟩); scope ⟨WH⟩, (*champ d'investigation* ⟨B⟩). Cf. **Gesichtsfeld.** | — **der Aufmerksamkeit,** field of (possible) attentive regard (cf. Ideen I, *105, l. 4-6*), attention's field of (possible) regard, (*champ du regard de l'attention* ⟨B⟩).

(Blicklinie), line of regard ⟨Bn⟩.

Blickpunkt, focus ot regard, (*foyer de regard* ⟨R⟩); (focus of vision ⟨BG⟩), (fixation point ⟨Bn⟩).

Blickrichtung, direction of regard ⟨Boring 1942, *230*⟩, (*direction de regard* ⟨B⟩), (*direction d'examen* ⟨B⟩), (line of regard ⟨Bn⟩, (*orientation du regard* ⟨R⟩); (line of vision). Not "direction of the mental glance" ⟨BG⟩. Cf. **Gesichtslinie, Richtung.** | **in der** — **auf,** when one directs one's regard to, (*dans la direction du regard sur* ⟨R⟩).

Blickstellung, focusing of regard, (*disposition du regard* ⟨R⟩), (*orientation* (ou *direction*) *d'examen* ⟨B⟩). Cf. **Einstellung.**

Blickstrahl, ray of regard, (*rayon du regard* ⟨R⟩); ray of vision. Cf. **Ichstrahl.** | — **des Ich,** ray of the Ego's regard, (*rayon du regard émis par le moi* ⟨R⟩). Cf. **Ich.**

Blickwendung, turn(ing) of regard, (*tourné* (ou *conversion*) *du regard* ⟨R⟩), turning one's regard. Not "directing of one's look (*or* the mental glance)" ⟨BG⟩, not "directing one's glance" ⟨BG⟩. Cf. **Wendung.**

bloss ⟨adj.⟩, mere ⟨WH, MS⟩, bare ⟨WH, MS⟩, sheer, (*simple* ⟨R, B⟩).

bloss ⟨adv.⟩, merely ⟨WH, MS⟩, just ⟨WH⟩, (*uniquement* ⟨B⟩).

Boden, basis ⟨WH, MS⟩, (*base* ⟨B⟩), ground ⟨MS 1, WH, BG⟩, footing ⟨WH, MS⟩, standpoint, field ⟨WH⟩, (*terrain* ⟨PL, B⟩), realm ⟨MS⟩. Cf. **Erdboden, Erfahrungsboden, Fundament, Fundierung, Grund, Grundlage, Seinsboden, Sinnesboden, Substruktion, Untergrund, Unterlage, Urboden, Urteilsboden, Weltboden.** | **auf dem** — **des natürlichen Denkens,** within the realm of ⟨MS⟩ natural thinking. | — **der Erfahrung,** experiential basis, (*base d'expérience* ⟨B⟩). | — **der Phänomenologie,** realm of phenomenology, (*domaine de la phénoménologie* ⟨R⟩. | **der** — **der Abstraktion,** the realm of abstraction. | **rein phänomenologischer** —, realm of pure phenomenology (*domaine purement phénoménologi-*

que ⟨R⟩). | **sich auf ihren — stellen,** to take them as one's basis, (*se placer sur le terrain* ⟨R⟩). | **von einem — des Gemeinsamen,** from a ground consisting in that which is common. Cf. **Gemeinsames.**
Boden-Form, basis-form.
Bodenkörper, basis-body.
bodenständig, (ant., zusammenge-

brochen:) standing on (*or* having) a solid basis, (fundamentally) sound.
Bodenständigkeit, footing on a solid basis.
Bodenstätte, basis-place, footing-place.
Bürgschaft, guarantee ⟨WH⟩, (*garantie* ⟨R⟩). Cf. **gewährleisten.**
Bürgschaftsleistung, guaranteeing. Cf. **Leistung.**

C

Charakter, characteristic ⟨WH 2⟩, character ⟨WH 1, MS 1, BG⟩, (*caractère* ⟨R, B, de M⟩). Cf. **Ablaufscharakter, Aktcharakter, Beschaffenheit, Bewusstseinscharakter, Evidenzcharakter, Geltungscharakter, Glaubenscharakter, Merkmal, Seinscharakter, Setzungscharakter, Typus, Vernunftcharakter, Wertcharakter.** | **— an etwas,** character stamped on something, (*caractère sur* ⟨R⟩). | **praktischer —,** practical

characteristic, (*aspect pratique* ⟨B⟩). Not "practicality" ⟨BG⟩.
Charaktereigenschaft, trait of character. Cf. **Eigenschaft, Merkmal.**
Charakterisierung, characteristic; (characterization ⟨?⟩ ⟨WH 1, BG⟩), (*caractérisation* ⟨R⟩).
Charakteristik, characterization ⟨WH 1⟩, (*caractérisation* ⟨B⟩).
Commercium, commerce. Cf. **Gemeinschaft.**

D

Dabei-sein, being-with, (*être-en-présence-de* ⟨B⟩). Cf. **Bei-ihm-selbst-sein.**
dahinfliessend, smoothy flowing.
dahingestellt bleiben, to remain undecided ⟨MS⟩.
Dahinleben, living along, (life). Not "urge of life" ⟨BG⟩. Cf. **Leben.**
dahinterliegend, lying further back than something else lies.
Daraufhinsetzen, positing-thereupon. Cf. **Hinsetzung, Setzen.**
Daraufsetzung, positing-thereupon. Cf. **Setzung.**
darstellen, (usually:) to present ⟨Bn, MS 1, WH⟩, (*présenter* ⟨B⟩), to set forth ⟨WH⟩, (*exposer* ⟨B⟩), to exhibit ⟨WH, MS⟩; to exemplify; to be; to represent ⟨WH 1, MS⟩, (*représenter* ⟨B⟩), (*figurer* ⟨R⟩); to state. Cf. **ausstellen, herausstellen, vergegenwärtigen, vorstellen, verweisen.** | **sich —,** to present itself ⟨L⟩, (*se présenter* ⟨B⟩). Cf. **auftreten,**

sich geben (*sub* geben), **Sich-selbstdarstellen, Sich-selbst-geben, vorliegen.**
darstellend (für), presentive (with respect to); (representing ⟨?⟩). Cf. **uneigentlich.**
Darstellung, (usually:) presentation ⟨Bn, WH 1, MS 1⟩, setting forth, exhibition ⟨Bn, MS 2⟩, (*exhibitio* ⟨K⟩); (*apparence* ⟨de M⟩); representation ⟨WH, MS⟩, (*figuration* ⟨R⟩); statement ⟨WH, MS⟩, (*exposé* ⟨B⟩), exposition ⟨WH, BG⟩; description ⟨WH⟩; (*analyse* ⟨R⟩). Cf. **Ausführung, Aussage, Gegenwärtigung, Herausstellung, Selbstdarstellung, Vergegenwärtigung, Vorstellung.**
Darstellungsfunktion, presentive function, (*fonction figurative* ⟨R⟩). Cf. **Funktion.**
Darstellungsmodus, mode of presentation.

daseiend, 1. factually existing, factually existent, (*existant,* ⟨R, B⟩). Save "existing" and "existent" for "seiend". 2. that is there, (*qui est là* ⟨B⟩), being there. Cf. **aktuell** ⟨adj.⟩ **2, faktisch, vorhanden, wirklich.** | (ein) **D ~es,** 1. something factually existing, a factual existent. Save "something that exists" and "an existent" for "ein Seiendes" (q.v. sub "seiend"). Not "an empirical being" ⟨L⟩. 2. something that is there. | **leibhaftig —,** being there in person, (*existant corporellement* ⟨R⟩). Not "corporally existent" ⟨BG⟩.

Dasein, *A.* (status:) 1. factual existence, (existence ⟨Bn, WH, MS, BG⟩), (*existence* ⟨R, B⟩), factual being. So far as possible save "existence" for "Existenz" and "Sein" ⟨q.v.⟩, and "being" ⟨L⟩ for "Sein" and "Wesen" ⟨q.v.⟩. 2. being there, (*être-présent* ⟨B⟩), thereness. *B.* (concretum:) factual being, factual existent, (*existant de la nature* ⟨R⟩). Save "existent" (n.) ⟨BG⟩ for "Seiend". Cf. **Bestehen, Mitdasein, Sein, Vorhandensein.** | **~setzung,** positing of (the) factual existence, (*position d'existence* ⟨R⟩). Cf. **Seinssetzung, Setzung.** | **~sthesis,** positing of factual existence, (*position d'existence* ⟨R⟩). Not "reference to concrete existence" ⟨BG⟩. Cf. **Thesis.**

Datum, Datum (capitalized). Cf. **Auffassungsdatum, Erlebnisdatum, Gegebenheit, Sinnendaten.**

Dauer, duration ⟨WH 1, MS 1⟩, (lastingness ⟨?⟩). Cf. **fortdauern, Hindauer, Tondauer, Zeitdauer.**

Dauereinheit, duration-unity. Cf. **Einheit.**

Dauerinhalt, duration-content. Cf. **Inhalt.**

Dauerstrecke, duration-extent. Cf. **Strecke.**

decken, | **sich —,** 1. to coincide ⟨WH 1, BG⟩ (with one another) ⟨Heath, *Euclid* I, 227; MS⟩, (*coïncider* ⟨R, B⟩), to be identical ⟨WH, MS⟩. 2. (of terms:) to have the same extension, (to be equivalent).

Deckung, coincidence ⟨F⟩, (*coïncidence* ⟨R, B⟩), coinciding; overlapping; (*recouvrement* ⟨B⟩). Cf. **Identitätsdeckung, Überdeckung, Übergreifen, Überschiebung.**

Deckungseinheit, union of coincidence. Cf. **Einheit.**

Deckungssynthesis, coincidental synthesis.

deduktiv ⟨adj.⟩, deductive ⟨WH 1, MS 1⟩, (*déductif* ⟨B⟩); deducible.

deduktiv ⟨adv.⟩, deductively, (*déductivement* ⟨B⟩); deducibly .| **— beschlossen in,** deducibly included in, (*déductivement impliqué dans* ⟨B⟩). Cf. **beschlossen in.**

definit, definite, ("*défini*" ⟨R, B⟩). Cf. **bestimmt.**

Definitheit, definiteness, (*définitude* ⟨B⟩). Cf. **Bestimmtheit.**

Denkakt, act of thinking, cogitative act.

denkbar, conceivable ⟨WH 1⟩, (*concevable* ⟨B⟩), thinkable ⟨WH, BG⟩. Cf. **denkmöglich, erdenklich, undenkbar.**

Denkbestimmung, determination effected by thinking, (*détermination que la pensée réalise* ⟨R⟩). Not "thought-determination" ⟨BG⟩. Cf. **Bestimmung.**

Denkbewusstsein, thinking consciousness.

Denkeinheit, unity for thinking, unity produced by thinking, (*unité de pensée* ⟨R⟩). Not "unity of thought" ⟨BG⟩; not "form of thought" ⟨BG⟩. | **konstruktive —,** constructional unity produced by thinking, (*construction de la pensée unificatrice* ⟨R⟩). Not "constructive form of thought" ⟨BG⟩. Cf. **konstruktiv** ⟨adj.⟩.

Denkeinstellung, attitude in thinking. Cf. **Denkhaltung, Einstellung.**

denken, to think ⟨WH 1, MS 1⟩, (*penser* ⟨R, B⟩), (*cogitare* ⟨Husserl⟩); to think of ⟨WH⟩, (*penser de* ⟨B⟩); to mean ⟨WH⟩; to conceive ⟨WH⟩, (*concevoir* ⟨B⟩); (to understand). Cf.

fassen, gedacht, Gedachtes, meinen, vermeinen, vorstellen 3. | sich —, to think of, to phantasy, (s'imaginer ⟨B⟩), (se figurer par la pensée ⟨R⟩), (se représenter ⟨B⟩), (concevoir ⟨B⟩). Cf. einbilden, fingieren, phantasieren, sich hineindenken (sub hineindenken), Sich-denken, vorstellen 2 and 3.

Denken, thinking ⟨WH 1, MS 1, BG⟩, (penser ⟨B⟩), process of thinking, (pensée ⟨R, B⟩|; phantasying. Save "thought" ⟨trln of Mill, quoted in LU II/1, Einl.; WH 2, L, BG⟩ for "Gedanke". Cf. Sich-denken, Umdenken.

Denkender, thinking subject, (sujet pensant ⟨R⟩), (celui qui pense ⟨B⟩).

Denkerlebnis, process of thinking. Cf. Erlebnis.

Denkfunktion, function for thinking, (fonction de la pensée ⟨B⟩). Cf· Funktion.

Denkgebilde, formation produced by thinking, (product of thinking), (thought-formations), (formation de pensée ⟨B⟩). Cf. Denkleistung, Gebilde.

Denkgegenständlichkeit, objectivity produced by thinking, (objectivité de pensée ⟨B⟩). Cf. Denkobjekt.

Denkhaltung, attitude in thinking, thinking attitude. Cf. Denkeinstellung, Haltung.

Denkhandlung, action of thinking, (activité de pensée ⟨B⟩). Cf. Handlung.

Denkintention, cogitative intention.

Denkleistung, production effected by thinking, (effectuation de la pensée ⟨B⟩), product of thinking; thinking (or cogitative) production, thinking productivity. Cf. Denkgebilde, Leistung.

Denkmal, monument ⟨WH 1, MS 1⟩, memorial ⟨WH 2, MS 2⟩.

denkmöglich, possible in thinking, thinkable, conceivable, (concevable ⟨B⟩). Cf. denkbar, erdenklich.

denknotwendig, necessary in thinking, (intellectually necessary ⟨?⟩ ⟨BG⟩).

Denkobjekt, Object of thinking, (objet de pensée ⟨B⟩). Cf. Denkgegenständlichkeit, Objekt.

Denkrichtung, direction of thinking. Cf. Richtung.

Denkstellungnahme, cogitative position-taking, (position adoptée par la pensée ⟨R⟩). Cf. Stellungnahme.

Denksynthesis, cogitative synthesis, (pensée synthétique ⟨R⟩). Not "synthetic thinking" ⟨BG⟩.

deskriptiv, (noetic, conceptual, or expressive:) descriptive ⟨WH 1⟩, (descriptif ⟨B⟩), of description; (of phenomena:) descriptional, (observable and) describable, (descriptif ⟨R⟩).

deutbar, interpretable ⟨WH⟩.

deuten, to interpret ⟨WH, MS⟩, (to construe ⟨WH, MS⟩). Cf. auffassen, ausdeuten, erklären.

deutlich, distinct ⟨MS 1, WH⟩, (distinct ⟨R⟩), plain ⟨WH⟩. Cf. undeutlich, verdeutlichen.

Deutlichkeit, distinctness ⟨MS 1, WH⟩, (distinction ⟨R, B, de M⟩), (caractère distinct ⟨B⟩). | blosse Evidenz der —, merely distinct evidence, (simple évidence de la distinction ⟨B⟩). | der —, of distinctness, (de la distinction ⟨B⟩); distinct. | Evidenz der —, distinct evidence, distinct evidentness; (évidence de la distinction ⟨B⟩). | Evidenz der — haben, to be distinctly evident, (avoir l'évidence de la distinction ⟨B⟩). | in der —, as distinct, (with distinctness), (dans la distinction ⟨B⟩). | zur — bringen, to make distinct, (amener à la distinction ⟨B⟩).

Deutlichkeitsevidenz, distinct evidence, (évidence de la distinction ⟨B⟩). | zur — bringen, to make distinctly evident, (amener à l'évidence de la distinction ⟨B⟩).

Deutung, interpretation ⟨MS 1, WH 2⟩. Cf. Andeuten, Auffassung, Ausdeutung, Umdeutung.

Dies(-)da, this(-)there ⟨see Ideen I, 34f.; BG⟩, (ceci-là ⟨R⟩). Cf. τόδετί.

Diesheit, (concretum:) this(-here); (determination:) thisness, (eccéité ⟨R⟩).

Differenz, differentia ⟨Br⟩; (different) species, different sort, difference ⟨WH 1, MS 1⟩, (différence ⟨R, B⟩). Cf. **Besonderung, Bewusstseinsdifferenz, Farbendifferenz, Unterschied, Verschiedenheit.** | **letzte** —, ultimate differentia, (ultima differentia ⟨Bn⟩); infima species; ultimate difference. | **letzte spezifische** —, ultimate specific differentia; infima species; ultimate specific difference. | **niederste** —, ultimate differentia; infima species; ultimate difference, (différence ultime ⟨R⟩). | **spezifische** —, specific differentia, (differentia specifica ⟨Br⟩); specifically different sort; specific difference.

differenzieren, (of a genus:) to divide.

differenzierend, differentiating, (qui différencie ⟨R⟩).

Dignität, rank, (dignité ⟨R⟩).

Ding, (concrete) physical thing; thing ⟨MS 1, WH, BG⟩, (chose ⟨R, B⟩). Cf. **Erfahrungsding, Etwas, Raumding, Sache, Sehding, Sinnending, Tastding.** | **— der Natur,** physical thing belonging to Nature, (chose située dans la nature ⟨R⟩). Cf. **Naturding.** | **physikalisches** —, physical thing as determined in physics, (chose selon la physique ⟨R⟩). Not just "physical thing" ⟨BG⟩. Cf. **physikalisch.**

Dingauffassung, physical-thing apprehension. Cf. **Auffassung.**

Dingbestimmung, determination of the physical thing, (détermination de la chose ⟨R⟩). Cf. **Bestimmung.**

Dingerfahrung, experience of a physical thing, (expérience de la chose ⟨B⟩). Cf. **Erfahrung.**

Dingerscheinung, physical-thing appearance. Cf. **Erscheinung.**

Ding-gegebenes, physical-thing datum, (donnée de chose ⟨R⟩). Not "thinggiveness" ⟨BG⟩.

Ding-gegebenheit, physical-thing datum. Cf. **Gegebenheit.**

dinglich, physical, of something physical, of a (or the) physical thing, of (physical) things, (des choses ⟨R⟩); thing- ⟨F⟩, (thingly ⟨not in OED⟩). Save "real" ⟨WH 1, MS 1⟩ for "real". Not "thinglike" ⟨BG⟩. Cf. **physikalisch, physisch, verdinglichen.** | **~es,** something physical. Save "reality" ⟨L⟩ for "Reales" and "Realität".

Dinglichkeit, 1. physicalness; (thinghood ⟨BG, not in OED⟩).
2. physical affair, physicality, (chose ⟨R⟩). Not "thing" ⟨L⟩; not "entity of the nature of a thing" ⟨BG⟩; not "potential thing" ⟨BG⟩. Save "reality" ⟨L⟩ for "Reales" and "Realität". Cf. **Sache.**

dinglich-real, physically real. Not "real after the manner of things" ⟨L⟩. Cf. **real.**

Dingrealität, physical reality; (thing-reality (?) ⟨BG⟩). Cf. **Reales.**

Dingwahrnehmung, perception of a physical thing, (perception de choses ⟨B⟩). Cf. **Wahrnehmung.**

Dingwelt, world of physical things, (monde des choses ⟨R⟩). Not "world of things" ⟨BG⟩.

disjunkt, mutually exclusive, excluded discrete, disjunctive. | **~e Teile,** discrete parts. Not "disjunct parts" ⟨F⟩.

Doppeldeutigkeit, double significancy, (ambiguity ⟨?⟩ ⟨BG⟩), (dualité de sens ⟨R⟩).

doppelseitig, two-sided, (à double orientation ⟨B⟩).

Doppelsinn, two senses, (double sense), (double sens ⟨B⟩). Not "twofold meaning" ⟨BG⟩. Cf. **Sinn.** | **korrelativer** —, two correlative senses, (double sens corrélatif ⟨B⟩).

Doxa, doxa, (doxa ⟨R⟩). Save "belief" for "Glaube". Cf. **Urdoxa.**

doxisch, doxic ⟨BG, not in OED⟩, (doxique ⟨R⟩).

Dreischichtung, threefold (or triple) stratification, (triple stratification ⟨B⟩), (stratification ternaire ⟨B⟩), division into three strata; distinguishing of three strata. Cf. **Schichtung.**

Dunkelheit, (lack of clarity:) obscurity ⟨MS⟩; (lack of light:) darkness ⟨WH 1, MS 1⟩.

Durchbruch, (sometimes:) emergence,

(*apparition* ⟨B⟩). | **zum — kommen,** to emerge, (*faire son apparition* ⟨B⟩). Cf. **sich herausheben** (*sub* **herausheben**).

Durchforschung, exploration ⟨WH 1⟩. Save "investigation" ⟨WH, L⟩ for "Forschung" (q.v.) and "Untersuchung". Cf. **Erforschung.**

durchgängig, pervasive, ubiquitous, complete, (*universel* ⟨B⟩), (*omnimodo* ⟨K⟩). Cf. **abgeschlossen, vollständig.**

durchgehend ⟨adj.⟩, running through-

out, all-inclusive, (*se faisant jour* ⟨B⟩). Cf. **universal.**

durchherrschen, to govern throughout.

durchleben, to live through ⟨WH 1, MS 1⟩. Cf. **erleben.**

durchstreichen, to cancel ⟨WH, MS⟩, (*biffer* ⟨R, B⟩), to strike out ⟨MS 1, WH⟩. Cf. **aufheben, negieren, Undurchstreichbarkeit.**

Durchstreichung, cancellation, (*biffage* ⟨B⟩), striking out. Cf. **Aufhebung, Vernichtung, Zunichtemachung.**

E

echt, genuine ⟨MS 1, WH⟩, (*véritable* ⟨PL⟩), (*vrai* ⟨B⟩), (*authentique* ⟨R⟩); (rarely:) legitimate ⟨MS⟩. Save "authentic" ⟨WH, MS, L⟩ for "ursprungsecht". Cf. **berechtigt, eigentlich, gesetzmässig, rechtmässig, reell, unecht, wirklich.**

Echtheit, genuineness ⟨MS 1⟩, (*authenticité* ⟨R, B, de M⟩). Save "authenticity" ⟨WH, MS⟩ for "Ursprungsechtheit". Cf. **Eigentlichkeit, Unechtheit.**

ego, ego (not capitalized). Cf. **Alterego, Ich.**

Eidetik, eidetics ⟨WH 1⟩, (*eidétique* ⟨R⟩).

eidetisch ⟨adj.⟩, eidetic ⟨WH 1⟩, (*eidétique* ⟨R⟩), eidetical.

eidetisch ⟨adv.⟩, eidetically, (*eidétiquement* ⟨B⟩), as eidetic.

Eidos, eidos, (*Eidos* ⟨R⟩).

eigen, own ⟨WH 1, MS 1, BG⟩, (*propre* ⟨R, B⟩), of one's own ⟨WH 3, MS 3, BG⟩, one's own ⟨MS 2⟩, (*nôtre* ⟨B⟩), (*qui est nôtre* ⟨B⟩), own peculiar, peculiar ⟨WH, MS⟩, (*original* ⟨R⟩), peculiar to, (own) proper ⟨BG⟩, (*authentique* ⟨R⟩), proper to ⟨WH, L⟩ appertinent, specific; intrinsic; particular ⟨WH, MS⟩, in particular, by itself, separate ⟨WH⟩, (*distinct* ⟨R⟩), in its own right; that belongs. Cf. **besondere, eigenheitlich, eigentümlich, für sich** (*sub* **für**), **selbsteigen, zugehörig.** | **die ihm**

selbst ~en, that are peculiar to it itself (*qui sont propre à quelque chose elle-même* ⟨B⟩), (its very own). | **~er Wesensgehalt,** essential contents proper. Cf. **Wesensgehalt.** | **E ~es,** see separate entry. | **ein ~er Akt,** a particular act, (*un acte original* ⟨R⟩). Not "an act proper" ⟨BG⟩. | **ein ihm ~es Recht,** a competence of its own. Not "an independent right of its own" ⟨BG⟩. Cf. **Recht.** | **eine ~e Welt,** a world of its own. | **eines ~en Wesens,** with an essence of its own. | **mein E ~es,** my own. | **mir ~es,** (peculiarly) my own. Cf. **Mir-Eigenes.**

Eigenart, own specific character, specific character of its own, (*caractères distinctifs* ⟨B⟩), character ⟨WH⟩; own specific peculiarity, (*spécificité* ⟨R⟩), peculiarity ⟨MS 1⟩; own sort. Cf. **Art, Charakter.**

eigenartig ⟨adj.⟩, own specific, specifically peculiar, (*spécifique* ⟨R⟩), (*propre* ⟨B⟩); of a peculiar sort, (*sui generis* ⟨R⟩), unique. | **prinzipiell —,** essentially unique. Cf. **prinzipiell** ⟨adv.⟩.

Eigenberechtigung, proper legitimacy ⟨?⟩. Cf. **Berechtigung.**

Eigenbestimmtheit, determination of its own, (*détermination propre* ⟨R⟩). Not "distinctive property of its own" ⟨BG⟩. Cf. **Bestimmtheit.**

Eigenes, (peculiarly) my ⟨*or* his⟩ own

⟨MS⟩, what is peculiar to me, owness Cf. **Mir-Eigenes, Nichteigenes, Selbsteigenes.** | **das Eigene,** (what is) my (*or* its) own, the property ⟨WH⟩, (*le caractère propre* ⟨R⟩), (*la caractéristique* ⟨B⟩); (the intrinsic nature (?) ⟨BG⟩). Cf. **Eigenschaft.** | **das mir Eigene,** what is my own, what is peculiar to me. | **diese Eigene,** this owness, this "my own". | **ihm —,** something peculiarly his own. | **mein —,** my own. | **mein primordial —,** what (*or* that which) is primordially my own, (*ce qui m'est propre en premier* ⟨B⟩).

Eigengehalt, own content, (*statut propre* ⟨R⟩). Not "individual content" ⟨BG⟩. Cf. **Gehalt.**

Eigengeltung, legitimacy ⟨?⟩. Cf. **Geltung.**

Eigenheit, owness ⟨in OED⟩, peculiar owness, own peculiarity, peculiarity ⟨WH, MS⟩, (*caractère propre* ⟨B⟩), (*particularité* ⟨B⟩), (property ⟨WH⟩), (*propriété* ⟨R⟩), (*spécificité* ⟨R⟩), (*originalité* ⟨R⟩). Save "singularity" ⟨WH, BG⟩ for "Einzelheit" (q.v.) and "Singularität" (q.v.). So far as possible save "property" for "Eigenschaft" (q.v.; cf. CM *132, l. 3–8*). Cf. **Besonderheit, Eigenheitlichkeit, Selbsteigenheit, Wesenseigenheit.** | **—en,** ownesses, components of my owness, features of my own, peculiarities, (*propriétés* ⟨R⟩).

eigenheitlich ⟨adj.⟩, (peculiarly) my (*or* his) own, included in my peculiar owness, within my owness, of my owness, owness. Cf. **eigen.** | **~e Natur,** Nature included in my peculiar owness. | **~e Präsentation,** presentation within my owness. | **~e Reduktion,** owness-reduction. Cf. **Eigenheitsreduktion.** | **~e Reinigung,** owness-purification. | **E ~es,** see separate entry. | **~es Wesen,** owness-essence. | **meine ~e Sphäre,** the sphere of my owness.

eigenheitlich ⟨adv.⟩, | **— gefasst,** taken as included in my owness. Cf. **fassen.** | **— konstituiert,** constituted

as part of my (peculiar) owness. | **— reduziert,** reduced to what is included in my owness.

Eigenheitliches, what is included in my owness, something included in my owness, owness. Cf. **Eigenheit.** | **das Eigenheitliche,** the owness, what is included in (*or* belongs to) my (peculiar) owness, what is my own. **mein —,** what is included in my owness.

Eigenheitlichkeit, (peculiar) owness. Cf. **Eigenheit.**

Eigenheitsreduktion, reduction to what is included in my owness. Cf. **eigenheitliche Reduktion** (*sub* **eigenheitlich** ⟨adj.⟩).

Eigenheitssphäre, sphere of my (peculiar) owness. Cf. **Eigensphäre.**

Eigenrecht, own legitimacy, (*droit propre* ⟨B⟩), independent legitimacy Cf. **Recht.**

Eigenschaft, property ⟨Bn; Gomperz trln of Mill, quoted in LU, II. Unters.; WH; MS; BG⟩, (*propriété* ⟨B, de M⟩), (*qualificative* ⟨R⟩), (own (*real*) property), trait, (*qualitas* ⟨K⟩). Save "quality" ⟨WH 1, MS 1⟩ for "Qualität". Cf. **Charaktereigenschaft, das Eigene** (*sub* **Eigenes**), **Wesenseigenschaft.** | (verborgene Eigenschaften), (*qualitates occultae* ⟨K⟩).

eigenschaftlich ⟨adj.⟩, | **~es Moment,** property-moment. | **~es Prädikat,** "adjectival" property-predicate, (*prédicat-attribut* ⟨R⟩).

eigenschaftlich ⟨adv.⟩, predicatively as having a property.

Eigenschaftlichkeit, the category of properties.

Eigensein, own (peculiar) being, (*être propre* ⟨R⟩), being that is peculiar (to something), (*originalité* ⟨R⟩). Cf. **Sein.** | **konkretes —,** own concrete being. | **primordiales —,** own primordial being.

Eigensphäre, sphere of (peculiar) owness. Cf. **Eigenheitssphäre.**

eigenständig ⟨adj.⟩, self(-)sufficient, independent, (*autonome* ⟨B⟩). Cf. **für sich, selbständig, unabhängig.**

eigenständig ⟨adv.⟩, self(-)sufficiently,

independently, (*d'une manière autonome* ⟨B⟩).

Eigenständigkeit, self(-)sufficiency, (*autonomie* ⟨B⟩), self-supportedness ⟨?⟩.

eigentlich ⟨adj.⟩, proper ⟨WH, MS⟩ (placed after the noun, if possible), (*propre* ⟨B⟩), true ⟨MS⟩, genuine ⟨F⟩, (*authentique* ⟨B⟩), strict ⟨WH, BG⟩, real ⟨MS⟩, (properly so-called ⟨BG⟩), (*proprement dit* ⟨B⟩), (*au sens propre du mot* ⟨R⟩). So far as possible save "true" for "wahr" and "wahrhaft", "genuine" for "echt" ⟨q.v.⟩, "strict" for "streng", "real" for "real". Cf. **wirklich, vereigentlichend.**

eigentlich ⟨adv.⟩, properly ⟨WH 1⟩, (*proprement* ⟨R, B⟩), truly, (*vraiment* ⟨B⟩), (*véritablement* ⟨B⟩), genuinely, strictly ⟨WH, BG⟩, (*exactement* ⟨B⟩), in strictness, just, really ⟨WH⟩, indeed, actually ⟨WH⟩, properly speaking ⟨WH 1, MS⟩, ((*d'une manière*) *à proprement parler* ⟨B⟩), (*à dire proprement* ⟨B⟩), (*proprement dit* ⟨R, B⟩). So far as possible save "truly" for "wahrhaft", "strictly" for "streng", "actually" for "wirklich". Cf. **uneigentlich** ⟨adv.⟩.

Eigentlichkeit, properness, trueness, genuineness, (*caractère propre* ⟨B⟩). So far as possible save "trueness" for "Wahrheit" ⟨q.v.⟩ and "genuineness" for "Echtheit".

eigentümlich ⟨adj.⟩, appertinent. Cf. **eigen, zugehörig.**

Eigentümlichkeit, peculiarity ⟨WH 1⟩, (*propriété distinctive* ⟨R⟩), (*trait caractéristique* ⟨R⟩), (*trait distinctif* ⟨R⟩). Cf. **Besonderheit.**

Eigenwesen, my (*or* his *or* its) own essence, proper essence, (*essence propre* ⟨R, B⟩). Cf. **Wesen.** | **das intentionale —,** its own intentional essence. | **sein reines —,** its own pure essence.

eigenwesentlich ⟨adj.⟩, own essential, included in (*or* belonging to) my (*or* its) own essence, that is a moment of my own essence, within my own

essence, pertaining to the proper essence, ((*qui lui est*) *essentiellement propre* ⟨B⟩). Cf. **Mir-Eigenwesentliches, wesentlich** ⟨adj.⟩.

eigenwesentlich ⟨adv.⟩, as moments (*or* as a moment *or* as part) of my own essence; in its own essence. Cf. **wesentlich** ⟨adv.⟩.

Eigenwesentliches, Cf. **Konkret-eigenwesentliches.** | **das Eigenwesentliche,** what is included in (*or* what appertains to) the own-essentiality, (*ce qui appartient essentiellement* ⟨B⟩), the own essentiality (*caractère essentiellement propre* ⟨B⟩), (*l'essence propre* ⟨B⟩). | **das Eigenwesentliche des Anderen,** what belongs to the Other's own essence. | **das mir Eigenwesentliche,** the own-essentiality belonging to me. Cf. **Mir-Eigenwesentliches.** | **das mir selbst Eigenwesentliche,** my peculiarly own essentiality. | **mein —,** what is included in my own essence.

Eigenwesentlichkeit, own-essentialness (*caractère essentiel propre* ⟨B⟩).

eignen, (governing the dative:) to be a property of, to characterize, (to belong to ⟨MS⟩), (*s'attacher à* ⟨R⟩).

einbeziehen in, to bring into ⟨WH 1⟩, to introduce into, (*insérer dans* ⟨B⟩), to include in ⟨WH 2⟩, (*inclure dans* ⟨B⟩), (*impliquer dans* ⟨B⟩), to make a part of, to incorporate in ⟨WH 3⟩, to organize within. Cf. **beschliessen, einlegen, Hereinziehung.**

einbilden, Cf. **hineinbilden.** | **sich —,** to imagine ⟨WH 2, MS 2⟩, (*feindre* ⟨R⟩); (to fancy ⟨WH 1, MS 3⟩). Cf. **fingieren, phantasieren, sich denken,** (*sub* **denken**), **vorstellen 3.**

Einbildung, 1. (noetic:) imagination, (*imagination* ⟨R⟩). 2. (object:) something imagined, (*fiction* ⟨R⟩). Cf. **Bild, Bildung, Erdichtung, Fiktion.**

(Einbildungskraft), (*facultas imaginandi* ⟨K⟩).

eindeutig, univocal, (*univoque* ⟨R⟩), unambiguous ⟨WH 1⟩.

Eindeutigkeit, univocalness, (*univocité*

⟨R⟩), unequivocalness ⟨WH 2⟩, unambiguousness ⟨WH 1⟩. Cf. **Vieldeutigkeit.**

Einfall, something coming (*or* that comes) to mind, (*idée qui vient* (ou *survient*) *à l'esprit* ⟨B⟩), (something occurring to one), conceit, (*idée* ⟨R, B⟩); having something come to mind. Cf. **Erinnerungseinfall.** | **apperzeptiver** —, something coming (*or* that comes) to mind apperceptionally, (*idée en tant que surgissement aperceptif* ⟨B⟩). Cf. **apperzeptiv** ⟨adj.⟩.

Einfall-Modifikation, modification, as something coming to mind, (*modification qui est une idée qui vient à l'esprit* ⟨B⟩), (*modification du type du surgissement d'une idée* ⟨B⟩).

einfallen, to come to mind ⟨MS⟩, (*passer par la tête* ⟨R⟩).

Einformung, | — **in etwas haben,** to be formed as entering into something, (*recevoir une forme à l'intérieur de quelque chose* ⟨B⟩). Cf. **Formung.**

einfühlen, | **sich** —, to feel oneself into, to empathize (with).

Einfühlen, empathizing, (*intropathie* ⟨R⟩).

Einfühlung, empathy ⟨WH 2, BG⟩, (*intropathie* ⟨R, B⟩), "empathizing".

Einfühlungsgemeinschaft, community of empathy, (*communion par intropathie* ⟨B⟩). Cf. **Gemeinschaft.**

einfühlungsmässig, empathic.

Einfühlungszusammenhang, nexus of empathy, (relation of empathy ⟨?⟩ ⟨BG⟩), (*rapport d'intropathie* ⟨R⟩). Cf. **Zusammenhang.**

eingelegt, attributed.

eingesehen, (intellectually) seen. Cf. **einsehen.**

eingestellt, in (*or* having) an attitude, focused, set, (orientated). | **arithmetisch** —, in the arithmetical attitude. | — **auf,** focused on. (*orienté vers* ⟨B⟩). | **erkennend-bewährend** —, set to cognize and to verify, (*orienté vers l'activité de connaissance et de vérification* ⟨B⟩). Cf. **bewähren, erkennen.** | **kritisch** — **sein,** to have a critical attitude, (*avoir une orien-*

tation critique ⟨B⟩). | **natürlich** —, in the natural attitude, (*placé dans l'attitude naturelle* ⟨R⟩). Not "at the natural standpoint" ⟨BG⟩. | **theoretisch** —, in (*or* having) a (*or* the) theoretical attitude, (interested in theory). | **wissenschaftstheoretisch** —, interested in a theory of science, (*dans une orientation épistémologique* ⟨B⟩).

eingreifen in, to engage with ⟨WH⟩ (*or* in ⟨WH⟩), (*empiéter sur* (ou *dans*) ⟨B⟩).

Einheit, (ant. Mehrheit:) unity ⟨MS 1, WH, BG⟩, (*unité* ⟨R, B, de M⟩), (*unitas* (trln of Leibniz, Arith *150*)); (mensuration or counting:) unit ⟨WH 1, MS 3⟩; union ⟨MS 2⟩; oneness ⟨WH⟩. Cf. **Alleinheit, Bedeutungseinheit, Dauereinheit, Deckungseinheit, Einigkeit, Erfahrungseinheit, Erfüllungseinheit, Erkenntniseinheit, Erlebniseinheit, Geltungseinheit, Lebenseinheit, Masseinheit, Sinneseinheit, Urteilseinheit.** | —**zwischen,** union between.

einheitlich ⟨adj.⟩, unitary ⟨WH⟩, (*unitaire* ⟨R, B⟩); united ⟨MS 1⟩, (*formant unité* ⟨B⟩), (*qui a une unité* ⟨B⟩). Not "unified". Cf. **zweiseitig-einheitlich.** | **prinzipiell** —, essentially unitory. Cf. **prinzipiell** ⟨adv.⟩.

einheitlich ⟨adv.⟩, unitarily, (*d'une manière unitaire* ⟨B⟩); unitedly, (as a unit). | — **erlebt,** lived unitedly. Cf. **erlebt.**

Einheitsbewusstsein, unity-consciousness, consciousness of (something's) unity.

Einheitsbildung, unity-formation. Cf. **Bildung.**

Einheitsform, unity-form, (*forme d'unité* ⟨B⟩); form of union; (*forme unitaire* ⟨B⟩), (*forme unitive* ⟨R⟩).

Einheitsfunktion, unity-function, (*fonction d'unité* ⟨B⟩). Cf. **Funktion, Funktionseinheit.**

Einheitsgestalt, unity-structure; (*type d'unité* ⟨B⟩). Cf. **Gestalt.**

Einheitspunkt, union-point. Not "rallying-point" ⟨L⟩.

Einheitssinn, sense of (something's) unity; (*sens d'unité* ⟨B⟩).

Einheitszusammenhang, connexion of unity, (*connexion* ⟨B⟩). Cf. **Zusammenhang.**

einige, some ⟨Bn, WH, MS⟩.

Einigkeit, oneness. Cf. **Einheit.**

Einigung, union ⟨WH 2⟩. | **Synthese der —,** uniting synthesis.

einklammern, to parenthesize ⟨WH, MS⟩, (*mettre entre parenthèses* ⟨R⟩).

Einklammerung, parenthesizing, (*mise entre parenthèses* ⟨R⟩). Not "bracketing" ⟨BG⟩.

(Einklang), unison ⟨Bn, WH 1, MS 1⟩.

einleben, cf. **hineinleben.** | **sich — in,** to enter into, to immerse oneself in.

Einleben in, making oneself conversant with.

einlegen, 1. (with dative:) to put within (something), to include in, (*inclure dans* ⟨R⟩), to attribute to, (*imposer à* ⟨R⟩).
2. (with "in":) to introduce into ⟨WH⟩. Cf. **einbeziehen in, zurechnen.**

einleuchtend, (intellectually) evident. Cf. **einsichtig, evident.**

einmalig, never repeatable, (*unique* ⟨R⟩). | **E∼es,** one-time affair.

einordnen, (with dative:) to fit to, (*ranger dans* ⟨B⟩), to make a member of. | **etwas dem Umfang —,** to make (something) a member of the extension. Cf. **Umfang.** | **sich — in,** to take place in, (*prendre place dans* ⟨B⟩), to find oneself a place in, to find its place within, (*s'insérer dans* ⟨R⟩), (*venir se ranger dans* ⟨B⟩). Cf. **sich einordnen unter** (*sub* **ordnen**).

Einordnung, | **— in eine Klasse,** putting in a class. | **— in einen Zusammenhang haben,** to have its place in a complex. | **historische ∼en,** historical connexions. Cf. **Zusammenhang.**

einsam, | **∼e Rede,** soliloquy. Not "solitary speech" ⟨F⟩. Cf. **Rede, Wechselrede.**

einschachteln, to encase ⟨MS⟩. Cf. **ineinanderschachteln, Schachtelung.**

Einschaltung, (ant. Ausschaltung ⟨LU,

V. Unters. *369, n. 2*⟩:) reinclusion, (*inclusion* ⟨B⟩), (insertion ⟨?⟩ ⟨WH 1, MS 1⟩).

einschliessen, to include; (logically:) to imply. Cf. **beschliessen, schliessen, nach sich ziehen** (*sub* **ziehen**).

einschränken, to restrict ⟨WH 1, MS 1⟩, (*restringere* ⟨K⟩), to limit, (*limitare* ⟨K⟩). Cf. **begrenzt, beschränken, binden.**

einsehbar ⟨adv.⟩, discernibly, (*d'une manière évidente* ⟨B⟩).

Einsehbarkeit, accessibility to insight, (*possibilité d'évidence* ⟨B⟩). Cf. **erschaubar.**

einsehen, to have insight into, to have the insight (that …), to see intellectually, to discern, to see ⟨WH, MS⟩, (*voir avec évidence* ⟨B⟩), (*saisir avec évidence* ⟨R⟩), (*perspicere* ⟨K⟩). Cf. **absehen, eingesehen, erschauen, sehen.**

Einsehen, (act of) insight, intellectual seeing, discerning, seeing. Not "seeing into" ⟨BG⟩; not "inseeing" ⟨BG⟩. Cf. **Einsicht, Erschauung, Schauung, Sehen.**

einsehend, with insight, intellectually seeing, discerning, seeing. Not "that which understands" ⟨BG⟩. Cf. **einsichtig** ⟨adj.⟩.

einseitig ⟨adj.⟩, (*unilatéral* ⟨R⟩).

einseitig ⟨adv.⟩, one-sidedly, (*sous une seule face* ⟨R⟩).

Einseitigkeit, one-sidedness ⟨WH 1, MS 1⟩.

Einsicht, insight ⟨MS, BG⟩, act of insight; intellectual sight (*or* seeing), (*vue intellectuelle* ⟨R⟩), (*intelligence* ⟨B⟩), something seen intellectually; discernment ⟨WH⟩, discerning, something discerned; (*évidence intellectuelle* ⟨R⟩ ou *rationnelle* ⟨B⟩ ou *apodictique* ⟨B⟩ ou *eidétique* ⟨R⟩), (*évidence* ⟨R, B⟩); (sight), (*vue* ⟨B⟩), (*idée évidente* ⟨B⟩), seeing, something seen; (*intuition* ⟨PL⟩); (*pouvoir de pénétration* ⟨B⟩). Though OED indicates that the relevant senses of "insight" are obsolete, to dispense with that word in translating "Einsicht" and cognate terms is undesirable. Save "intuition" for "Anschauung" (q.v.). Cf. **Struktureinsicht, Wesenseinsicht.** | **subjektive Reflexion auf** —, reflection on subjective insight, (*réflexion subjective sur l'évidence rationnelle* ⟨B⟩). Cf. **Reflexion.** | **zur** — **bringen,** to make seen, to make evident, (*porter à l'évidence* ⟨R⟩). Not "to bring home to insight" ⟨BG⟩.

einsichtig ⟨adj.⟩, with insight, given in insight, a matter (*or* an object) of insight, having the quality of insight, clarified by insight; intellectually seeing, intellectually seen; discerning, discerned; apodictically evident, (*apodictiquement* (ou *absolument*) *évident* ⟨B⟩); evident, (*évident* ⟨R, B⟩), (*compris avec évidence* ⟨B⟩). Cf. **einzusehend** ⟨adj.⟩, **evident** ⟨adj.⟩, **uneinsichtig.** | **in ~er Weise,** with insight ⟨BG⟩, in the manner peculiar to intellectual seeing. Cf. **einsehend.** | **mittelbar** —, (noetic:) with insight, (*d'évidence médiate* ⟨R⟩). | **möglicherweise** —, with possible insight, with possible intellectual seeing; possibly seen intellectually (*or* apodictically). | **unmittelbar** —, (noematic:) an object of immediate insight, immediately evident, (*immédiatement évident* ⟨B⟩), (*dont l'évidence est immédiate* ⟨R⟩).

einsichtig ⟨adv.⟩, with insight ⟨BG⟩, in insight, by insight; with intellectual seeing; with apodictic evidence, (*avec une évidence absolue* ⟨B⟩); with evidence, (*avec évidence* ⟨R, B⟩, (evidently). Cf. **evident** ⟨adv.⟩. | — **begründet,** established by insight, (*fondé avec une évidence absolue* ⟨B⟩). Cf. **begründet.** | — **gegeben,** given in insight, (*donné avec évidence* ⟨B⟩).

Einsichtigkeit, insight, (insightfulness ⟨?⟩ ⟨F; not in OED⟩); intellectual seenness, apodictic evidentness, evidentness, (*évidence* ⟨B⟩). Cf. **Evidenz, Uneinsichtigkeit.**

einstellen, 1. to put in ⟨WH 2⟩ (its place) ⟨MS 1⟩; to set, to adjust ⟨WH MS⟩, to focus ⟨WH, MS⟩, (to orientate).
2. to drop, to discontinue ⟨WH, MS⟩. Cf. **eingestellt, gestellt sein, orientieren, richten nach** (*sub* **richten**). | **sich** —, 1. to set oneself, to take an attitude, to orientate oneself (toward(s)).
2. to take place, to occur. | **sich** — **auf,** to focus on, (*s'orienter vers* ⟨B⟩).

Einstellung, attitude ⟨Bn, Boring 1950, WH⟩, (*attitude* ⟨R, B⟩), focusing ⟨WH⟩, focus ⟨WH⟩, attitude or focus, orientation ⟨L⟩, (*orientation* ⟨B⟩), (set ⟨Boring 1950⟩), setting ⟨WH⟩, disposition ⟨Bn⟩, stand ⟨F; cf. Krisis, *153, l. 21-31*⟩, (*position* ⟨B⟩), (*tournée* ⟨B⟩). Not "position" ⟨BG⟩; not "standpoint" ⟨L, BG⟩; not "point of view" ⟨BG⟩. Cf. **Blickstellung, Denkeinstellung, Inneneinstellung, Erfahrungseinstellung, Erkenntniseinstellung, Haltung, Orientierung, Richtung, Stellung, Umstellung, Urteileinstellung.** | **abstraktive** —, abstractive focusing, (*attitude abstractive* ⟨B⟩). | **apophantische** —, focusing on the apophansis, (apophantic focusing), (*attitude* (ou *position*) *apophantique* ⟨B⟩). | **eidetische** —, eidetical attitude. | — **auf Sinne,** focusing on senses, (*attitude orientée vers le sens* ⟨B⟩). | — **der Weltlichkeit,** world-accepting attitude Cf. **Weltlichkeit.** | **gegenständliche** —, focusing on what is objective, objective focus, (*orientation vers l'objet* ⟨B⟩). Cf. **gegenständlich.** | **in der noematischen** —, when focused on the noematic, (*dans l'attitude noématique* ⟨B⟩). | **in der phänomenologischen** —, in the phenomenological attitude, as meant in the phenomenological attitude. Not "from the phenomenological point of view" ⟨L⟩. | **in einer verschiedenen** —, as meant in different attitudes. | **in empirisch-psychologischer** —, as accepted in the attitude appropriate to empirical psychology. | **in noematischer** —, while focusing on the noematic aspect, (*dans une attitude noématique* ⟨B⟩). | **in ontischer** —, when (thinking is) focused on the existent, (*dans l'attitude ontique* ⟨B⟩). | **naturale** —, focusing on Nature. | **natürliche** —, natural attitude, (*attitude naturelle* ⟨R⟩). Not "natural standpoint" ⟨BG⟩; not "natural setting" ⟨BG⟩. | **normative** —, normative attitude, (*orientation normative* ⟨B⟩). | **objektiv-ideale** —, focusing on what is objective and ideal, (*tourné vers l'objectivité idéale* ⟨B⟩). | **ontologische** —, ontological focusing, (*attitude ontologique* ⟨B⟩). | **psychophysikalische** —, psychophysical attitude. | **subjektive** —, focusing on what is subjective, subjective focus, (*attitude subjective* ⟨B⟩). | **thematische** —, focusing on a theme, thematizing (*or* thematical) focusing, (*orientation* (ou *attitude*) *thématique* ⟨B⟩). Cf. **thematische Umstellung** (*sub* **thematisch**).

Einstellungsänderung, alteration (*or* change) of one's attitude (*or* of attitude *or* focus), (*changement* (ou *modification*) *d'attitude* ⟨B⟩), (*modification d'orientation* ⟨B⟩).

einstimmig ⟨adj.⟩, harmonious, (*harmonique* ⟨B⟩), (*concordant* ⟨R, B⟩), (*cohérent* ⟨R⟩). Cf. **stimmen mit.**

einstimmig ⟨adv.⟩, harmoniously, (*harmonieusement* ⟨R⟩), (*d'une manière harmonique* ⟨B⟩), with one voice.

Einstimmigkeit, harmony, accord ⟨WH 1⟩, accordance, (*concordance* ⟨R, B⟩), agreement ⟨WH 2⟩. | **in** —, harmonious.

Einteilung, (logical:) division ⟨WH 1, MS 1⟩, (*division* ⟨B⟩). Cf. **Teilung, Zerstückung.**

Einverstehen, | **— in den Anderen,** understanding of what occurs in others. Cf. **verstehen.**

einverstehend, | **jeder sich in das Subjekt E~e,** everyone who puts himself (understandingly) in the subject's place.

Einwand, objection ⟨Bn, WH 1, MS

1⟩. | **richtiger** —, valid objection. Cf. **richtig.**

Einwendung, objection ⟨Bn, MS 1, WH 2⟩.

(Einwirkung), action ⟨WH 1, MS⟩ on ⟨Bn⟩. Cf. **Gegenwirkung, Tätigkeit, Wirkung.**

einwohnen, (with dative:) to inhere in ⟨WH, MS⟩, (*résider en* ⟨R⟩), (*habiter en* ⟨R⟩). Cf. **in etwas liegen,** (*sub* **liegen**), **innewohnend.**

Einzelanschauung, intuition of a single particular (*or* of single particulars), (*intuition individuelle* ⟨R⟩). Save "particular intuition" ⟨BG⟩ for "Sonderanschauung". Cf. **Anschauung.**

Einzelfall, single case, (*cas particulier* ⟨B⟩). Not "individual instance" ⟨L⟩.

Einzelheit, 1. (concretum:) single, single particular, single case, (*cas particulier* ⟨R⟩), (singular), (*individualité* (*singulière*) ⟨B⟩), (particular ⟨WH⟩), (*élément particulier* ⟨B⟩), (*élément individuel* ⟨B⟩), (*cas individué* ⟨B⟩). The relevant sense of "singularity" is obsolete ⟨OED⟩. 2. (property:) singleness ⟨WH 1⟩, singularity ⟨MS 1, WH 2⟩. Not "individuality" ⟨Bn, MS 2, WH 3⟩. Cf. **Besonderheit, Besonderung, ein Einzelnes,** (*sub* **einzeln**), **Erfahrungseinzelheit, Vereinzelung.** | **— der Form,** single particular subsumed under the Form, (*cas particulier de la forme* ⟨B⟩). | **in** —, singly, (*considéré individuellement* ⟨B⟩). Cf. **einzeln** ⟨adv.⟩.

Einzelidee, (with reference to Berkeley:) particular idea (Ueberweg trln, quoted in LU, II. Unters.).

einzeln ⟨adj.⟩, 1. single ⟨MS 1, WH⟩, of the single particular (*or* individual), (singular), (particular ⟨Ueberweg trln of Berkeley, quoted in Arith and LU, II. Unters.; Schultze trln of Hume, followed by Husserl in LU, II. Unters.; MS 2; WH⟩), (*particulier* ⟨B⟩), (individual ⟨Schultze trln of Hume, followed by Husserl in LU, II. Unters.; WH⟩). So far as possible save "particular" for

"besondere" ⟨q.v.⟩ and "individual" for "individuell". 2. (contradictory of "kommunikativ" ⟨q.v.⟩:)
solitary ⟨WH⟩, (*isolé* ⟨B⟩), (*pris
isolément* ⟨B⟩).
3. (logic:) singular, (*singularis* ⟨K⟩).
Cf. **singular.** | der **E~e,** the single
subject, (*l'individu* ⟨B⟩). | ein **E~es,**
a single (particular). Cf. **Einzelheit.** |
~e Subjektivität, single subjectivity,
subjectivity of the single individual,
(*subjectivité individuelle* ⟨B⟩); solitary subjectivity, (*subjectivité prise
isolément* ⟨B⟩). Cf. **Einzelsubjektivi-
tät.** | **~es Urteil,** singular judgment,
(*judicium singulare* ⟨K⟩). | im **~en,**
(strict sense:) in respect of single
particulars.
einzeln ⟨adv.⟩, singly ⟨MS 1, WH,
BG⟩, (*sur un cas particulier* ⟨B⟩),
(*séparément* ⟨B⟩), (*isolément* ⟨R⟩),
(*en tant qu'êtres isolés* ⟨B⟩); in detail.
⟨Consult WH⟩. Cf. in **Einzelheit** (*sub
Einzelheit*).
einzelpersonal, private, (*individuel*
⟨B⟩).
Einzelpraxis, instance of practice,
(*praxis particulière* ⟨B⟩). Cf. **Praxis.**
Einzelsache, single matter, (*chose particulière* ⟨B⟩). Cf. **Sache.**
Einzelsubjekt, single subject, (*sujet
particulier* ⟨B⟩).
einzelsubjektiv ⟨adj.⟩, single-subjec-
tive, (*individuel* ⟨B⟩).
einzelsubjektiv ⟨adv.⟩, privately to a
single (*or* particular) subject. Cf.
einzelpersonal.
Einzelsubjektivität, (ant. Intersubjek-
tivität:) single subjectivity. Cf.
einzelne Subjektivität (*sub* **einzeln**
⟨adj.⟩).
Einzelvorstellung, (mental) objectivation of a single particular,
singular objectivation, single ob-
jectivation. | **individuelle —,** (men-
tal) objectivation of a single individual.
einzig, unique ⟨WH⟩, (*unique* ⟨R⟩);
single ⟨MS 1, WH, BG⟩.
einzigartig, unique ⟨WH 1, MS 1⟩,
(*exceptionnel* ⟨R⟩).
einzusehend ⟨adj.⟩, that which can be

discerned (*or* seen). Cf. **einsichtig**
⟨adj.⟩.
Elementarschluss, elementary ⟨WH⟩
argument, (*déduction élémentaire*
⟨B⟩). Cf. **Schluss 1.**
empfinden, to sense ⟨WH⟩, (*se rendre
compte* ⟨B⟩). Cf. **empfunden, fühlen.**
Empfindlichkeit, sensibility, ⟨MS 1;
WH; "the recognized translation"
— Bn⟩. Cf. **Sinnlichkeit.**
Empfindnis, feeling; sentiment (re-
gularly translated as "Empfind-
nis"). Cf. **Gefühl, Gemüt.**
Empfindung, sensation ⟨WH 1, MS⟩,
(*sensation* ⟨R⟩), (*sensatio* ⟨Wolff, K,
Hamilton⟩), (*perceptio* ⟨Wolff⟩). Cf.
Sinnesempfindung, Tonempfindung.
Empfindungs-, of sensation(s), (*de sensation* ⟨R, B⟩), sensation-, sensational, (*sensuel* ⟨R⟩), (sensed). Cf. **sen-
suell, sinnlich.**
Empfindungsdatum, Datum (capitalized) of sensation, (*datum de sensation* ⟨R, B⟩). Not "sensory datum"
⟨BG⟩. Cf. **Datum.**
Empfindungsfarbe, sensational color,
sensed color, (*couleur en tant que
sensation* ⟨B⟩).
Empfindungsinhalt, sensation-content.
Cf. **Inhalt.**
Empfindungskomplexion, complex (*or*
combination) of sensations, sen-
sation-complex ⟨F⟩. Cf. **Komplexion.**
empfunden, sensed, (*ressenti* ⟨B⟩),
(felt). Cf. **empfinden, fühlen.**
Empirie, *empeiria* (italicized), the empirical, (empirical inquiry), (experience (of matters of fact)), (field of
experienceable matters of fact),
(*procès* (ou *processus*) *empirique*
⟨B⟩), (*démarche empirique* ⟨B⟩).
empirisch-konkret ⟨adj.⟩, | **~e Tat-
sachenerkenntnis,** empirical cognition of concrete matters of
fact, (*connaissance concrète de type
empirique portant sur des faits* ⟨R⟩).
endgültig ⟨adj.⟩, ultimately valid,
(definitive ⟨WH 2, L⟩).
Endgültigkeit, final validity, definitive
validity, definitiveness. Cf. **Gültigkeit.**
endlich ⟨adj.⟩, finite ⟨WH 1, MS 2⟩,

(*fini* ⟨B⟩); (*achevé* ⟨B⟩); (hoped-for). Cf. **begrenzt, unendlich.**

endlos, endless ⟨WH 1, MS 2⟩. Cf. **unendlich.** | **offen —,** openly endless, (*jamais achevé* ⟨B⟩).

entfalten, to explicate, to unfold ⟨WH, MS⟩, (*déployer* ⟨B⟩), to develop ⟨WH, MS⟩, to display ⟨WH, MS⟩; to exercise. Cf. **auseinanderlegen, auslegen, explizieren, herausstellen.** | **eine Funktion —,** to exercise a function. Cf. **Funktion.**

Entfaltung, explication, unfolding ⟨MS 1, WH⟩, (*déploiement* ⟨B⟩), development ⟨WH, MS⟩, display ⟨WH, MS⟩, displaying in detail. Cf. **Auseinanderlegung, Auslegung, Explikation, Explizierung, Verdeutlichung.**

entfernen, Cf. **fern.** | **sich —,** to move away.

Entfernung, moving away.

enthalten, | **sich —,** to abstain ⟨WH 1, MS 1⟩, (*s'abstenir* ⟨PL⟩). Cf. **Mich-Enthalten.**

Enthaltung, abstention ⟨WH 1, MS 1⟩. Cf. **Urteilsenthaltung.**

enthüllen, to uncover ⟨WH 1, MS 1⟩, to disclose ⟨WH, MS⟩, (*dévoiler* ⟨PL⟩), (*mettre à nu* ⟨B⟩). | **sich —,** to become disclosed, (*se révéler* ⟨B⟩).

Enthüllen, uncovering ⟨MS 1⟩, disclosing ⟨MS⟩. Cf. **Herausstellen.**

enthüllend, revelatory.

Enthüllung, uncovering ⟨MS 1⟩, (*dévoilement* ⟨B⟩), (*révélation* ⟨PL⟩).

Entkräftigung, refutation, (*infirmation* ⟨R⟩). Cf. **Bekräftigung, Kraft.**

entnehmen aus, to take from, to draw from ⟨WH⟩, (*tirer de* ⟨B⟩), to obtain from, (*en dégager* ⟨R⟩).

Entrechnung, (*invalidation* ⟨R⟩).

Entscheidbarkeit, (*décidabilité* ⟨B⟩). Cf. **Zweifelsentscheidung.**

Entschliessung, deciding.

Entschluss, decision ⟨Bn, WH 1⟩, (*décision* ⟨R⟩).

entsprechend, corresponding ⟨WH, MS, L, BG⟩, (*correspondant* ⟨R, B⟩), answering; appropriate ⟨WH⟩, suitable ⟨WH, MS⟩, (*adéquat* ⟨B⟩).

entspringen, to originate ⟨MS⟩, to arise ⟨MS 1⟩, (*prendre naissance* ⟨B⟩), (*jaillir* ⟨B⟩), (governing the dative:) to derive from, (*en provenir* ⟨B⟩). Cf. **sich ergeben,** (*sub* **ergeben**), **stammen.** | **— aus,** to spring from ⟨WH, MS⟩, (*prendre leur source dans* ⟨B⟩), to originate from, ⟨WH, MS⟩, (*provenir de* ⟨B⟩), (*procéder de* ⟨R⟩), (*résulter de* ⟨B⟩). | **— durch,** to arise by virtue (*or* because) of. | **—in,** to originate in ⟨MS⟩. Cf. **seinen Ursprung haben in** (*sub* **Ursprung**).

entstehen, to come into being.

Entstehung, origin ⟨WH, MS⟩, (genesis ⟨WH, MS, BG⟩ ⟨?⟩), (*genèse* ⟨R⟩). Not "occurrence" ⟨L⟩. Cf. **Ursprung.**

enttäuschen, to undeceive. | **sich —,** to be disappointed ⟨MS⟩, (*être désillusionné* ⟨B⟩).

enttäuschend, undeceiving, (*qui détrompe* ⟨B⟩). Cf. **täuschend.**

Enttäuschung, undeception ⟨in OED⟩, disappointment ⟨WH 1, MS⟩, disillusion ⟨WH 2⟩. Save "deception" ⟨L⟩ for "Täuschung" ⟨q.v.⟩.

Entwährung, infirmation. Cf. **Bewährung.**

Entwertung, devaluation ⟨WH 2⟩. Not "depreciation" ⟨Bn, WH 1, MS 1⟩. Cf. **Bewertung, Wertung.**

Entwicklung, development ⟨WH 1, MS 1⟩, (*développement* ⟨R, B⟩); (esp. biological:) evolution ⟨WH, BG⟩, (*évolution* ⟨B⟩); (*explicatio* ⟨K⟩). Cf. **geworden.**

Entwicklungslehre, doctrine of evolution ⟨WH 1⟩. Not "theory of development" ⟨L⟩.

erblicken, to regard ⟨WH⟩, (*regarder* ⟨R⟩), (to descry ⟨WH, MS, BG⟩). Cf. **Blick, betrachten.**

Erdboden, ground ⟨WH, MS⟩. Cf. **Boden, Grund.**

erdenklich, that can be phantasied, imaginable ⟨MS 1, WH 2⟩, (*imaginable* ⟨B⟩); conceivable ⟨WH 1, MS 2⟩, (*concevable* ⟨B⟩). Cf. **denkbar, denkmöglich, phantasiert.**

Erdenklichkeit, imaginableness; conceivability, (*concevabilité* ⟨B⟩).

Erdichtung, fiction ⟨Schultze trln of

Locke, quoted in LU II. Unters.; WH 1⟩. Cf. **Einbildung, Fiktion.**

Erdraum, terrestrial space.

erfahren ⟨vb.⟩, to experience ⟨WH⟩, (*expérimenter* ⟨R, B⟩; to undergo ⟨WH, MS, BG⟩, (*subir* ⟨R, B⟩), to be subjected to, (to be the (*or* an) object of), (*porter* ⟨R⟩). Cf. **erleben, leiden.**

Erfahren, experiencing, process of experiencing, ((*activité d'*)*expérience* ⟨B⟩). Save "experience" ⟨L⟩ for "Erfahrung" ⟨q.v.⟩. Cf. **Erfahrung.**

erfahrend, experiencing, (*empirique* ⟨R⟩). Save "empirical" ⟨BG⟩ for "empirisch".

Erfahrender, experiencing subject, (*celui qui expérimente* ⟨B⟩).

Erfahrung, experience ⟨MS 1, WH⟩, (*expérience* ⟨R, B, de M⟩), experiencing. Cf. **Dingerfahrung, Erfahren, Fremderfahrung, Naturerfahrung, Selbsterfahrung, Welterfahrung.** | **Boden der —,** experiential basis, (*base d'expérience* ⟨B⟩). Cf. **Boden, Erfahrungsboden.** | **Welt reiner —,** world given in pure experience, (*monde d'expérience pure* ⟨B⟩). Cf. **Erfahrungswelt.**

Erfahrungsbegriff, experiential concept. Not "experimental concept" ⟨L⟩. Cf. **Begriff.**

Erfahrungsbewährung, experiential confirmation, (*vérification de l'expérience* ⟨B⟩). Cf. **Bewährung.**

Erfahrungsbewusstsein, experiential consciousness. Not "empirical consciousness" ⟨L⟩. Cf. **Bewusstsein.**

Erfahrungsboden, experiential basis. Cf. **Boden, Boden der Erfahrung** (*sub* **Erfahrung**).

Erfahrungsding, experienced physical thing. Cf. **Ding.**

Erfahrungseinheit, (sometimes:) experienced unity. Cf. **Einheit.**

Erfahrungseinstellung, attitude in experiencing; experiential attitude. Cf. **Einstellung.** | **in der —,** as meant in the experiential attitude. Not "from the empirical point of view" ⟨L⟩.

Erfahrungseinzelheit, single experiential particular. Not "empirical detail" ⟨L⟩. Cf. **Einzelheit.**

Erfahrungserlebnis, (mental) experience-process, (mental) process of experience, (*vécu de l'expérience* ⟨B⟩). Cf. **Erlebnis, Wahrnehmungserlebnis.**

Erfahrungsevidenz, experiential evidence, evidence of experience, (*évidence de l'expérience* ⟨B⟩). | **natürliche —,** evidence of natural experience.

Erfahrungsfeld, | **transzendentales —,** field of transcendental experience.

Erfahrungsgegebenheit, datum of experience. Cf. **Gegebenheit.** | **naïve —,** datum of naïve experience. Not "naïve empirical datum" ⟨L⟩.

Erfahrungsgegenstand, object of experience, (*objet de l'expérience* ⟨B⟩), experienced object. Cf. **Erfahrungsobjekt.**

Erfahrungsgegenständlichkeit, experienced objectivity; experiential objectivity.

Erfahrungsgesetzlichkeit, empirical law, (*légalité empirique* ⟨B⟩). Cf. **Gesetzlichkeit.**

Erfahrungsgestalt, experience-formation, (*formation d'expérience* ⟨B⟩). Cf. **Gestalt, Urteilsgestalt.**

Erfahrungshintergrund, experiential background, (*arrière-plan d'expérience* ⟨R⟩). Not "background in experience" ⟨BG⟩. Cf. **Hintergrund.**

Erfahrungshorizont, experiential horizon, horizon of experience. Cf. **Horizont.**

Erfahrungskraft, force of experience, (*force de l'expérience* ⟨R⟩). Cf. **Kraft.**

Erfahrungskunde, experiential cognizance, (*information de l'expérience* ⟨R⟩). Cf. **Kunde.**

erfahrungslogisch ⟨adj.⟩, experiential (-)logical. Not "empirically logical" ⟨L⟩.

erfahrungslogisch ⟨adv.⟩, conformably to experiential logic, (*en termes de la logique expérimentale* ⟨R⟩). Not "in terms of the logic of experience" ⟨BG⟩.

erfahrungsmässig ⟨adj.⟩, according to

experience, derived from experience, experientially given, experienced, (*par expérience* ⟨R⟩).

Erfahrungsobjekt, Object of experience, (*objet d'expérience* ⟨B⟩), experienced object. Cf. **Erfahrungsgegenstand.**

Erfahrungsquelle, experiential source, (*source d'expérience* ⟨B⟩).

Erfahrungsschluss, experiential conclusion. Not "empirical conclusion" ⟨L⟩. Cf. **Schluss 2.**

Erfahrungssphäre, sphere of experience ⟨L⟩. | **transzendentale** —, sphere of transcendental experience.

Erfahrungsteil, experiential judgment, (*jugement d'expérience* ⟨B⟩). Cf. **Urteil, Wahrnehmungsurteil.**

Erfahrungswelt, experiential world, experienced world, (*monde de l'expérience* ⟨B⟩). Cf. **eine Welt reiner Erfahrung** (*sub* **Erfahrung**).

Erfahrungswissenschaft, experiential science, (*science issue de l'expérience* ⟨R⟩).

erfahrungswissenschaftlich, of experiential science, done by experiential science.

Erfahrungszusammenhang, nexus of experience, continuity of experience. Cf. **Wahrnehmungszusammenhang, Zusammenhang.**

erfassen, to grasp ⟨MS 1, WH, BG⟩, (*saisir* ⟨R, B⟩), (to gather); to seize upon ⟨WH⟩; (to designate). Save "to apprehend" ⟨BG⟩ for "fassen" ⟨q.v.⟩. Cf. **auffassen, befassen, begreifen, greifen, herausfassen, inne sein** (*od.* **werden**), **selbst-erfasst.**

erfassen aus, to gather from, (*saisir à partir de* ⟨B⟩). | **unter einem Titel** —, to designate by a name. Cf. **Titel.**

erfassend, grasping; seizing (upon), (*qui saisit* ⟨R⟩), (*de saisie* ⟨B⟩). Not "that apprehends" ⟨BG⟩. | **im ∼en Sinn,** in the sense of a seizing-upon.

Erfassung, grasping ⟨WH⟩, grasp, (*saisie* ⟨R, B⟩); seizing upon. Save "apprehending" ⟨BG⟩ for "Auffassung" ⟨q.v.⟩. Cf. **Griff, Selbsterfassung, Wesenserfassung.**

erfolgend, (logically) consequent, (*dé-*

duit ⟨B⟩). Cf. **folgend 1, konsequent.**

erforschen, to explore ⟨WH 1, MS 1⟩, (*explorer* ⟨R, B⟩), (*rechercher* ⟨B⟩). Save "to investigate" ⟨WH, MS, L⟩ for "nachgehen" ⟨q.v.⟩ and "untersuchen" ⟨q.v.⟩; save "to study" ⟨BG⟩ for "studieren". | — **nach,** to seek out, (*examiner* ⟨B⟩).

Erforschung, exploration ⟨WH 1, MS 1⟩, (*exploration* ⟨B⟩), exploring, (*recherche* ⟨B⟩). Not "inquiry" ⟨BG⟩, not "study" ⟨BG⟩. Cf. **Durchforschung, Forschung, Wesenserforschung.**

erfragen, to inquire for, (*mettre en question* ⟨R⟩). Not "to question" ⟨BG⟩.

erfreulich, gladsome ⟨WH 2⟩, (*réjouissant* ⟨R⟩), (*ce qui réjouit* ⟨R⟩); gratifying ⟨WH⟩. Not "joyous" ⟨BG⟩; "enjoyed" ⟨BG⟩. Cf. **Freude, gefällig.**

erfüllen, to fulfil ⟨WH, MS⟩, to fill ⟨WH 1, MS 1⟩, (*remplir* ⟨B⟩), (*satisfaire* ⟨B⟩); (to attain). Cf. **ausfüllen, bedeutungerfüllend.** | **sich** —, to become fulfilled, (*se remplir* ⟨B⟩).

erfüllend-bewährend, fulfilling and verifying. Cf. **bewährend.**

erfüllt, fulfilled ⟨F⟩, (sometimes, when contrasted with "leer":) filled, (*rempli* ⟨B⟩). Not "filled out" ⟨BG⟩. Cf. **sinnerfüllt.**

Erfülltheit, filledness, fulfilledness, state of fulfilment ⟨F⟩.

Erfüllung, 1. (process:) fulfilling, (*accomplissement* ⟨B⟩).
2. (result:) fulfilment ⟨WH, MS⟩.
3. (state:) fulfilment; fullness (Ideen I, *336, l. 22–25*⟩.
4. (without distinction ⟨?⟩:) (*remplissement* ⟨R, B, de M⟩). Cf. **Ausfüllung, Bedeutungserfüllung, Fülle, Füllung.** | **besinnliche** —, clear sense-fulfilment, (*remplissement effectué par la prise de conscience* ⟨B⟩). Cf. **besinnlich.**

Erfüllungseinheit, unity of fulfilling (*or* fulfilment). Cf. **Einheit.**

Erfüllungserlebnis, mental fulfilling process. Cf. **Erlebnis.**

Erfüllungsleistung, production of fulfilment, (action de remplissement ⟨R, B⟩).

Erfüllungsrichtung, direction in which (the) fulfilment lies. Cf. **Richtung.**

Erfüllungssynthese, synthesis of fulfilment, (synthèse de remplissement ⟨B⟩).

ergeben, to yield ⟨WH 1, MS 1⟩, to result in, to give rise to, (donner lieu à ⟨B⟩), (to produce ⟨MS 2⟩), (produire ⟨B⟩, (engendrer ⟨B⟩), (faire apparaître ⟨R⟩), (fournir ⟨B⟩), (donner ⟨B⟩). Save "to give" ⟨BG⟩ for "geben" ⟨q.v.⟩. Cf. **erzeugen, herstellen, leisten, schaffen.** | **sich als etwas —,** to turn out to be something, (se donner comme quelque chose ⟨B⟩). | **sich —,** to be yielded, to emerge ⟨WH⟩, to result ⟨MS⟩, to arise ⟨WH⟩, (se livrer ⟨B⟩), (se produire ⟨B⟩), (se dégager ⟨R⟩), (se former ⟨R⟩), (se présenter ⟨B⟩), (apparaître ⟨B⟩). Not "to present itself" ⟨BG⟩, not "to be reached" ⟨BG⟩. Cf. **entspringen.**

Ergebnis, result ⟨WH 1, MS 1, BG⟩, (résultat ⟨B⟩), (conséquence ⟨B⟩), conclusion, (conclusion ⟨R⟩). Cf. **Auswirkung, Erkenntnisergebnis, Folge 4, Leistung, Scheinergebnis, Schlussergebnis, Urteilsergebnis.**

ergriffen, taken hold of. Cf. **greifen.**

erhalten, to preserve ⟨WH⟩, to keep ⟨WH⟩; to get ⟨WH⟩, to receive ⟨WH, L⟩. Cf. **bewahren.**

Erhaltung, preservation ⟨WH 2⟩, (maintien ⟨B⟩). | **unter —,** while preserving (or conserving).

erinnern, to remember ⟨WH 1, BG⟩, to be mindful of, to bring to mind. | **an etwas —,** to bring something to mind, to put one in mind of something, (faire songer à quelque chose ⟨B⟩), to call attention to something. | **sich — an,** to remember ⟨Bn, WH 1, MS 1⟩, to remind oneself, to be mindful of, (se souvenir ⟨B⟩), (se rappeler ⟨B⟩).

erinnernd, (at least sometimes:) recollective.

Erinnerung, memory ⟨Bn, MS, BG⟩, (souvenir ⟨R, B⟩), (mémoire ⟨R⟩),

remembering, quasi-memory, mindfulness. Save "recollection" ⟨WH 1, L, BG⟩ for "Wiedererinnerung". Cf. **Rückerinnerung, Vorerinnerung.**

Erinnerung an, memory of ⟨WH⟩.

Erinnerungsauffassung, memorial apprehension. Cf. **Auffassung.**

Erinnerungsbewusstsein, memorial consciousness. Not "recollective consciousness" ⟨BG⟩.

Erinnerungseinfall, something that comes to mind memorially, (souvenir qui revient à l'esprit ⟨B⟩). Cf. **Einfall.**

Erinnerungsgeltung, memorial acceptance. Cf. **Geltung.** | **in — haben,** to accept in memory, Cf. **in Geltung haben** (sub **Geltung**).

erinnerungsmässig ⟨adj.⟩, memorial. Cf. **wiedererinnerungsmässig.**

erinnerungsmässig ⟨adv.⟩, memorially, (par voie de souvenir ⟨R⟩). Not "by way of recollection" ⟨BG⟩.

Erinnerungsnoesis, remembering noesis, (noèse de souvenir ⟨R⟩). Cf. **Wahrnehmungsnoesis.**

Erinnerungsphänomen, memory phenomenon.

Erinnerungssinn, sense of the remembering, (sens du souvenir ⟨R⟩). Cf. **Phantasiesinn, Wahrnehmungssinn.**

Erinnerungsvergegenwärtigung, something made present memorially (or in a remembering), (présentification du type souvenir ⟨R⟩). Cf. **Vergegenwärtigung.**

Erinnerungswelt, world of memory. Cf. **Phantasiewelt.**

erkennbar, cognizable, (connaissable ⟨B⟩), (reconnaissable ⟨B⟩).

erkennen, to cognize ⟨WH⟩, (connaître ⟨B⟩), (cognoscere ⟨K⟩), to know ⟨WH, MS, BG⟩; to recognize ⟨MS 1, WH⟩, (reconnaître ⟨R, B⟩); to discover ⟨WH⟩ (discerner ⟨B⟩). Cf. **kennen, wissen.**

erkennend, cognitive, cognizing, (connaissant ⟨B⟩), (qui connaît ⟨B⟩), (au service de la connaissance ⟨B⟩). Cf. **erkenntnismässig, urteilend-erkennend.**

erkennend-bewährend ⟨adv.⟩, | **— ein-**

gestellt, set to cognize (*or* know) and
(to) verify, (*orienté vers l'activité de
connaissance et de vérification* ⟨B⟩).
Cf. **bewähren, eingestellt.**
erkennend-prädizierend ⟨adv.⟩, cogni-
tive-predicating, (*prédicatif dirigé
vers la connaissance* ⟨B⟩). Cf. **prädizieren, urteilend-erkennend.**
Erkennender, cognizing (*or* cognitive)
subject, (*être connaissant* ⟨B⟩). Cf.
Erkenntnissubjekt.
Erkenntnis, cognition ⟨WH, MS⟩,
(*connaissance* ⟨R, B⟩), (*cognitio* ⟨K⟩),
cognizing, knowledge ⟨MS 1, BG⟩
(of the truth) ⟨WH⟩, (knowledge
about ⟨Bn⟩), (knowing about);
recognition. Cf. **Anerkennung, Erkennung, kennen, Kenntnis, Kunde,
matter-of-fact-Erkenntnis, Seinserkenntnis, Tatsachenerkenntnis,
Vorkenntnis, Wesenserkenntnis,
Wissen.** | Intention auf —, intention
aimed at cognition, (*intention dirigée
vers la connaissance* ⟨B⟩). Cf. **Er-
kenntnisintention, Intention.** | zur —
bringen, to make cognized, (*faire
connaître* ⟨R⟩).
Erkenntnisakt, cognitional act. Not
"act of knowledge" ⟨L⟩.
Erkenntnisanalyse, analysis of cognition, (*analyse de la connaissance*
⟨B⟩).
Erkenntnisarbeit, work of cognition,
(*travail de connaissance* ⟨B⟩). Cf.
**Arbeit, Erkenntnisleistung, Urteils-
arbeit.**
Erkenntnisbegründung, grounding of
cognition. Cf. **Begründung.**
Erkenntnisbestand, stock of cognitions, (*connaissances* (*accumulées*)
⟨R⟩). Not "knowledge accumu-
lated" ⟨BG⟩. Cf. **Bestand.**
Erkenntniseinheit, unity of a cognition. Cf. **Einheit.**
Erkenntniseinstellung, focusing on
cognition, (*attitude de connaissance*
⟨B⟩), (*orientation de la connaissance*
⟨B⟩). Cf. **Einstellung.** | in der —,
when cognition is the goal, (*dans
l'attitude de connaissance* ⟨B⟩).
Erkenntnisergebnis, cognitional result,
(*résultat (de la sphère) de la connais-*

sance ⟨B⟩); resultant cognition,
(knowledge-result), (*résultat théori-
que* ⟨R⟩). Not "theoretical result"
⟨BG⟩.
Erkenntniserlebnis, process of cognition. Cf. **Erlebnis.**
Erkenntniserwerb, cognitional acqui-
sition, (*gain de la connaissance* ⟨B⟩),
(knowledge-acquisition).
Erkenntnisforschung, scientific inquiry into cognition, (*recherche de la
connaissance* ⟨B⟩), investigation of
cognition. Cf. **Forschung.**
Erkenntnisfülle, fullness of cognition,
(*plénitude de la connaissance* ⟨B⟩).
Erkenntnisfunktion, conditional
functioning, function pertaining to
cognition, (*fonction de la connaissan-
ce* ⟨B⟩). Cf. **Funktion.** | in — stehen,
to function cognitionally. | in —
treten, to take on functions for
cognition. | mögliche —, functions
pertaining to possible cognition.
Erkenntnisgebiet, province of cognition, (*domaine de connaissance* ⟨B⟩),
province of knowledge, knowledge-
province. Cf. **Gebiet.**
Erkenntnisgebilde, cognitional formation, (*formation (de la sphère) de
la connaissance* ⟨B⟩), (*formation de
connaissance* ⟨B⟩), knowledge-formation. Cf. **Gebilde, Wissengebilde.**
Erkenntnisgegenstand, cognitional object, object of cognition. Cf. **Erkenntnisgegenständlichkeit, Erkenntnisobjekt, Erkenntnisobjektivität.**
Erkenntnisgegenständlichkeit, cognitional objectivity, objectivity for
cognition. Cf. **Erkenntnisgegenstand, Erkenntnisobjekt, Erkenntnisobjektivität.**
Erkenntnisgemeinschaft, cognitive
community, (*communauté de la connaissance* ⟨B⟩). Cf. **Gemeinschaft.**
Erkenntnisgestalt, cognition formation, (*forme de connaissance* ⟨B⟩).
Cf. **Gestalt, Urteilsgestalt.**
Erkenntnisintention, intention aimed
at cognition (*or* cognizing), (intention aimed at knowing), (*intention de la connaissance* ⟨B⟩). Cf.

Intention auf Erkenntnis (*sub* **Erkenntnis**).

Erkenntnisinteresse, cognitional interest, (*intérêt de connaissance* ⟨B⟩), interest in cognizing (*or* in knowing).

Erkenntnislehre, epistemology ⟨WH⟩, theory of cognition, (theory of knowledge). Cf. **Erkenntnistheorie.**

Erkenntnisleistung, cognitive performance, work of cognition, what something produces as a cognition, (cognitional result ⟨?⟩). Cf. **Erkenntnisarbeit, Leistung.**

erkenntnismässig, cognitional(ly), (*cognitif* ⟨R⟩), from the standpoint of cognition, (*du point de vue de la connaissance* ⟨B⟩), epistemic(ally). Save "cognitive" for "erkennend" ⟨q.v.⟩.

Erkenntnismaterie, cognition-material, (*matière de la connaissance* ⟨B⟩). Cf. **Materie.**

Erkenntnisobjekt, Object of cognition, cognitional Object, cognized Object. Cf. **Erkenntnisgegenstand, Erkenntnisgegenständlichkeit, Erkenntnissubjekt.**

erkenntnis-praktisch ⟨adj.⟩, | ⁓e **Bedeutung für,** significance for the cognitive practice of, (*importance épistémologique pratique pour* ⟨R⟩). Cf. **Bedeutung.**

erkenntnis-praktisch ⟨adv.⟩, in the practice of cognition, (*dans la pratique de la connaissance* ⟨R⟩), with respect to cognitive practice, epistemo-practically. Not "in practical knowledge" ⟨BG⟩.

Erkenntnisprätention, claim to being a cognition; (pl.:) claims to being cognitions.

Erkenntnisquelle, cognitional source.

Erkenntnissinn, cognitional sense, sense of (a) cognition.

Erkenntnisstrebung, cognitional striving, striving for cognition, (*effort de la connaissance* ⟨B⟩). Cf. **streben.**

Erkenntnisstufe, cognitional level. Cf. **Stufe.**

Erkenntnissubjekt, cognizing subject, (*sujet de la connaissance* ⟨R⟩). Not

"subject of knowledge" ⟨BG⟩. Cf. **Erkennender, Erkenntnisobjekt.**

erkenntnistheoretisch, epistemological ⟨BG⟩, (*épistémologique* ⟨R⟩). Cf. **wissenschaftstheoretisch.**

Erkenntnistheorie, theory of cognition ⟨WH 1⟩, (*théorie de la connaissance* ⟨B⟩), epistemology ⟨WH 2⟩, (theory of knowledge). Cf. **Erkenntnislehre.**

Erkenntnisurteil, cognitive judgment, (*jugement visant à la connaissance* ⟨B⟩), cognitional judgment.

Erkenntniswert, cognition-value. Cf. **Wert.**

Erkenntniswillen, will to cognize, (*volonté de connaître* ⟨B⟩). Cf. **Willen.**

Erkenntnisziel, cognitional goal, (*but de la connaissance* ⟨B⟩). Cf. **Ziel.**

Erkenntniszusammenhang, cognition-complex, (*enchaînement de connaissance* ⟨B⟩), (knowledge-complex). Cf. **Zusammenhang.**

Erkennung, recognition ⟨MS 1, WH⟩. Cf. **Anerkennung, Erkenntnis.**

(Erkennungszeichen), recognition mark ⟨BN⟩. Cf. **Kennzeichen.**

erklärbar, explainable ⟨WH 1, MS 1⟩, (*explicable* ⟨B⟩).

erklären, to explain ⟨WH 1, MS 1⟩; to elucidate ⟨MS 2⟩; (to interpret ⟨Bn, MS⟩); to declare ⟨WH, L⟩. Cf. **aufklären, auslegen, ausdeuten, deuten, klarlegen, klarstellen.** | **für gültig —,** to declare valid. Cf. **gültig.**

erklärend, explanatory ⟨WH 1⟩, (*explicatif* ⟨B⟩); elucidative. | ⁓e **Wissenschaft,** explanatory science, (*science explicative* ⟨B⟩).

Erklärung, explanation ⟨WH 1, MS 1, BG⟩, (*explication* ⟨R, B⟩), (*explicitation* ⟨B⟩), elucidation ⟨MS 2⟩, (*definitio* ⟨Wolff, K⟩). Cf. **Aufklärung, Auslegung, Explikation, Explizierung.**

Erklärungsgebilde, explanatory construct. Cf. **Gebilde.**

erklingen, to sound ⟨WH 1⟩, (*retentir* ⟨B⟩).

erläuternd, elucidative ⟨WH 1⟩, (*explicatif* ⟨B⟩); vocal, (*commenté* ⟨B⟩).

erleben, 1. to live (something) (mentally), (*vivre* ⟨R⟩); to undergo ⟨MS⟩

(mentally), (*éprouver* ⟨B⟩); to have really immanent in one's (mental) life (*or* in one's stream of mental processes).

2. (loose sense, rarely:) to witness ⟨WH, MS⟩, "to experience". So far as possible, save "to experience" ⟨WH 1, MS⟩ for "erfahren" (q.v.). Cf. **durchleben, erlebt, leiden.**

Erleben, mental living, mental undergoing; mental process; (*vécu* ⟨R, B⟩); inward having; (rarely:) consciousness. So far as possible, save "experience" ⟨BG⟩ for "Erfahrung"; save "experiencing" for "Erfahren" and "Erfahrung". Cf. **Bewusstsein, Erlebnis, Evidenzerleben, Leben, Leiden.** | im —, with our inward having (of). | **psychisches —,** psychic living. | **urteilendes —,** judging mental process, judging consciousness, (*vécu du jugement* ⟨B⟩). Cf. **Urteilserlebnis.**

Erlebnis, 1. mental process (*or* occurrence), (something lived), (*vécu* ⟨R, B, de M⟩), (mental) life-process, part of mental life, really immanent process or occurrence; something undergone (mentally); (rarely:) consciousness (*or* awareness).

2. (loose sense, rarely:) "experience". So far as possible save "experience" ⟨WH 1, L, F, BG⟩ for "Erfahrung". Cf. **Bedeutungserlebnis, Bewusstseinserlebnis, Denkerlebnis, Erleben, Erfahrungserlebnis, Erfüllungserlebnis, Erkenntniserlebnis, Erscheinungserlebnis, Evidenzerlebnis, Gefallenserlebnis, Icherlebnis, Urteilserlebnis, Vorstellungserlebnis, Wahrnehmungserlebnis, Zeiterlebnis.** | — **von dem Papier,** mental process pertaining to the sheet of paper, (*vécu du papier* ⟨R⟩). Not "experience of the paper" ⟨BG⟩. | **intentionales —,** intentional process. | **physische und psychische ∼se,** physical and mental "experiences". | **psychisches —,** psychic (life-)process (*or* occurrence), (*vécu psychique* ⟨R⟩). | **seine ∼se,** his mental life-

processes, the processes making up his mental life.

Erlebnisart, sort (*or* species) of mental process, (*mode du vécu* ⟨R⟩). Cf. **Art.**

Erlebnisdatum, really immanent (mental) Datum, (*datum du vécu* ⟨R⟩). Not "datum of expérience" ⟨BG⟩. Cf. **Datum.**

Erlebniseinheit zwischen, union in mental life between. Cf. **Einheit.**

Erlebnisfaktum, mental process qua fact, (*fait brut du vécu* ⟨R⟩). Not "experimental fact as lived" ⟨BG⟩. Cf. **Faktum.**

Erlebniskomplexion, complex (*or* combination) of lived (*or* mental) processes (*or* occurrences). Cf. **Komplexion.**

erlebnismässig, as a mental (or really immanent) process (*or* occurrence).

Erlebnisprozess, mental process, (*processus vécu* ⟨B⟩).

Erlebnissituation, in such a state of mental life, (*situation vécue* ⟨R⟩). Cf. **Zustand.**

Erlebnisstrom, stream of mental processes (*or* occurrences), (*flux (du) vécu* ⟨R⟩). Not "stream of experience(s)" ⟨BG⟩; not "experience-stream" ⟨BG⟩. Cf. **Strom.**

Erlebnissubjektivität, subjectivity such as characterizes mental processes, (*subjectivité d'un vécu* ⟨R⟩). Not "experiential subjectivity" ⟨BG⟩.

Erlebnisweise, mode of consciousness. Not "mode of experiencing" ⟨BG⟩. Cf. **Bewusstseinsweise, Weise.**

Erlebniszeitlichkeit, temporality such as belongs to a mental process, (internal temporality). Cf. **Zeitlichkeit.**

Erlebniszusammenhang, complex of lived (*or* mental) processes, (*enchaînement des vécus* ⟨R⟩). Not "connexion of experience" ⟨BG⟩. Cf. **Zusammenhang.**

erlebt, (that is) undergone (mentally); lived, that is being lived, that one is living, (really) immanent in one's (mental) life (*or* in one's stream of mental processes). Save "experienced" for "erfahren". | **als Motiv**

—, undergone as a motive. | **einheit-lich** —, lived unitedly. Cf. **einheit-lich** ⟨adv.⟩. | — **sein**, to be lived, to occur in mental life. | **subjektiv** —, really immanent in subjective life.

Erörterung, discussion ⟨MS 1, WH, L, BG⟩, (*discussion* ⟨R, B⟩), exposition, (*expositio* ⟨K⟩), treatment, explanation.

erregen, to excite ⟨Gomperz trln of Mill, quoted in LU, II. Unters.; MS 1; WH 2⟩.

Erregung, excitation ⟨Bn, WH 1⟩. Cf. **Aktregung, Regung.**

erschaubar, seeable, that can be seen. Cf. **Einsehbarkeit, sichtlich.**

erschauen, to see ⟨MS 1, WH⟩, (*voir* ⟨R, B⟩), to view ⟨L⟩, (*discerner* ⟨R⟩). Not "to perceive" ⟨BG⟩. Save "to intuit" ⟨L⟩ for "anschauen". Cf. **absehen, auffassen, betrachten, schauen, sehen.**

Erschauung, seeing, viewing. Cf. **Anschauung, Schau, Schauen, Schauung, Wesenserschauung.**

erscheinen, to appear ⟨WH 1, MS 2⟩, (*apparaître* ⟨R⟩), (*paraître* ⟨B⟩). Cf. **auftreten, sich zeigen** (*sub* **zeigen**).

Erscheinung, appearance ⟨WH 1, MS, BG⟩, (*apparence* ⟨R, de M⟩), (*apparentia* ⟨K⟩), appearing. So far as possible save "phenomenon" ⟨WH⟩ for "Phänomen". Cf. **Auftreten, Apparenz, Ausdruckserscheinung, Fernerscheinung, Selbsterscheinung, Sondererscheinung, Wahrnehmungserscheinung.** | **zur** — **bringen**, to make appear, (*faire apparaître* ⟨B⟩). | **zur** — **kommen**, to make its appearance. Cf. **auftreten, sich zeigen,** (*sub* **zeigen**).

Erscheinungsabhängigkeit, phenomenal dependence (*or* dependency), (*relation de dépendance entre les apparences* ⟨R⟩). Not "relations of dependence among appearances" ⟨BG⟩.

Erscheinungsbestimmtheit, determination of the appearance, (apparent determination ⟨?⟩ ⟨BG⟩), (*détermination apparente* ⟨R⟩). Cf. **Bestimmtheit.**

Erscheinungserlebnis, mental appearance-process, (*vécu de l'apparence* ⟨R⟩). Cf. **Erlebnis.**

Erscheinungsweise, mode (*or* manner) of appearance (*or* appearing), (*mode* (ou *manière*) *d'apparaître* ⟨R⟩). Cf. **Weise.** | **sinnliche** —, mode of sensuous appearance (*or* appearing), (*manière d'apparaître sensible* ⟨R⟩), (sensuous manner of appearing). Not "sensory way of appearing" ⟨BG⟩. Cf. **sinnlich.**

Erscheinungszusammenhang, phenomenal complex, (*connexion entre les apparences* ⟨R⟩). Not "connexion between appearances" ⟨BG⟩. Cf. **Zusammenhang.**

erschliessbar, discoverable.

erschliessen, 1. (logical:) to infer ⟨WH, MS, BG⟩, (*inférer* ⟨R⟩), to deduce ⟨WH⟩, (*déduire* ⟨B⟩), to conclude ⟨WH, MS⟩, (*dériver* ⟨R⟩). Cf. **ableiten, beschliessen, folgern, herleiten, schliessen.**
2. (non-logical:) to open up ⟨WH⟩, (*se faire jour* ⟨B⟩), to uncover, to make accessible ⟨MS⟩, to make available; to discover; to derive ⟨WH⟩. Cf. **unerschlossen.** | **sich** —, 1. to be deduced, 2. to be opened up, (*se révéler* ⟨R⟩).

Erschliessung, (with gen:) disclosure ⟨WH 1⟩ brought by, (*apparition de* ⟨B⟩).

ersehen (an), to descry (in), (*apercevoir* (*sur*) ⟨B⟩), (*voir* (*de*) ⟨B⟩), to see (when one considers).

ersichtlich ⟨adj.⟩, apparent, (*évident*, ⟨B⟩).

erst ⟨adv.⟩, not until ⟨WH⟩, only ⟨WH, MS⟩, (*uniquement* ⟨B⟩), (*seulement* ⟨B⟩), for the first time, in the first place, (*d'abord* ⟨B⟩), still.

Erstarken, increasing strength.

Erstreckung, extension ⟨MS 1⟩. Cf. **Ausbreitung, Ausdehnung, Erweiterung, Strecke.**

erwachsen, to grow up ⟨MS 1⟩, (*se former* ⟨B⟩), to accrue ⟨WH⟩, (*résulter* ⟨B⟩), to arise ⟨WH⟩, to spring up ⟨MS 2⟩, (*naître* ⟨B⟩), (*prendre connaissance* ⟨B⟩), (*se faire jour* ⟨B⟩), to

develop ⟨WH⟩, (se développer ⟨B⟩).
Cf. **Zuwachsen.** | **einem —,** to accrue
to someone ⟨WH⟩. | **— aus,** to
accrue from ⟨MS⟩, to arise from
⟨MS 1⟩, (provenir de ⟨B⟩), (to spring
from ⟨MS 3, WH⟩), (naître de ⟨B⟩),
(to proceed from ⟨MS 2⟩). | **— durch,**
to accrue through, (provenir de ⟨B⟩).
| **— in,** to accrue by, (devoir son dé-
veloppement à ⟨B⟩).

Erwägung, deliberation ⟨MS 3⟩, consideration ⟨WH 1, MS 1⟩. Cf. **Betrachtung, Überlegung, Vorerwä-
gung.**

erwartet, expected, awaited, (attendu
⟨R⟩).

Erwartung, expectation ⟨Gomperz
trln of Mill, quoted in LU, II. Unters.;
WH 1⟩, (expectatio ⟨K⟩), (attente
⟨R⟩). Cf. **Vorerinnerung, Vorerwartung, Vormeinung.**

Erweckung, awakening ⟨WH⟩. Cf.
Weckung.

Erweis, demonstration ⟨WH 1⟩, showing. Cf. **Ausweis, Beweis, Nachweis,
Nachweisung.**

erweisen, to show ⟨WH⟩, (prouver
⟨B⟩). Cf. **aufweisen, beweisen, nach-
weisen, weisen.** | **— als,** to show to
be, to make evident as. | **sich —
dass,** to turn out that, (se manifester
que ⟨B⟩). | **sich zu stark —,** to prove
too strong.

erweitern, to enlarge ⟨MS 1, WH⟩,
(élargir ⟨B⟩), to amplify, (amplifi-
care ⟨K⟩), to broaden, to extend
⟨WH 1⟩, (étendre ⟨B⟩).

erweitert, | **~e Analytik,** enlarged
analytics. | **~e "Weltanschauung",**
enlarged "world view". | **~er Be-
griff,** amplified concept. | **~er Sinn,**
amplified sense, (sens élargi ⟨B⟩),
(sens étendu ⟨R⟩). Not "extended
meaning" ⟨BG⟩.

Erweiterung, enlargement ⟨MS 1,
WH⟩, (élargissement ⟨B⟩), amplifi-
cation, broadening, extension ⟨WH
1, MS 2⟩, (extension ⟨B⟩). Cf. **Ausbreitung, Ausdehnung, Erstreckung.**
| **— auf,** extension to, (extension à
⟨B⟩), broadening to cover. | **— um,**

broadening to include, (extension
pour constituer ⟨B⟩).

(Erweiterungsurteil), ampliative judgment ⟨Bn⟩.

erzeugbar, producible ⟨WH 1, MS 2⟩,
generable ⟨MS 2⟩, (engendrable ⟨B⟩).

erzeugen, to produce ⟨WH, MS⟩, (produire ⟨R, B⟩), (créer ⟨R⟩), (faire apparaître ⟨R⟩), (former ⟨R⟩), to
generate ⟨WH 2, MS, BG⟩, (engen-
drer ⟨R, B⟩), (donner naissance à
⟨B⟩). Cf. **ergeben, herstellen, leisten,
schaffen.**

erzeugend, productive, (producteur
⟨B⟩), generative; (being generated).
Cf. **bildend, leistend.** | **in ~er Weise,**
in the manner of something that is
being produced (or generated), (d'une
manière productrice ⟨B⟩).

Erzeugnis, generated product, product
⟨WH, MS⟩, (production ⟨B⟩), (cre-
ation ⟨WH, MS⟩). Cf. **Gebilde,
Leistung, Originalerzeugnis.**

Erzeugung, production ⟨MS⟩, (production ⟨PL, R, B⟩), producing, product,
generation ⟨MS 2⟩, generating. Cf.
Genesis, Leistung, Nacherzeugung.

Erziehung, upbringing ⟨WH 2⟩, edu-
cation ⟨MS 1, WH⟩, (éducation ⟨B⟩).

erzielen, to attain ⟨WH 2, MS 2⟩, (atteindre ⟨B⟩), (parvenir à ⟨B⟩), (to
obtain ⟨WH 3, MS 3, F⟩ ⟨?⟩). Cf.
gewinnen.

Erzielung, attainment ⟨MS 1⟩, (atteinte
⟨B⟩), (obtention ⟨R⟩).

etablieren, | **sich —,** to be set up, to get
started, (s'établir ⟨R⟩).

ethisch, ethical, (éthique ⟨R⟩), of
ethics. | **rein ~er Satz,** proposition
of pure ethics, (proposition purement éthique ⟨B⟩).

etwa, perchance ⟨MS⟩, perhaps ⟨WH,
MS⟩, (peut-être ⟨B⟩), (tel ⟨R⟩), in
some cases, let us say ⟨WH⟩. | **nicht
—,** not perchance, obviously not.

Etwas, Something ⟨BG⟩, (quelque(-)
chose ⟨R, B⟩), anything ⟨WH, MS⟩,
(aliquid). Cf. **Ding.** | **beliebiges —,**
anything you please, (un quelque
chose arbitraire ⟨B⟩). | **irgend —,**
(just) anything, something or other
⟨WH 1⟩, (quelque chose ⟨B⟩).

Etwas(-)überhaupt, anything(-)whatever, (*quelque chose en général* ⟨B⟩). Cf. **Gegenstand überhaupt** (*sub* **Gegenstand**), **Gegenständlichkeit überhaupt** (*sub* **Gegenständlichkeit**), **Gegenstand-überhaupt, überhaupt.**

evident ⟨adj.⟩, 1. (noematic:) evident ⟨WH 1, MS 1⟩, evidently true. 2. (noetic:) evidential.

evident ⟨adv.⟩, 1. (noematically:) evidently ⟨MS 1⟩. 2. (noetically:) evidentially. 3. (without distinction:) (*d'une manière évidente* ⟨B⟩), (*avec évidence* ⟨B⟩). | — **erfahrend,** evidentially experiencing.

evidentermassen, evidently, (*d'une manière évidente* ⟨B⟩).

Evidentmachung, process of making evident, (*processus qui rend évident* ⟨B⟩).

Evidenz ⟨f.⟩, evidence ⟨WH 1, MS 1⟩, (*évidence* ⟨R, B, de M⟩); (rarely:) evidentness. Not "evidential vision" ⟨BG⟩; not "self-evidence" ⟨BG⟩. Cf. **Deutlichkeitsevidenz, Einsichtigkeit, Erfahrungsevidenz, Urteilsevidenz.** | — **für,** evidence appropriate to, evidence with respect to, (*évidence pour* ⟨B⟩). | — **haben,** to be evident, (*avoir l'évidence* ⟨B⟩). | **in** —, in (acts) of evidence. Not "on the basis of evidence" ⟨L⟩. | **mit** —, evidentially.

Evidenzbewusstsein, evidential consciousness, (*conscience d'évidence* ⟨B⟩). Cf. **Evidenzerleben.**

Evidenzcharakter, evidence-characteristic. Not "character of evidential vision" ⟨BG⟩. Cf. **Charakter.**

Evidenzerleben, evidential consciousness, (*vie de l'évidence* ⟨B⟩). Cf. **Erleben, Evidenzbewusstsein.**

Evidenzerlebnis, mental evidence-process, (*vécu de l'évidence* ⟨B⟩). Cf. **Erlebnis.**

Evidenzfunktion, evidential function, (*fonction de l'évidence* ⟨B⟩). Cf. **Funktion.**

Evidenzleistung, evidential performance, (*effectuation d'évidence* ⟨B⟩).

Cf. **die Leistung der Evidenz** (*sub* **Leistung**).

Exaktheit, exactitude ⟨WH 2, MS 2⟩.

exemplarisch ⟨adj.⟩, of examples; of an example; (serving or fit to serve as an example:) exemplary ⟨WH 1, MS 1⟩, (*qui sert d'exemple* ⟨B⟩), (taken) as an example, (*pris comme* (ou *à titre*) *d'exemple* ⟨B⟩), (*cité à titre d'exemple* ⟨R⟩), (*exemplifié* ⟨B⟩); (furnishing an example:) exemplificative. Not "of illustrations" ⟨BG⟩. | ~e **Anschauung,** intuition of examples, (*intuition prise à titre d'exemple* ⟨B⟩). | ~e **Kritik,** criticism of examples, (*critique qui s'appuie sur des exemples* ⟨B⟩). | ~es **Bewusstsein,** consciousness of an example. | ~es **Feld,** field of examples, (*champ d'exemples* ⟨B⟩). | **konkrete** ~e **Anschauung von Gegenständen,** intuition of objects as concrete examples.

exemplarisch ⟨adv.⟩, as an example, (*à titre d'exemple* ⟨R⟩), as examples; in an exemplary manner.

existential ⟨adj.⟩, | ~e **Setzung,** positing (of something) as existent, (existential positing ⟨L⟩). Cf. **Setzung.**

existential ⟨adv.⟩, | — **mitsetzen,** to co-posit as existent (*or* existentially).

Existenz, existence ⟨WH 1, MS 1, BG⟩, (*existence* ⟨R, de M⟩). Cf. **Dasein, Bestehen, Sein.**

Explikat, explicate ⟨not in OED⟩, (*explicatum*), (*explicat* ⟨B⟩). Cf. **Verdeutlichung 2.**

Explikation, explication ⟨WH 1⟩, (*explication* ⟨de M⟩), (*explicitation* ⟨R, B⟩). Save "explanation" ⟨WH 1, BG⟩ for "Erklärung" ⟨q.v.⟩. Cf. **Auseinanderlegung, Auslegung, Entfaltung.**

explizieren, to explicate, (*expliciter* ⟨R, B⟩). Cf. **auseinanderlegen, auslegen, entfalten, erklären, verdeutlichen.**

Explizierung, explication, explicating. Cf. **Auseinanderlegung, Auslegung, Entfaltung, Erklärung.**

Fachwissenschaft, special science. Cf. **Sonderwissenschaft.**

Fähigkeit, 1. (in an agent:) ability ⟨WH 1, MS 2⟩, (faculty ⟨MS⟩), (*capacité* ⟨B⟩). Cf. **Vermögen.** 2. (passive:) capacity ⟨MS 1, WH⟩.

faktisch ⟨adj.⟩, de facto (Logik, *175*), (*de fait* ⟨R, B⟩), factual ⟨WH 1, BG⟩, actual ⟨WH 2, MS⟩, (*existant* (*en fait*) ⟨B⟩), (*contingent* ⟨R⟩), (*concret* ⟨B⟩). Not "concrete" ⟨BG⟩; not "given" ⟨BG⟩. Cf. **aktuell** ⟨adv.⟩ **2, daseiend, wirklich** ⟨adj.⟩. | **ein F ~es,** something factual, (*ce qui est fait* ⟨B⟩). Not "an element of fact" ⟨BG⟩.

faktisch ⟨adv.⟩, de facto ⟨WH⟩, (*de fait* ⟨B⟩), in fact ⟨MS⟩, (*en fait* ⟨B⟩), (*effectivement* ⟨B⟩). Cf. **aktuell** ⟨adv.⟩ **2, wirklich** ⟨adv.⟩.

Faktizität, factualness, (*facticité* ⟨R, B⟩); the factual. Not "fact-character" ⟨BG⟩. Save "actuality" ⟨BG⟩ for "Aktualität" ⟨q.v.⟩ and "Wirklichkeit" ⟨q.v.⟩.

Faktum, fact ⟨WH 1, MS 1, BG⟩, (*fait* ⟨R, de M⟩), (*fait de l'existence* ⟨B⟩), factual. Not "fact-world" ⟨BG⟩. Cf. **Erlebnisfaktum, Tatsache, Wirklichkeit.**

fällen, | **ein Urteil —,** to make a judgment, (*porter un jugement* ⟨B⟩). Cf. **ein Urteil vollziehen** (*sub* **vollziehen**).

falsch, false ⟨WH 1, MS 1, L⟩, (*faux* ⟨B⟩), (of a proof or an argument:) fallacious, erroneous, (*erroné* ⟨R⟩), mistaken.

Farbendifferenz, | **niederste —,** infima species of color. Not "ultimate difference of color" ⟨L⟩. Cf. **niederste Differenz** (*sub* **Differenz**).

Farbenspezies, color-species. Cf. **Formspezies.**

Färbung, coloring ⟨MS 1, WH⟩, coloration ⟨WH⟩, (of expressions:) tone.

fassbar, apprehensible, that can be laid hold of, (*saisissable* ⟨B⟩), (*susceptible d'être saisi* ⟨R⟩); comprehensible ⟨WH 1, MS⟩; formulable. Cf. **fasslich, greifbar.**

fassen, 1. to apprehend ⟨WH, MS⟩, to lay hold of, (*saisir* ⟨R, B⟩). 2. to comprehend ⟨WH, MS⟩, (*comprendre* ⟨B⟩). 3. to conceive ⟨Gomperz trln of Mill, quoted in LU, II. Unters.; WH; MS; BG⟩, (*concevoir* ⟨R, B⟩), to frame ⟨WH⟩. 4. to formulate, (*exprimer* ⟨B⟩). 5. to take ⟨WH, MS⟩, (*prendre* ⟨R, B⟩). Save "to grasp" ⟨WH, L⟩ for "begreifen" ⟨q.v.⟩ and "erfassen" ⟨q.v.⟩. Cf. **auffassen, begreifen, denken, erfassen, gefasst, herausfassen, mitfassen, umgreifen, zusammenfassen.** | **als Prätentionen —,** to take as claims, (*prendre comme des prétentions* ⟨R⟩). | **an** (*oder* bei) **der Hand —,** to take by the hand. | **den Begriff —,** to frame the concept, (*concevoir le concept* ⟨B⟩); to take the concept; (*saisir le concept* ⟨B⟩). | **den Sinn —,** to apprehend the sense. | **ein Wesen —,** to apprehend an essence. | **eine Frage —,** to conceive a question. | **eine Idee —,** to conceive an idea. | **eine Meinung —,** to conceive an opinion; to formulate an opinion. | **einen Ausdruck weit —,** to take an expression broadly, (*prendre une expression dans un sens large* ⟨B⟩). | **einen Gedanken —,** to conceive a thought. | **in Begriffe —,** to comprehend in concepts, (*saisir dans des concepts* ⟨B⟩). | **in Formen —,** to apprehend in forms, (*saisir dans des formes* ⟨B⟩); to put into forms. | **in sich —,** to include ⟨WH, MS⟩, (*renfermer en soi* ⟨B⟩), to comprise ⟨WH, MS⟩. | **ins Auge —,** to fix one's eye (*or* regard) on: to have in view ⟨MS⟩, to consider (doing) ⟨WH⟩, (*considérer* ⟨R⟩). | **mit Begriffen —,** to comprehend with concepts. | **prädikativ —,** to conceive as a predicate, (*saisir sous forme prédicative* ⟨B⟩). | **reflektiv —,** to apprehend reflectively, (*saisir dans la réflexion* ⟨B⟩). | **rein —,** to apprehend purely (*or* in its purity), (*saisir avec pureté* ⟨B⟩), (*saisir en toute pureté* ⟨B⟩), to purify. | **unter Begriffe** —, to comprehend under concepts.

fassend, | **eidetisch zu** —, eidetically apprehensible, (*qui doit être saisi eidétiquement* ⟨B⟩). | **rein zu** —, that can be apprehended purely.

fasslich, apprehensible; comprehensible ⟨WH 1, MS 1⟩; conceivable ⟨WH 2, MS 2⟩. Cf. **fassbar.**

Fassung, 1. apprehension ⟨WH 1⟩, (*appréhension* ⟨R⟩), (*apprehensio* ⟨K⟩), (*saisie* ⟨B⟩). 2. comprehension ⟨WH, MS⟩. 3. conception, (*conception* ⟨B⟩), framing. 4. formulation, wording ⟨WH, MS⟩. 5. taking. Cf. **Auffassung, Erfassung, Sonderfassung, Unverständnis, Wesensfassung.** | **begriffliche** —, conceptual comprehension, (*appréhension conceptuelle* ⟨R⟩). Not "conceptual grasp" ⟨L⟩. | **ideale** —, taking ideally.

Fehlschluss, fallacious argument; fallacious inference.

fern, distant ⟨WH, MS⟩, (remote ⟨WH, MS, BG⟩); alien, (*étranger* ⟨B⟩). Cf. **entfernen, fremd, sachfern.**

Ferne, distance ⟨WH 1, MS 1, L⟩. Cf. **Bewusstseinsferne, Ichferne.**

Fernerscheinung, distance-appearance.

fest, solid, firm, stable, fixed, (*immuable* ⟨R⟩). Save "definitive" ⟨L⟩ for "endgültig". | **~e Artung,** fixed species, (*espèce immuable* ⟨R⟩). | **~e Aussage,** firm statement. | **~er Begriff,** firm concept. | **~es Axiom,** fixed axiom. | **~e Spezies,** fixed species.

festgehalten, | **~es,** something retained.

festhalten, dass, to keep it firmly in mind that, to stipulate that, (*maintenir que* ⟨B⟩).

Festhaltung, holding on, (*maintien* ⟨R⟩); retention.

Festigkeit, stability ⟨WH⟩.

Festsetzung, ascertainment ⟨MS 1⟩, ascertaining.

feststellen, 1. to ascertain ⟨WH 1, MS⟩, (*constater* ⟨R⟩), to establish ⟨WH, MS, BG⟩, (*établir* ⟨B⟩); to discover ⟨WH⟩, (*découvrir* ⟨R⟩). Save "to fix" ⟨BG⟩ for "fixieren". 2. to assert. Cf. **aussagen, begründen, behaupten, gründen, meinen, prädizieren.**

Feststellung, 1. ascertainment ⟨WH 1⟩. 2. assertion, (*position* ⟨R⟩). Save "determination" ⟨WH, L⟩ for "Bestimmung" and "Beschaffenheit". Cf. **Aussage, Behauptung.**

Fiktion, fiction ⟨WH 1, MS 1, L, BG⟩, (*fiction* ⟨R, de M⟩), phantasy, (feigning), (*imagination* ⟨R⟩). Not "fancy" ⟨BG⟩. Cf. **Einbildung, Erdichtung, Phantasie.**

fiktiv, fictional, fictitious ⟨MS 1, WH 2⟩. Cf. **fingiert.**

Fiktum, figment, (*fictum* ⟨R⟩).

Fingierbarkeit, (abstract:) phantasiableness, (concrete:) phantasiable. Cf. **Vorstellbarkeit.**

fingieren, to phantasy, (to feign ⟨WH 1, MS 1⟩), (*feindre* ⟨R⟩), (*forger fictivement* ⟨R⟩), (to invent). Cf. **einbilden, phantasieren, sich denken** (*sub* denken), **sich hineindenken** (*sub* hineindenken), **umfingieren, vorstellen 2.**

fingierend, inventive, (*créateur* ⟨R⟩), (*qui forme la fiction* ⟨R⟩), (*du type de la fiction* ⟨R⟩). | **~e Phantasie,** inventive phantasy, (*imagination créatrice* ⟨R⟩), (*jeu d'imagination* ⟨R⟩). Not "play of fancy" ⟨BG⟩.

fingiert, phantasied, invented, (feigned), (*fictif* ⟨R⟩). Not "fancied" ⟨BG⟩. Cf. **fiktiv.**

Fixierung, fixing ⟨WH 2⟩, (*fixation* ⟨R⟩). Not "fixation" ⟨WH 1⟩.

Fliehen, (ant. Begehren:) shunning, (aversion ⟨BG⟩), (*aversion* ⟨R⟩).

Flüchtigkeit, fleetingness ⟨WH 1⟩; instability.

Fluss, flow ⟨WH 1, MS, L⟩, (*flux* ⟨B⟩). Cf. **Ablauf, Belauf, Bewusstseinsfluss, Bewusstseinslauf, Strom, Verlauf.**

Folge, 1. (logical:) consequence ⟨WH, MS⟩, (*conséquence* ⟨R, B⟩), conse-

quentness, consequent ⟨Bn, BG⟩, (*proposition conséquente* ⟨B⟩); (inference ⟨MS⟩); (implication), (implicate). Not "conclusion" ⟨L⟩. Cf. **Folgerung, Folgesatz, Nachsatz, Schluss 1, Schlussfolge, Schlussfolgerung, Widerfolge.**
2. (temporal:) succession ⟨WH, MS⟩, (*succession* ⟨R, B⟩), sequence ⟨WH⟩, sequel ⟨WH, MS⟩, train.
3. (serial:) succession ⟨WH, MS, BG⟩, (*suite* ⟨B⟩), series ⟨WH, MS⟩, sequence, train. Cf. **Satzfolge, Stufenfolge.**
4. (causal:) consequence ⟨Bn, WH, MS⟩, (*conséquence* ⟨B⟩), (result ⟨WH, MS⟩), (effect ⟨WH, MS⟩. Cf. **Auswirkung, Ergebnis, folgenlos, Leistung, Wirkung.**

Folgekomplex, consequent-whole, (*complexe de conséquence* ⟨B⟩).

folgend, 1. (logical:) following, consequent, (consequential), (implied). Cf. **erfolgend, folgerecht, konsequent.**
2. (temporal or serial:) following ⟨WH, MS⟩, subsequent ⟨WH, MS⟩, successive ⟨MS⟩.
3. (causal:) following ⟨WH⟩, consequent ⟨WH⟩, ensuing ⟨MS⟩, (resultant ⟨WH⟩).
4. (motivational:) obeying.

folgenlos, without result ⟨WH⟩. Cf. **Folge 4.**

folgenreich, having important consequences ⟨MS⟩, (*lourd de conséquences* ⟨B⟩), telling.

folgerecht, consequential(ly), consistent(ly) ⟨WH, MS⟩, (conclusive(ly) ⟨MS⟩), (valid(ly)). Cf. **konsequent, schluss(ge)recht, schlussrichtig.**

Folgerichtigkeit, consequentiality, consistency ⟨Bn, WH, MS⟩, (validity).

folgern, to deduce ⟨WH, MS⟩, to infer ⟨WH, MS⟩. Cf. **ableiten, beschliessen erschliessen 1, herleiten, schliessen. | aus etwas —,** to draw an inference from something.

Folgern, deducting ⟨MS⟩, inferring ⟨WH 2, BG⟩, inference ⟨WH 1, MS⟩. Cf. **Schliessen.**

Folgerung, deduction ⟨WH, MS⟩, (con-

sécution ⟨B⟩), inference ⟨WH, MS⟩, (*conclusion* ⟨R⟩). Not "consequential reasoning" ⟨BG⟩. Cf. **Folge 1, Schluss 3, Schlussfolge, Schlussfolgerung.**

Folgesatz, consequent, (geometry:) corollary ⟨MS⟩, deduction ⟨MS⟩, conclusion ⟨MS⟩, (implicate). Cf. **Folge 1, Nachsatz, Schlusssatz.**

Folgeurteil, consequent judgment, (implied judgment).

folgewidrig, inconsistent ⟨MS 1, WH⟩, (logically) invalid. Cf. **inkonsequent, schlusswidrig.**

folglich, consequently ⟨MS 1, WH⟩, hence ⟨WH, MS⟩.

Form, form ⟨WH 1, MS 1⟩, (*forme* ⟨R, B⟩). Save "order" ⟨BG⟩ for "Ordnung" ⟨q.v.⟩. Cf. **Boden-form, Funktionsform, Ganzheitsform, Gebilde, Gestalt, Grundform, Sonderform, Urform. | (der — nach),** (*formaliter* ⟨K⟩). | **— der Wissenschaft,** (at least sometimes:) science-form, (*forme de la science* ⟨B⟩). Cf. **Wissenschaftsform.**

formal, formal ⟨WH 1, MS 1⟩, (*formel* ⟨R, B⟩). | **das F∼e,** the formal, ((*le*) *formel* ⟨B⟩); the (*or* its) formalness.

formal-allgemein ⟨adj.⟩, formally universal. Cf. **allgemein.**

formal-apriorisch ⟨adj.⟩, Cf. **apriorisch** ⟨adj.⟩. | **das F∼e,** the formal Apriori, (*le caractère apriorique formel* ⟨B⟩). Cf. **Apriori.**

formal-inkonsequent ⟨adj.⟩, formally inconsistent, (*inconséquent sur le plan formel* ⟨B⟩). Cf. **inkonsequent.**

formal(-)logisch ⟨adj.⟩, of (*or* proper to *or* on) formal logic, (*de* (ou *sur*) *la logique formelle* ⟨B⟩); formally logical, formal-logical, (*logico-formel* ⟨B⟩); as formal logic. Cf. **analytisch-logisch, apophantisch-logisch, logisch, rein-logisch.**

formal-logisch ⟨adv.⟩, from the standpoint of (*or* according to) formal logic, (*dans la perspective de la logique formelle* ⟨B⟩); in the manner proper to a formal logic.

formal-mathematisch, of (*or* comprised in *or* making up) formal mathematics, formal mathematical, (*mathématique formel* ⟨B⟩).

formal-ontologisch, belonging to formal ontology, formal-ontological, (*ontologico-formel* ⟨B⟩).

Formbegriff, form-concept, concept of form, (*concept formel* ⟨B⟩). Cf. **Formidee.**

formbildend, form-productive, form-constructive, (*qui construit des formes* ⟨B⟩), (*édificateur de formes* ⟨B⟩). Cf. **aufbauend, bildend.**

Formbildung, form-construction, (*construction de formes* ⟨B⟩). Cf. **Bildung, Bildungsform, Formenbildung.**

Formenabwandlung, modifying forms, (*variation de formes* ⟨B⟩). Cf. **Abwandlung, Formenverwandlung.**

Formenbildung, construction of forms, (*construction de formes* ⟨B⟩), form-construction. Cf. **Bildung, Formbildung.** | **sukzessive —,** successively produced forms.

Formenlehre, theory of (the) forms, form-theory, (*morphologie* ⟨R, B, de M⟩). Save "morphology" ⟨WH 1⟩ for "Morphologie". | **apophantische —,** theory of apophantic forms, (*morphologie apophantique* ⟨B⟩). | **— der Bedeutungen,** theory of the forms of significations, (*morphologie des significations* ⟨B⟩)⟩. Cf. **Bedeutungsform.** | **— der Urteile,** theory of judgment-forms, (*morphologie des jugements* ⟨B⟩). Cf. **Urteilsform.** | **reine —,** theory of (the) pure forms, (pure theory of forms), (*morphologie pure* ⟨B⟩). | **reine logische —, rein-logische —,** form-theory of pure logic, (*morphologie pure logique* ⟨B⟩). Cf. **rein-logisch.**

Formenverknüpfung, connecting forms, (*liaison de formes* ⟨B⟩). Cf. **Verknüpfung.**

Formenverwandlung, change of forms, (*changement de formes* ⟨B⟩), transformation. Cf. **Formenabwandlung, Verwandlung.**

Formgesetz, law of form, law governing the forms, form-laws, formal law, (*loi formelle* ⟨B⟩). Cf. **Gesetzform.**

Formgesetzlichkeit, laws of form, (set of) formal laws, (*légalité formelle* ⟨B⟩). Cf. **Gesetzlichkeit.**

Formgleichheit, perfect (*or* complete) likeness of form, (*similitude formelle* ⟨B⟩). Cf. **Gleichförmigkeit, Gleichheit.**

Formidee, form-idea, (*idée de forme* ⟨B⟩), (*idée formelle* ⟨B⟩).

Formspezies, form-species.

Formstruktur, formal structure.

Formtypik, formal types, (*typique formelle* ⟨B⟩). Cf. **Typik.**

Formtypus, formal stamp, form-type, (*type formel* ⟨B⟩). Cf. **Typus.**

Formung, forming ⟨WH 2⟩, (*imposition de forme* ⟨B⟩), formation ⟨MS 1, WH 3⟩, (*formation* ⟨R⟩), (*mise en forme* ⟨B⟩), (*information* ⟨B, de M⟩); being formed; (form). Cf. **Ausgestaltung, Bildung, Einformung, Ganzheitsformung, Gebilde, Gestalt, Gestaltung.**

forschen, to carry on research ⟨WH⟩, to inquire ⟨WH 1⟩ scientifically, to investigate ⟨L⟩. Cf. **sich besinnen** (*sub* **besinnen**), **nachgehen, untersuchen.**

Forschen, inquiring, (*activité de recherche* ⟨B⟩).

Forschender, investigator, person investigating, (*chercheur* ⟨B⟩).

Forscher, (scientific) investigator, researcher ⟨WH⟩, (*savant* ⟨R⟩). Save "scientist" and "man of science" ⟨BG⟩ for "Wissenschaftler"; save "scholar" ⟨L⟩ for "Gelehrte(r)". Cf. **Naturforscher.**

Forschung, research ⟨WH 1, L⟩, (*recherche* ⟨B⟩), scientific inquiry, inquiry ⟨BG⟩, investigation ⟨WH 2, L⟩, (examination), (*étude (de)* ⟨R⟩), (*science* ⟨R⟩). Cf. **Bewusstseinsforschung, Durchforschung, Erforschung, Erkenntnisforschung, Untersuchung, Ursprungsforschung, Wesensforschung.** | **subjektive —,** investigation of the subjective.

Forschungsgebiet, field of research ⟨WH 1, MS⟩, (*domaine de recherche* ⟨B⟩). Cf. **Gebiet.**

Fortbewegung, motion away. Cf. **Bewegung.**

Fortbildung, further(-)forming, (*façonnement progressif* ⟨B⟩). Cf. **Bildung.**

fortdauern, (*perdurer* ⟨R⟩). Cf. **Dauer.**

Fortgang, continuation ⟨WH⟩, (further) course, (*cours* ⟨B⟩); progression ⟨WH⟩. Cf. **Ablauf, Verlauf.**

fortgelten, to go on being accepted, (*continuer à être valable* ⟨B⟩). Cf. **gelten.**

fortgeltend, continuingly accepted, continuingly held, (continuingly operative). Cf. **geltend.**

Fortgeltung, continuing acceptance; continuing validity, (*valeur qui persiste* ⟨B⟩); (*valeur qui se prolonge* ⟨B⟩). Cf. **Geltung, Nochgeltung.**

fortlaufend, unbroken, (*ininterrompu* ⟨R⟩); (*continu* ⟨B⟩); progressive. Not "prolonged" ⟨BG⟩.

Fortpflanzung, propagation ⟨WH 1, MS 1⟩, transmission ⟨Bn, WH, MS⟩.

fortwerdende, still developing, (*qui continue à être* ⟨B⟩). Cf. **geworden, werden.**

Frage, question ⟨WH 1, MS 1, BG⟩, (*question* ⟨R, B⟩), inquiry ⟨MS⟩, problem ⟨WH⟩, (asking), (questioning), (*interrogation* ⟨R⟩). | **ausser —sein,** not to be in question, (*être hors de question* ⟨B⟩), to be beside the question; to be beyond question. | **die — nach,** the question of, (the question concerning ⟨BG⟩); inquiry about. | **eine — stellen,** to put (*or* ask) a question. | **in — haben,** to ask about, (*s'occuper de* ⟨B⟩). | **in — kommen,** to come into question ⟨WH 1⟩; to be involved ⟨WH 2⟩, (*intervenir* ⟨R⟩). | **in — sein,** to be in question, (*être en question* ⟨B⟩); to lie within the sphere of inquiry. Cf. **nicht in Frage sein.** | **in — stehen,** to be questioned, to be called in question. | **in — stellen,** to call in question ⟨WH 1⟩, (*mettre en question* ⟨B⟩), to question ⟨MS 1, WH 2⟩. | **nicht in — sein,** (sometimes:) to be out of the question ⟨WH 1⟩. Cf. **in Frage sein.**

Fragestellung, inquiry, (*question* (*posée*) ⟨B⟩); mode of inquiry, line of

inquiry; problem. Not "questioning" ⟨L⟩. Cf. **Problemstellung.**

fraglich, questionable ⟨WH, MS, BG⟩, (*problématique* ⟨R, B⟩), (*douteux* ⟨B⟩)

Fraglichkeit, questionability ⟨BG⟩, questionableness, (*caractère problématique* ⟨B⟩), (*ce qui est considéré comme douteux* ⟨B⟩). | **mit ~en behaftet,** questionable in some respects.

fraglos ⟨adj.⟩, without question, (*qui ne fait pas question* ⟨B⟩), unquestioned. Cf. **selbstverständlich.**

fraglos ⟨adv.⟩, undoubtedly.

fremd, other ⟨WH, MS⟩, another's ⟨WH⟩, (*d'autrui* ⟨R, B⟩), on the part of another, that belongs to others, (of others ⟨BG⟩), of someone else; (not one's own ⟨WH⟩); alien ⟨WH, BG⟩, foreign ⟨WH 1, MS, BG⟩, (strange ⟨MS 1, BG⟩), (*étranger* ⟨R, B⟩), with which one is unacquainted. Cf. **fern, geistesfremd, ichfremd.** | **die ~en Akte,** another's acts, (*les actes d'autrui* ⟨R⟩), the acts of others ⟨BG⟩). | **F~es,** something alien, (*élément étranger* ⟨B⟩). | **mir —,** other than mine (alone), not mine.

Fremderfahrung, experience of someone else; experience of something other (*or* alien).

Fremdgeistiges, other-spiritual. Cf. **geistig.**

Fremdheit, otherness.

Fremdsubjekt, other subject.

Freude, gladness ⟨MS 1, WH 2⟩, joy ⟨WH 1, MS 2, BG⟩, (*joie* ⟨R⟩). Cf. **erfreulich, Sichfreuen.**

fühlen, to feel ⟨WH 1, MS 1, BG⟩, to sense ⟨WH⟩, (*sentir* ⟨R⟩). Cf. **empfinden, Gefühl.**

Fülle, fullness ⟨WH, MS, F, L, BG⟩, (*plénitude* ⟨R, B⟩), (*plein* ⟨R⟩); filledness; (non-technical, sometimes:) wealth ⟨WH, BG⟩, (*abondance* ⟨R⟩). Cf. **Erfüllung, Erkenntnisfülle, Klarheitsfülle.** | **in der —,** in its fullness, (*rempli* ⟨B⟩).

Füllung, filling ⟨WH, MS⟩. Cf. **Ausfüllung, Erfüllung.**

Fundament, foundation ⟨WH, MS⟩,

(fundamentum (Arith, trln of Mill)), (*fondement* ⟨R, B⟩), (ground). Mill translates "fundamentum" as "foundation" and as "ground". So far as possible save "ground" for "Grund" ⟨q.v.⟩. Cf. **Boden, Fundierung, Grundlage, Motivationsfundament, Unterlage.**

Fundamentalbetrachtung, Cf. **Betrachtung.** | die phänomenologische —, considerations fundamental to phenomenology, (*considérations phénoménologiques fondamentales* ⟨R⟩). Not "fundamental phenomenological outlook" ⟨BG⟩.

Fundamentalwissenschaft, | — **der Philosophie,** science fundamental to philosophy.

fundieren, to found ⟨WH 1, MS, BG⟩, (*fonder* ⟨R, B⟩). Not "to consolidate" ⟨WH, MS, BG⟩. Save "to ground" ⟨WH, BG⟩ for "begründen" ⟨q.v.⟩ and "gründen" ⟨q.v.⟩.

Fundierung, founding, relationships of founding, foundation ⟨WH⟩, (*acte de fondation* ⟨B⟩). Save "grounding" ⟨F⟩ for "Begründung" ⟨q.v.⟩. Cf. **Fundament, Grund, Grundlage, Grundlegung.**

Funktion, function ⟨WH 1, MS 1⟩, (*fonction* ⟨R, B, de M⟩), functioning, performing, functional activity ⟨BG⟩, activity ⟨WH 2⟩, rôle ⟨WH⟩, capacity. Cf. **Abbildungsfunktion, Ausdrucksfunktion, Bedeutungsfunktion, Beruf, Darstellungsfunk-**tion, **Denkfunktion, Erkenntnisfunktion, Evidenzfunktion, Leistung, Tätigkeit.** | in der — stehend, having the function. | in —, functioning, (*ayant fonction* ⟨B⟩). | **intentionale** —, intentional functioning, (*fonction intentionelle* ⟨B⟩). | **kundgebende** —, cognizance-giving function. Cf. **kundgebend.** | **lebendige** —, actual functioning. Cf. **lebendig** ⟨adj.⟩.

Funktionseinheit, functional unity, (*unité fonctionelle* ⟨B⟩). Cf. **Einheitsfunktion.**

Funktionsform, functional form, (*forme fonctionelle* ⟨B⟩).

Funktionswandel, functional change (*or* alteration). Cf. **Wandel.**

für, | — **sich,** by itself ⟨WH, MS, L⟩, ((*considéré*) *pour soi* ⟨B⟩), all by itself, alone ⟨WH, MS⟩, separate(ly) ⟨WH⟩, ((*considéré*) *à part* ⟨B⟩), (on its own account ⟨?⟩ ⟨WH, BG⟩), distinct, singly, particular(ly); as something selfsufficient, independent(ly), (*indépendant* ⟨B⟩), (*en soi* (ou *lui*) *-même* ⟨R⟩). Cf. **an sich** (*sub* **an**), **an und für sich, eigen, eigenständig, selbständig, unabhängig.** | — **gelten,** to be accepted all by itself; to obtain alone. Cf. **gelten.** | — **meinen,** to mean particularly. Cf. **meinen.** | — **sein,** to exist all by itself.

Für-wahrscheinlich-halten, considering probable.

G

ganz, whole ⟨WH 1, MS 1⟩, (*tout* ⟨R, B⟩), (*total* ⟨B⟩), as a whole, ((*pris*) *dans sa totalité* ⟨B⟩), (*dans son ensemble* ⟨R⟩), entire ⟨WH 2, MS 2⟩, (*entier* ⟨B⟩), complete ⟨WH⟩, (*complet* ⟨B⟩). Cf. **überhaupt.**

Ganzes, whole ⟨WH 1⟩, (*tout* ⟨B⟩), (*totalité* ⟨B⟩), whole complex.

Ganzheit, entirety ⟨WH 2, MS 2⟩, wholeness ⟨WH 4⟩; whole, (*totalité* ⟨B, de M⟩). Save "totality" ⟨WH, MS⟩ for "Gesamtheit" ⟨q.v.⟩. Cf. **Ganzes.**

ganzheitlich ⟨adj.⟩, of wholes, in a whole, integral ⟨WH⟩, (*conduisant à des totalités* ⟨B⟩).

ganzheitlich ⟨adv.⟩, in the whole, (*en une totalité* ⟨B⟩).

Ganzheitsform, form appertaining to wholeness, form of wholeness, (*forme de totalité* ⟨B⟩); form of the whole.

Ganzheitsformung, forming of the whole, (*mise sous forme de totalité* ⟨B⟩). Cf. **Formung.**

Ganzheitsproblem, problem of entirety, (*problème de totalité* ⟨B⟩).

Gattung, genus ⟨WH 1, MS⟩, (kind ⟨MS 1, WH⟩), (*genre* ⟨R, B, de M⟩). Cf. **Wesensgattung.**

Gattungsbestimmtheit, generic determinateness. Cf. **Bestimmtheit.**

Gattungsidee, generic idea.

Gattungsmerkmal, generic characteristic. Cf. **Merkmal.**

Gattungszahlen, (*numeralia specialia* (Arith)).

geartet, | so —, of such a character, (*de telle façon* ⟨R⟩).

Gebaren, manifest behavior. Cf. **Gehaben, Sichverhalten, Verhalten, Verhaltung.**

Gebäude, edifice. Cf. **Bau, Lehrgebäude.**

gebaut, Cf. **bauen.** | so —, having this structure. Cf. **Bau.**

geben, to give ⟨WH 1, MS 1⟩, (*donner* ⟨R⟩); to bestow ⟨MS⟩, (*conférer* ⟨B⟩). Cf. **gegeben, ergeben, verleihen.** | **sich** —, to present itself, (*se donner* ⟨R, B⟩); to be given. Cf. **auftreten, sich darstellen** (*sub* **darstellen**), **Sich-selbst-geben, vorliegen.**

gebend, giving, (*donateur* ⟨R, B⟩), presentive, (presenting); bestowing. Not "dator" ⟨BG⟩. Cf. **bedeutunggebend, selbstgebend, sinngebend, verleihend.** | originär ~e Anschauung, originally presentive intuition, (*intuition donatrice originaire* ⟨R⟩). Cf. **originär** ⟨adv.⟩. | **selbst** —, that gives something-itself. Cf. **selbstgebend.**

Gebiet, province ⟨WH⟩, field ⟨WH, L⟩, (realm), (*domaine* ⟨B⟩), (*marge* ⟨R⟩). Save "domain" ⟨WH⟩ for "Bereich" ⟨q.v.⟩ and "Domäne". Cf. **Erkenntnisgebiet, Forschungsgebiet, Gegenstandsgebiet, Objektgebiet, Reich, Sachgebiet, Sondergebiet, Tragweite, Umfang, Universalgebiet, Urteilsgebiet.**

Gebietsbegriff, concept defining the province, (*concept propre du domaine* ⟨B⟩).

Gebilde, produced formation, formation produced, formation ⟨WH 1; MS; Boring 1950, trln of Stumpf⟩, (*formation* ⟨B⟩), product ⟨MS 2⟩, (*produit de construction* ⟨R⟩); structure ⟨WH, F⟩; form ⟨WH 2, MS⟩. Not "creation" ⟨MS 1, BG⟩. Cf. **Aufbau, Ausgestaltung, Bau, Bedeutungsgebilde, bilden, Bildung, Denkgebilde, Erkenntnisgebilde, Erklärungsgebilde, Formung, Gegenstandsgebilde, Geistesgebilde, Gestalt, Gestaltung, Kerngebilde, Kulturgebilde, Lautgebilde, Leistung, Leistungsgebilde, Partialgebilde, Raumgebilde, Satzgebilde, Sinngebilde, Sondergebilde, Urteilsgebilde, Vernunftgebilde, Wissensgebilde, Wortgebilde, Zahlengebilde.** | aktives —, formation produced actively, (*formation active* ⟨B⟩). | ein — vollziehen, to produce a formation, (*effectuer une formation* ⟨B⟩). Cf. **vollziehen.** | geistiges —, formation produced by mind (*formation spirituelle* ⟨B⟩). Cf. **Geistesgebilde, geistig.** | logisches —, formation with which logic is concerned, logical formation, (*formation logique* ⟨B⟩). Cf. **logisch** ⟨adj.⟩. | psychisches —, psychically produced formation, (*formation psychique* ⟨B⟩), psychic (*or* mental) product, product of the mind; psychic structure. Cf. **psychisch.** | sprachliches —, verbal formation, (*formation de langage* ⟨B⟩). Cf. **sprachlich** ⟨adj.⟩. | subjektives —, subjectively produced formation, (*formation subjective* ⟨B⟩). | syntaktisches —, syntactical formation, (*formation syntaxique* ⟨B⟩).

Gebrauchsobjekt, Object for use, (*objet usuel* ⟨R⟩).

gebunden, prescribed ⟨WH⟩, (*commandé* ⟨R⟩). Cf. **verbunden.** | — an, restricted to (*or* by), limited to (*or* by); tied to ⟨WH, MS⟩, (*lié à* ⟨R, B⟩), bound to ⟨WH 1⟩ (*or* by), (*attaché à* ⟨B⟩), (fettered to ⟨?⟩ ⟨BG⟩); bound up with; inseparable from. Cf. **Bindung an.**

Gebundenheit (an), restriction ⟨WH⟩ (to), combination (with), (*attaché* ⟨B⟩). Cf. **Bindung an.**

gedacht, thought of; phantasied. Cf.

denken. | ~er Gegenstand, object thought of.

Gedachtes, what is thought, (*chose pensée* ⟨B⟩); something thought of. Cf. denken.

Gedachtsein, being thought of.

Gedanke, thought ⟨MS 1, WH 2⟩, (*pensée* ⟨R⟩), (*pensée effectuée* ⟨B⟩), (*pensée produite* ⟨B⟩). Cf. Denken, Satzgedanke, Vorstellung 7.

gedankenlos ⟨adj.⟩, (at least sometimes:) unthinking ⟨WH 2, MS, BG⟩.

gedankenlos ⟨adv.⟩, (at least sometimes:) without thinking, (*machinalement* ⟨B⟩).

Gedankenmotive (pl.), motivating thoughts.

Gedankenzusammenhang, nexus of thoughts. Cf. Zusammenhang.

gedanklich ⟨adv.⟩, intellectually.

gefallen, to please, (*prendre plaisir* ⟨R⟩).

Gefallen, liking ⟨WH⟩, (*plaire* ⟨R⟩), (*plaisir* ⟨R, B⟩). Not "approval" ⟨BG⟩. Cf. Missfallen, Wohlgefallen.

gefallend, liking; liked, (*qui plaît* ⟨R⟩), (*agréable* ⟨R⟩). Not "approving" ⟨BG⟩. | das G~e, the liked, (*le plaisant* ⟨R⟩).

Gefallen-haben, liking. Cf. An-etwas-Gefallen-haben, Gefallen.

Gefallenserlebnis, mental process of liking, (*vécu de plaisir* ⟨R⟩). Cf. Erlebnis.

gefällig, pleasant ⟨MS 2⟩, (*plaisant* ⟨R⟩), (pleasing ⟨BG⟩). Save "agreeable" ⟨MS 3, WH, BG⟩ for "angenehm". Cf. erfreulich, missfällig.

gefasst, See fassen. | eigenheitlich —, taken as included in my ownness. Cf. eigenheitlich ⟨adv.⟩.

Gefühl, feeling ⟨Gomperz trln of Mill, quoted in LU, II. Unters.; Br; MS 1; WH; BG⟩, affect, (pl. sometimes:) sentiments ⟨WH, MS⟩, (*sentiment* ⟨R, B⟩), (*sensibilité* ⟨B⟩). Cf. Empfindnis, fühlen, Gemüt, Sinnesempfindung. | (sittliches —), moral feeling. Not "moral sense" ⟨Bn⟩.

Gefühls-, feeling-, affective, (*affectif* ⟨R⟩). So far as possible save "em-

otional" ⟨WS 1⟩ for "Gemüts-" ⟨q.v.⟩.

Gefühlswertung, affective valuation, (*appréciation affective* ⟨R⟩). Not "valuation in terms of feeling" ⟨BG⟩. Cf. Wertung.

gegeben, given. Cf. geben. | ein absolut G~es, something given absolutely, (an absolute datum ⟨?⟩ ⟨L⟩). | ein G~es, something given, a datum. Cf. Datum, Gegebenheit.

Gegebenheit, 1. (concretum:) datum ⟨WH 1⟩, (*donnée* ⟨B⟩); something given, (what is given), data. 2. (status:) givenness, (*donnée* ⟨B⟩), (presentedness). Not "given material" ⟨BG⟩. Cf. Datum, Dinggegebenheit, Erfahrungsgegebenheit, Mitgegebenheit, Selbstgegebenheit, Vernunftgegebenheit, Vorgegebenheit, Wesensgegebenheit. | eine Sphäre absoluter —, a sphere of absolute data. zur — kommen, to become given. | zur — bringen, to make given, (*élever au rang de donnée* ⟨R⟩). Not "to bring to givenness" ⟨BG⟩. | zur — bringen lassen, to admit of becoming given.

Gegebenheitsbewusstsein, consciousness of givenness ⟨L⟩.

Gegebenheitsmodus, mode of givenness, (*mode de donnée* ⟨B⟩).

Gegebenheitsweise, manner of givenness, manner in which (something) is given, (*façon dont (quelque chose) se donne* ⟨R⟩), (mode of givenness ⟨BG⟩), (mode of being given ⟨L⟩), (*mode de donnée* ⟨B⟩). Not "form of givenness" ⟨BG⟩. Cf. Weise. | intentionale —, manner of intentional givenness, (*mode intentionnel de donnée* ⟨B⟩). | subjektive —, manner of subjective givenness, (*mode subjectif de donnée* ⟨B⟩). | ursprüngliche —, manner of original givenness, manner in which (something) is given originally, (*mode originel de donnée* ⟨B⟩). Cf. ursprünglich ⟨adj.⟩.

Gegenbild, (*contre-partie* ⟨R⟩).

Gegenmotif, (*contre-motif* ⟨R⟩).

Gegennoema, (*contre-noème* ⟨R⟩).

Gegensachverhalt, correlative (predi-

catively formed) affair-complex, ("*état-de-choses*"-*conséquence* ⟨B⟩). Cf. **Sachverhalt.**
Gegensätzlichkeit, mutual opposition.
Gegenstand, object ⟨WH 1, MS 1, BG⟩, (*objet* ⟨R, B⟩), (that which stands over against the subject ⟨BG⟩). Cf. **Erfahrungsgegenstand, Thema, Urteilsgegenstand, Wahrnehmungsgegenstand.** | — überhaupt, any object whatever, object as a universal, object as such, (*objet en général* ⟨B, de M⟩), (*vis-à-vis du sujet en général* ⟨R⟩). Cf. **Etwas(-)überhaupt, Gegenständlichkeit überhaupt (*sub* Gegenständlichkeit), Gegenstandüberhaupt, überhaupt.**
gegenständlich ⟨adj.⟩, objective ⟨MS 1, WH, BG⟩, (*objectif* ⟨R⟩), of an (*or* the) object, of (the) objects, objectival, object-; (having an existent or valid object). Cf. **objektiv, sachlich, vorstellig.** | das G~e, objective something, the objective affair, (*l'objet* ⟨B⟩). Not "the objective content" ⟨BG⟩, not "the objective factor" ⟨BG⟩. Cf. **das Objektive** (*sub* **objektiv** ⟨adj.⟩). | ~e Auffassung, objectival construing. Cf. **Auffassung.** | ~e Beziehung, 1. (Beziehung, welche eine Gegenständlichkeit ist:) objective relation.
2. (Beziehung eines Ausdrucks bzw. eines Satzes auf Gegenständliches:) relation to something objective, object-relation, (*relation aux objets* ⟨B⟩), (*référence à l'objet* ⟨B⟩).
3. having an existent or valid object. Cf. **Beziehung, Gegenständlichkeit 2, gegenstandslos.**
| ~e Einstellung, focusing on what is objective, (*orientation vers l'objet* ⟨B⟩), objective focusing. Cf. **Einstellung.** | ~e Kategorie, object-category, (*catégorie d'objet* ⟨B⟩), (*catégorie objective* ⟨B⟩). Cf. **Gegenstands-Kategorie.** | ~e Richtung, directedness (*or* direction) to something objective, (objective reference). Cf. **Richtung.** | ~er Totalbegriff, concept of a totality of objects, (*concept total d'objet* ⟨B⟩). | ~e Vorstellung, objectivation having an

existent object. Cf. **Vorstellung 1.** | ~er Sinn, object-sense; objective sense, (*sens objectif* ⟨R, B⟩). | ~es Moment, moment of the object, (*moment de l'objet* ⟨R⟩), object moment.
gegenständlich ⟨adv.⟩, | — erfasst, grasped as an object (*or* as objects), (*saisie à la façon d'un objet* (ou *comme objets*) ⟨R⟩). | — gerichtet, directed to something objective, (*dirigé vers ce qui est objet* ⟨B⟩), (*dirigé vers l'objet* ⟨B⟩), directed to objects. | — vor dem Blick haben, to have before one as one's object. | — zusammenhängen, to hang together by virtue of their objects, (*être en connexion objective* ⟨B⟩). Cf. **zusammenhängen.**
Gegenständlichkeit, 1. objectivity ⟨F, BG⟩, (*objectivité* ⟨R, de M⟩), (*objectité* ⟨B⟩), (*caractère d'objet* ⟨B⟩), something (*or* anything) objective.
2. having an existent or valid object (*or* existent or valid objects). Cf. **Denkgegenständlichkeit, Erfahrungsgegenständlichkeit, Erkenntnisgegenständlichkeit, Gegenstandslosigkeit, Objektivität, Sachlichkeit, Urgegenständlichkeit, Urteilsgegenständlichkeit.** | — überhaupt, See Gegenständlichkeit-überhaupt.
Gegenständlichkeit-überhaupt, any objectivity whatever, (*objectivité en général* ⟨R⟩), (*objectité en général* ⟨B⟩), anything objective whatever. Cf. **Etwas(-)überhaupt, Gegenstand(-)überhaupt, überhaupt.**
Gegenstandsbewusstsein, consciousness of objects, (*conscience d'objet* ⟨R⟩).
Gegenstandsbildung, fashioning of an object, (*organisation d'objets* ⟨B⟩). Cf. **Bildung.**
Gegenstandsform, object-form, (*forme d'objet* ⟨B⟩). Cf. **Bedeutungsform.**
Gegenstandsgebiet, object-province, (*domaine d'objets* ⟨R, B⟩). Cf. **Gebiet, Objektgebiet.**
Gegenstandsgebilde, (produced) object-formation, (*formation d'objet* ⟨B⟩). Cf. **Gebilde, Urteilsgebilde.**
Gegenstands-Kategorie, object-cate-

gory ⟨L⟩. Cf. **gegenständliche Kategorie,** (*sub* **gegenständlich**).
Gegenstandslehre, theory of objects, (*doctrine de l'objet* ⟨B⟩).
gegenstandslos, without an object, objectless; having no existent or valid object; having no objective basis. | — **machen,** to deprive (something) of (its) objective basis. | ~e **Vorstellung,** objectivation having no (*or* that lacks an) existent nor valid object. Cf. **gegenständlich 3, Vorstellung 1.**
Gegenstandslosigkeit, being without an (existent or valid) object, lack of an (existent or valid) object, Cf. **Gegenständlichkeit 2.**
Gegenstandssphäre, sphere of objects.
Gegenstand-überhaupt, any object whatever; object as a universal; (*objet-en-général* ⟨B⟩). Cf. **Etwas(-) überhaupt, Gegenständlichkeit-überhaupt, überhaupt.**
Gegenthesis, (*contre-thèse* ⟨R⟩).
Gegenüber, counterpart ⟨Sch⟩; vis-à-vis ⟨WH⟩. | **mein** —, my vis-à-vis ⟨WH 1⟩, what faces me.
Gegenwart, present ⟨WH, MS, BG⟩, (*présence* ⟨R, B⟩). Cf. **Aktualität 1, Bewusstseinsgegenwart, Gegenwärtigkeit, Präsenz, Selbstgegenwart.**
gegenwärtig ⟨adj.⟩, present ⟨WH 1, MS 1⟩, (*présent* ⟨R, B⟩). Cf. **aktuell** ⟨adj.⟩ **1, jetzig, mitgegenwärtig, selbstgegenwärtig, vorgegenwärtig, vorliegend.** | **G~es,** something present (in original intuition).
Gegenwärtigen, making (originally) present, (original) presenting. Cf. **darstellen, vergegenwärtigen.**
gegenwärtigend ⟨adv.⟩, presentively. Not "by presenting" ⟨L⟩. Cf. **vergegenwärtigend.**
Gegenwärtigkeit, (concrete:) present. Cf. **Gegenwart, Präsenz.**
Gegenwärtigung, making (originally) present, (original) presentation, (*présentation* ⟨R⟩). Cf. **Darstellung, Mitgegenwärtigung, Vergegenwärtigung, Vorstellung 3.**
Gegenwartshorizont, horizon of the present. Cf. **Horizont.** | **unser** —, horizon of our present.
Gegenwesen, (*contre-essence* ⟨R⟩). Cf. **Wesen.**
(Gegenwirkung), reaction against ⟨Bn⟩. Cf. **Einwirkung, Wirkung.**
gegliedert, (many-)membered, (*pourvu de membres* ⟨B⟩), articulate(d), (*articulé* ⟨R⟩), articulated as having members, (organized), (*organisé* ⟨B⟩). Cf. **gliedern.**
Gehaben, conduct, way of acting. Cf. **Gebaren, Sichverhalten, Verhalten, Verhaltung.**
Gehalt, content ⟨WH 1⟩, (*contenu* ⟨B⟩), contents ⟨MS⟩, constituents ⟨MS 1⟩, (*élément(s) constitutif(s)* ⟨B⟩), (*état constitutif* ⟨B⟩), (*statut* ⟨R⟩), (*teneur* ⟨B⟩). Cf. **Bedeutungsgehalt, Eigengehalt, Inhalt, Kerngehalt, Sinngehalt, Wasgehalt, Wesensgehalt.**
gehörig, belonging ⟨WH 1, MS 1⟩ (to *or* with), that belongs (to *or* with), appertaining ⟨MS⟩, (*appartenant* ⟨B⟩), pertinent ⟨Bn, WH, MS⟩, pertaining, that pertains; corresponding (to); concomitant (with); (*convenant* (*à*) ⟨B⟩). Cf. **anhaftend, zugehörig, zusammengehörig.** | **ein G~es,** an appertinent. Cf. **ein Zugehöriges** (*sub* **zugehörig**).
Geist, mind ⟨"in phil." — Bn; Schultze trln of Locke, quoted in LU; Gomperz trln of Mill, quoted in LU, I. Unters.; WH; MS⟩; spirit ⟨WH 1, MS 2, L⟩, (*esprit* ⟨R, B⟩), intellect ⟨WH⟩. Cf. **Gesinnung, Seele.**
Geistesfremd, intellectually alien. Cf. **fremd.**
Geistesgebilde, formation produced by the mind, (*formation psychique* ⟨B⟩). Cf. **geistiges Gebilde** (*sub* **Gebilde**).
Geistesgestalt(ung), socio-cultural formation. Cf. **Gestalt, Gestaltung.**
Geistesleben, cultural life, socio-cultural life.
Geistesleistung, production on the part of the mind, (*effectuation spirituelle* ⟨B⟩). Cf. **Leistung.**
Geistesmotivation, socio-cultural motive. Cf. **Motivation.**

Geisteswelt, cultural world, (world of spirit), (intellectual world ⟨?⟩ ⟨WH 1⟩). Cf. **geistige Welt** (*sub* **geistig**).

Geisteswerk, work of the mind.

Geisteswissenschaften, socio-cultural sciences, cultural sciences, moral sciences, (mental and moral sciences ⟨?⟩ ⟨Bn⟩). Not "mental sciences" ⟨BG⟩. (Dilthey, *Einl. i.d. Geisteswissenschaften*, indicates that he regards the terms "Geisteswissenschaften" and "moral sciences" (Mill) as synonyms). Cf. **Kulturwissenschaft.**

geistig, mental ⟨WH, MS, BG⟩, (*mental* ⟨R⟩), of the mind ⟨WH, BG⟩, spiritual ⟨WH 1, MS 1⟩, (*spirituel* ⟨B⟩), (*de l'esprit* ⟨R, B⟩), intellectual ⟨WH, MS⟩; cultural, socio-cultural. Cf. **Fremdgeistiges, intellektiv, psychisch, seelisch.** | ~e **Welt** cultural world, spiritual world, (intellectual world ⟨?⟩). Cf. Logik, *18*: "die sogenannte geistige oder Kulturwelt". Cf. **Geisteswelt.** | ~er **Blick,** mental regard, (*regard de l'esprit* ⟨R⟩). | ~es **Gebilde,** formation produced by the mind, (*formation spirituelle* ⟨B⟩). Cf. **Gebilde.**

geliebt, loved, (beloved ⟨?⟩ ⟨WH 1, BG⟩). | das **G**~e, the loved, (*ce qui est aimé* ⟨R⟩). Not "the beloved" ⟨BG⟩.

gelten, to be accepted, to be taken, (to be posited), to be in force ⟨MS⟩, (*s'imposer* ⟨R⟩), (to carry weight), to be in operation ⟨MS⟩, to be operative, to obtain ⟨MS⟩, to hold good ⟨WH, BG⟩, to be valid ⟨WH, MS⟩, (*être valable* ⟨B⟩), (*valoir* ⟨R, B⟩), to be true, (to pertain). Cf. **Bestehen, Geltung haben** (*sub* **Geltung**). | **als etwas** —, Equivalent to "für etwas gelten 1" ⟨WH, MS⟩, ⟨q.v.⟩. Cf. **in Geltung sein als** (*sub* **Geltung**). | **den Substraten** —, to pertain to the substrates. | **einem wenig** —, to carry little weight for someone. | **es gilt,** it is a question (*or* a matter) of ⟨WH⟩, it depends on ⟨WH⟩, it is to be ⟨WH⟩, it is necessary ⟨WH⟩. | **für etwas** —, 1. to be accepted (or taken) as something, to be taken (*or* held) to be something, to have the status of something, to pass for something ⟨WH 1, MS 1⟩, (*valoir comme quelque chose* ⟨B⟩), (*être valable en tant que quelque chose* ⟨B⟩). 2. Equivalent to "von etwas gelten" ⟨WH⟩, q.v. | **für mich** —, to be accepted by me; to hold good for me, (*valoir pour moi* ⟨B⟩). | **für sich** —, to obtain all by itself, to obtain alone. Cf. **für sich.** | — **lassen,** to accept, (*admettre* ⟨B⟩), (*accorder validité à* ⟨B⟩), to let pass ⟨WH 1, MS⟩, (to approve (of) ⟨MS 1, WH 2⟩), (*déclarer valable* ⟨B⟩). Cf. **anerkennen, annehmen, hinnehmen, in Geltung haben** (*sub* **Geltung**), **in Geltung halten** (*sub* **Geltung**). | **mir — (als),** to be accepted by me (as), to be taken by me (to be), (*valoir pour moi* (*comme*) ⟨B⟩). Cf. **als etwas gelten.** | **von etwas** —, to obtain in the case of something; to apply in the case of (*or* to ⟨WH 1, MS⟩) something, to hold good for (*or* of ⟨WH, MS⟩) something, to be true of something ⟨MS⟩, (*être vrai pour quelque chose* ⟨B⟩), (particularly of a law:) to be valid for something, ⟨WH, MS⟩, (*être valable pour quelque chose* ⟨B⟩), (*valoir pour quelque chose* ⟨R, B⟩).

Gelten, Equivalent to "Geltung", q.v. | **mir** —, acceptance by me, (*valoir pour moi* ⟨B⟩). Cf. **mir geltend** (*sub* **geltend**).

geltend, accepted ⟨WH 1⟩, (posited), in force ⟨MS⟩, in operation ⟨MS⟩, operative, obtaining ⟨MS⟩, valid ⟨WH, MS⟩, (*valable* ⟨B⟩), (*valant* ⟨B⟩), (brought out), (apparent). Cf. **anerkannt, fortgeltend, gesetzt, gültig, mitgeltend, seiend-geltend.** | **für mich** —, accepted, by me, that I accept, my accepted, (*qui vaut pour moi* ⟨B⟩). Cf. **mir Gelten** (*sub* **Gelten**). | — **zu machen ist,** should be brought out ⟨L⟩. | **mir** —, accepted by me (*valant pour moi* ⟨B⟩), that I accept. Cf. **mir Gelten** (*sub* **Gelten**). | **noch** ~**es Urteilen,** judging that is still in

force, (*juger qui est encore valable*
⟨B⟩). Cf. **in fester Geltung verbleiben**
(*sub* **Geltung**). | **sich — machen,** to
become apparent, (*apparaître* ⟨B⟩).
Geltung, acceptance, acceptedness,
something accepted, acceptance or
status, status ⟨F⟩, (rôle ⟨?⟩ ⟨F⟩),
position, (*positio* (see Logik, *143*)),
positedness, what is posited, being
in force, being in operation, oper-
ativeness, obtaining, validity ⟨WH,
L⟩, (*validité* ⟨R, B⟩), legitimacy ⟨?⟩,
application; (value ⟨WH, MS⟩).
(*valeur* ⟨B⟩), importance ⟨MS 3,
WH⟩. Cf. **Anerkennung, Eigengeltung, Erinnerungsgeltung, Fortgeltung, Gültigkeit, Mitgeltung, Noch-
geltung, Satzgeltung, Seinsgeltung,
Umgeltung, Wert, Wirklichkeits-
geltung, Zusammengeltung.** | **als et-
was — haben,** to be accepted as something. Cf. **als etwas gelten** (*sub* **gel-
ten**), **in Geltung sein als.** | **ausser —
bleiben,** to remain unaccepted (*or*
inoperative), (*être mis en suspens*
⟨PL⟩). | **ausser — setzen,** to deprive
of acceptance, (to render inoper-
ative). Cf. **Aussergeltungsetzung.** |
— haben, to be valid ⟨WH⟩, (*avoir
une validité* ⟨B⟩). Cf. **gelten.** | **in
bleibender — haben,** to accept abid-
ingly, to involve abiding acceptan-
ce of. Cf. **in Geltung haben.** | **in fester
— verbleiben,** to remain firmly in
force, (*persister avec une validité
stable* ⟨B⟩). Cf. **in Geltung bleiben,
noch geltendes Urteilen** (*sub* **gel-
tend**). | **in — behalten,** to maintain
acceptance (of something). | **in —
belassen,** to go on accepting, (*conti-
nuer d'admettre comme valable* ⟨B⟩). |
in — bleiben, to remain accepted, to
hold good ⟨WH 1⟩ still, (*rester valable* ⟨B⟩). Cf. **in fester Geltung verbleiben, in Seinsgeltung bleiben** (*sub*
Seinsgeltung). | **in — bringen,**
Equivalent to "zur Geltung bringen",
q.v. | **in — haben,** to accept, (*ad-
mettre comme valable* ⟨PL⟩), to believe in, to have in force. Cf. **anerkennen, annehmen, hinnehmen, in bleibender Geltung haben, in Erinne-**

rungsgeltung haben (*sub* **Erinnerungsgeltung**), **In-Geltung-haben, in
Seinsgeltung haben** (*sub* **Seinsgel-
tung**). | **in — halten,** to accept. Cf.
the terms referred to *sub* **in Geltung
haben.** | **in — lassen,** to go on ac-
cepting. | **in — sein,** to be accepted,
(*être valable* ⟨B⟩). | Cf. **gelten, in
Geltung stehen.** | **in — sein als,** to be
accepted as. Cf. **als etwas gelten** (*sub*
gelten), **als etwas Geltung haben.**
| **in — setzen,** to give acceptance to,
to posit, (*poser comme valable* ⟨B⟩).
Cf. **in Seinsgeltung setzen** (*sub* **Seins-
geltung**), **setzen.** | **in — stehen,** to
be accepted. Cf. **gelten, in Geltung
sein.** | **in naiv-sachlicher —,** naively
accepted as having objective validi-
ty. Cf. **sachlich.** | **objektive —,** Ob-
jective validity, (*validité objective*
⟨B⟩). Cf. **objektiv.** | **zur — bringen,**
to bring to bear ⟨WH 1⟩, (a demand,
a law:) to enforce. | **zur — kommen,**
to win (*or* gain) acceptance, (*arriver
à une autorité* ⟨B⟩), (*parvenir à la
validité* ⟨B⟩), (*s'affirmer* ⟨R⟩); to
find application.
Geltungsbereich, (of a concept:) extension. Cf. **Umfang.**
Geltungsbewusstsein, acceptive consciousness ⟨?⟩, positive consciousness ⟨?⟩.
Geltungscharakter, validity-character-
istic, (*caractère de validité* ⟨B⟩). Cf.
Charakter, Gültigkeitsprädikat.
Geltungseinheit, accepted unity, (posited unity), unity-of-obtaining,
valid unity ⟨F⟩, (unity of validity
⟨?⟩), (*étalon de validité* ⟨R⟩), (*princi-
pe unificateur ayant une validité* ⟨R⟩).
Not "validity system" ⟨BG⟩.
Geltungsfrage, question about validity.
Cf. **Frage.**
Geltungsgrund, ground for acceptance,
basis of validity ⟨?⟩. Cf. **Grund.**
Geltungsleben, life of acceptance, (*vie-
ayant-une-valeur* ⟨B⟩). Cf. **Leben.**
Geltungslehre, theory of validity, (*doc-
trine de la validité* ⟨B⟩).
Geltungsleistung, accepted product
⟨?⟩. Cf. **Leistung.**
Geltungsmodifikation, acceptance-

modification, positional modification ⟨?⟩.

Geltungsmodus, mode of acceptance.

Geltungsphänomen, acceptance-phenomenon, acceptedness-phenomenon; validity-phenomenon.

Geltungssphäre, positional sphere, (*plan où une validité est en jeu* ⟨R⟩).

Geltungswert von etwas, value at which something is accepted, acceptance-value, (*valeur d'autorité* ⟨B⟩). Cf. **Wert.**

Gemeinbild, generic image ⟨?⟩ ⟨Bn⟩. Cf. **Bild.**

Gemeinsames, what is common, (*ce qui est commun* ⟨B⟩), common element. | **von einem Boden des Gemeinsamen,** from a ground consisting in what is common. Cf. **Grund.**

Gemeinsamkeit, community ⟨WH 2⟩, commonness ⟨WH 1⟩, something in common, common character, (common element (*or* point)). Cf. **Gemeinschaft.** | **eine — des Wesens,** some commonness of essence.

Gemeinschaft, community ⟨WH 1, MS 1⟩, (*communauté* ⟨B⟩), communion ⟨WH, MS⟩, (*communio* ⟨K⟩), commerce, (*commercio* ⟨K⟩), commonness. Cf. **Allgemeinschaft, Commercium, Einfühlungsgemeinschaft, Erkenntnisgemeinschaft, Gemeinsamkeit, Urteilsgemeinschaft, Vergemeinschaftung, Wechselgemeinschaft, Wesensgemeinschaft.** | **in —,** in common, (*en commun* ⟨B⟩), (*en communauté* ⟨B⟩); in communion, (*en tant qu'êtres faisant partie d'une communauté* ⟨B⟩).

Gemeinschaftlichkeit, (concrete:) common thing.

Gemeinschaftsakt, cooperative act.

Gemeinschaftsbewusstsein, community consciousness. Not "social consciousness" ⟨L⟩. Cf. **Bewusstsein.**

gemeint, 1. (consciously) meant, (intended), (*visé* ⟨R, B⟩), (*désigné* ⟨B⟩). 2. (doxically, sometimes:) believed, (*pensé* ⟨B⟩), (supposed). Cf. **Bewusstseins-Gemeintes, meinen.** | **bedeutungsmässig —,** signifyingly meant. Cf. **bedeutungsmässig** ⟨adv.⟩. | **das**

G~e, the (consciously) meant, (the intended), (the supposed), (*ce qui est pensé* ⟨B⟩). Cf. **das Vermeinte** (*sub* **vermeint**). | **urteilsmässig —,** meant judgingly, (*visé dans le jugement* ⟨B⟩). Cf. **urteilsmässig** ⟨adv.⟩.

Gemeintheit, meantness. Save "intentionality" ⟨L⟩ for "Intentionalität".

Gemeintheitsweise, manner of meantness. Cf. **Weise.**

Gemüt, 1. emotion ⟨WH⟩, emotions, (*affectivité* ⟨R, B⟩), (*sphère affective* ⟨B⟩), (feeling ⟨MS 1, WH⟩), (sentiments). 2. (sphere of) emotion and volition, (feeling and desire ⟨BH⟩). Not "affective-conative disposition or function" ⟨Bn⟩. Save "sentiment" ⟨WH, MS, BG⟩ for "Empfindnis". Cf. **Gefühl, Gemütsbewegung.** | **des ~s,** of emotion, of the emotions, emotional, affective, (*de l'affectivité* ⟨B⟩). Cf. **Gefühls-, Gemüts-.**

Gemüts-, emotional ⟨WH 1⟩, of emotion, affective, (*affectif* ⟨B⟩), (*de l'affectivité* ⟨B⟩). Cf. **Gefühls-, des Gemüts** (*sub* **Gemüt**).

Gemütsakt, affective act, (*acte de l'affectivité* ⟨B⟩), act of emotion.

Gemütsbewegung, emotion ⟨WH 1⟩, (in Brentano's sense:) affective-conative phenomenon. Not "act of sentiment" ⟨BG⟩. Cf. **Gemüt.**

Gemütsmodalität, modality of emotion, (*modalité de l'affectivité* ⟨B⟩). | **~en,** modalities of emotion and volition.

Gemütstätigkeit, emotional activity. Cf. **Tätigkeit.**

genau ⟨adj.⟩, precise ⟨MS 3, WH 5⟩; (*exact* ⟨R⟩). Save "exact" ⟨MS 1, WH 3, BG⟩ for "exakt".

genau ⟨adv.⟩, precisely ⟨WH 3⟩, (*précisément* ⟨B⟩), (*exactement* ⟨R⟩), (*stricte* ⟨K⟩). Not "exactly" ⟨WH 2, BG⟩. Cf. **geradehin, geradezu.**

Generalisierung, generalization, (*généralisation* ⟨R, de M⟩). Cf. **Verallgemeinerung.**

Generalität, generality ⟨MS 1⟩, (*géné-*

ralité ⟨R⟩), (*le général* ⟨R⟩). Cf.
Allgemeinheit.
Generalthesis, general positing, (*posi-
tion générale* ⟨R⟩), (*thèse générale*
⟨R⟩). Cf. **Thesis.**
generell ⟨adj.⟩, general, generic, ge-
nerical. | ∼e **Aussage,** generical
statement. Cf. **Aussage.** | ∼e **Vor-
stellung,** generical objectivation. Cf.
Vorstellung 1.
generell ⟨adv.⟩, universally. Cf. **allgemein** ⟨adv.⟩.
Genesis, genesis, ⟨MS 1, WH⟩, (*genèse*
⟨B⟩); generating, generation. Cf.
**Bewusstseinsgenesis, Erzeugung,
Seinsgenesis, Sinnesgenesis, Werden.**
genetisch ⟨adv.⟩, genetically, (*du point
de vue génétique* ⟨B⟩), in the generating.
gerade ⟨adj.⟩, (ant. reflektiv:) straightforward ⟨WH, MS⟩; direct ⟨WH,
MS⟩, (*direct* ⟨B⟩), (*immédiat* ⟨B⟩);
straight ⟨MS 1, WH⟩, rectilinear,
even ⟨WH 1, MS⟩. | — **Thematik,**
straightforward thematizing activity. Cf. **Thematik.**
geradeaus, (ant. reflektierend:) straight
forwardly, (*directement* ⟨R⟩).
geradehin, (ant. reflektiv:) straight-
forwardly; directly, (*de façon directe*
⟨B⟩), (*immédiatement* ⟨B⟩); (precisely ⟨BG⟩), (*exactement* ⟨R⟩). Cf.
genau ⟨adv.⟩, **geradezu.**
geradezu, directly ⟨BG⟩, (*directe* ⟨K⟩),
simply ⟨WH⟩, (*tout bonnement* ⟨B⟩),
(*franchement* ⟨R⟩), precisely ⟨BG⟩,
(*exactement* ⟨R⟩), even, (just ⟨BG⟩).
Cf. **genau** ⟨adv.⟩, **geradehin.**
Gerechtigkeit, justice ⟨WH 1, MS 1⟩,
justness ⟨WH⟩, legitimacy ⟨MS⟩,
(*légitimité* ⟨B⟩), justification ⟨WH,
MS⟩. Cf. **Recht, Rechtfertigung, Berechtigung.**
geregelt, governed, subjected to rules;
regular. Cf. **regeln.**
gerichtet, Cf. **richten, Richtung.** | **im-
manent** —, directed to something
immanent, (*dirigé de* (ou *d'une*) *façon
immanente* ⟨R⟩). Not "immanently
directed" ⟨BG⟩. Cf. **immanent**
⟨adv.⟩. | **gegenständlich** —, directed
to something objective, (*dirigé vers*

ce qui est objet (ou *vers l'objet* ⟨B⟩),
directed to objects. | — **auf,** directed
to, (directed towards ⟨?⟩), (*dirigé
vers* ⟨R, B⟩), aimed at, (*tourné vers*
⟨R⟩), concerned with, paying at-
tention to. | **objektiv-ideal** —, di-
rected to the Objective and ideal,
(*dirigé vers l'objectivité idéale* ⟨B⟩). |
subjektiv —, directed to the subjective, (*dirigé vers le subjectif* (ou
vers la subjectivité ou *du côté subjectif*
ou *du côté de la subjectivité*) ⟨B⟩);
relating to (*or* concerning) the sub-
jective. | **subjektiv** ∼e **Thematik,**
thematizing activity directed to the
subjective, thematizing of the subjective, (*thématique dirigée vers la
subjectivité* ⟨B⟩). Cf. **Thematik.** |
subjektiv-phänomenologisch —, directed phenomenologically to the
subjective, (*dirigé vers la subjectivité
dans la perspective phénoménologique*
⟨B⟩). | **transzendent** —, directed to
something transcendent, (*dirigé de
façon transcendantale* ⟨R⟩). Not
"transcendently directed" ⟨BG⟩.
Gerichtetsein auf, directedness to (*or*
towards ⟨BG⟩), being directed to (*or*
towards), (*être dirigé sur* ⟨R⟩), being
aimed at, being pointed at (*or* towards). Cf. **richten auf, Richtung.**
gesamt, (sometimes:) as a whole.
Gesamt-, total, (*total* ⟨R, B⟩), col-
lective, aggregate ⟨Bn⟩, composite
⟨Bn⟩. See compound words, *infra.*
Gesamtform, total form, (*forme totale*
⟨B⟩).
Gesamtglied, total member, (*membre
complexe* ⟨B⟩).
Gesamtheit, totality ⟨WH, MS⟩, (*tota-
lité* ⟨B⟩), every one (of the). Cf. **All-
heit, Ganzheit.**
Gesamthorizont, collective horizon.
Gesamtinbegriff, sum-total, (*somme*
⟨R⟩). Save "totality" ⟨BG⟩ for
"Gesamtheit" (q.v.). Cf. **Inbegriff.**
Gesamtkomplexion, total combination.
Cf. **Komplexion.**
Gesamtleistung, total effect. Cf. **Lei-
stung.**
Gesamttitel, collective title (*or* name).
Cf. **Titel.**

Gesamtvorstellung, aggregate idea. Cf. **Vorstellung 4 & 7.**

Geschehen, happening, (process), (event).

Geschichte, story, history ⟨WH⟩, (*histoire* ⟨R⟩), science of history. Cf. **historisch.**

geschlossen ⟨adj.⟩, closed ⟨WH 1⟩, (*clos* ⟨B⟩). Cf. **abgeschlossen, schliessen 1.** | **in sich —,** self-contained, (*fermé sur soi* ⟨B⟩), (*autonome* ⟨B⟩). Cf. **in sich abgeschlossen** (*sub* **abgeschlossen**).

geschlossen ⟨adv.⟩, self-containedly.

Gesetzesform, law-form; (pl.:) law-forms, (*formes légales* ⟨B⟩). Cf. **Formgesetz, Gesetzform.**

Gesetzesnorm, normative law, (*loi normative* ⟨B⟩).

Gesetzform, law-form, (*loi ayant pour forme* ⟨B⟩). Cf. **Formgesetz, Gesetzesform.**

gesetzlich ⟨adj.⟩, according to a law; as a law; regulative; of a law, of laws. Cf. **wesensgesetzlich.**

gesetzlich ⟨adv.⟩, | **— gültig,** having the force of a law. Cf. **gültig.**

Gesetzlichkeit, (set of) laws, law; lawfulness ⟨WH 1⟩, (*légalité* ⟨B⟩). Cf. **Erfahrungsgesetzlichkeit, Formgesetzlichkeit, Grundgesetzlichkeit, Wesensgesetzlichkeit.**

gesetzmässig ⟨adj.⟩, conforming to (or in conformity with) law(s), (*qui se conforme à des lois* ⟨B⟩), regulated, regular, (legitimate ⟨Bn, WH, MS⟩). Cf. **berechtigt, echt, rechtmässig.**

gesetzmässig ⟨adv.⟩, conformably to law(s), regulatedly, regularly.

Gesetzmässigkeit, conformity to law(s), (*légalité* ⟨B⟩), regulatedness, regularity, legitimacy ⟨WH, MS⟩, (regulated necessity); set (or system) of laws, law(s), (*lois* ⟨B⟩). Cf. **Bewusstseinsgesetzmässigkeit, Gesetzlichkeit, Wesensgesetzmässigkeit.** | **passiv modifizierende —,** law of passive modification, (*légalité qui introduit des modifications passives* ⟨B⟩). Cf. **modifizierend.**

gesetzt, posited ⟨Bn, BG⟩, (*posé* ⟨R, B⟩). Cf. **geltend, Satz, setzen.**

Gesetzurteil, law-judgement.

Gesicht, vision ⟨Bn, WH 2, MS 2⟩; sight ⟨WH 1, MS 1⟩. Cf. **Blick, Sehen.** | **zu — bekommen,** to get sight of ⟨WH 1⟩. | **zu — bringen,** to bring to sight, (*envisager* ⟨B⟩).

Gesichtsfeld, field of vision ⟨WH 1⟩. Cf. **Blickfeld.**

Gesichtskreis, sphere of vision, (*horizon* ⟨B⟩). Save "field of vision" ⟨Bn⟩ for "Blickfeld" ⟨q.v.⟩ and "Gesichtsfeld"; save "horizon" ⟨MS 1, WH⟩ for "Horizont".

Gesichtslinie, line of vision. Not "visual axis" ⟨Bn⟩. Cf. **Blicklinie, Blickrichtung.**

Gesichtspunkt, point of view ⟨WH 1⟩; respect. Cf. **Hinsicht, Standpunkt.** | **unter den idealen ~en eines Gesetzes betrachtet,** considered with respect to their relationships to an ideal law ⟨?⟩.

Gesinnung, disposition ⟨Bn, MS 1⟩, spirit, (*sentiment* ⟨B⟩). Cf. **Geist.**

Gestalt, shape ⟨WH, MS⟩, formation ⟨MS⟩, structure, configuration ⟨MS⟩, (*configuration* ⟨B⟩), form ⟨WH, MS⟩, (*forme* ⟨B⟩), type, (*type* ⟨B⟩), (*genre* ⟨R⟩), (figure), (*figure* ⟨R⟩), (*contour* ⟨R⟩). Not "shape and figure" ⟨BG⟩. Cf. **Ableitungsgestalt, Abwandlungsgestalt, Ausgestaltung, Bau, Bildung, Einheitsgestalt, Erkenntnisgestalt, Form, Formung, Gebilde, Gestaltung, Geistesgestalt, Grundgestalt, Kulturgestalt, Nachgestalt, Raumgestalt, Sinngestalt, Sondergestalt, Stufengestalt, Systemgestalt, Typus, Urteilsgestalt, Vorgestalt, Vorstellungsgestalt, Wesensgestalt, Zusammenhang.** | **geometrische —,** geometrical shape, (*forme géométrique* ⟨B⟩).

gestalten, to shape ⟨MS 3, WH⟩, to fashion ⟨WH 1, MS 3⟩, (*façonner* ⟨B⟩), to give shape (or form or figure) to, (*donner forme à* ⟨B⟩), (to form ⟨WH 2⟩), (*former* ⟨B⟩). Cf. **ausgestalten, bilden, herausarbeiten, neugestaltet, umgestalten.** | **sich —,** to take shape ⟨MS⟩, (*se former* ⟨B⟩). Cf. **sich umgestalten** (*sub* **umgestal-**

ten). | sich — in, to fashion itself into.

gestaltend, shaping, fashioning, formative ⟨WH⟩, (formant ⟨B⟩). Cf. bildend, zugestaltend.

Gestaltqualität, form-quality (Boring 1950), (shape-quality).

Gestaltung, shaping ⟨MS 2, WH 4⟩, (mise en forme ⟨B⟩), fashioning ⟨WH 1, MS 3⟩, formation ⟨MS 1, WH 5⟩, (formation⟨B⟩), (figure ⟨R⟩), forming, (configuration ⟨R, B⟩), (transformation ⟨R⟩), organization, (organisation ⟨B⟩). Save "form" ⟨L⟩ for "Form" and "Gestalt" ⟨q.v.⟩. Cf. Ausgestaltung, Bewusstseinsgestaltung, Bildung, Formung, Gebilde, Kulturgestaltung, Neugestaltung, Raumgestaltung, Sondergestaltung. | syntaktische —, syntactical fashioning, (configuration syntaxique ⟨B⟩).

gestellt sein, to be placed, to be in a position. Cf. eingestellt, einstellen, stellen.

gewahren, to perceive attentively, (s'apercevoir ⟨R⟩), (to notice ⟨WH 1, MS⟩). Not "to become aware of" ⟨BG⟩. Cf. aufmerken, beachten, merken, wahrnehmen.

Gewahren, attentive perceiving. Not "(explicit) awareness" ⟨BG⟩. Cf. Gewahrung.

gewahrend, attentive.

gewährleisten, to guarantee, (garantir ⟨R⟩). Cf. Bürgschaft.

Gewahrung, attentive perceiving, (acte de s'apercevoir ⟨B⟩). Cf. Gewahren.

geweckt, Cf. wach, Weckung. | das G∼e, the awakened (object), (ce qui est évoqué ⟨B⟩).

gewendet, turned, (orienté ⟨PL⟩); (stated). Cf. sich wenden (sub wenden). | subjektiv —, turned toward(s) the subject himself, (orienté vers le sujet ⟨PL⟩); stated subjectively.

gewesen, Cf. Gleichzeitgewesenes. | Wahrgenommen G∼es, was perceived

Gewesenheit, beenness.

gewinnen, to gain ⟨WH 1, MS 1⟩, to acquire ⟨WH, MS⟩, (acquérir ⟨B⟩),

to obtain ⟨WH, MS⟩, (obtenir ⟨B⟩), to get ⟨WH, MS⟩, to attain, (atteindre ⟨B⟩); to reach ⟨WH⟩, (parvenir à ⟨B⟩). Cf. erzielen.

Gewissheit, (usually:) certainty ⟨WH 1, MS 1, BG⟩, (certitude ⟨R, B⟩), (subjective or noetic, sometimes:) certitude. Cf. Glaubensgewissheit, Seinsgewissheit, Urteilsgewissheit. | in —, as a certainty, (avec certitude ⟨R⟩).

Gewissheitslogik, certainty-logic, (logique de la certitude ⟨B⟩). Cf. Wahrheitslogik.

Gewissheitsurteil, judgment (made) with certainty, (jugement-certitude ⟨B⟩). Cf. Urteil, Urteilsgewissheit.

gewöhnlich, customary, (habituel ⟨B⟩), ordinary ⟨WH, MS⟩. Save "common" ⟨WH 1, MS⟩ for "gemeinsam".

gewohnt, accustomed ⟨WH 1, MS 1⟩, habitual ⟨WH⟩, (habituel ⟨B⟩). Cf. habituell.

geworden, having become, that has come into being (or into existence), (as it has) developed, (qui s'est développé ⟨B⟩), (qui a eu un développement ⟨R⟩), (already) generated, (né ⟨B⟩), (qui a été ⟨B⟩). Cf. fortwerdend, werden.

giltig, Equivalent to "gültig" ⟨q.v.⟩.

Glaube(n) (masc.), belief ⟨WH 1, MS 1⟩, (croyance ⟨R, B⟩), believing, (foi ⟨PL, B⟩). Not "faith" ⟨WH 2, MS 2⟩. Cf. Glaubensweise, Meinen, Meinung, Seinsglaube(n), Sonderglaube, Wahrheitsglaube.

Glauben (neut.), believing. Cf. Glaubensweise, Meinen, Seinsglauben ⟨neut.⟩. | im —, believingly. | Cf. im Seinsglauben (sub Seinsglauben ⟨neut.⟩. | im — sein, to be believed in.

Glaubenscharakter, belief-characteristic, (caractère de croyance ⟨R⟩). Not "character distinctive of belief" ⟨BG⟩. Cf. Charakter.

Glaubensgewissheit, certainty of believing (or belief ⟨BG⟩), (certitude de croyance ⟨R, B⟩), doxic certainty.

Not "believing certitude" ⟨BG⟩. Cf. **Gewissheit.**

Glaubensmodalität, doxic modality, (*modalité de la croyance* ⟨R, B⟩).

Glaubensmodifikation, modification of believing, (*modification de croyance* ⟨B⟩).

Glaubensthesis, doxic positing, (*thèse de croyance* ⟨B⟩). Cf. **Thesis.**

Glaubensweise, manner of believing, (*croyance* ⟨R⟩). Not "way of believing" ⟨BG⟩.

gleich ⟨adj.⟩, (that are) perfectly (*or* completely *or* quite) alike, alike ⟨Gomperz trln of Mill, quoted in LU, II. Unters.; WH; MS⟩, like ⟨WH, MS⟩, (*semblable* ⟨B⟩), equal ⟨Ueberweg trln of Berkeley, quoted in LU, II. Unters.; WH 1,MS⟩, (the same ⟨WH, MS⟩), (*même* ⟨B⟩), (one and the same ⟨MS⟩), (*identique* ⟨B⟩). Cf. **ähnlich, wesensgleich.** | **G ~es,** things that are quite alike, thing that is perfectly like another, (*quelque chose qui est semblable* ⟨B⟩). | **immer —,** unvarying, (*toujours le même* ⟨B⟩).

gleichartig, (that are) of the same sort, (that are) alike in kind, ((a)like). Cf. **ähnlich.**

Gleichartigkeit, specific likeness.

gleichbedeutend, (that are) (perfectly) alike in signification. Not "meaning the same thing" ⟨BG⟩. Cf. **bedeutend, tautologisch.**

Gleichförmigkeit, perfect (*or* complete) likeness of form, (uniformity ⟨Bn, MS 1, WH 2⟩). Cf. **Formgleichheit.**

Gleichheit, perfect (*or* complete) likeness, likeness ⟨WH, MS⟩, equality ⟨Bn, MS 1, WH⟩, (*égalité* ⟨B⟩), parity ⟨Bn, MS 2, WH⟩; (concrete): perfectly like thing. Cf. **Ähnlichkeit, Formgleichheit.** | **in —,** without change, (*en restant les mêmes* ⟨B⟩). | **von — zu — übergehen,** to go from one thing to another that is perfectly like it. Cf. **übergehen zu.**

Gleich-Jetzigkeit, same nowness. Cf. **Jetzigkeit.**

Gleichordnung, parity.

gleichsam, as it were ⟨WH 1⟩, quasi, (*quasi* ⟨R⟩).

Gleichzeitiggewesen, Were-Simultaneous.

Gleichzeitigkeit, (a) simultaneity.

Glied, member ⟨WH, MS⟩, (*membre* ⟨PL, B⟩); link ⟨WH, MS⟩; (*élément* ⟨B⟩), Cf. **Bauglied, Hauptglied, Nebenglied, Subjektglied, Substratglied.**

Gliederform, membership-form, (*forme de membres* ⟨B⟩).

gliedern, Cf. **abgliedern, gegliedert, zergliedern.** | **sich —,** to be articulated, to be membered, (*se décomposer* ⟨B⟩). | **sich in Teile —,** to be articulated as having parts, to be so articulated that it has parts, (*se décomposer en parties* ⟨B⟩).

Gliederung, articulation ⟨WH 1, MS⟩, (*articulation* ⟨R, B⟩), (*articulatio* ⟨K⟩), memberedness, memberedness or articulation, (member), (division ⟨WH⟩), (differentiation), (organization ⟨MS⟩), (*organisation (complexe)* ⟨B⟩), (*démembrement (possible)* ⟨B⟩), (*décomposition (en membres)* ⟨B⟩). Cf. **Abgliederung, Problemgliederung.** | **— in,** articulation as comprising, (*organisation en* ⟨B⟩).

gliedweise, member by member, (*membre par membre* ⟨B⟩).

Glück, happiness ⟨WH, MS⟩.

Glückseligkeit, happiness ⟨Bn, WH⟩.

Gradualität, degree(s), (*degré(s)* ⟨B⟩), (*graduation* ⟨B⟩), gradations; gradual diminution. Cf. **Stufe.**

grammatisch ⟨adj.⟩, verbal, lingual, of language, linguistic; of grammar, (*grammatical* ⟨B⟩). Cf. **rein-grammatisch, rein-logisch-grammatisch, sprachlich.** | **~er Gegenstand,** linguistic object. | **~er Satz,** sentence, (*proposition grammaticale* ⟨B⟩). Cf. **Satz 2.**

grammatisch ⟨adv.⟩, verbally, in its lingual aspect, linguistically, (*au point de vue grammatical* ⟨B⟩), (*sur le plan grammatical* ⟨B⟩).

greifbar, seizable ⟨WH 1, MS 1⟩, (*saisissable* ⟨B⟩), tangible ⟨Gomperz trln of Mill, quoted in LU; WH; MS⟩. Cf. **fassbar, fasslich.**

greifen, to seize ⟨MH 1, WH⟩, to grip

⟨WH⟩. Cf. begreifen, erfassen, ergriffen, herausgreifen, umgreifen, vergreifen, zurückgreifen auf, Zusammengreifen.

Grenzbegriff, limit-concept, (concept-limite ⟨B⟩), limiting concept. Not "limiting notion" ⟨Bn⟩.

Grenze, limit ⟨Bn, MS 1, WH⟩, (limite ⟨R, B, de M⟩). Cf. Abgrenzung, abschliessen, Begrenzung, Rahmen, Umgrenzung.

Grenzpunkt, limit, (point limite ⟨B⟩).

Griff, grip ⟨WH, MS⟩, (emprise du moi ⟨R⟩). Cf. Erfassung, Im-Griff-behalten, Noch-im-Griff, Noch-im-Griff-behalten, Noch-im-Griff-haben, Noch-im-Griff-halten. | im —, in one's grip. | in den — bekommen, to lay hold of, (reprendre en main ⟨B⟩).

Grösse, magnitude ⟨Br, WH, MS⟩, (grandeur ⟨B⟩); size; (particularly in mathematics:) quantity ⟨Bn, WH, MS⟩, (quantitas ⟨K⟩). Cf. Massgrösse, Sehgrösse.

Grössenschätzen, estimating size. Not "measure" ⟨L⟩. Cf. Schätzung.

Grössenzahl, quantitative number. Cf. Masszahl.

Grund, 1. (wherever possible:) ground ⟨WH, MS, BG⟩, grounds ⟨WH⟩. 2. bottom ⟨WH 1, MS⟩, (fond ⟨B⟩). Cf. Boden. 3. (Hintergrund:) ground, background ⟨MS 1⟩. 4. (Fundament:) basis ⟨WH 1, BG⟩, (base ⟨R⟩), foundation ⟨MS 1⟩, (fondement ⟨R, B⟩). So far as possible save "basis" for "Boden" ⟨q.v.⟩ and "foundation" for "Fundament" ⟨q.v.⟩. 5. (Latin ratio:) reason ⟨trln of Mill in LU II/1, Einl.; Bn; WH; MS⟩, (raison ⟨R, B⟩), (ratio ⟨Wolff⟩), (droit ⟨B⟩). a. (Beweggrund:) reason, (motive ⟨WH 1, MS 1⟩), (motif ⟨B⟩). b. (Ursache:) reason ⟨WH 2⟩, (cause ⟨MS 1⟩). c. (Veranlassung:) reason, occasion ⟨MS 1, WH 2⟩.

6. (Grundsatz:) fundamental principle, (principe ⟨B⟩). 7. (Grundurteil, ant. Folge:) (logical) antecedent. 8. realm. Not "strength" ⟨WH, MS, BG⟩. Cf. Begründung, Boden, Erdboden, Fundierung, Geltungsgrund, Grundlage, Grundlegung, Grundsatz, Grundurteil, Grundurteilen, Rechtsgrund, Untergrund, Unterlage, Urgrund, Ursache, Wahrscheinlichkeitsgrund, (Weltgrund), Wesensgrund, zugrunde. | auf absolutem —, in a realm that is absolute. | auf dem intuitiven ~e, on the basis of the intuiting. | auf — der Einsicht in, grounded on the insight. | aus assoziativen ~en, because of associations (du fait de l'association ⟨B⟩). Cf. assoziativ. | im ~e, at bottom ⟨MS 1, WH⟩, (au fond ⟨B⟩). | nach ~en und Folgen, in their relationships as grounds to consequences. Not "as principles and conclusions" ⟨L⟩. Cf. Folge 1. | zu ~e liegen, to be at the basis of, to underlie. Cf. zugrunde liegen (sub zugrunde). | zureichender —, sufficient reason.

Grundart, fundamental sort, (fundamental kind ⟨L⟩). Cf. Art.

Grundbegrifflichkeit, (set of) fundamental concepts, (concepts fondamentaux ⟨B⟩), (appareil conceptuel fondamental ⟨B⟩). Cf. Begrifflichkeit.

gründen, to ground ⟨WH⟩, to be grounded ⟨BG⟩; to base ⟨WH⟩, to be based, (to establish ⟨WH, MS⟩), (to found ⟨WH 1, MS 1⟩), (fonder ⟨R⟩). So far as possible save "to found" for "fundieren". Cf. begründen, feststellen. | (sich) in etwas —, to have a (or its or their) basis in something, (se fonder dans quelque chose ⟨R⟩).

Grundform, fundamental form, (forme fondamentale ⟨R, B⟩), (basic form ⟨WH, BG⟩).

Grundgesetz, fundamental law ⟨MS 1⟩, (loi fondamentale ⟨B⟩), (ultimate) principle. Save "axiom" ⟨Bn⟩ for "Axiom". Cf. Grundsatz.

Grundgesetzlichkeit, (set of (homogeneous)) fundamental laws, fundamental law, ((fundamental) principles), (*légalité fondamentale* ⟨B⟩). Cf. **Gesetzlichkeit.**

Grundgestalt, fundamental type, (*forme fondamentale* ⟨B⟩), (*configuration fondamentale* ⟨B⟩). Cf. **Gestalt.**

Grundlage, groundwork ⟨MS 1, WH 2⟩, foundation ⟨MS 2, WH⟩, (*fondement* ⟨PL, B⟩), basis ⟨WH 1⟩, (pl., sometimes:) fundamentals ⟨WH⟩. Cf. **Anschauungsgrund, Auffassungsgrund, Boden, Fundament, Fundierung, Grund, Motivationsgrundlage, Substruktion, Untergrund, Unterlage, Vorstellungsgrundlage.**

Grundlagenproblem, problem of fundamentals, problem of the foundations, (*problème des fondements* ⟨B⟩).

Grundlagensphäre, sphere of fundamentals. | **prinzipielle** —, sphere of eidetically necessary fundamentals. Cf. **prinzipiell.**

Grundlegung, laying of a foundation ⟨MS⟩, foundation ⟨WH 1, MS⟩, (*fondation* ⟨B⟩), basing, (establishing), (founding). So far as possible save "founding" for "Fundierung" ⟨q.v.⟩. Cf. **Begründung.**

Grundsatz, fundamental principle, principle ⟨Bn, Kemp Smith trln of Kant, WH 1, MS 2⟩, (*principe* ⟨B⟩), law ⟨Bn⟩; fundamental thesis. Cf. **Grund 6, Grundgesetz, Satz.**

Gründung, grounding.

Grundurteil, antecedent judgment, (*jugement qui est prémisse* ⟨B⟩). Cf. **Grund 7.**

Grundurteilen, judging the antecedent,

(*jugement-prémisse* ⟨B⟩). Cf. **Grund 7.**

Grundverfassung, fundamental composition ⟨?⟩.

Grundwissenschaft, fundamental science, (*science fondamentale* ⟨R⟩). | — **für,** science fundamental to.

Grundzahl, cardinal number ⟨WH 1, cf. Arith, 3⟩.

Grundzug, fundamental trait. Not "principle" ⟨L⟩. Cf. **Zug.**

gültig, valid ⟨WH 1, MS 1, BG⟩, (*valable* ⟨PL, R, B⟩), good ⟨WH, MS⟩, holding good, having force, (*rigoureux* ⟨R⟩). Cf. **geltend.** | **für — erklären,** to declare valid. | **gesetzlich** —, having the force of a law. | — **machen,** to make valid ⟨MS 1⟩, to validate. | Cf. **Gültigmachen.** | — **sein für,** to hold good for ⟨MS 1⟩, to be valid in the case of, (*valable pour* ⟨B⟩), (to apply to ⟨MS⟩).

Gültigkeit, validity ⟨WH 1, MS 1, BG⟩, (*validité* ⟨R, B⟩). Cf. **Endgültigkeit, Geltung.**

Gültigkeitsprädikat, validity-predicate (*prédicat de validité* ⟨B⟩). Cf. **Geltungscharakter.**

Gültigmachen, validating, validation ⟨MS 1⟩.

gut, | **das G⁓e,** the morally (*or* practically) good. Cf. **Wert.** | **ein G⁓es,** something good. | **Güter,** moral (*or* practical) goods, goods ⟨Bn⟩, (*biens* ⟨B⟩). Cf. **Wert.**

Güte, goodness ⟨Bn, WH 2, MS 2⟩, (*bonté* ⟨R⟩). Cf. **Wert.**

Güterwelt, world of moral (*or* practical) goods, (world of goods ⟨BG⟩), (*monde des biens* ⟨R⟩). Cf. **Wertewelt.**

Gut-sein, being morally (*or* practically) good.

H

Habe, having, possession, (*possession* ⟨B⟩). Cf. **Selbsthabe.**

Habitualität, habituality ⟨not in OED⟩, (*habitus* ⟨B, de M⟩), (state of the Ego). Cf. **Aktualität 3, Beschaffenheit, Habitus, Zustand.**

habituell, habitual ⟨WH 1⟩, (*habituel* ⟨B⟩), as a habituality, (*comme une habitude* ⟨B⟩), (*sous forme d'habitude* ⟨B⟩); in the realm of habit; lasting. Cf. **gewohnt.**

Habitus, *habitus* ⟨MS⟩ (italicized), (*ha-*

bitus ⟨de M⟩), state, (*Zustand* ⟨K⟩), (condition). Not "habit" ⟨WH⟩. Cf. **Beschaffenheit, Habitualität, Zustand.**

haftend an, attaching itself to.

Halt, support ⟨WH, MS, BG⟩, (*prise* ⟨R⟩).

Haltung, attitude ⟨WH, MS⟩. Cf. **Denkhaltung, Einstellung.**

handeln, to act ⟨WH 1, MS 1⟩, (*agir* ⟨R⟩).

Handeln, acting ⟨BG⟩, action ⟨WH 1, MS 1⟩, doing. Cf. **Handlung, Tun.** | realisierendes —, (*faire* ⟨de M⟩).

handelnd ⟨adj.⟩, acting, (active ⟨WH 1⟩). Cf. **aktiv, aktuell** ⟨adj.⟩, **tätig.** | der H~e, the acting subject, (*celui qui agit* ⟨B⟩), the agent ⟨MS 2⟩, the doer.

handelnd ⟨adv.⟩, in acting, (*en agissant* ⟨B⟩), in doing (something).

Handlung, action ⟨MS 1, WH 2, BG⟩, (*action* ⟨R, B⟩), acting, (*activité* ⟨B⟩), deed ⟨WH 3, MS 4⟩, (*acte* ⟨B⟩). Save "act" ⟨Bn, WH 1, MS 3⟩ for "Akt". Not "conduct" ⟨Bn⟩. Cf. **Denkhandlung, Handeln, Tat, Tätigkeit.**

Haufen, (with reference to Hume:) bundle or collection, (*amas* ⟨B⟩).

Haupt-, chief ⟨WH 2⟩, principal ⟨WH⟩, (*principal* ⟨B⟩), highest.

Hauptbegriff, highest concept, (*concept principal* ⟨B⟩), (*terminus* ⟨K⟩). Cf. **Begriff.**

Hauptglied, principal member, (*membre principal* ⟨B⟩). Cf. **Nebenglied.**

Heimatstätte, home place.

her, | **vom Ego her,** proceeding (*or* deriving) from the ego.

Herabsinken, (temporal:) sinking into the past.

herabsinkend, subsiding, (*qui tombe* ⟨B⟩).

heranbringen an, to confront with, (*amener en contact avec* ⟨B⟩).

herausarbeiten, to work out ⟨MS 1, WH, L⟩, (*élaborer* ⟨R⟩), to disengage, (*dégager* ⟨B⟩), to fashion, to work into shape. Cf. **bilden, gestalten.**

herausbestimmen, to bring out and determine ⟨?⟩.

herausfassen, to single out and seize, to seize and pick out, to pick out, (*extraire* ⟨R⟩), (*détacher de leur fond* ⟨R⟩), to single out ⟨BG⟩. Cf. **erfassen, fassen.**

herausgreifen, to seize and pick out, (*extraire* ⟨R⟩), to single out ⟨MS 2⟩. Cf. **greifen.**

herausheben, to pick out, to single out ⟨WH⟩, to stress, (*souligner* ⟨R, B⟩), (*prélever* ⟨R⟩). | sich —, to emerge. Cf. **zum Durchbruch kommen** (*sub* **Durchbruch**).

herauskonstruieren, to bring out and construct ⟨?⟩.

herausschauen, to abstract visually; to single (*or* pick) out intuitively, (*dégager intuitivement* ⟨R⟩). Cf. **schauen.**

herausstellen, to bring out ⟨WH⟩, (*faire ressortir* ⟨R⟩), (*mettre en relief* ⟨B⟩), to exhibit, to display, to bring to light, (*faire apparaître* ⟨R⟩), (*mettre en évidence* ⟨B⟩), to expose, to discover. Not "to set out" ⟨BG⟩. Save "to express" ⟨L⟩ for "ausdrücken". Cf. **ausstellen, darstellen, entfalten, klarlegen, sichtbar machen.** | sich —, to come out, to turn out (*or* prove) to be ⟨WH, MS⟩, to come to light ⟨MS⟩, (*être mis en évidence* ⟨B⟩), to become apparent, (*se manifester* ⟨B⟩), (*ressortir* ⟨R⟩), to transpire, to show oneself ⟨MS⟩. Cf. **auftreten, sich zeigen** (*sub* **zeigen**).

Herausstellung, bringing out, exhibition, (*mise en évidence* ⟨B⟩), discovery. Cf. **Darstellung.**

Hereinziehung, bringing in, (introduction ⟨L⟩). So far as possible save "introduction" for "Einführung", "Einbeziehung" and "Einleitung".

herleiten, to deduce ⟨WH⟩, to derive ⟨WH, MS⟩. Cf. **ableiten, erschliessen, folgern.**

Herrschaftsbereich, dominion. Cf. **Bereich.**

herstellen, to make ⟨WH, MS⟩, to make up ⟨WH⟩, (*constituer* ⟨R⟩), to assemble, to bring about ⟨WH⟩, to effect, to produce ⟨WH, MS⟩, to establish ⟨WH⟩, (*établir* ⟨B⟩), (*instaurer* ⟨B⟩), (to set up ⟨BG⟩), (*poser*

⟨B⟩), (*introduire* ⟨B⟩). Cf. **ergeben, erzeugen, leisten, schaffen, vollziehen, wirken, zustandebringen.**

hervortreten, to come to the fore ⟨WH, MS⟩, to come out ⟨WH⟩, (*ressortir* ⟨B⟩), (*apparaître* ⟨B⟩), to stand out ⟨WH⟩, (*être* (ou *se trouver*) *mis en relief* ⟨B⟩), (*se dégager* ⟨B⟩), (*se détacher* ⟨B⟩), to emerge ⟨WH⟩, (*se dessiner* ⟨B⟩), to be brought out. Cf. **sich abheben** (*sub* **abheben**). | — **lassen,** to cause to emerge. | **synthetisch** —, to be brought out by the synthesis, (*se dégager synthétiquement* ⟨B⟩). Cf. **synthetisch** ⟨adv.⟩.

hinanreichen an etwas, to be adequate to something.

Hinausreichen über, transcending of, (reaching out beyond ⟨?⟩ ⟨BG⟩). Cf. **Transzendenz 1.**

hinauswollen auf, to aim at ⟨WH 1, MS 1⟩, (*tendre* ⟨B⟩). Cf. **absehen, Abzielen** (**auf**).

Hinblick, looking, regard ⟨WH, MS⟩, (*considération* ⟨B⟩). Not "consideration" ⟨MS⟩. Cf. **Blick.** | **durch** — **auf,** through looking at. | **durch** ∼**e auf,** by regards directed to. | **in** — **auf,** in looking at, with regard to ⟨WH⟩. Not "in considering" ⟨L⟩. Cf. **in Beziehung auf** (*sub* **Beziehung**).

Hindauern, duration, (lastingness). Cf. **Dauer.**

hindeuten, to point at ⟨MS 1, WH 2⟩, to indicate ⟨WH, MS⟩. Cf. **andeuten, anzeigen, bedeuten, bezeichnen 4, hinweisen auf, zeigen.**

Hindeutung, indicating ⟨WH, MS⟩. Cf. **Anzeigen.**

hineinbilden, Cf. **einbilden.** | **etwas in eine Phantasiewelt** —, to imagine something in a phantasy world.

hineindenken, | **sich** —, (in phantasy) to immerse oneself in, (*se transporter dans* ⟨B⟩), to phantasy clearly. Cf. **sich denken,** (*sub* **denken**), **fingieren, phantasieren, Sichhineindenken.**

hineinleben, Cf. **einleben.** | **sich** — **in,** to immerse oneself in, to become immersed in, to project oneself into, (*se familiariser avec* ⟨B⟩). Not "to familiarize oneself with" ⟨MS 1⟩.

Hingabe, devotedness ⟨MS⟩. Not "devotion" ⟨WH, MS⟩.

hinmeinen auf, 1. (noetic:) to aim at. 2. (noematic:) to point to, (*viser à* ⟨B⟩). Cf. **absehen, beabsichtigen, hinweisen auf, hinzeigen.**

hinnehmen, to accept ⟨WH 1⟩, (*accueillir* ⟨R⟩). Cf. **anerkennen, annehmen, gelten lassen** (*sub* **gelten**), **in Geltung haben** (*sub* **Geltung**), **in Geltung lassen** (*sub* **Geltung**).

Hinsetzung, setting down. Cf. **Daraufhinsetzen.**

Hinsicht, respect ⟨WH⟩, aspect, (*point de vue* ⟨R⟩). Cf. **Gesichtspunkt, Standpunkt.** | **in dieser** —, in this respect ⟨WH 2⟩; regarding this. | **in ethisch-religiöser** —, in its ethico-religious aspect, (from an ethico-religious point of view ⟨L⟩). | **in noetischer** —, in its noetic aspect, (*au point de vue noétique* ⟨R⟩). | **in subjektiver** —, in its subjective aspect, with respect to the subjective (*or* to subjectivity), (*dans la perspective subjective* ⟨B⟩).

hinstellen, to put down ⟨WH 2⟩, to set down ⟨WH 3⟩, (to state), to set up ⟨L⟩. Save "to express" ⟨BG⟩ for "ausdrücken". Cf. **aussagen.** | **etwas** — **wie,** to make something out to be, (*traiter quelque chose comme* ⟨R⟩).

hinstreben, Cf. **streben, zustreben.** | — **auf,** to strive toward, to tend toward, (*tendre vers* ⟨B⟩). | — **zu,** to strive to reach, (*tendre vers* ⟨B⟩).

Hintergrund, background ⟨WH 1, MS 1, BG⟩, (*arrière-plan* ⟨R⟩), substratum. Cf. **Erfahrungshintergrund, Grund 7, Untergrund.**

Hintergrundbewussthaben, background consciousness-of. Cf. **Bewussthaben, Vordergrundbewussthaben.**

(Hinüberschaffen), (in logic:) transposition ⟨Bn⟩.

hinüberweisend zu, pointing beyond (itself) to, (*renvoyant par-delà (lui-même) à* ⟨B⟩).

Hinweis, pointing, indication ⟨WH⟩ of

⟨MS⟩, reference ⟨WH, F⟩. Cf.
Anzeichen, Anzeige.
hinweisen auf, to point to ⟨Gomperz
trln of Mill, quoted in LU, I. Unters.;
WH; BG⟩, (*or* toward(s) ⟨MS⟩), to
indicate ⟨WH, MS⟩, (*indiquer* ⟨B⟩),
to point out ⟨WH⟩, to refer to ⟨WH,
MS⟩, (*se référer à* ⟨R⟩), (*renvoyer* à
⟨R⟩). Cf. **anzeigen, bedeuten, bezeichnen, hindeuten, hinmeinen auf,
hinzeigen, verweisen, zeigen.**
Hinweisen, pointing.
Hinweisung, | **Hin- und Rückweisung,**
pointing back and forth.
hinzeigen, to point ⟨MS⟩. Cf. **hinmeinen auf, hinweisen auf, vordeuten.**
Historie, historical understanding.
historisch ⟨adj.⟩, historical ⟨MS 1,
WH⟩, historically existing (*or* given),

(*rencontré dans l'histoire* ⟨B⟩), as a
historical fact, (*traditionnel* ⟨B⟩). Cf.
Geschichte.
historisch ⟨adv.⟩, historically, as a
historical fact, (*dans le passé* ⟨B⟩).
Hof, halo, fringe, (*aire* ⟨R⟩). Not
"zone" ⟨BG⟩. Cf. **Zeithof.**
Horizont, horizon ⟨WH 1, MS 1, BG⟩,
(*horizon* ⟨R, B⟩; vista. Not "en-
circling sphere" ⟨BG⟩; not "depth
or fringe" ⟨BG⟩. Cf. **Aussenhorizont,
Erfahrungshorizont, Gegenwartsho-
rizont, Sinneshorizont, Zeithorizont.**
Horizonthaftigkeit, horizonedness.
Hyle, hyle, (*hylé* ⟨R⟩). Cf. **Stoff.**
Hyletik, hyletics, (*hylétique* ⟨R⟩).
hyletisch ⟨adj.⟩, hyletic, hyletical. Cf.
stofflich.
hyletisch ⟨adv.⟩, hyletically.

I

Ich, Ego (capitalized) ⟨BG⟩, I, (*je*
⟨R⟩), (*moi* ⟨R, B⟩). Save "self"
⟨WH, MS, BG⟩ for "Selbst". Cf.
Bewusstseins-Ich, Ego.
Ichakt, Ego's act, act of an Ego,
(*acte*(-)*du*(-)*moi* ⟨R, B⟩), Ego act.
Ichaktualität, Ego's actionality, (*actualité du moi* ⟨R⟩). Cf. **Aktualität 3.**
Ich-all, Cf. **All.** | transzendentales —,
universe of transcendental egos, (*to-
talité transcendentale des mois* ⟨B⟩).
ichartig ⟨adv.⟩, as egoical ⟨in OED
but not as expressing Husserl's
sense⟩. Cf. **ichlich** ⟨adj.⟩.
Ichblick (auf), Ego's regard (to), (*regard du moi* (*en direction de*) ⟨R⟩),
Ego-regard (to). Not "glancing of
the Ego" ⟨BG⟩. Cf. **Blick.**
Icherlebnis, Ego-process, (process lived
in by the Ego), (*vécu subjectif* ⟨R⟩).
Not "experience of the Ego" ⟨BG⟩.
Cf. **Erlebnis.**
Ichferne, distance from the Ego. Cf.
Bewusstseinsferne, Ferne, Ichnähe.
ichfremd ⟨adv.⟩, as other than the
Ego's own, (*comme* (ou *en tant
qu'*)*étranger au moi* ⟨B⟩). Cf. **fremd.**

Ich-fremdes, | nichts —, nothing other
than my Ego's own.
ichlich ⟨adj.⟩, Ego-, egoical ⟨in OED
but not as expressing Husserl's
sense⟩, of the Ego. Cf. **ichartig**
⟨adv.⟩.
Ichlichkeit, egoicalness.
Ichnähe, nearness to the Ego. Cf. **Ichferne.**
Ich-sein, being as an Ego.
Ichstrahl, Ego-ray. Cf. **Blickstrahl.**
Ichsubjekt, Ego-subject ⟨BG⟩, (*sujet
personnel* ⟨R⟩).
Ichzugehörigkeit, (*appartenance au moi*
⟨R⟩). Cf. **Zugehörigkeit.** | — haben,
to be appertinent to the Ego, (*comporter une appartenance au moi* ⟨R⟩).
ideal ⟨adj.⟩, ideal ⟨WH 1, MS 1⟩,
(*idéal* ⟨R, B⟩), of the ideal, as ideal.
Cf. **ideell** ⟨adj.⟩, **mathematisch-ideal**
⟨adj.⟩. | ∼e **Verwirklichung,** actu-
alization of the ideal.
ideal ⟨adv.⟩, | — **zu reden,** to speak of
the ideal.
ideal-identisch ⟨adj.⟩, ideally identical.
ideal-objektiv ⟨adj.⟩, of ideal Objects,
(*idéal objectif* ⟨B⟩). Cf. **objektiv-ideal.**
Idealwissenschaft, science of idealities,

(*science de l'idéal* ⟨R⟩), (*science idéale* ⟨B⟩). Cf. **Realwissenschaft.**
ideell ⟨adj.⟩, ideal ⟨WH 1, MS 1⟩, (*idéel* ⟨R⟩). Cf. **ideal.**
ideell ⟨adv.⟩, ideally ⟨WH 1⟩, idealiter.
ideierend, ideative.
Identifizierbarkeit. | ursprüngliche —, possibility of original identification, (*capacité originelle d'identification* ⟨B⟩).
identifizierend-kopulierend, identifyingly copulative. Cf. **kopulierend.**
identisch, Cf. **sinnesidentisch.** | I ~es, identical something (*or* moment).
Identitätsbezüglichkeit, identity-relatedness, (*relation d'identité* ⟨B⟩). Cf. **Bezüglichkeit.**
Identitätsdeckung, coincidence of identity, (*coïncidence d'identité* (ou *d'identification*) ⟨B⟩). Cf. **Deckung.**
Identitätspol, identical pole, (*pôle d'identité* ⟨B⟩).
Identitätssinn, identity-sense.
Identitätssynthesis, identifying synthesis, (*synthèse identificatrice* ⟨B⟩).
Im-geistigen-Blick-haben, having the mind's eye on, (*avoir-sous-le-regard-de-l'esprit* ⟨R⟩). Not "mentally scrutinizing" ⟨BG⟩. Cf. **geistiger Blick** (*sub* **geistig**), **im Blick haben** (*sub* **Blick**).
Im-Griff-behalten, keeping in one's grip. Cf. **Griff, Noch-im-Griff-behalten.**
immanent ⟨adj.⟩, immanent, (*immanent* ⟨R, B⟩), immanental, of (*or* to) something immanent. | ~e **Analyse,** immanental analysis. | ~e **Beziehung,** relation to something immanent. | ~e **Deskription,** "immanental" description. | ~e **Erfahrung,** immanental experience, experience of something immanent. | ~e **Wahrnehmung,** immanental perception, perception of something immanent, (*perception immanente* ⟨R⟩). Not "immanent perception" ⟨L, BG⟩. Cf. **transzendent** ⟨adj.⟩. | ~e **Wesensanalyse,** immanental eidetic analysis. | ~er **Art,** of the immanent sort. Cf. **Art.** | ~es **Schauen,** immanental viewing (*or*

seeing). Not "immanent view" ⟨L⟩. Cf. **Schauen.** | ~es **Wesen,** immanent essence, (*essence immanente* ⟨R⟩). | ~es **Zeitobjekt,** Object in immanent time. Cf. **Objekt.**
immanent ⟨adv.⟩, Cf. **transzendent** ⟨adv.⟩. | ein — **Konstituiertes,** something constituted immanentally (*or* as immanent). | — **bezogen,** relating to something immanent, (*rapporté de façon immanente* ⟨R⟩). | Not "immanently related" ⟨BG⟩. Cf. **transzendent bezogen** (*sub* **transzendent** ⟨adv.⟩). | — **erforschend,** that explores (something) in respect of what is immanent (in it). | — **gerichtet,** directed to something immanent, (*dirigé de* (ou *d'une*) *façon immanente* ⟨R⟩). Not "immanently directed" ⟨BG⟩.
immanent-psychologisch, | in echtem **Sinn** —, pertaining to a genuinely immanental psychology, (*psychologique immanent au sens authentique* ⟨R⟩).
immanent-zeitlich ⟨adj.⟩, of (*or* in) immanent time, (*dont la temporalité est immanente* ⟨B⟩).
immanent-zeitlich ⟨adv.⟩, as in immanent time.
Immanenz, 1. (condition or quality:) immanence ⟨WH 1, MS 1⟩.
2. (something immanent:) immanency.
3. (without distinction:) (*immanence* ⟨R, B⟩). Cf. **Transzendenz.** | reelle —, real immanence. Cf. **reell.**
immer, | — **neu,** always … in new.
impliziert, implicated, (*impliqué* ⟨B⟩), involved; implied.
imputieren, (at least sometimes:) to involve. Cf. **beschliessen.**
in, | — **sich,** intrinsically, in itself, (*en soi* ⟨B⟩). Cf. **an sich** (*sub* **an**).
Inadäquatheit, inadequateness. Cf. **Adäquatheit.**
Inaktualität, 1. non-actionality, inactivity, (*inactualité* ⟨R⟩). Not "non-actuality" ⟨BG⟩, not "marginal actuality" ⟨BG⟩, not "dormant actuality" ⟨BG⟩. Cf. **Aktualität 3.**

2. (inactuality). Cf. **Aktualität 2, Unwirklichkeit.** | **Modus der** —, non-actionality mode, (*mode de l'inactualité* ⟨R⟩). Cf. **Aktualitätsmodus.**

Inaktualitätsmodifikation, non-actionality modification, inactivity-modification, (*modification d'inactualité* ⟨R⟩). Not "modal form of marginal actuality" ⟨BG⟩.

inaktuell, non-actional, inactive, (*inactuel* ⟨R⟩). Not "marginal" ⟨BG⟩, not "dormant" ⟨BG⟩. Cf. **aktuell** ⟨adj.⟩ 3.

Inanspruchnahme, laying claim to ⟨MS 1⟩, claiming, (*revendication* ⟨B⟩), assuming. Cf. **Anspruch.**

Inbegriff, sum ⟨MS 1, WH 3⟩, (totality ⟨MS 3, F⟩), (*totalité* ⟨B⟩), (*complexus* ⟨K⟩). So far as possible save "totality" for "Allheit" ⟨q.v.⟩ and "Gesamtheit" ⟨q.v.⟩. Save "aggregate" ⟨Heath, *Euclid, 125*⟩ for "Aggregat". Save "sum-total" ⟨L⟩ for "Gesamtinbegriff". But "aggregate" may be the best trln.

indem ⟨adv.⟩, at the moment ⟨MS 1, WH 5⟩; during that time ⟨MS 2⟩, meantime ⟨WH 1⟩, meanwhile ⟨WH 2, MS 3⟩, in the mean time ⟨WH 3, MS 4⟩; by that time ⟨WH 4⟩. Cf. **indessen** ⟨adv.⟩.

indem ⟨conj.⟩, 1. (simultaneity:) *a.* (different subjects:) as ⟨WH 1⟩, when ⟨MS 3⟩. *b.* (same subject:) while ⟨with verb, MS 2⟩, while ⟨with present participle, WH 2, MS 4⟩.
2. (means:) by ⟨with present participle, WH 1, MS 1⟩, in ⟨with present participle, WH 2⟩.
3. (reason:) as ⟨WH 1, MS 2⟩, since ⟨MS 1, WH 2⟩, because ⟨WH 3⟩.

indes(sen) ⟨adv.⟩, during that time ⟨MS 1⟩, meantime ⟨WH 1⟩, meanwhile ⟨WH 2, MS 2⟩, in the mean time ⟨WH 3, MS 3⟩; by that time ⟨WH 4⟩; at that moment ⟨WH 5⟩. Cf. **indem** ⟨adv.⟩.

indes(sen) ⟨conj.⟩, 1. (coordinative:) *a.* (dennoch:) nevertheless ⟨MS 1, WH 4⟩, for all that ⟨MS 2⟩; *b.* (dessenungeachtet:) despite all that

⟨MS 3⟩, after all ⟨WH 2⟩, all the same ⟨WH 3⟩; *c.* (immerhin:) yet ⟨MS 4, WH 6⟩, still ⟨WH 5, MS 5⟩, however ⟨WH 1, MS 6⟩, (*cependant* ⟨R, B⟩), though ⟨at end of sentence, WH 7⟩.
2. (subordinative, verb at end of clause:) while ⟨WH 1, MS 2⟩; whereas ⟨WH 2⟩. Cf. **indem** ⟨conj.⟩ 1.

individuell ⟨adj.⟩, | ~**e Anschauung,** intuition of something individual (*or* of individuals), (*intuition de l'individu* ⟨R⟩), individual intuition ⟨BG⟩, (*intuition individuelle* ⟨B⟩). | ~**e Vorstellung,** objectivation of something individual. Cf. **individuell-anschauliche Vorstellung** (*sub* **individuell-anschaulich** ⟨adv.⟩). | **I**~**es,** an individual. | ~**es Meinen,** meaning something individual. Cf. **Meinen.**

individuell ⟨adv.⟩, individually (*sous forme individuelle* ⟨R⟩). | **das** — **Sichtige,** what is sight as an individual.

individuell-anschaulich, | ~**e Vorstellung,** intuitive objectivation of something individual. Cf. **individuelle Vorstellung** (*sub* **individuell** ⟨adj.⟩).

Individuum, *individuum* (italicized), concrete individual, individual ⟨WH 1, MS 1⟩, (*individu* ⟨R, B, de M⟩).

induktiv ⟨adj.⟩, inductive ⟨WH 1, MS 1⟩, inductively inferred.

Ineinander, intermingling, interpenetration, complexity, (*emboîtement* ⟨R, B⟩); (*complexe* ⟨R⟩), (nexus ⟨?⟩ ⟨BG⟩). Cf. **Miteinander, Zusammenhang.**

ineinanderschachteln, Cf. **einschachteln.** | **sich** —, to be encased one in another. Not "to dovetail into one another" ⟨BG⟩.

Ineinanderschachtelung, encasement of one in another.

In-Geltung-haben, believing in something, (*croyance* ⟨B⟩). Cf. **in Geltung haben** (*sub* **Geltung**).

Inhalt, content ⟨WH, BG⟩, (*contenu* ⟨R, B, de M⟩), contents ⟨WH 1, MS 1⟩. Cf. **Auffassungsinhalt, Bedeu-**

tungsinhalt, Dauerinhalt, Empfindungsinhalt, Gehalt, Phantasie-
inhalt, Urteilsinhalt, Wahrneh-
mungsinhalt. | intendierender —,
intentive content.
inhaltlich ⟨adj.⟩, content-, of con-
tent(s), contentual. | ~er Bestand,
stock of contents, (contenu ⟨R⟩). Cf.
Bestand.
inhaltlich ⟨adv.⟩, in (respect of (its))
content, (quant au (ou à son) contenu
⟨B⟩).
inhaltlich-leer, (de)void of content.
inhaltreich, rich in content, (riche de
contenu ⟨R⟩), (possessing content
⟨?⟩ ⟨BG⟩).
Inhaltsbestand, stock of content, (contenu ⟨R⟩). Cf. inhaltlicher Bestand
(sub Bestand).
Inhaltslogik, intensional logic.
Inhaltsstrom, stream of contents, (flux
de contenus ⟨R⟩).
inkonsequent, inconsistent ⟨MS 1,
WH⟩, (inconséquent ⟨B⟩). Cf. folgewidrig, formal-inkonsequent, konsequent, schlusswidrig.
Inkonsequenz, inconsistency ⟨MS 1,
WH⟩, (non-conséquence ⟨B⟩). Cf.
Konsequenz, Konsequenzlosigkeit,
Unstimmigkeit, Widerfolge.
inne, | — sein (oder werden), to grasp,
(se rendre compte de ⟨B⟩). Cf. erfassen.
innen ⟨adv.⟩, (ant. aussen:) inside
⟨WH 2, MS 2⟩, (intérieurement ⟨B⟩).
Cf. innere ⟨adj.⟩. | von — her, from
inside, (de l'intérieur ⟨B⟩).
Inneneinstellung, focusing on what
lies inside, (attitude tournée vers l'intériorité ⟨B⟩). Cf. Einstellung.
Innenleben, inner life ⟨WH 1⟩, inner
living. Cf. Innerlichkeit, Leben.
Innenpsychologie, internal psychology.
innere ⟨adj.⟩, (ant. ausser:) internal
⟨Bn, WH 3, MS⟩, (interne ⟨R, B⟩),
(internus ⟨K⟩), of (the or something)
internal, (intérieur ⟨R⟩), (inner ⟨WH
1, MS 2, F, BG⟩), (inward ⟨Gomperz
trln of Mill, quoted in LU, II. Unters.; WH; MS⟩); intrinsic ⟨WH,
MS⟩. Cf. reell ⟨adj.⟩. | das I~, the
interior ⟨WH 1, MS 1⟩, the inside

⟨WH2, MS 2⟩. | —Erfahrung, experi-
ence of something internal, internal
experience, (expérience intérieure
⟨R⟩). | — Gattung, intrinsic genus,
(genre interne⟨B⟩). | ~r Sinn, internal
sense. | ~s Bewusstsein, conscious-
ness of the internal. | ~s Bild, in-
ternal image, (portrait interne ⟨R⟩).
Cf. Bild. | ~s Zeitbewusstsein, con-
sciousness of internal time. Cf. Zeit-
bewusstsein.
innerlich ⟨adj.⟩, internal ⟨WH, MS⟩,
(interne ⟨B⟩); intrinsic ⟨Bn, WH,
MS⟩.
innerlich ⟨adv.⟩, internally ⟨WH 1,
MS 2⟩, (de façon (ou d'une manière)
interne ⟨B⟩), intrinsically, inwardly
⟨MS 1, WH 3, BG⟩, from within,
(dans son intimité ⟨R⟩).
Innerlichkeit, internality, (intériorité
⟨PL, B⟩), interior, inwardness ⟨MS
1, WH 2⟩, (inner life). Cf. Äusser-
lichkeit, Innenleben. | eine seelische
—, an internal psychic life, (une intériorité psychique ⟨B⟩). Cf. seelisch.
innerste, intimate ⟨WH⟩.
innewohnend, lodged in, inherent in.
Cf. einwohnen, in etwas liegen (sub
liegen).
insofern als, in so far as ⟨WH, MS⟩,
(dans la mesure où ⟨R⟩), in as much
as, since. Cf. sofern.
Installierung, establishing ⟨?⟩, (installation ⟨?⟩), (installation ⟨R⟩).
intellektiv, intellectual. Cf. geistig.
intendieren, to intend to.
intendierend, intentive, (intending).
Cf. intentional.
intendiert, intended to.
Intention, intention ⟨WH 1, MS⟩,
(intention ⟨R, B⟩), bare intention,
(tendency). Cf. Auffassungsintention, Bedeutungsintention, Denkintention, Erkenntnisintention, Tendenz, Vorintention, Vorstellung 1,
Vorstellungsintention. | — auf Er-
kenntnis, intention aimed at cognition, (intention dirigée vers la con-
naissance ⟨B⟩). Cf. Erkenntnis. | mit
der — auf, with its intention aimed
at, (dans une intention dirigée vers
⟨B⟩), tending toward.

intentional ⟨adj.⟩, intentional, (*intentionnel* ⟨R, de M⟩), of intentionality, of intentionalities, (noetic, sometimes:) intentive. Cf. **intendierend.** | ~e **Analyse,** intentional analysis. | **das I~e,** the intentional (sense), (*l'élément intentionnel* ⟨R⟩). | **I~es,** Equivalent to "das Intentionale". | **solche ~e Untersuchungen,** investigation of such intentionalities, (*telles recherches intentionnelles* ⟨B⟩). Cf. **Untersuchung.**

intentional ⟨adv.⟩, intentionally. Cf. **bewusst** ⟨adv.⟩.

Intuition, Intuition (capitalized), (*intuition* ⟨R, de M⟩), Intuiting (capitalized). Cf. **Anschauung, Signifikation.**

intuitiv ⟨adj., adv.⟩, Equivalent to "anschaulich" ⟨adj., adv.⟩, q.v.

intuitiv-eidetisch ⟨adj.⟩, intuitable eidetic, (*intuitif éidétique* ⟨B⟩).

Invarianz, unvaryingness.

irgend ein, some ... or other ⟨WH 1⟩, any(other).

irgend etwas, (just) anything, something or other ⟨WH 1⟩, (*quelque chose* ⟨B⟩). Cf. **Etwas.**

irreal, irreal ⟨not in OED, though "irrealizable" is listed⟩, (*irréel* ⟨B⟩). Cf. **irreell, real.**

irreell, non-real, non-really immanent, (*intentionnel* ⟨de M⟩). Cf. **reell.** | ~es **Beschlossensein,** being non-really included, (*inclusion intentionnelle* ⟨de M⟩). Cf. **Beschlossensein.**

Iteration, (unlimited) reiteration, (*itération* ⟨B⟩), (*redoublement* ⟨R⟩). Cf. **Wiederholung.**

iterativ ⟨adj.⟩, reiterable (without limit), endlessly reiterated, reiterational, (*itératif* ⟨B⟩).

iterativ ⟨adv.⟩, reiteratedly (without limit); reiteratively, (*par itération* ⟨B⟩).

iterierbar, reiterational, (*itérable* ⟨B⟩).

J

jedermann, everyone ⟨WH 1⟩, (*tout être* ⟨B⟩), (*tout le monde* ⟨B⟩). Not "anyone" ⟨WH⟩; see Logik, *210.*

jetzig, now ⟨MS⟩, present ⟨WH 1, BG⟩, (*présent* ⟨B⟩), (*actuel* ⟨B⟩), (*d'aujourd'hui* ⟨R⟩). Cf. **aktuell** ⟨adj.⟩ 1, **gegenwärtig, vorliegend.** | ~e **Dauer,** duration now.

Jetzigkeit, nowness. Cf. **Gleich-Jetzigkeit.**

jeweilig ⟨adj.⟩, 1. (temporal:) of (*or* on) the actual (*or* particular) occasion, actual current, currently intended, of the moment, momentary, (for the time being ⟨WH, L⟩), (occasional ⟨MS 1⟩).
2. (atemporal:) indicated, (*considéré* ⟨B⟩), in question, (*qui est en question*

⟨B⟩), (*dont il s'agit* ⟨B⟩), (*en jeu* ⟨B⟩), certain, particular, specified ⟨BG⟩, (specific ⟨WH 2⟩); pertinent, relevant, corresponding, concomitant, respective, (*respectif* ⟨B⟩), various, this or that ⟨BG⟩, such and such.

jeweilig ⟨adv.⟩, 1. (temporal:) occasionally, currently.
2. (atemporal:) in the particular case, (*dans un cas donné* ⟨R⟩).

Jeweiligkeit, transiency ⟨?⟩.

jeweils, in the (*or* any) particular case, always, (*chaque fois* ⟨R, B⟩), at the (*or* a *or* any) (particular) time, (at times ⟨MS 1⟩), (occasionally ⟨MS 2⟩), (from time to time ⟨?⟩). Not "as occasion suggests" ⟨BG⟩.

K

kalkulativ ⟨adv.⟩, in terms of calculational operations, (*au moyen de calculs* ⟨B⟩).

kalkulatorisch ⟨adj.⟩, calculative, (*calculateur* ⟨B⟩). Cf. **rechnerisch.**

kategorial, categorial, (*catégorial* ⟨R, B⟩). Not "categorical" ⟨BG⟩.

kategorisch, categorical ⟨WH 1, MS 1⟩, (*catégorique* ⟨B⟩).

kennen, to know ⟨WH 1, MS 1⟩ (by acquaintance ⟨Bn⟩), to be acquainted with, (*connaître* ⟨B⟩), (*noscere* ⟨K⟩). Cf. **erkennen, wissen.**

kenntlich, (sometimes:) easy to recognize ⟨WH, MS⟩. | — **machen,** to make known, ⟨MS 1, WH 2⟩. Cf. **bekunden, kundgeben, kundtun.**

Kenntnis, cognizance ⟨WH 5, MS⟩, notice ⟨WH 4, MS⟩, something (*or* fact *or* truth) of which one is cognizant, information ⟨Gomperz trln of Mill, quoted in LU, I. Unters.; MS 2; WH 3⟩, (*connaissances* ⟨R⟩). Cf. **Erkenntnis, Kunde, Vorkenntnis, Wissen.**

Kenntnisnahme, cognizance ⟨WH 1, MS 2⟩ (taken), (process of) taking cognizance, cognizance-taking. Cf. **Kundnahme.**

Kennzeichen, symptom ⟨WH, MS⟩, recognition-sign, (criterion ⟨Bn⟩), (*Kriterium* ⟨K⟩). Cf. **Anzeichen, Zeichen.**

kennzeichnen, to characterize, (*caractériser* ⟨B⟩); to stamp; to distinguish Cf. **abheben, anzeichnen, bezeichnen, eignen, unterscheiden, zeichnen.**

Kern, core ⟨WH, MS⟩, (nucleus ⟨Bn, WH 2, MS 2, BG⟩), (*noyau* ⟨R, B⟩), (*élément* ⟨B⟩). Cf. **Sinneskern.** | — **zu einem Kometenschweif,** head attached to a comet tail.

Kernbestand, core-component, (*fonds nucléaire* ⟨R⟩). Cf. **Bestand.**

Kernform, core-form, (*forme-noyau* ⟨B⟩).

Kerngebilde, core-formation, (*formation-noyau* ⟨B⟩). Cf. **Gebilde.**

Kerngehalt, nuclear content, (*contenu qui en est le noyau* ⟨B⟩). Cf. **Gehalt.**

kernhaft, 1. (special:) nuclear, of the cores, (*qui a trait aux noyaux* ⟨B⟩). 2. (général:) solid ⟨WH, MS⟩, (*substantiel* ⟨B⟩).

kernhaftig, of the core(s), nucleated, nuclear.

Kernstoff, core-stuff, (*matériau-noyau* ⟨B⟩). Cf. **Stoff.**

(Kettenschluss), sorites ⟨Bn, WH 2, MS 2⟩. Cf. **Schluss 1.**

Klangfarbe, timbre ⟨Bn, WH 1, MS 2⟩, (*timbre* ⟨B⟩).

Klarheit, clarity ⟨WH⟩, (*clarté* ⟨R, B⟩), (clearness ⟨WH 1⟩), (lucidity ⟨WH⟩). | **zur — bringen,** to make clear, (*amener à la clarté* ⟨B⟩). | **zur — kommen,** to become clear.

Klarheitsfülle, full clarity, (*plénitude de clarté* ⟨R, B, de M⟩). Cf. **Fülle.**

klarlegen, to clear up ⟨WH 1⟩, to make clear, (*éclaircir* ⟨B⟩); to bring to light. Save "to uncover" ⟨L⟩ for "enthüllen" ⟨q.v.⟩. Cf. **aufklären, erklären, herausstellen, klarstellen, sichtbar machen.**

Klarlegung, clearing up.

klarstellen, to clear up ⟨WH 1⟩, to make clear, (*poser clairement* ⟨B⟩), to elucidate. Cf. **aufklären, erklären, klarlegen.**

Klärung, clarification ⟨WH 1⟩, (*clarification* ⟨R, B, de M⟩), clarifying, making clear, clearing. Save "elucidation" ⟨WH, L⟩ for "Aufklärung" ⟨q.v.⟩, "Erklärung" ⟨q.v.⟩, etc. Cf. **Ursprungsklärung.**

Koexistenz, (simultaneous) coexistence.

Kolligation, collecting, (*colligation* ⟨R⟩), (*acte de colligation* ⟨B⟩).

kolligieren, to collect ⟨BG⟩, (*colliger* ⟨R, B⟩).

Kombination, combination ⟨WH 1, MS 1⟩ (in the mathematical sense of the word), (*combinaison* ⟨B⟩). Cf. **Komplexion, Verbindung, Verflechtung.**

kombinatorisch, combinative, (*combinatoire* ⟨B⟩).

kombinieren, to combine ⟨WH 1, MS 1⟩ mathematically, (*combiner* ⟨B⟩). Cf. **verbinden, verflechten.**

Kommunikationsgesetz, (Druckfehler ⟨?⟩) law of commutation.

kommunikativ, (contradictory of "einzeln":) in communication, (*pris dans sa possibilité de communication* ⟨B⟩), communicative. | ∼e **Intention,** intention to communicate.

komplex ⟨adj.⟩, (at least sometimes:) combined, (*complexe* ⟨B⟩). Cf. **verbunden.**

Komplexion, complex, (*assemblage complexe* ⟨B⟩), combination; complication. Cf. **Empfindungskomplexion, Erlebniskomplexion, Gesamtkomplexion, Kombination, Lautkomplexion, Relation, Urteilskomplexion, Verbindung, Verflechtung, Verhalt, Verwebung, Zusammenhang.**

Komplikation, complication ⟨WH 1⟩, complexity, (*complexité* ⟨B⟩).

kompliziert, complicated; intimately combined.

Konkret-eigenwesentliches, concrete own-essentially, (*caractère concret, essentiellement propre* ⟨B⟩). Cf. **Eigenwesentliches.**

Konkretion, concreteness ⟨BG⟩; concretion ⟨MS 1, L⟩, (*concrétion* ⟨R⟩), (*unité* (ou *totalité*) *concrète* ⟨B⟩), (*ensemble* (ou *assemblage*) *concret* ⟨B⟩). Not "full development" ⟨BG⟩. | **volle —,** full concreteness ⟨BG⟩, (*plénitude concrète* ⟨R⟩); full concretion. Not "concrete fullness" ⟨BG⟩.

Konkretum, concretum, (*concret* ⟨R⟩).

konsequent, consequent, (*conséquent* ⟨B⟩); consistent ⟨MS 1, WH 2⟩, consequential, consistently maintained, systematic. Cf. **erfolgend, folgend 1, folgerecht, inkonsequent, schluss(ge)recht, schlussrichtig.** | **~er Schluss,** consequent argument. Cf. **Schluss 1.** | **mir —,** self-consistent, (*conséquent à l'égard de moi-même* ⟨B⟩).

konsequenterweise, to be consistent, (*par voie de conséquence* ⟨R⟩), (*d'une manière conséquente* ⟨B⟩), as consistency would require.

Konsequenz, consequence ⟨WH 1, MS 2⟩, (*conséquence* ⟨R, B, de M⟩), consequence-relationship(s); consistency ⟨MS 1, WH⟩, (*suite* ⟨B⟩), (*cours* ⟨B⟩); consequence or consistency; consequence-relationships and consistency; *Konsequenz.* Cf. **Folge 1, Folgerichtigkeit, Inkonsequenz,**

Konsequenzlosigkeit, Selbstimmigkeit, Übereinstimmung, Urteilskonsequenz. | **analytische —,** analytic consequence-relationship(s), (case of) analytic consistency, (*conséquence analytique* ⟨B⟩). | **Analytik der —,** analytics of consequence-relationships, (*analytique de la conséquence* ⟨B⟩). | **in —,** with consequence; (*dans la conséquence* ⟨B⟩), as standing in a consequence-relationship (*or* in consequence-relationships); consistently, (*avec l'esprit de suite* ⟨B⟩). | **— der Wahrheiten,** consequence-relationship of truths. | **Verhältnis der —,** consequence-relationship, (*relation de conséquence* ⟨B⟩). Cf. **Konsequenzverhältnis.**

Konsequenzgesetz, consequence-law, (*loi de la conséquence* ⟨B⟩).

Konsequenzlehre, consequence-theory, (*doctrine de la conséquence* ⟨B⟩).

Konsequenzlogik, consequence-logic, (*logique de la conséquence* ⟨B⟩), (*logique formelle de la conséquence* ⟨de M⟩).

Konsequenzlosigkeit, lack of consistency. Cf. **Inkonsequenz.**

Konsequenzverhältnis, consequence-relationship, (*rapport de conséquence* ⟨B⟩). Cf. **Verhältnis.**

konstituieren, to constitute ⟨WH 1, MS 1⟩. Cf. **mitkonstituieren, vorkonstituieren.** | **sich —,** to become constituted, (rarely:) to constitute itself ⟨BG⟩, (*se constituer* ⟨R, B⟩).

konstitutierend, constituting ⟨BG⟩, (*constituant* ⟨R, B⟩), constitutive, constituent. | **~es Merkmal,** constituent mark, (*caractère constituant* ⟨B⟩). Cf. **Merkmal.**

Konstitution, constitution ⟨WH 1⟩, (*constitution* ⟨B⟩), constituting.

konstitutiv, 1. (intentional konstituierend:) constitutive, constituting 2. (die Konstitution betreffend:) constitutional, of constitution. 3. (ausmachend:) constituent. 4. (without distinction ⟨?⟩:) (*constitutif* ⟨R, B⟩).

Konstruktion, construction ⟨MS 1, WH 2⟩, (*construction* ⟨R, B⟩), con-

structing. Cf. **Aufbau, Bau, Bildung.**
konstruktiv ⟨adj.⟩, constructional,
(*constructif* ⟨B⟩). Cf. **aufbauend,
bildend.** | ∼e Denkeinheit, construc-
tional unity produced by thinking,
(*construction de la pensée unificatrice*
⟨R⟩). Not "constructive form of
thought" ⟨BG⟩.
konstruktiv ⟨adv.⟩, by construction,
(*par construction* ⟨B⟩).
Kontinuität, continuity ⟨WH 1⟩; continuum. Cf. **Auffassungskontinuität.**
Kontradiktion, (at least sometimes:)
contradictory (opposite).
Kopulation, copulative combining,
(*liaison copulative* ⟨B⟩), copular
form, copular formation, copulative.
⟨OED reports that the non-sexual
senses of "copulation" are obs.⟩.
kopulativ ⟨adj.⟩, copular; copulative,
(*copulatif* ⟨B⟩).
kopulativ ⟨adv.⟩, copulatively, (*d'une
manière copulative* ⟨B⟩).
kopulierend, copulative, (*copulatif*
⟨B⟩); copular. Cf. **identifizierend-
kopulierend.**
Körper, 1. (physical:) body, (*corps*
⟨B⟩).
2. (geometrical:) solid.
Cf. **Bodenkörper, Leib, Leibkörper,
Nullkörper.**
Körperlichkeit, (*corporéité* ⟨R⟩).
Körperwelt, corporeal world ⟨WH 1,
L⟩. Not "world of bodies" ⟨L⟩.
Korrelat, perfect correlate, correlate,
⟨WH 1, MS⟩, (*corrélat* ⟨R, B⟩); correlative ⟨WH 2⟩.
Korrelation, perfect correlation, corre-
lation ⟨WH 1, MS 1⟩, (*corrélation*
⟨R, B⟩). Cf. **Zusammengehörigkeit.** |
in — zu, correlated with, (*en corréla-
tion avec* ⟨R⟩).
korrelativ ⟨adj.⟩, perfectly correlated,
(*corrélatif* ⟨B⟩).
korrelativ ⟨adv.⟩, as perfect correlates.
Kraft, force ⟨WH 2, MS⟩, (*force* ⟨R,
B⟩), (Lockean sense:) power ⟨WH 3,
MS 3⟩, strength ⟨WH 1, MS 1⟩, (*vis*
⟨Wolff⟩). Cf. **Erfahrungskraft.** | (le-
bendige —), *vis viva* ⟨Bn⟩, (living
force ⟨Bn⟩).
Kreis, circle ⟨WH 1, MS 1, BG⟩, (*cercle*

⟨R, B⟩); (in figurative senses, usually:) sphere, (*sphère* ⟨B⟩). Cf. **Bereich, Gesichtskreis, Rahmen, Umfang.**
Kritik, (usually:) criticism ⟨WH 1,
MS 1⟩, (with explicit reference to
K:) critique ⟨WH 2, MS 2⟩, (*critique*
⟨B⟩), critical discrimination, critical
determination, critical evaluation.
Cf. **Erkenntniskritik.** | **an etwas —
üben,** to submit something to
criticism.
Kulturgebilde, cultural formation,
(*produit de la civilisation* ⟨R⟩). Not
"cultural creation" ⟨BG⟩, not "cul-
tural expression" ⟨BG⟩. Cf. **Gebilde.**
Kulturgestalt, cultural formation, (*for-
me culturelle* ⟨B⟩). Cf. **Gestalt.**
Kulturgestaltung, cultural formation.
Not "cultural structure" ⟨L⟩. Cf.
Gestaltung.
Kultur-Phänomen, cultural phenomenon, (*phénomène de civilisation* ⟨R⟩).
Kulturwissenschaft, science of culture,
(*science de la civilisation* ⟨R⟩). Cf.
Geisteswissenschaft.
Kunde, cognizance, knowledge ⟨WH 1,
MS⟩. Cf. **Erfahrungskunde, Erkenntnis, Kenntnis, Naturkunde, Wissen.**
Kundgabe, giving cognizance of,
(making known); that of which
cognizance is given, (what is made
known). Not "manifestation" ⟨F⟩.
Cf. **Kundnahme.**
kundgeben, to give cognizance of, (to
make known ⟨WH 1, MS 3⟩. Cf.
**bekunden, kenntlich machen, kund-
tun.**
kundgebend, cognizance-giving,
(making known). Not "manifesting"
⟨F⟩. | ∼e Funktion, cognizance-
giving function. Cf. **Funktion.** | ∼e
Leistung, cognizance-giving function. Cf. **Leistung.**
Kundgebung, giving cognizance,
(making known).
kundgegeben, given cognizance of,
(made known).
Kundnahme, taking cognizance, cognizance (taken). Cf. **Kenntnisnahme,
Kundgabe.**
kundnehmen, to take cognizance.

kundtun, to give cognizance of, (to make known). Cf. **bekunden, kenntlich machen, kundgeben.**

Kunst, art ⟨WH 1, MS 1⟩, (*art* ⟨de M⟩), *technè*; artifice ⟨MS⟩, (*artifice* ⟨B⟩). Cf. **Messkunst, Technik.**

Kunstlehre, technology, (*technologie* ⟨B⟩), (practical discipline). **kunstmässig** ⟨adj.⟩, technical ⟨WH 2⟩, (*selon les règles d'un art* ⟨B⟩).

L

Laut, sound ⟨Bn, WH 1, MS 1⟩. Cf. **Ton, Wortlaut.**
Laut-, sound-, (phonetic ⟨Bn⟩).
Lautgebilde, sound-formation. Cf. **Gebilde.**
Lautkomplexion, sound-complex. Cf. **Komplexion.**
Leben, life ⟨WH 1, MS 1⟩, (*vie* ⟨B⟩); living ⟨WH⟩, (*vivre* ⟨R⟩). Cf. **Bewusstseinsleben, Dahinleben, Erleben, Geltungsleben, Innenleben, Nachleben.** | **Menschen des natürlichen ~s,** human beings who are living naturally. Cf. **Mensch.**
lebendig ⟨adj.⟩, living ⟨WH 1, MS 1⟩, (*vivant* ⟨R, B⟩), alive ⟨WH 2, MS 2, BG⟩, (lively ⟨WH⟩), (livingly active ⟨?⟩ ⟨BG⟩); awakened; actual. Cf. **aktuell** ⟨adj.⟩ 2, **unlebendig, wirklich.** | **~e Funktion,** actual functioning. Cf. **Funktion.** | **~e Rede,** actual conversation. Cf. **Rede 1.** | **~e Vergangenheit,** living past. Not "alive past" ⟨BG⟩.
lebendig ⟨adv.⟩, livingly, (*d'une manière vivante* ⟨B⟩), vitally, actually. | **— fungierend,** actually functioning. | **— gegenwärtig,** livingly present.
Lebendigkeit, aliveness ⟨WH 1⟩, vitality ⟨WH⟩, (*caractère vivant* ⟨B⟩).
Lebenseinheit, unity of life, life-unity. Not "vital unity" ⟨L⟩. Cf. **Einheit.**
Lebensform, life-form.
Lebensumwelt, surrounding life-world. Cf. **Umwelt.**
Lebensverfassung, | **Form der —,** form in which life is ordered. Not "form of life-interpretation" ⟨L⟩.
Lebenswelt, life-world, (*monde de la vie* ⟨B⟩). Cf. **Lebensumwelt.**
(**Lebhaftigkeit**), (vividness ⟨?⟩ ⟨Bn⟩).
Leerauffassung, empty apprehension,

empty apprehending. Cf. **Auffassung**
Leere, emptiness ⟨WH 1, MS 1⟩.
leer-formal ⟨adj.⟩, of empty forms, empty-formal, (*formel vide* ⟨B⟩).
Leervorschweben, empty intendedness, (*être présent à l'esprit d'une manière vide* ⟨B⟩). Cf. **vorschweben.**
leervorstellig, empty objective. Not "represented emptily" ⟨L⟩. Cf. **vorstellig.**
Leervorstellung, empty objectivation. Cf. **Vorstellung 1.**
Lehrgebäude, edifice of doctrine.
Leib, (animate) organism, (body ⟨WH 1, MS 1, L, BG⟩), (*corps* ⟨R⟩). Not "living body" ⟨BG⟩. So far as possible save "body" for "Körper". Cf. **Leibkörper, Leiblichkeit.** | **sprachlicher —,** verbal body. Cf. **sprachlich.**
leibhaft(ig) ⟨adj.⟩, (")in person(") ⟨WH 4, BG⟩, (")personal("), (*vif* ⟨R⟩), (*corporel* ⟨R⟩). Save "bodily" ⟨WH 1, BG⟩ and "corporeal" ⟨WH 3, BG⟩ for "körperlich". | **~e Gegebenheit,** givenness (")in person(").
leibhaft(ig) ⟨adv.⟩,(")in person("), (in one's own person ⟨WH 1⟩), (*corporellement* ⟨R⟩). Save "bodily" ⟨WH 2, BG⟩ for "körperlich". Cf. **sinnlich-leibhaft.**
Leibkörper, animate body. Cf. **Körper, Leib.**
leibkörperlich, of the (*or* an) animate body, animate-bodily.
leiblich ⟨adj.⟩, organismal.
Leiblichkeit, (animate) organism. Cf. **Leib, Leibkörper.**
leiden, to undergo ⟨WH⟩, (*pâtir* ⟨R⟩). Cf. **erfahren, erleben.**
Leiden, undergoing, suffering ⟨WH 1, MS 1⟩. Cf. **Erleben.**

leidend, undergoing, (passive ⟨WH, MS, BG⟩), (*passif* ⟨R⟩).

leisten, to produce; to perform ⟨WH 2, MS 2⟩; to do ⟨WH 1, MS 1⟩; to effect ⟨MS 3, WH 5⟩, (*effectuer* ⟨B⟩); to carry out ⟨WH 4, MS 4⟩; to make ⟨WH, MS⟩; to bring about; (to accomplish ⟨WH 3, MS 3, L⟩), (to solve), (to achieve ⟨MS, WH⟩); (*agir* ⟨R⟩); (*fournir* ⟨B⟩); (*fixer* ⟨R⟩). Cf. **ergeben, erzeugen, herstellen, schaffen, tun, vollziehen, wirken, zustandebringen.**
Leisten, producing, (production); performing; doing ⟨MS 1⟩; effecting, ((*acte d'*)*effectuation* ⟨B⟩); carring out; making; bringing about; (accomplishing), (achieving). | **urteilendes** —, judicative producing, judicative doing, (*effectuation de jugement* ⟨B⟩). Cf. **urteilend, urteilende Leistung** (*sub* Leistung), **urteilendes Tun** (*sub* Tun), **Urteilsleistung.**
leistend, productive, producing; performing; that does; effective, effecting, (*effectuant* ⟨B⟩), efficient; that carries out; that makes; that brings about; (accomplishing), (achieving). Cf. **bildend, erzeugend, sinnleistend.** | ~e **Intentionalität,** productive (*or* effective) intentionality, (*intentionnalité effectuante* ⟨B⟩). | ~es **Tun,** productive doing, (*activité d'effectuation* ⟨B⟩).
Leistung, production, product, producing, productivity; performance, ⟨WH 1, MS 2⟩, something done, doing ⟨MS 1⟩; effective performance, performance effected; effect ⟨WH⟩, (*effectuation* ⟨B⟩), produced effect, effect produced ⟨MS 6⟩; (result); (*action* (*d'effectuation*) ⟨B⟩); work done ⟨MS 5⟩, work; (Dienstleistung:) function, (*fonction* ⟨R⟩); (of an expression:) what it conveys; (accomplishment ⟨WH 2, MS 4⟩), (achievement ⟨MS⟩). Cf. **Aktleistung, Arbeit, Auswirkung, Bewusstseinsleistung, Bildung, Bürgschaftsleistung, Denkleistung, Erfüllungsleistung, Erzeugnis, Erzeugung, Folge 4, Funktion, Gebilde, Geistesleistung,**

Geltungsleistung, Gesamtleistung, Tätigkeit, Urteilsleistung, Vernunftleistung, Vollziehung, Vollzug, Werkleistung, Wirkung. | **die** — **der Evidenz,** what evidence does, (*l'action de l'effectuation de l'évidence* ⟨B⟩). Cf. **Evidenzleistung.** | **die** — **des Bewusstseins,** what consciousness does, (*l'action de l'effectuation de la conscience* ⟨B⟩). Cf. **Bewusstseinsleistung.** | **habituelle** —, effect produced in the realm of habit. | **konstitutive** —, constitutional effect, (*action pour la constitution* ⟨B⟩). | **kundgebende** —, cognizance-giving function. Cf. **kundgebend.** | — **der Erfahrung,** product of experience. | **noematische** —, noematic effect, (*fonction noématique* ⟨R⟩). | **theoretische** — **des Allgemeinen,** theoretic function of the universal. | **urteilende** —, judicative performance, (*effectuation de jugement* ⟨B⟩. Cf. **urteilend, urteilendes Leisten** (*sub* Leisten), **Urteilsleistung.** | **vollzogene** —, performance brought about, (*effectuation accomplie* ⟨B⟩). Cf. **eine Leistung vollziehen** (*sub* vollziehen).
Leistungsfähigkeit, productivity ⟨WH 2⟩, productive power ⟨MS 1, WH 3⟩; ability to perform ⟨MS 2⟩; efficacy, (of a scientific instrument:) efficiency ⟨WH 1, MS 6⟩.
Leistungsgebilde, produced formation, (*formation formée par une effectuation de conscience* ⟨B⟩). Cf. **Gebilde, Leistung.**
Leistungssinn, performance-sense.
Leitfaden, clue ⟨WH 1, MS 1⟩, (*fil conducteur* ⟨B⟩), (*index* ⟨de M⟩). | — **für,** clue for, (*fil conducteur pour* ⟨B⟩), clue to guide.
Leitidee, guiding idea, (*idée directrice* ⟨PL, B⟩).
Liebe, love ⟨WH 1, MS 1, BG⟩, loving (*aimer* ⟨R⟩). | **Akt der** —, act of loving, (*acte d'aimer* ⟨R⟩). Not "act of love" ⟨BG⟩.
liegen, | **in etwas immanent** —, to lie immanently in something, (*résider à titre "immanent" dans* ⟨R⟩). | **in etwas** —, to be inherent in some

thing, to lie in something, (*reposer dans quelque-chose* ⟨R⟩), (*résider dans quelque-chose* ⟨R⟩), to be implicit in something. Cf. **einwohnen, innewohnend.**

Lobatschewski, Lobachevski (Webster), (*Lobatchevski* ⟨B⟩), (Lobachewski (Heath, *Euclid*)).

logisch ⟨adj.⟩, logical ⟨WH 1, MS 1⟩, (*logique* ⟨R, B⟩), of logic, (*de logique* ⟨B⟩), pertaining to logic, for logic, with which logic is concerned, taken by logic. Cf. **analytisch-logisch, apophantisch-logisch, erfahrungslogisch** ⟨adj.⟩, **formal-logisch, objektiv-logisch, rein-logisch, rein-logisch-grammatisch, schluss(ge)-recht, schlussrichtig, umfangslogisch.** | alles **L**~e, any thing with which logic is concerned. | ~e **Idee,** idea of logic, (*idée de logique* ⟨B⟩); idea with which logic is concerned, (*idée logique* ⟨B⟩). | ~e **Thematik,** themes of logic; logical thematizing.

Cf. **Thematik.** | ~e **Theorie,** theory of logic. | ~e **Vorstellung,** idea with which logic is concerned. Cf. **Vorstellung.** | ~er **Begriff,** concept pertaining to logic. | ~er **Satz,** proposition of logic, (*proposition logique* ⟨R⟩). | ~es **Datum,** Datum for logic. Cf. **Datum.** | ~es **Gebilde,** formation with which logic is concerned; logical formation, (*formation logique* ⟨B⟩). Cf. **Gebilde.** | rein ~e **Einsicht,** insight pertaining to pure logic, (*évidence purement logique* ⟨R⟩). Cf. **Einsicht.**

logisch ⟨adv.⟩, logically ⟨WH 1, MS 1⟩, to logic, by logic, from the standpoint of logic, (*du point de vue logique* ⟨B⟩), (*dans la perspective logique* ⟨B⟩). Cf. **erfahrungslogisch** ⟨adv.⟩, **formal-logisch** ⟨adv.⟩, **natur-logisch** ⟨adv.⟩.

logisch-unmittelbar ⟨adj.⟩, immediate logical ⟨BG⟩, (*logique immédiat* ⟨R⟩).

M

mannigfach ⟨adj.⟩, various, (*de toutes sortes* ⟨R⟩).

mannigfach ⟨adv.⟩, variously. Not "diversely" ⟨L⟩.

mannigfaltig, multiple ⟨MS 3⟩, (*multiple* ⟨B⟩), manifold ⟨WH 1, MS 1⟩, various ⟨WH 2, L⟩, (many ⟨Gomperz trln of Mill, quoted in LU, II. Unters.⟩). Cf. **mehrfältig, verschieden, vielfältig.**

Mannigfaltigkeit, multiplicity ⟨MS, WH, L⟩, (*multiplicité* ⟨R, B⟩), manifoldness ⟨WH 1, MS 1⟩, (*divers* ⟨R⟩). Cf. **Mehrheit, Vielfachheit, Vielheit.**

Mannigfaltigkeitsform, form of multiplicities.

Mannigfaltigkeitslehre, (*doctrine de la multiplicité* ⟨R, B⟩), theory of multiplicities, multiplicity-theory.

Mass, measure ⟨WH 1, MS 1⟩, (*mesure* ⟨R⟩), standard ⟨WH⟩; degree ⟨WH, MS⟩. Cf. **Stufe.** | in fortschreitendem ~e, progressively.

Mass-, metrical, of measure, measuring.

Masseinheit, unit of measure ⟨WH 1⟩. Cf. **Einheit.**

massgebend, determining, (*qui commande* ⟨R⟩); normative.

Massgrösse, metrical quantity. Cf. **Grösse.**

Massstab, measuring rod, (standard ⟨Bn, WH⟩), (criterion ⟨Bn⟩).

Masszahl, metrical number. Cf. **Grössenzahl.**

Materie, material, matter ⟨MS 1⟩, (*matière* ⟨R, B, de M⟩), (*contenu* ⟨B, de M⟩). Cf. **Aktmaterie, Erkenntnismaterie, Sache, Satzmaterie, Seinsmaterie, Stoff, Urteilsmaterie, Verhältnis.** | (der — nach), (*materialiter* ⟨K⟩).

materiell, (*matériel* ⟨R⟩).

mathematisch-ideal ⟨adj.⟩, Cf. **ideal.** | ~e **Erkenntnis,** cognition of mathematical-ideal (objects), (*connaissance idéale de type mathématique* ⟨R⟩).

mathematisierend, mathematizing ⟨not in OED⟩.

matter-of-fact-Erkenntnis, cognition of matters of fact. Cf. Erkenntnis, Tatsachenerkenntnis.

mehrere, a plurality of, several ⟨WH 1⟩.

mehrfach ⟨adj.⟩, a number of, (*un certain nombre de* ⟨R⟩).

mehrfältig, multiple (*multiple* ⟨R⟩). Cf. mannigfaltig.

Mehrheit, (ant. Einheit:) plurality ⟨MS 1, WH 2⟩, (*pluralité* ⟨B⟩), majority ⟨WH 1⟩, (*plupart* ⟨R⟩), number. Cf. Vielheit.

meinen, 1. (usually:) to mean ⟨WH, MS, BG⟩ (mentally), (*viser* ⟨B⟩), (*envisager* ⟨B⟩), (*vouloir dire* ⟨B⟩), (*signifier* ⟨B⟩). Cf. verstehen.
2. (doxically, sometimes:) to mean or opine, (to opine), (*opiner* ⟨B⟩), (*penser* ⟨B⟩); to believe ⟨WH, MS⟩; (to assert ⟨WH⟩).
Cf. aussagen, behaupten, denken, feststellen, gemeint, mitmeinen, prädizieren, vermeinen, vormeinen, zumeinen.

Meinen, 1. (usually:) mental meaningprocess, (mental) process (*or* act) of meaning, (where there is no danger of ambiguity:) meaning.
2. (doxic, sometimes:) meaning or opining, opining, (*opiner* ⟨B⟩), (*acte d'opinion* ⟨B⟩); believing. Cf. Vermeinen. | individuelles —, meaning (of) something individual. | naturales —, believing about Nature, (*opinion naturelle* ⟨B⟩). Cf. natural, natürlich. | spezifisches —, meaning (of) something specific. | urteilendes —, judging process of meaning (*activité d'opinion qui juge* ⟨B⟩), (*intention du jugement* ⟨B⟩). Cf. urteilend, urteilende Meinung (*sub* Meinung).

Meinung, A. (equivocally:) meaning. B. (noematic:) 1. (usually:) meaning (intended to), (*visée* ⟨R⟩), (*intention* ⟨B⟩), (something meant).
2. (doxic, sometimes:) meaning or opinion, opinion ⟨WH 1, MS 1⟩, (*opinion* ⟨B⟩), belief ⟨WH, MS⟩.

C. (noetic:) Equivalent to "Meinen" ⟨q.v.⟩.
Cf. Glaube(n), Mitmeinung, Seinsmeinung, Sinn, Ursache-Meinung, Sachverhaltsmeinung, Teilmeinung, Vormeinung, Willensmeinung, Wortmeinung, Wunschmeinung. | urteilende —, judging process of meaning, (judicative meaning), (*jugement en tant qu'opinion* ⟨B⟩). Cf. urteilend, urteilendes Meinen (*sub* Meinen), Urteilsmeinung.

Menge, 1. (math:) set ⟨WH 1⟩, (*groupe* ⟨R⟩), (*ensemble* ⟨B⟩). Not "multiplicity" ⟨Bn⟩.
2. (non-math:) multitude ⟨MS 3, WH⟩, many.
Cf. Mannigfaltigkeit, Ordnung, Vielfachheit, Vielheit.

Mengenlehre, theory of sets ⟨WH 1⟩, (*théorie des groupes* ⟨R⟩), (*théorie des ensembles* ⟨B⟩).

Mensch, human being ⟨MS 1, WH 2⟩, man ⟨Gomperz trln of Mill, quoted in LU, II. Unters.; WH 1; MS 2; BG⟩, (*homme* ⟨R⟩). | ~en des natürlichen Lebens, men (who are) living naturally.

Menschentum, 1. mankind, human race ⟨WH 1, MS 1⟩.
2. humanity ⟨Gomperz trln of Mill, quoted in LU, II. Unters.; WH 2; MS 2⟩; (*le règne de l'humain* ⟨B⟩).

Menschheit, 1. humanness, human nature ⟨MS 1, WH⟩.
2. humanity ⟨BG⟩, (*humanité* ⟨R, B⟩), mankind ⟨Bn, WH 2⟩.
Cf. Allmenschheit.

Menschheitlichkeit, humanness.

merken, to note, (to notice ⟨WH, MS⟩), (*remarquer* ⟨R, B⟩), (*entrevoir* ⟨B⟩). Not "to discern" ⟨Bn⟩. Cf. ansehen, aufmerken, bemerken, gewahren.

Merkmal, distinctive trait, trait, mark ⟨Bn, WH 1, MS 1⟩; (in original sense:) character ⟨F⟩, characteristic ⟨WH 3, MS⟩; mark of distinction ⟨MS 2⟩; (in logic, where it is a trln of Latin *nota* ⟨K⟩:) note. Cf. Beschaffenheit, Charakter, Gattungsmerkmal, Zeichen. | charakteristisches —, characteristic mark. Cf.

charakteristische Beschaffenheit (*sub* Beschaffenheit). | konstituierendes —, constituent mark, (*caractère constituant* ⟨B⟩). Cf. konstituierend.

Merkmalmoment, trait-moment.

Merkzeichen, distinctive sign ⟨MS 2⟩, distinctive mark⟨MS 3⟩. Cf. Zeichen.

messen, | sich — an, to be fitted to.

Messkunst, mensurational art. See Krisis, *35*, *l.* *1*—*5*. Cf. Kunst.

Methodik, method(s); (*méthodique* ⟨B⟩), (methodics ⟨MS 1, not in OED⟩), (methodology ⟨WH 1, MS 2⟩).

methodisch ⟨adj.⟩, of (the) method, (*de méthode* ⟨R, B⟩), (*de la méthode* ⟨B⟩), pertaining to method, method-⟨Bn⟩; according to (a) method, in the method, methodic (though lexicographers do not recognize the relevant sense of this word), (*méthodique* ⟨B⟩); methodological ⟨L, BG⟩, (*méthodologique* ⟨B⟩); (rarely:) methodical ⟨WH 1, MS 1, L⟩. | die ∼e Art, nature of the method, (*type de méthode* ⟨B⟩). | in diesem ∼en Stil einer Mathematik, by this method in the style of a mathematics, (*dans ce style méthodique d'une mathématique* ⟨B⟩). | ∼er Schritt, step in the method. Not "methodical step" ⟨L⟩.

methodisch ⟨adv.⟩, in respect of method, methodically, in the method. | — unerfahren, inexperienced in the method. | — vollkommen, perfect in respect of method.

Mich-Enthalten, abstaining, (*abstention* ⟨PL⟩). Cf. sich enthalten (*sub* enthalten).

Mir-Eigenes, | das —, my own, what is peculiarly my own. Cf. eigen, Eigenes, mir selbsteigen (*sub* selbsteigen).

Mir-Eigenwesentliches, | das —, that which belongs to my own (peculiar) essence; the own essentiality belonging to me. Cf. Eigenwesentliches.

Missbilligung, disapprobation ⟨WH 2, MS 2⟩, (*désapprobation* ⟨R⟩), disap-

proval ⟨WH 1, MS 1, BG⟩. Cf. Billigung.

Missfallen, disliking, (*déplaisir* ⟨B⟩), (*désagrément* ⟨R⟩). Save "disapproval" ⟨BG⟩ for "Missbilligung" ⟨q.v.⟩. Cf. Gefallen, Wohlgefallen.

missfällig, unpleasant ⟨MS 2, WH 3⟩, (*déplaisant* ⟨R⟩). Save "disagreeable" ⟨WH 2, MS 3, BG⟩ for "unangenehm". Cf. gefällig.

mitaufgefasst, co-apprehended. Not "along with which they are grasped" ⟨L⟩. Cf. auffassen.

Mitbedeutung, co-signification. Save "connotation" ⟨MS, L⟩ for "Mitbezeichnung". Cf. Bedeutung.

(mitbegreifen), to include ⟨WH 1⟩, (to connote ⟨Bn⟩). Cf. begreifen, mitbezeichnen, miteinbegreifen, mitmeinen, umgreifen.

mitbeschlossen in, included in ⟨L⟩, (*enfermé dans* ⟨B⟩), (*impliqué dans* ⟨B⟩). Cf. beschlossen in.

mitbewusst, of which there is (*or* I have) (a) co-consciousness, (*coprésent à ma conscience* ⟨R⟩). Not "co-perceived" ⟨BG⟩. Cf. bewusst.

mitbezeichnen, to connote ⟨Gomperz trln of Mill, quoted in LU, II. Unters.; WH 1⟩. Cf. bezeichnen, mit ausdrücken (*sub* ausdrücken), mitbegreifen, miteinbegreifen.

mitbezeichnend, connotative ⟨Gomperz trln of Mill, quoted in LU, I. Unters.⟩. Cf. bezeichnend.

Mitbezeichnung, connotation ⟨Gomperz trln of Mill, quoted in LU, I. Unters.⟩. Cf. Bezeichnung.

Mitbeziehung, concomitant relation. Cf. Beziehung. | intentionale —, concomitant intentional relation, (*référence intentionelle qui se trouve là impliquée* ⟨B⟩).

Mit-da, "there-too", there-too.

Mitdasein, being-there-too. Cf. Dasein, Mit-sein.

Miteinander, togetherness. Cf. Ineinander.

(miteinbegreifen), to connote ⟨Bn⟩. Cf. mitbegreifen, mitbezeichnen, mitmeinen.

mitfassen, to apprehend along with, (*grouper ensemble* ⟨R⟩). Cf. **fassen.**

Mitgegebenheit, co-givenness. Cf. **Gegebenheit 2.**

mitgegenwärtig, co-present ⟨BG; in OED⟩, (*co-présent* ⟨R⟩). Cf. **gegenwärtig.**

Mitgegenwärtigung, making co-present, (*co-présentation* ⟨R⟩). Not "co-representation" ⟨BG⟩. Cf. **Gegenwärtigung.**

mitgeltend, co-accepted, accepted along with, in force along with, etc. See geltend ⟨q.v.⟩.

Mitgeltung, co-acceptance, co-acceptedness, something accepted along with, etc. See Geltung. ⟨q.v.⟩. Cf. **Zusammengeltung.** | **zu angemessener — kommen,** to be given a due share of importance.

mitgeschaut, seen along with, (*co-perçu* ⟨R⟩). Not "co-perceived" ⟨BG⟩. Cf. **schauen.**

mitkonstituieren, to be a constituent of. Cf. **konstituierend.**

mitmachen, to join in ⟨WH⟩.

mitmeinen, to mean (mentally) along with; (to involve the assumption of). Cf. **meinen.**

Mitmeinung, attendant (*or* accompanying) meaning; co-intending. Save "connotation" ⟨L⟩ for "Mitbezeichnung".

Mit-sein, coexistence. Cf. **Mitdasein, Sein.**

mitsubstruieren, to co-hypothesize, (to co-substruct). Cf. **substruieren.**

mitteilend, communicative; to communicate. | ~**e Intention,** intention to communicate.

mittelbar ⟨adj.⟩, mediate ⟨WH 1, L⟩, (*médiat* ⟨R, B⟩); mediative.

mittelbar ⟨adv.⟩, | — **gebildet,** formed at a mediated level.

(Mittelbegriff), middle term ⟨Bn⟩, (*terminus medius* ⟨K⟩).

Mittelsetzung, (process of) willing a means. Cf. **Setzung, Zwecksetzung.**

mitverflochten, combined with (it). Cf. **verflechten.**

modifizierend, modifying, modificational modification. | **passiv** ~**e Gesetzmässigkeit,** law of passive modification, (*légalité qui introduit des modifications passives* ⟨B⟩). Cf. **Gesetzmässigkeit.**

modifiziert ⟨adv.⟩, | — **genommen,** taken as modified.

Modus, mode ⟨WH 1, MS 1⟩, (*mode* ⟨R, B, de M⟩), manner ⟨WH 2⟩. Cf. **Aktmodus, Art, Darstellungsmodus, Gegebenheitsmodus, Geltungsmodus, Setzungsmodus, Urmodus, Weise.**

Möglichkeit, Cf. **Seinsmöglichkeit.** | **in** —, in the mode of possibility, (*quant à la possibilité* ⟨B⟩).

Möglichkeitsabwandlung, possibility-variant, possible variant, (*variante possible* ⟨B⟩). Cf. **Abwandlung.**

Moment, moment, (*moment* ⟨R, B⟩), (abstract part), (*aspect* ⟨R⟩), (*facteur* ⟨B⟩). Save "aspect" ⟨BG⟩ for "Seite" ⟨q.v.⟩, "phase" ⟨BG⟩ for "Phase". Not "factor" ⟨F⟩. Cf. **Identisches, Merkmalsmoment, Stück, Urmoment, Ursprungsmoment.**

monothetisch, monothetic, (*monothétique* ⟨R⟩). Cf. **thetisch.**

Motivation, motivation, motive. Cf. **Geistesmotivation, Motivierung.**

Motivationsfundament, motivational foundation, (*fondement de la motivation* ⟨B⟩).

Motivationsgrundlage, motivational foundation, (*fondement de motivation* ⟨B⟩). Cf. **Grundlage.**

Motivationszusammenhang, 1. nexus of motivation, motivational complex (*or* nexus), (*ensemble total de la motivation* ⟨B⟩). 2. motivational coherence. Cf. **Motivierungszusammenhang, Zusammenhang.**

Motivierung, motivating, motivation. Cf. **Motivation.**

Motivierungseinheit, motivational unity.

Motivierungszusammenhang, nexus of motivation, motivational complex (*or* nexus). Cf. **Motivationszusammenhang, Zusammenhang.**

N

Nachbild, copy ⟨WH 1, MS 1⟩; afterimage (Boring, 1942). Cf. **Abbild.**
Nacherzeugung, regenerating, reproduction ⟨L⟩. Cf. **Erzeugung.**
nachgehen, to trace, to follow up ⟨WH 2, BG⟩, to pursue ⟨WH, BG, L⟩, (*poursuivre* ⟨R⟩), (*venir après* ⟨B⟩), to investigate ⟨WH 1⟩. Save "to consider" ⟨BG⟩ for "betrachten" and "to concern oneself with" ⟨L⟩ for "sich beschäftigen mit". Cf. **forschen, sich besinnen** (*sub* **besinnen**), **untersuchen.** | **einer Idee —,** to pursue an idea.
Nachgestalt, formation subsequent to. Cf. **Gestalt, Vorgestalt.**
nachkommend, ex post facto, (*venant après coup* ⟨B⟩), (*qui vient en second lieu* ⟨B⟩); subsequent, (*qui vient après* ⟨B⟩).
nachleben, | **die fremden Akte —,** to live another's acts after him, (*revivre les actes d'autrui* ⟨R⟩). Cf. **fremd.**
Nachleben, reliving ⟨L⟩. Cf. **Leben.**
Nachsatz, 1. (logic:) consequent (Ziehen, see Logik), (proposition), (*conséquent* ⟨B⟩). 2. (grammar:) apodosis. Cf. **Folge 1, Folgesatz, Satz, Vordersatz.**
nachschauen, to follow with one's regard. Cf. **schauen.**
Nachsprechen, following in speaking. Cf. **Quasi-nachsprechen.**
nachveranschaulichend, making (something) intuited afterwards. Cf. **veranschaulichen, vorveranschaulichen.**
nachverstehen, to follow and understand, to understand in following (another), (*comprendre à leur suite* ⟨B⟩); to follow in understanding, (*comprendre après* ⟨B⟩); to understand regeneratively, (*ré-comprendre* ⟨B⟩). Cf. **verstehen.**
Nachverstehen, following and understanding, understanding-in-following-another, (*comprendre-après* ⟨B⟩), (*ré-comprehension* ⟨B⟩).
nachvollzogen, that one performs in "following".

Nachweis, pointing out, showing, demonstration, (*preuve* ⟨B⟩). | **der —, dass,** showing that.
nachweisbar, demonstrable ⟨MS 1, WH 2⟩. Cf. **aufweisbar, ausweisbar, nachweislich.**
nachweisen, to point out ⟨WH 1, MS 2⟩, (*indiquer* ⟨B⟩), to show ⟨WH 3, BG, L⟩, to demonstrate ⟨WH 4⟩, (*prouver* ⟨R, B⟩), to authenticate ⟨WH, MS⟩. Cf. **aufweisen, erweisen.** | **— als,** to show to be; to authenticate as ⟨MS⟩.
Nachweisen, showing, demonstrating.
nachweislich, demonstrable ⟨MS 1, WH 2⟩. Cf. **aufweisbar, ausweisbar, nachweisbar.**
Nachweisung, showing, demonstration ⟨MS 4⟩, (*preuve* ⟨B⟩), (*justification* ⟨R⟩), (indication ⟨MS 2⟩), (*indication* ⟨B⟩). Cf. **Ausweisung, Erweis.**
naheliegend, obvious ⟨WH 1, MS 4⟩, ready, likely, natural. Cf. **natürlich, urwüchsig, vermutlich.**
naiv-sinnlich, | **in ~er Erscheinung,** naïvely accepted as it appears sensuously.
Name, name ⟨WH 1, MS 1, BG⟩, (with reference to Hume ⟨Lipps trln, quoted in LU, II. Unters.⟩ or Mill ⟨Gomperz trln, quoted *loc. cit.*⟩:) term, (*vocable* ⟨R⟩). Cf. **Terminus.**
Natur, nature (capitalized ⟨BG⟩ when it denotes the totality of Nature). Cf. **Allnatur, Art, Artung, Beschaffenheit, Sosein.**
natural ⟨adj.⟩, of (*or* belonging to, *or* relating to, *or* on, *or* about) Nature, (natural), (*naturel* ⟨B⟩). Cf. **naturhaft, natürlich.** | **~e Einstellung,** focusing on Nature. Cf. **Einstellung.** | **~e Erfahrung,** experience (*or* experiencing) of Nature, Nature-experience, (*expérience naturelle* ⟨B⟩). Cf. **Naturerfahrung.** | **~es Meinen,** believing about Nature, (*opinion naturelle* ⟨B⟩). Cf. **Meinen.** | **~es Sein,** the being of Nature, (*être naturel* ⟨B⟩). | **rein ~e Erfahrung,**

experience purely of Nature, (*expérience purement naturelle* ⟨B⟩).
natural ⟨adv.⟩, in Nature.
Naturbezug, relation to Nature.
Naturding, physical thing belonging to Nature. Not "thing of nature" ⟨L⟩. Cf. Ding der Natur (*sub* Ding), Natursache.
Naturerfahrung, Nature-experience, (*expérience de la nature* ⟨B⟩). Cf. Erfahrung.
Naturforscher, scientific investigator of Nature, (*savant dans les sciences de la nature* ⟨R⟩). Not "student of nature" ⟨BG⟩, not "scientific worker" ⟨BG⟩. Cf. Forscher.
naturhaft ⟨adj.⟩, natural.
Naturkausalität, causality in Nature.
Naturkunde, cognizance of Nature. Not "nature study" ⟨L⟩. Cf. Kunde.
natürlich, natural ⟨WH 1, MS 1⟩, (*naturel* ⟨R, B⟩), (*naturalis* ⟨K⟩), (ant. philosophisch:) of the natural sort. Cf. naheliegend, natural, naturhaft, urwüchsig. | Menschen des ∼en Lebens, human beings who are living naturally. Cf. Mensch. | ∼e Wissenschaft, science of the natural sort. Cf. Naturwissenschaft.
natur-logisch ⟨adv.⟩, | — leitend, guiding in the manner proper to a logic of Nature.
Naturobjekt, Object belonging to Nature, (*objet de la nature* ⟨R⟩). Cf. Objekt.
Natur-Objektivität, Nature-Objectivity. Cf. Objektivität.
Natursache, mere thing belonging to Nature, (*chose naturelle* ⟨R⟩). Cf. Naturding, Sache.
Natursphäre, sphere of Nature ⟨BG⟩, (*sphère de la nature* ⟨R⟩).
Naturwissenschaft, natural science ⟨WH 1, MS 1⟩, science of Nature. Cf. natürliche Wissenschaft (*sub* natürlich).
Nebenglied, collateral member, (*membre adjoint* ⟨B⟩). Cf. Hauptglied.
Negat, negatum, (*negatum* ⟨R⟩), (*ce qui est nié* ⟨B⟩); negative, (*négation* ⟨B⟩). Not "what is negated" ⟨BG⟩.

negierbar, | nicht —, incapable of being negated.
negieren, to negate ⟨WH 2, BG⟩, (*nier* ⟨R⟩), to deny ⟨WH 1, MS 1, BG⟩, (*aboutir à supprimer* ⟨R⟩). Cf. verneinen.
Neigung, tendency ⟨WH, MS, BG⟩, (*tendance* ⟨R, B⟩), inclination ⟨WH, MS⟩, (propensity ⟨Bn, WH, MS⟩).
neugestaltet, refashioned.
Neugestaltung, refashioning. Cf. Gestaltung.
Nichteigenes, what is not (peculiarly) my (*or* his) own. Cf. Eigenes.
nichtig, null ⟨WH 1, MS⟩, (*nul* ⟨R, B⟩). Not "not at all" ⟨BG⟩. Cf. Null.
Nichtigkeit, nullity ⟨WH 2, MS⟩, (*nullité* ⟨B⟩), (*néant* ⟨R⟩). Cf. aufheben.
Nichtig-sein, being null, nullity.
Nichtsollen, should not. Cf. Sollen.
(Nichtwissen), nescience ⟨Bn⟩. Cf. Wissen.
Noch-Bewusstsein, being still an object of consciousness. Cf. Bewusstsein 2.
Noch-Geltung, continuing acceptance, (*validité persistant encore* ⟨B⟩). Cf. Fortgeltung, Geltung.
Noch-im-Griff, (the) still-in-one's-grip. Cf. im Griff (*sub* Griff).
Noch-im-Griff-behalten, still-keeping-in-one's-grip. Cf. Griff, Im-Griff-behalten.
Noch-im-Griff-haben, still-having-in-one's-grip. Cf. Griff.
Noch-im-Griff-halten, still-holding-in-one's-grip. Cf. Griff.
Noema ⟨n.⟩, noema ⟨BG⟩, (*noème* ⟨R, de M⟩). Cf. Gegennoema, Wahrnehmungsnoema.
noematisch ⟨adj.⟩, noematic, (*noématique* ⟨R, B⟩), noematical, about a noema. | in ∼er Einstellung, while focusing on the noematic aspect, (*dans une attitude noématique* ⟨B⟩). Cf. Einstellung. | ∼e Aussage, statement about a noema, (*énoncé noématique* ⟨R⟩). Cf. Aussage.
noematisch ⟨adv.⟩, noematically, (*noématiquement* ⟨B⟩), as noematic, on the noematic side, (*du point de vue noématique* ⟨B⟩).

Noesis ⟨f.⟩, noesis ⟨BG⟩, (noèse ⟨R, de M⟩).
Noetik, noetics ⟨WH 1⟩, (noétique ⟨R⟩).
noetisch ⟨adj.⟩, noetic, (noétique ⟨B⟩), noetical, of noeses (or of a noesis). | ∼e Objekte, Objects of noeses, (objets noétiques ⟨R⟩). | ∼e Reflexion, reflection on the noesis, noetical reflection, (réflexion noétique ⟨B⟩).
noetisch ⟨adv.⟩, noetically, (noétiquement ⟨B⟩), as noetic, on the noetic side, (au point de vue noétique ⟨B⟩).
noetisch-noematisch, noetico-noematic, (noético-noématique ⟨R⟩).
nominal, naming; nominal ⟨MS 1⟩. | ∼e Vorstellung, naming objectivation of something as named. Cf. Vorstellung 1, Wortvorstellung.
normal ⟨adj.⟩, normal; right.
normativ ⟨adj.⟩, normative, (normatif ⟨B⟩), by norms, in furnishing norms.
normativ ⟨adv.⟩, | — gemeint, meant as normative.
normieren, to be (or furnish) a norm for, to apply a norm to, to test (by a norm), to square (with a norm).
normierend, which furnishes norms, (qui est la norme ⟨B⟩), testing.
normiert, | N ∼es, something to which a norm is applied.
Normierung, testing by a norm (or by norms).
Notwendigkeitszusammenhang, necessary connexion (with); nexus of necessity. Cf. Zusammenhang. | realer —, necessary real connexion (with), (enchaînement réel d'ordre nécessaire ⟨R⟩); real nexus of necessity. Not "real necessary connexion." ⟨BG⟩.
Nuance, shade ⟨WH 1⟩, nuance ⟨L⟩, (nuance ⟨R⟩), | leiseste —, slightest shade, (moindre nuance ⟨R⟩). | letzte —, finest nuance ⟨L⟩.
Null, zero ⟨MS 1, WH⟩. Cf. nichtig.
Nullkörper, zero body.
Nutzen, utility ⟨MS 1, WH 2⟩; advantage ⟨WH, MS⟩.
Nützlichkeit, usefulness ⟨WH 1, MS 2⟩, utility ⟨WH 2⟩.

O

oben, | von — her, (empty …) from on high, (effectué de haut ⟨B⟩).
Oberbegriff, superordinate (or higher) concept, (concept suprême ⟨B⟩); (major term ⟨Bn⟩), (terminus major ⟨K⟩). Cf. Unterbegriff.
Obersatz, principle, first principle ⟨MS 1⟩; (logic:) major premise ⟨Bn, WH, MS⟩, (propositio major ⟨K⟩). Cf. Satz, 1 & 4, Untersatz.
Oberschicht, upper stratum ⟨WH 1⟩. Cf. Unterschicht.
Objekt, Object (spelled with a capital to distinguish between "Objekt" and "Gegenstand"), (objet ⟨R, B⟩), (complément ⟨B⟩). Cf. Gebrauchsobjekt, Naturobjekt, Thema, Vorstellungsobjekt, Weltobjekt, Zeitobjekt.
Objektität, (abstract:) Objectiveness, (concrete:) Object. Cf. Gegenständlichkeit, Objektivität, Wertobjektität.
objektiv ⟨adj.⟩, Objective, (objectif ⟨B⟩), of something Objective. Cf. gegenständlich, sachlich, vorstellig. | das O ∼e, the Objective something, (l'objet ⟨R⟩). | ∼e Erfahrung, experience of something Objective, Objective experience, (expérience objective ⟨B⟩). | ∼e Wissenschaftslehre, theory of Objective science, (doctrine objective de la science ⟨B⟩).
objektiv ⟨adv.⟩, Objectively, as Objective, to the Objective, on the Objective side, (du côté objectif ⟨B⟩), (dans la perspective objective ⟨B⟩). | — hinstellen, to set up as Objective, Cf. hinstellen.
objektiv-logisch, pertaining to Objective logic. Cf. logisch.
Objektivation, Objectivation, (objecti-

vation ⟨R⟩). Save "objectification" ⟨BG⟩ for "Vergegenständlichung". Cf. **vorstellig machen** (*sub* **vorstellig**), **Vorstellung.**
objektiv-ideal ⟨adj.⟩, Cf. **ideal-objektiv.** | ∼e **Einstellung,** focusing on what is Objective and ideal, (*tournée vers l'objectivité idéale* ⟨B⟩). Cf. **Einstellung.**
objektiv-ideal ⟨adv.⟩, | — gerichtet, directed to what is Objective and ideal.
Objektivierung, Objectivation, (*objectivation* ⟨R, B⟩). See comment and references *sub* Objectivation.
Objektivität, Objectivity, (*objectivité* ⟨R, B, de M⟩), that which is objective. Cf. **Gegenständlichkeit, Natur-Objektivität, Objektität, Sachlichkeit.**
objektiv-zeitlich ⟨adv.⟩, in Objective time, (*dans la temporalité objective* ⟨B⟩); in Objective temporal respects. Not "objectively-temporally" ⟨L⟩.
Objekt-schlechthin, Object pure and simple, (*objet en tant que tel* ⟨B⟩). Cf. **schlechthin.**
obwaltend, | ∼es **Verhältnis,** obtaining relationship. Cf. **Verhältnis.**
ohne weiteres, without more ado, simply ⟨WH⟩, (without further thought ⟨BG⟩), (*sans autre examen* ⟨R⟩). Save "immediately" for "unmittelbar".
offen-beliebig, open to choice. Cf. **beliebig.**
ontisch ⟨adj.⟩, ontic ⟨BG, not in OED⟩, (*ontique* ⟨R, B⟩). | **in** ∼er **Einstellung,** when (thinking is) focused on the existent, (*dans l'attitude ontique* ⟨B⟩). Cf. **Einstellung.**
ontisch ⟨adv.⟩, | — gerichtet, directed to what exists.
Ontologie, | — im **realem Sinne,** ontology in the sense, ontology of realities, (*ontologie au sens réel* ⟨B⟩). Cf. **Realontologie.**
ontologisch ⟨adj.⟩, ontological, (*ontologique* ⟨R⟩), of ontology. | **rein** ∼er **Satz,** proposition of pure ontology, (*proposition purement ontologique* ⟨R⟩).

operativ, operative ⟨WH 1, MS⟩, (*opératoire* ⟨B⟩); operational ⟨WH 2⟩.
ordnen, | **sich** — **unter,** to find one's place under. Cf. **sich einordnen in** (*sub* **einordnen**).
Ordnung, order ⟨WH 2, MS⟩, (*ordre* ⟨B⟩); (math:) ordered set; orderliness ⟨MS⟩, organization. Cf. **Anordnung, Menge, Regelordnung, Seinsordnung, Stufenordnung.** | **dingliche** — **und Beziehung,** physical order and connexion. Cf. **dinglich, Beziehung.**
Ordnungszahl, ordinal number ⟨WH 1, MS 1⟩, (pl.:) (*numeralia ordinalia* ⟨Arith⟩).
orientieren, to adjust, to place, (to orientate ⟨WH⟩), (*orienter* ⟨B⟩). Cf. **richten nach** (*sub* **richten**). | — **an,** to adjust to, (*orienter vers* ⟨B⟩). | — **nach,** to adjust (e.g. a concept) to. | **sich** — **nach,** to direct one's attention to; to pattern oneself on; (*s'orienter d'après* ⟨B⟩).
orientiert, adjusted, placed. | — **nach,** adjusted to; patterned on; (*orienté vers* ⟨B⟩).
Orientierung, adjustment; orientation ⟨WH 1, MS 1, L⟩, (*orientation* ⟨R⟩). Cf. **Einstellung, Richtung.** | — **an,** adjustment to, (orientation by), (*orientation vers* ⟨B⟩). | — **auf,** orientation toward.
original, original ⟨WH 1, MS 1⟩, originary, (originative), (originant). Cf. **originär, ursprünglich, urtümlich.**
Originalerzeugnis, originally generated product, (*produit original* ⟨B⟩). Cf. **Erzeugnis.**
Originalität, originality ⟨WH 1, MS 1⟩, originariness, originativeness, originative activity. Cf. **Originärität, Ursprünglichkeit.**
originär ⟨adj.⟩, originary, (*originaire* ⟨R⟩), original, in an original manner. Not "of origins" ⟨L⟩. Save "primordial" ⟨BG⟩ for "primordi(n)al". Cf. **original, Ur-, ursprünglich** ⟨adj.⟩.
originär ⟨adv.⟩, originarily, (*originairement* ⟨R⟩), (*de façon originaire* ⟨B⟩), originally, (originaliter), as the origi-

nal (object) itself. Save "primordially" ⟨BG⟩ for "primordi(n)al" ⟨adv.⟩. Cf. **ursprünglich** ⟨adv.⟩. | — **erfassen,** to grasp (something) as the original (object) itself. | — **gebend,** originarily (*or* originally) giving, (*donateur originaire* ⟨R⟩). | — **ge-**

geben, given originarily (*or* originally), (*originairement donné* ⟨R⟩), (given originaliter). **Originarität,** originariness, (*originarité* ⟨R⟩), originalness. Cf. **Originalität, Ursprünglichkeit.** **orthoid,** "rectilinear".

P

Paarung, pairing ⟨WH 1, MS 1⟩. Cf. **Kopulation.** **partial** ⟨adj.⟩, component, (*partiel* ⟨B⟩). Cf. **partiell.** **Partialanschauung,** intuition of a part. **Partialgebilde,** component formation, (*formation partielle* ⟨B⟩). Cf. **Gebilde.** **partiell** ⟨adj.⟩, partial ⟨WH 1, MS 1⟩, (*partiel* ⟨R, B⟩). Cf. **partial.** **perzeptiv** ⟨adj.⟩, 1. (noetic only:) perceptive. 2. (noetic or noematic:) perceptual, of perception, (*perceptif* ⟨B⟩). Cf. **wahrnehmungsmässig** ⟨adj.⟩. | **das P∼e,** the perceptual object, (*l'élément perceptif* ⟨B⟩). **perzeptiv** ⟨adv.⟩, perceptually ⟨BG⟩, (*de façon perceptive* ⟨R⟩). Cf. **wahrnehmungsmässig** ⟨adv.⟩. **phänomenologisch** ⟨adj.⟩, | **in echtem Sinn** —, pertaining to a genuine phenomenology. **Phantasie,** phantasy, (*imagination* ⟨R, B, de M⟩), (*image* ⟨R⟩). Not "fantasy" and not "fancy" ⟨WH 1, MS 2, BG⟩; see Bn, OED, and MEU. Save "imagination" ⟨MS 1, WH 2, L⟩ for "Einbildung". Cf. **Fiktion.** **Phantasiebild,** phantasy image. Cf. **Bild.** **Phantasieinhalt,** phantasy-content. **phantasieren,** to phantasy (not in OED, which reports that the relevant sense of "fancy" ⟨BG⟩ is obs.), (*imaginer* ⟨R⟩). Cf. **einbilden, fingieren, sich denken** (*sub* denken), **sich hineindenken** (*sub* hineindenken), **vorstellen 2.** **phantasierend,** phantasying, (*imageant* ⟨R⟩).

phantasiert, phantasied, (*imaginé* ⟨R⟩), (*imaginaire* ⟨R⟩). Not "fancyshaped" ⟨BG⟩. Cf. **erdenklich.** **Phantasiesichtigkeit,** something in phantasy, (*aperçu de l'imagination* ⟨R⟩). **Phantasiesinn,** sense of the phantasy, (*sens de l'imagination* ⟨R⟩). Cf. **Erinnerungssinn, Wahrnehmungssinn.** **Phantasiewelt,** world of phantasy, (*monde de l'imaginaire* ⟨R⟩). Cf. **Erinnerungswelt.** | **blosse** —, world of mere phantasy. **Phantasma,** phantasma (pl. -as or -ata), (*phantasma* ⟨R⟩). Cf. **Urphantasma.** **phantastisch,** | **∼e Modifikation,** phantasy modification. **philosophisch** ⟨adj.⟩, philosophic ⟨WH 1⟩, philosophical ⟨WH 2, L⟩, of the philosophic sort. | **∼e Wissenschaft,** science of the philosophic sort. **Phoronomie,** phoronomy, kinematics, (*cinématique* ⟨R⟩). **physikalisch** ⟨adj.⟩, of physics, pertaining to physics, (*physicaliste* ⟨B⟩), as conceived (*or* determined) in physics, (*selon la physique* ⟨R⟩), in the manner peculiar to physics, dealt with in physics, implicit in physics, (*physique* ⟨R⟩). Save "physical" ⟨WH 1, MS 1, BG⟩ for "physisch". | **∼e Bestimmung,** determination by means of concepts peculiar to physics, (*détermination physique* ⟨R⟩). Not "physical determination" ⟨BG⟩. | **∼es Ding,** physical thing as determined in physics, (*chose selon la physique* ⟨R⟩), (*chose physique* ⟨R⟩). Not just "physical thing" ⟨BG⟩. Cf. **Ding.**

physikalisch exakt ⟨adj.⟩, as having the exactness ascribed in physics. Not "physically exact" ⟨L⟩.
physisch, physical ⟨WH 1, MS 1⟩, (*physique* ⟨B⟩), of the physical, of something physical. Cf. dinglich. | ~e Erfahrung, experience of something physical, (*expérience physique* ⟨B⟩). Not "physical experience" ⟨L⟩. | ~es Phänomen, phenomenon of something physical. | ~e Sphäre, sphere of the physical, (physical sphere ⟨L⟩).
pointieren, to express pointedly ⟨WH 2⟩, to emphasize.
Pointierung, emphasis.
Polarisierung, polarity, (*polarisation* ⟨B⟩).
polythetisch, polythetic (*polythétique* ⟨R⟩). Cf. thetisch.
Position, positing ⟨Bn⟩, position ⟨WH 1, MS 1⟩, (*position (au sens strict)* ⟨B⟩). Cf. Setzen, Setzung, Stellung, Stellungnahme, Thesis.
Positivität, positiveness, positivity, (*positivité* ⟨B⟩).
(Postulat), 1. (Forderung:) requirement, demand ⟨MS 1⟩.
2. (math): postulate ⟨WH 1⟩.
prädikativ, predicative ⟨MS 1, BG⟩, (*prédicatif* ⟨R, B⟩), predicational, as a predicate. | ~e Wahrheit, predicational truth.
prädizieren, to predicate; to assert. Cf. aussagen, behaupten, erkennendprädizierend, feststellen, meinen, zusprechen.
prägnant, strict, (*qui est pris au sens fort* ⟨B⟩), (*fort* ⟨R, B⟩), (*par excellence* ⟨B⟩). Not "meaningfull" ⟨BG⟩, nor "pregnant" ⟨WH 1, MS 1, BG⟩.
Prägung, stamp, version. Cf. Wendung.
präjudizieren, to prejudge ⟨MS 1, WH 2⟩, (*préjuger* ⟨PL, B⟩) ; to presuppose. | — für, to make an advance judgment in favor of; to make it certain in advance that.
Praktik, theory of practice, practice ⟨MS 1⟩, (*pratique* ⟨B⟩), action, theory of action. Cf. Praxis.
praktisch ⟨adj.⟩, practical ⟨WH 1, MS

1⟩, (*pratique* ⟨B⟩), produced by practice.
praktisch ⟨adv.⟩, practically, (*du point de vue pratique* ⟨B⟩), (*dans la perspective pratique* ⟨B⟩), in practice, as a basis for practice. Cf. erkenntnispraktisch ⟨adv.⟩.
Präsenz, present; presence ⟨MS 1⟩. Cf. Bewusstseinspräsenz, Gegenwart, Gegenwärtigkeit, Vorhandensein.
Präsumption, (*pré-somption* ⟨de M⟩).
prätendieren, to claim ⟨MS 2⟩, (*prétendre* ⟨R⟩). Cf. den Anspruch erheben (*sub* Anspruch).
prätendiert ⟨adj.⟩, ostensible, (*prétendu* ⟨B⟩).
prätendiert ⟨adv.⟩, ostensibly.
Prätention, claim ⟨WH 2, MS 2⟩, (*présumé* ⟨B⟩), (*prétention* ⟨B⟩), (*pré-tention* ⟨de M⟩). Cf. Anspruch, Erkenntnisprätention.
Praxis, (*praxis* ⟨B⟩), practice ⟨WH 1, MS 1⟩, realm of practice, (action), (*discipline pratique* ⟨PL⟩). Cf. Einzelpraxis, Praktik.
Primitivität, primitiveness.
prinzipiell ⟨adj.⟩, fundamental, of fundamentals, essential, fundamentally essential, radical, eidetically necessary, absolute, in principle ⟨MS 2⟩, as a principle, (as) concerned with principles, of principles, (*de principe* ⟨R, B⟩), (*par principe* ⟨B⟩), (*principiel* ⟨B⟩), (fundamental essential), (essentially necessary), ((eidetically) universal), (pertaining to principles), (pertaining to the highest (*or* the most radical) universalities and necessities ⟨Ideen I, 96⟩). Cf. wesensmässig ⟨adj.⟩, wesentlich ⟨adj.⟩. | ~e Allgemeinheit, fundamental (*or* absolute) universality, universality (of something) as concerned with principles, (*généralité principielle* ⟨B⟩). | ~e Allgemeinheiten, the universality of principles. | ~e Analyse, fundamental analysis. | ~e Ausgestaltung, fundamental development. | ~e Besinnung, investigation of (the) essential sense. Cf. Besinnung. | ~e Definition, fundamental definition. | ~e Di-

mension, fundamental dimension. |
~e **Eigentümlichkeit,** radical pe-
culiarity, (*caractères essentiels*
⟨R⟩). | ~e **Einsicht,** insight into
principles, (*évidence principielle*
⟨B⟩). Cf. **Einsicht.** | ~e **Einseitig-
keit,** essential one-sidedness. | ~e
Erörterung, fundamental treatment.
Cf. **Erörterung.** | ~e **Form,** form as
a principle; essential form. | ~e
Grundlagensphäre, sphere of eideti-
cally necessary fundamentals. | ~e
Klärung, fundamental clarification,
(*clarification principielle* ⟨B⟩). | ~er
Kontrast, fundamental contrast,
(*contraste principiel* ⟨B⟩). | ~e **Kri-
tik,** radical criticism. | ~e **Leitung,**
fundamental guidance. | ~e **Metho-
de,** fundamental method, essential
method. | ~e **Möglichkeit,** essential
possibility, (in principle the possibil-
ity), (*possibilité de principe* ⟨R⟩). | ~e
Neugestaltung, fundamental re-
fashioning. | ~es **Organon,** essential
organon. | ~e **Probleme,** fundamen-
tally essential problems. | ~e
Rechtfertigung, fundamental justi-
fication. Cf. **Rechtfertigung.** | ~er
Sinn, fundamental sense, essential
sense, (*sens principiel* ⟨B⟩). | ~e
Sonderung, essential separation. |
~e **Struktureinsichten,** insights that
grasp the essential structure, (*évi-
dences structurelles principielles* ⟨B⟩).
Cf. **Einsicht.** | ~es **Thema,** funda-
mental theme, (*thème principiel*
⟨B⟩). | ~e **Verantwortlichkeit,** radi-
cal responsibility. Cf. **verantwort-
lich.** | ~e **Verwurzelung,** rooted-
ness in principles. | ~e **Wissen-
schaftslehre,** theory of science, con-
cerned with principles. | ~e **Ziele,**
essential goals. Cf. **Ziel.** | das P~e,
the fundamental essentials, radical
universalities and necessities, principles, the matter of principles, (*le
caractère principiel* ⟨B⟩). | dem
P~en nach, essentially, (*par principe* ⟨R⟩).
prinzipiell ⟨adv.⟩, fundamentally, (*fon-
damentalement* ⟨B⟩), essentially, by
(*or* according to) its essential nature,

necessarily, by essential (*or* eidetic)
necessity, on radical principles, according to principles, radically, on
principle ⟨WH 1, MS 1⟩, (*principiel-
lement* ⟨B⟩), (*d'une manière principielle* ⟨B⟩), (*par principe* ⟨R⟩). Not
"in principle" ⟨BG⟩. Cf. **wesensmäs-
sig** ⟨adv.⟩, **wesentlich** ⟨adv.⟩. | —
anders, fundamentally and essential-
ly different. | — **ausgeschaltet,** ex-
cluded on principle. | — **begründet,**
grounded on radical principles. Cf.
begründet. | — **betrachtet,** consider-
ed fundamentally. | — **eigenartig,**
essentially unique. | — **einheitlich,**
essentially unitary. Cf. **einheitlich.** |
— **evident,** radically evident, (*prin-
cipiellement évident* ⟨B⟩). | — **ge-
klärt,** fundamentally clarified, (*cla-
rifié d'une manière principielle* ⟨B⟩). |
— **im Unendlichen liegen,** to lie
necessarily at infinity. | — **möglich,**
essentially possible. | — **neuartig,** of
a radical novel sort. | — **nicht ne-
gierbar,** essentially incapable of
being negated. | — **nicht zugäng-
lich,** essentially inaccessible. | — **un-
abhängig,** necessarily independant. |
— **unerkennbar,** essentially un-
cognizable, essentially unknowable.
| — **unterschieden,** essentially differ-
entiated, (*distingué de façon princi-
pielle* ⟨B⟩). | — **wahrnehmbar,** es-
sentially perceivable. | — **zu recht-
fertigen,** to justify according to
principles. | sich — **scheiden,** to be
set apart essentially.
Prinzipienfrage, | die logischen ~n,
the questions that concern the
principles of logic, (*les questions lo-
giques des principes* ⟨B⟩).
Problematik, problems, (*problèmes*
⟨PL⟩), set (*or* complex, *or* field, *or*
sequence) of problems, problem,
(problematic(s) ⟨not in OED⟩),
(*problématique* ⟨R, B⟩), (*position des
problèmes* ⟨PL⟩), (inquiry ⟨?⟩). Not
"form of inquiry" ⟨BG⟩.
Problemgliederung, differentiation of
problems. Cf. **Gliederung.**
Problemlinie, line of inquiry.
Problemsphäre, | unbequeme　　—,

sphere of uncomfortable problems, (*ensemble de problèmes gênants* ⟨R⟩). **Problemstellung,** setting (of) a (*or* the) problem, manner of setting a (*or* the) problem, inquiry. Not "problematization" ⟨L⟩. Cf. **ein Problem stellen** (*sub* **stellen**), **Fragestellung, Stellung.**
psychisch ⟨adj.⟩, psychic ⟨WH 1, MS 1⟩, (*psychique* ⟨B⟩), of the psychic.

Cf. **geistig, seelisch.** | ∼**e Sphäre,** sphere of the psychic, psychic sphere. | **P** ∼**es,** something psychic. | ∼**es Gebilde,** psychically produced formation, (*formation psychique* ⟨B⟩), psychic product; Cf. **Gebilde. psychologisch,** psychological ⟨WH 1, MS 1⟩, of psychology. | ∼**e Sphäre,** sphere of psychology, (*sphère psychologique* ⟨R, B⟩).

Q

qualitativ, qualitative; qualitied. | ∼**e Konfiguration,** qualitied configuration.
quantitätslos, non-quantitative.
Quasi-nachsprechen, following in a quasi-speaking, (*quasi-répétition* ⟨B⟩). Cf. **Nachsprechen.**
Quelle, source ⟨MS 1, WH 3⟩, (*source*

⟨R, B⟩), (*principium* ⟨Wolff⟩). Cf. **Erfahrungsquelle, Erkenntnisquelle, Sinnesquelle, Urquelle, Ursprung.** | **aus** ∼**n der,** by virtue of sources in (*or* belonging to), (*aux* (ou *à partir de*) *sources de* ⟨B⟩).
Quellpunkt, source-point.

R

Radikalismus, radicalness, (*radicalisme* ⟨PL, B⟩). Not "radicalism" ⟨MS 1⟩. Cf. **Relativismus.**
Rahmen, frame ⟨WH 1, MS 1⟩, (*cadre* ⟨R, B⟩), outer frame, boundary, boundaries, bounds ⟨WH⟩, limits ⟨BG⟩, (*limites* ⟨R⟩), sphere. Cf. **Bereich, Grenze, Kreis, Umfang.**
Rätsel, enigma ⟨WH 3, MS 3, BG⟩, (*énigme* ⟨R, B⟩). Not "riddle" ⟨WH 1, MS 1⟩. Cf. **unverständlich.**
Raum, space ⟨WH 2, MS 2⟩, (*espace* ⟨R⟩); room ⟨WH 1, MS 1⟩.
Raumanschauung, intuition of space; (natural-scientific:) view of space. Cf. **Anschauung, Zeitanschauung.**
Raumding, spatial thing ⟨BG⟩, (*chose spatiale* ⟨R⟩). Cf. **Ding.**
Raumgebilde, spatial formation, (*configuration spatiale* ⟨B⟩). Cf. **Gebilde.**
Raumgestalt, spatial shape, (*forme spatiale* ⟨B⟩). Cf. **Gestalt.**
Raumgestaltung, spatial formation, (*figure spatiale* ⟨R⟩). Cf. **Gestaltung.**
Raumwirklichkeit, (realm of) spatial actuality, (*réalité spatiale* ⟨R⟩).

real ⟨adj.⟩, real ⟨Bn, WH 1, MS 4, BG⟩, (*réel* ⟨R, B⟩), of the real, with respect to something real, in something real, (*naturel* ⟨B⟩). Cf. **irreal, reell, wirklich.** | **ein R** ∼**es,** something real, (*une réalité naturelle* ⟨R⟩). | **im** ∼**en Sinne,** really, in the sense of realities. Cf. **reell** ⟨adj.⟩. | **Ontologie im** ∼**en Sinne,** ontology in the real sense, ontology of realities, (*ontologie au sens réel* ⟨B⟩). Cf. **Realontologie.** | ∼**e Bedeutung,** significance with respect to what is real. | ∼**e Immanenz,** immanence in something real. Cf. **Immanenz, reelle Immanenz** (*sub* **reell**). | **R** ∼**es,** real, reality, (*réalité* ⟨R⟩).
Realisierung, reification; realization ⟨MS 1⟩, (*réalisation* ⟨B⟩). Cf. **verdinglichen, Verwirklichung.**
Realitätsauffassung, apprehension of something as a reality. Cf. **Auffassung.**
Realontologie, ontology of realities, (*ontologie "réelle"* ⟨B⟩). Cf. **Ontologie im realen Sinne** (*sub* **real**).

Realwissenschaft, science of realities, (*science du réel* ⟨R⟩). Cf. **Idealwissenschaft.**

Rechenkonvention, computational convention, (*convention de calcul* ⟨B⟩).

rechnen, to compute ⟨WH, MS⟩, (*computer* ⟨B⟩), to calculate ⟨WH, MS⟩, (*calculer* ⟨B⟩).

Rechnen, reckoning ⟨WH 1⟩. Cf. **Verrechnen.**

rechnerisch, computational ("rare"— OED), (*dans le calcul* ⟨B⟩). Cf. **kalkulatorisch.**

Rechnung, reckoning ⟨WH 1⟩, computation ⟨WH 3⟩, (calculus ⟨Bn⟩).

recht ⟨adj.⟩, right ⟨WH 1, MS 1⟩, (*juste* ⟨B⟩), rightful, due ⟨WH⟩, (*convenable* ⟨B⟩), true ⟨WH⟩, correct ⟨WH, MS⟩, (*exact* ⟨B⟩). Cf. **rechtmässig, richtig, schluss(ge)-recht.**

Recht, 1. legitimacy, (*légitimité* ⟨B⟩), right ⟨WH 1, MS 1⟩, (*droit* ⟨R, B, de M⟩), justness, justice ⟨WH, MS⟩, rightness; competence ⟨MS⟩, (*autorité* ⟨R⟩).
2. law ⟨WH, BG⟩, (*droit* ⟨R⟩). Save "justification" ⟨L⟩ for "Berechtigung" ⟨q.v.⟩, "Gerechtigkeit" ⟨q.v.⟩, and "Rechtfertigung" ⟨q.v.⟩. Cf. **Eigenrecht, Richtigkeit, Unrecht.** | **ein ihm eigenes** —, a competence of its own. Not "an independent right of its own" ⟨BG⟩. Cf. **eigen.** | **mit** —, legitimately ⟨WH 1⟩, rightly ⟨WH, MS⟩, justly, with a legitimacy.

rechtausweisend, that shows legitimacy. Cf. **ausweisen.**

rechtfertigen, to justify ⟨WH 1, MS 1⟩, (*justifier* ⟨B⟩), to vindicate ⟨WH, MS⟩.

Rechtfertigung, justification ⟨Bn, WH 1, MS 1⟩, (*justification* ⟨B⟩), (*légitimation* ⟨B⟩), (*justification intuitive* ⟨de M⟩), vindication, (verification). Cf. **Berechtigung, Bewährung, Gerechtigkeit.**

rechtgebend, legitimating, that legiti-

mates, (*qui fonde le droit* ⟨B⟩), (*justificateur* ⟨B⟩). Cf. **ausweisen.**

Rechtgebung, legitimation. Cf. **Ausweisung, Begründung, Berechtigung, Rechtsprechung.**

rechtmässig ⟨adj.⟩, right, legitimate ⟨WH 2, MS 4⟩, (*légitime* ⟨PL, B⟩), (*legitimus* ⟨K⟩), (*ayant une légitimité* ⟨B⟩), (legitimated), rightful ⟨WH 4, MS 3⟩. Cf. **berechtigt, echt, gesetzmässig, recht, richtig, unrechtmässig.**

Rechtsanspruch, claim. Cf. **Anspruch.**

Rechtsausweisung, legitimation, (proof of legitimacy ⟨L⟩). Cf. **Ausweisung.**

Rechtsentscheidung, adjudication ⟨?⟩.

Rechtsfrage, question about (*or* of ⟨L⟩) legitimacy, (*question du droit* ⟨B⟩).

Rechtsgrund, legitimizing basis, (*fondement de la légitimité* ⟨B⟩), legitimate (*or* legitimizing) ground. Save "justification" ⟨L⟩ for "Berechtigung" ⟨q.v.⟩, "Gerechtigkeit" ⟨q.v.⟩, and "Rechtfertigung" ⟨q.v.⟩. Cf. **Grund.**

Rechtssprechung, legitimation, (*juridication* ⟨R⟩). Cf. **Begründung, Berechtigung, Rechtgebung.**

Rede, 1. speech ⟨WH 1, MS 1⟩, (*langage* ⟨B⟩), discourse ⟨WH, MS⟩, (*discours* B⟩), (pregnant sense ⟨LU, I. Unters. *33, l. 9*⟩:) conversation ⟨WH, MS⟩. Cf. **Sprache, Wechselrede.** | **das, wovon die** — **ist,** that which is spoken of (*or* about), (*ce dont il est question* ⟨B⟩), the theme. Cf. **Thema.** | **einsame** —, soliloquy. Cf. **Wechselrede.** | **in** — **stehend,** referred to (in speaking). | **lebendige** —, actual conversation. Cf. **lebendig.** | **monologische** —, soliloquy.
2. locution, (*expression* ⟨R, B⟩), phraseology, parlance, manner of speaking, (word), (term), (*terme* ⟨B⟩), (*dénomination* ⟨B⟩), (phrase); statement ⟨BG⟩, (*énoncé* ⟨R⟩). Cf. **Aussage, Terminus, Wendung, Wunschrede.** | **die alte** —, the old phraseology. | **die Einheit der** (*oder* einer) —, the unity of the (*or* a) locution. | **die ganze** —, the entire locution. | **die geredete** —, the

spoken locution. | **die jeweilige** —, the locution used on the particular occasion. | **die** —, **dass**, the statement that ⟨BG⟩. | **die** — **von**, (*le terme de* ⟨R⟩), (use of) the word(s) (*or* the phrase), (*usage du mot* ⟨R⟩), (*le mot*⟨R⟩), speaking of, to speak of, (verbal) reference to, (*l'expression de* ⟨B⟩) ⟨R⟩), (statements about). | **die** — **von Sollen**, should-statements. | **eine grössere** —, a more extensive locution. | **in der** —, in the locution. | **in der logischen** —, in logical parlance, (*en s'exprimant d'une manière logique* ⟨B⟩). | **relative** —, relative term, (*expression relative* ⟨B⟩). | **traditionelle** —, traditional phraseology, (*langage traditionnel*⟨B⟩). | **wissenschaftliche** ∼**n**, scientific locutions.

reden, speaking ⟨WH 1, MS 1⟩, to speak, (*parler* ⟨B⟩). | **Vermögen des R**∼**s**, ability to speak.
Redezusammenhang, context. Cf. **Zusammenhang.**
reell ⟨adj.⟩, (ant. ideell:) real ⟨WH, BG⟩, (*réel* ⟨R, B⟩), genuine ⟨WH⟩; really immanent, really intrinsic. Cf. **echt, innere, irreell, real, wirklich.** | ∼**e Analyse**, analysis into real parts (*or* real components), analysis into really immanent parts, (*analyse réelle* ⟨R, B⟩). | ∼**e Immanenz**, real immanence, (*immanence réelle* ⟨B⟩). Cf. **Immanenz, reale Immanenz** (*sub* **real** ⟨adj.⟩).
reell ⟨adv.⟩, really, (*à titre réel* ⟨R⟩). Cf. **im realen Sinn** (*sub* **real** ⟨adv.⟩).
Referat, (*objet de référence* ⟨R⟩).
Referent, (*centre de référence* ⟨R⟩).
reflektierend ⟨adj.⟩, (sometimes:) reflectively grasped.
reflektierend ⟨adv.⟩, reflectively, (*par réflexion* ⟨R⟩).
reflektiert, reflected on (*or* upon) ⟨BG⟩, (*réfléchi* ⟨R⟩), reflectively modified ⟨see Ideen, I, § 78⟩, reflective. Cf. **unreflektiert.**
reflektiv ⟨adj.⟩, reflective, reflectional. Cf. **reflexiv.**
Reflexion, reflection ⟨WH 1, MS⟩, (*réflexion* ⟨B⟩), act of reflection, (re-

flective focusing); (physical only ⟨MEU⟩:) reflexion ⟨MS⟩. Cf. **Besinnung, Sinnesreflexion.** | **subjektive** — **auf Einsicht**, reflection on subjective insight, (*réflexion subjective sur l'évidence rationelle* ⟨B⟩). Cf. **Einsicht.**
Reflexionsthematik, reflective thematizing (activity). Cf. **Thematik.**
reflexiv, reflective, (*réflexif* ⟨B⟩). Not "reflexive" ⟨WH 1, MS 1, BG⟩. Cf. **reflektiert, reflektiv.**
Regelmässigkeit, regularity ⟨WH 1, MS 1, L⟩. Cf. **Regelung.**
regeln, (*régler* ⟨B⟩), to govern; to ascertain rules for. Cf. **beherrschen, geregelt.**
Regelordnung, regular order ⟨ ? ⟩, (*ordre et régulation* ⟨R⟩). Cf. **Ordnung.**
Regelung, regulation ⟨WH 1, MS 1⟩, (*régulation* ⟨R⟩), (governing) rule(s), (*règle qui ordonne* ⟨R⟩); regularity. Not "norm" ⟨L⟩. Cf. **Regelmässigkeit.** | ∼**en absoluter Erlebnisse**, regularities of absolute mental processes, (*règles qui ordonnent les vécus absolus* ⟨R⟩). Cf. **Erlebnis.**
Regung, stirring ⟨MS 1, WH⟩, (*amorce* ⟨R⟩). Cf. **Aktregung, anregen, Erregung.**
Reich, realm, (*domaine* ⟨B⟩), (*règne* ⟨B⟩), (*pouvoir* ⟨R⟩). Not "republic" ⟨Lipps trln of Hume, quoted in LU, II. Unters.⟩. Cf. **Bereich, Gebiet.**
rein ⟨adj.⟩, pure ⟨MS 1, WH⟩. | **der** ∼**e Logiker**, the logician busied with pure logic. | ∼**e Reduktion**, reduction to purity.
rein-grammatisch, of pure grammar, (purely grammatical), (*grammatical pur* ⟨B⟩). Cf. **grammatisch.**
Reinheit, | **in der phänomenologischen** —, (at least sometimes:) purely phenomenologically, (*dans sa pureté phénoménologique* ⟨R⟩).
rein(-)logisch, of pure logic, pertaining to pure logic, (*pure logique* ⟨B⟩), (*logique pure* ⟨B⟩). Cf. **analytisch-logisch, apophantisch-logisch, formallogisch, logisch.** | ∼**e Grammatik**, grammar of pure logic.
rein-logisch-grammatisch, in the

sphere of (*or* in accordance with) the grammar of pure logic, (*relevant de* (ou *conformement à*) *la grammaire pure logique* ⟨B⟩). Cf. **grammatisch, logisch.**

Reiz, stimulus ⟨WH⟩.

rekurrieren auf, to have recourse to, (*avoir recours à* ⟨B⟩), to resort to, (*revenir à* ⟨B⟩), to fall back on, to appeal to.

Relation, relational complex; relationship ⟨MS⟩, (*relation* ⟨B⟩). Cf. **Beziehung, Komplexion, Verhalt, Verhältnis, Zusammenhang.**

Relationalität, the category of relationships, relationality.

Relationsprädikat, relationship-predicate, (*prédicat de relation* ⟨B⟩).

relativ ⟨adj.⟩, relative ⟨WH 1, MS 1⟩, (*relatif* ⟨B⟩); (grammar, sometimes:) relatival, (*de relation* ⟨B⟩); comparative. | ~**es Prädikat,** relatival predicate, (*prédicat de relation* ⟨B⟩).

relativ ⟨adv.⟩, relatively, (*d'une manière relative* ⟨B⟩), as relative, comparatively. | — **nehmen,** to take as relative.

Relativismus, (sometimes:) relativeness. Cf. **Radikalismus.**

Relativsatz, relative clause ⟨WH 1⟩, (*proposition relative* ⟨B⟩). Cf. **Satz 2.**

Relativum, relative, (*terme de relation* ⟨B⟩), (*adjectif de relation* ⟨B⟩).

reproduktiv ⟨adj.⟩, 1. (noetic or noematic:) reproductional, (*réproductif* ⟨R⟩).
2. (noetic only:) reproductive.

reproduktiv ⟨adv.⟩, in reproduction.

Restitution, restoration, (*restitution* ⟨B⟩).

(Restmethode), method of residues ⟨Bn⟩.

richten, Cf. **gerichtet, Richtung.** | — **an,** (of words:) to address to ⟨WH 1, MS⟩. | — **auf,** to direct to ⟨WH, MS⟩, to direct toward(s), (*diriger vers* ⟨B⟩), to aim at ⟨WH⟩, (to point at ⟨WH⟩). Cf. **Gerichtsein auf.** | — **nach,** to adjust to ⟨MS 1⟩, (*diriger vers* ⟨B⟩). Cf. **orientieren.** | **sich** — **auf,** 1. (of persons:) to direct oneself to, (*se diriger sur* ⟨R⟩); (to attend

to); to direct oneself toward(s) ⟨BG⟩, (*se diriger vers* ⟨R⟩).
2. (of processes or things:) to be directed to (*or* toward), (*s'appliquer sur* ⟨R⟩). | **sich** — **nach,** to be adjusted (*or* to adjust itself) to, to be governed by ⟨WH, MS⟩, (*se régler sur* ⟨B⟩), (to conform with ⟨WH, MS⟩), (*se conformer à* ⟨B⟩), (to depend on ⟨WH, MS⟩).

Richten, adjustment ⟨MS 1⟩. Cf. **Richtung.**

richtig, correct ⟨MS 2, WH⟩, valid, right, (*juste* ⟨B⟩), (*exact* ⟨B⟩). Cf. **Berichtigung, recht, rechtmässig, schlussrichtig, unrichtig.** | ~**er Einwand,** valid objection.

Richtigkeit, correctness ⟨WH, MS⟩, rightness ⟨WH 1, MS 1⟩, (*justesse* ⟨B⟩). Cf. **Recht, Unrichtigkeit, Urteilsrichtigkeit.**

Richtigkeitsausweisung, showing of (the) correctness. Cf. **Ausweisung.**

Richtlinien, guiding lines.

Richtung, adjustment ⟨MS 1⟩, (orientation); direction ⟨WH 1, MS, L, BG⟩, (*direction* ⟨R, B⟩), directedness, (bent ⟨WH, MS⟩), tendency, (*tendance* ⟨PL⟩), (interest), line (of thought) ⟨WH, MS⟩; dimension, side. Cf. **Anschauungsrichtung, Blickrichtung, Denkrichtung, Einstellung, Erfüllungsrichtung, gerichtet, Gerichtetsein, Orientierung, Seite, richten, Willensrichtung.** | **gegenständliche** —, directedness (*or* direction) to something objective, (objective reference). | **in subjektiver** —, on the subjective side, (*dans la direction subjective* ⟨B⟩). | **in thematischer** — **auf etwas,** when one directs oneself to something as one's theme. Cf. **sich richten auf** (*sub* richten). | — **auf,** directedness to, (*direction vers* ⟨B⟩), interest in. | — **auf etwas haben,** to be directed to something. | — **einer Thematik,** direction of a thematizing activity.

Richtungslinie, line of direction ⟨WH 1, MS 1⟩.

rot, (adjectival:) red, (*rouge* ⟨B⟩).

Röte, redness ⟨WH 1, MS 1⟩, (*rougeur* ⟨B⟩).

Rückbesinnung, (retrospection ⟨?⟩). Cf. **Besinnung.**

Rückbeziehung, backward relation, backward relating, reflex(ive) relation, relation to something antecedent, backward reference, (reference backward), (*rétro-référence* ⟨R⟩), (*caractère référentiel* ⟨B⟩). Cf. **Beziehung.** | — **auf,** relation back to ⟨L⟩.

Rückbezogenheit, backward relatedness, reflexiveness, relation. Cf. **Beziehung, Bezogenheit, Verhältnis.**

Rückerinnerung, (*rétro-souvenir* ⟨R⟩). Cf. **Erinnerung, Vorerinnerung, Wiedererinnerung.**

Rückfrage, inquiry back, regressive inquiry, asking back, retrospective inquiry. Cf. **Frage, zurückfragen.**

Rückführung, tracing back, carrying back. Save "reduction" for "Reduktion".

Rückgang, going back, (*retour* ⟨PL, B⟩), resort, recourse, regress ⟨WH 2⟩, regression, retrogression ⟨WH 1, MS⟩, recurrence (to); resorting.

Rückkehr, reversion ⟨WH⟩, (*régression* ⟨B⟩).

(Rückschlag), reversion ⟨Bn⟩.

Rückschluss, inference. Cf. **Schluss 3.**

Rückseite, back ⟨WH 1, MS 1⟩, rear (aspect). Cf. **Seite, Vorderseite.**

Rückverwandlung, reconversion, (*retour* ⟨B⟩). Cf. **Verwandlung.**

Rückweis auf, pointing back to.

rückweisen auf, to point back to (*or* at). Cf. **weisen auf, zurückweisen auf.**

Rückweisung, pointing back, (*renvois* ⟨B⟩). Cf. **Weisung.** | **Hin- und —,** pointing back and forth.

S

Sachbeschaffenheit, merely material determination, (*propriété matérielle* ⟨R⟩). Cf. **Beschaffenheit.**

Sachbewusstsein, consciousness of a mere thing, (*conscience de chose* ⟨R⟩). Not "consciousness of a subject-matter" ⟨BG⟩.

sachbezüglich, related to subject-matter (*or* to affairs). Cf. **bezüglich, Sache.**

Sachbezüglichkeit, relatedness to subject-matter (*or* to affairs), (*référence aux choses* ⟨B⟩). Cf. **Bezüglichkeit, Sache.**

Sache, matter ⟨MS 1, WH 4, BG⟩, affair ⟨WH 5, MS 5⟩, (*affaire* ⟨B⟩), materially determinate affair, matter in question, (particularly as trln of pl.:) subject-matter ⟨BG⟩, thing, ⟨WH 1, MS 2, L, BG⟩, (*chose* ⟨R, B, de M⟩), (*res* ⟨K⟩), thing itself, mere thing, materially determinate thing, case, job ⟨WH⟩, (*tâche* ⟨R⟩), work ⟨WH⟩, undertaking, (*situation* ⟨B⟩). Cf. **Ding, Dinglichkeit, Einzelsache, Materie, Natursache, Sachbewusstsein, Sachvorstellen, Stoff, Tatsache,**

Verhältnis. | **blosse —,** mere thing, (*chose brute* ⟨R⟩), (*simple chose* ⟨R, B⟩). Not "mere fact" ⟨BG⟩, not "mere material" ⟨BG⟩. | **die ∼n selbst,** the things themselves.

Sachenwelt, world of mere things, (*monde des choses* ⟨R⟩). Not "world of facts and affairs" ⟨BG⟩.

sachfern, remote from things. Cf. **fern.**

Sachgebiet, material province, (*domaine concret* ⟨B⟩). Cf. **Gebiet, Sachsphäre.**

Sachgehalt, material content(s), (*contenu matériel* ⟨B⟩), (*teneur matérielle* ⟨B⟩), (*contenu concret* ⟨B⟩), (*teneur concrète* ⟨B⟩), (*se rapportant au concret* ⟨B⟩). Cf. **Gehalt.**

sachhaltig ⟨adj.⟩, with a material content, having (*or* that has) material content(s), (*ayant un contenu matériel* ⟨B⟩), materially filled (*or* determinate), material, (*matériel* ⟨B⟩), (*se référant aux choses* ⟨B⟩), (*déterminé concrètement* ⟨B⟩), (*concret* ⟨B⟩). Cf. **sachlich, stofflich.** | **∼e Form,** material form.

sachhaltig ⟨adv.⟩, materially, (*matériel-lement* ⟨B⟩).

Sachhaltigkeit, object with a material content, (*élément concret* ⟨B⟩).

Sachlage, state of affairs ⟨WH 1, MS 1⟩, situation ⟨BG⟩, (*situation* ⟨R, B⟩), concrete situation, how matters (*or* affairs *or* things) lie, lay of things, pre-syntactical state-of-affairs, (*propriété* ⟨R⟩). Not "whole matter" ⟨BG⟩. Cf. **Sachverhalt, Wesenslage, Zustand.**

sachlich ⟨adj.⟩, material ⟨WH, MS⟩, (*se rapportant aux choses* ⟨B⟩), ("*in re*" ⟨B⟩), (objective ⟨WH, MS⟩). (concrete ⟨?⟩), (*concret* ⟨B⟩). Cf. **gegenständlich, sachhaltig, stofflich, Versachlichung, vorstellig. | das S ∼e,** the material, (*ce qui est concret* ⟨B⟩). **| ∼e Evidentmachung,** process of making materially evident, (*processus qui rendent évident au contact des choses* ⟨B⟩). **| ∼e Geltung,** objective validity. Cf. **Geltung. | ∼er Zusammenhang,** (objective connexion between (*or* among) affairs (*or* affair-complexes); materially coherent whole, (*ensemble cohérent de choses* ⟨B⟩). Cf. **Zusammenhang.**

sachlich ⟨adv.⟩, materially, (*matérielle-ment* ⟨B⟩); (objectively).

Sachlichkeit, materiality, (*ensemble de choses* ⟨B⟩), (*chose* ⟨B⟩), (objectivity ⟨WH, MS⟩), (concreteness ⟨?⟩).

Sachsphäre, material sphere, (*sphère des choses* ⟨B⟩), (*sphère concrète* ⟨B⟩). Cf. **Sachgebiet.**

Sachverhalt, predicatively formed affair-complex, predicational complex of affairs, affair-complex, (particularly when equivalent to "Sachlage" ⟨q.v.⟩:) state of affairs ⟨MS 1, WH⟩ (hyphenated if ambiguous otherwise), (*état(-)de(-)choses* ⟨B⟩), (*état de chose* ⟨R⟩), facts ⟨WH 1⟩. Not "positive fact" ⟨BG⟩. Cf. **Gegensachverhalt, Relation, Sache, sachlicher Zusammenhang** (*sub* **Zusammenhang**), **Seinsverhalt, Urteilsverhalt, Verhalt, Wertsachverhalt, Wertverhalt, Wesenssachverhalt,**

Wesensverhalt, Wirklichkeitsver-halt.

Sachverhaltsmeinung, complex-of-affairs meaning, (*état des choses en tant qu'opinion* ⟨B⟩).

Sachvorstellen, (mental) objectivating of the mere thing, (*représentation de la chose* ⟨R⟩). Not "representation of the matter in question" ⟨BG⟩. Cf. **Sache, Vorstellen 1.**

Satz, 1. (Urteil:) proposition ⟨Bn; trln of Mill in LU II/1, Einl.; Ueberweg trln of Berkeley, quoted in LU II, Unters.; WH; MS; BG⟩, asserted proposition, thesis ⟨WH⟩, (*proposition* ⟨R, B⟩),
2. (grammar:) sentence ⟨WH 1, MS⟩, (*proposition (grammaticale)* ⟨B⟩); clause, (*phrase* ⟨B⟩).
3. (broad sense, Einheit von Sinn u. thetischem Charakter:) positum, (what is posited, as posited), (*proposition* ⟨R⟩). Not "position" ⟨BG⟩.
4. law.
5. (Lehrsatz:) theorem.
Cf. **Ansatz, Aussagesatz, Behauptungssatz, Folgesatz, gesetzt, Grundsatz, Nachsatz, Obersatz, Relativsatz, Satzfolge, These, Thesis, Untersatz, Urteilssatz, Vordersatz. | gesprochener —,** spoken sentence (*proposition parlée* ⟨B⟩). **| grammatischer —,** sentence, (*proposition grammaticale* ⟨B⟩). **| — des Widerspruches,** law of contradiction, (*principe de contradiction* ⟨B⟩), (*principium contradictionis*). **| sprachlicher —,** sentence.

Satzbedeutung, signification of the sentence.

Satzbegriff, | kategorialer —, concept of the categorial proposition, (*concept catégorial de proposition* ⟨B⟩).

Satzelement, propositional element, (*élément de la proposition* ⟨B⟩).

Satzfolge, sentence-sequence, (*suite de phrases* ⟨B⟩). Cf. **Folge 2 & 3.**

Satzform, proposition-form, (*forme de proposition* ⟨B⟩), (*forme propositionnelle* ⟨B⟩).

Satzganzes, propositional whole, (*totalité propositionnelle* ⟨B⟩).

Satzgebilde, propositional formation, (*formation propositionelle* ⟨B⟩). Cf. **Gebilde.**

Satzgedanke, propositional thought, (*pensée qui s'exprime par la phrase* ⟨B⟩).

Satzgeltung, acceptance of a proposition, (*validité d'une proposition* ⟨B⟩). Cf. **Geltung.**

Satzmaterie, proposition-material, (*matière d'une proposition* ⟨B⟩). Cf. **Materie.**

Satzsinn, | **kategorialer** —, sense of the categorial proposition, (*sens que peut avoir la proposition catégoriale* ⟨B⟩).

Satzzusammenhang, proposition-complex, (*enchaînement de propositions* ⟨B⟩); complex of sentences. Cf. **Zusammenhang.**

Schachtelung, encasement, (*emboîtement* ⟨R⟩). Cf. **einschachteln.**

Schachtelungsstufe, encasement-level, (*couche emboîtée dans une autre* ⟨R⟩). Cf. **Stufe.**

schaffen, to create ⟨MS 1, WH 3⟩, (*créer* ⟨B⟩), (*donner naissance à* ⟨B⟩), to make ⟨WH 1⟩, to produce ⟨WH 4, MS 5⟩, to bring about ⟨WH⟩, to contrive. Cf. **ergeben, erzeugen, herstellen, leisten, vollziehen.**

schalten, to rule ⟨WH, MS⟩. Cf. **beherrschen, walten.**

Schatten, (*ombre* ⟨R⟩).

Schattenbild, (*ombre* ⟨R⟩).

Schätzung, estimation, ⟨WH 1, MS 1⟩. Cf. **abschätzig, Grössenschätzen, Wertschätzung.**

Schau, seeing, (*vision* ⟨B⟩), viewing. Cf. **Blick, Erschauung, Wesensschau.**

schauen, to see ⟨WH 1, MS 1, BG⟩, (*voir* ⟨R⟩), to view ⟨MS⟩, to look ⟨WH 2, MS 5⟩. Cf. **absehen, auffassen, anschauen, betrachten, erschauen, herausschauen, mitgeschaut, nachschauen, sehen.**

Schauen, seeing, viewing. Cf. **Erschauung, Wesensschauen.**

schauend ⟨adv.⟩, seeingly. Save "intuitively" ⟨L⟩ for "anschaulich" ⟨q.v.⟩ and "intuitiv".

Schauung, seeing, (*vision* ⟨R⟩), viewing. Not "awareness" ⟨BG⟩. Save

"intuition" ⟨L⟩ for "Anschauung" ⟨q.v.⟩. Cf. **Einsehen, Erschauung, Sehen, Wesensschauung.**

scheiden, to separate ⟨MS 1, WH 2⟩; to distinguish ⟨L⟩, (*distinguer* ⟨B⟩). Cf. **abscheiden, kennzeichnen, unterscheiden.** | **sich** —, to become separated, (*se séparer* ⟨B⟩), to be set apart.

Scheidung, separation ⟨WH 1, MS 1⟩, (*séparation* ⟨B⟩), (*clivage* ⟨R⟩), distinction, (*distinction* ⟨B⟩), division, differentiation. Cf. **Abscheidung, Unterscheidung, Unterschied.**

Schein, illusion ⟨Kemp Smith trln of K; WH; BG⟩, (rarely:) semblance ⟨Bn, WH, MS⟩, (*semblant* ⟨PL⟩), (*simulacre* ⟨R⟩), (*apparence* ⟨B⟩). Not "seeming" ⟨BG⟩. Cf. **Sinnenschein, Täuschung, Trug.**

(Scheinbarkeit), (*versimilitudo* ⟨K⟩).

Scheinergebnis, illusory result. Not "apparent result" ⟨L⟩.

Schicht, stratum ⟨WH, MS⟩, (*couche* ⟨R, B⟩). Cf. **Oberschicht, Unterschicht.**

Schichtendisziplinen, strata-disciplines, (*stratification des disciplines* ⟨B⟩).

Schichtung, stratification ⟨WH, MS⟩, (*stratification* ⟨R, B⟩), distinction between strata. Cf. **Dreischichtung.**

schlechthin, pure and simple, purely and simply, (*pure(ment) et simple-(ment)* ⟨R, B⟩), taken simply ⟨BG⟩, simple, simply ⟨WH 1, MS 2⟩, (*tout simplement* ⟨B⟩), just, without restriction, without particularization, *per se*, unqualified, complete, absolutely. Cf. **Objekt-schlechthin, schlicht.**

schlechtweg, Equivalent to "schlechthin" ⟨q.v.⟩.

schlicht ⟨adj.⟩, unqualified, unmodified, simpliciter⟩ pure and simple, (*pur et simple* ⟨B⟩), (pure), (plain ⟨WH 1, BG⟩), (simple ⟨WH 2, MS 2⟩), (*simple* ⟨R⟩). Not "plain" where confusion with "clear" is possible. Not "sheer" ⟨BG⟩. So far as possible save "simple" for "einfach".

schlicht ⟨adv.⟩, (purely and) simply.

Not "plainly" ⟨BG⟩. Cf. **schlechthin.** | — **anschauend,** in a pure and simple intuition.

schliessen, 1. to conclude ⟨WH, MS⟩, (*conclure* ⟨B⟩), to draw a conclusion ⟨MS⟩, (*déduire* ⟨B⟩), to infer ⟨WH⟩, to argue ⟨WH, MS⟩, (to reason ⟨WH, MS⟩). 2. to close ⟨MS 1, WH 2⟩, (*fermer* ⟨B⟩). Cf. **ableiten, abschliessen, beschliessen, erschliessen 1, folgern, geschlossen.** | **in sich** —, to include, (*inclure* ⟨R⟩), to imply ⟨Gomperz trln of Mill, cited in LU, I. Unters.; WH; MS⟩. Cf. **beschliessen, einschliessen, nach sich ziehen** (*sub* **ziehen**).

Schliessen, concluding, (*déduire* ⟨B⟩), inferring, (*inférence* ⟨B⟩), (reasonning.). Cf. **Folgern.**

Schluss, 1. argument, implicative argument; (syllogism ⟨Br, WH, MS⟩); (*déduction* ⟨B⟩). 2. conclusion ⟨WH, MS⟩, (*conclusion* ⟨B⟩). 3. inference ⟨WH, MS⟩, (*consequentia* ⟨K⟩). Cf. **Beweis, Elementarschluss, Erfahrungsschluss, Fehlschluss, Folge, Folgerung, Folgesatz, (Kettenschluss), Rückschluss, Schlusssatz, Schlussurteil, Trugschluss, (Vernunftschluss), (Vorschluss), Wahrscheinlichkeitsschluss.** | **konsequenter** —, consequent argument. Cf. **konsequent.** | **unmittelbarer** —, immediate inference, (*consequentia immediata* ⟨K⟩). | **zum** —, in conclusion ⟨WH 1, MS 2⟩, finally ⟨WH, MS⟩.

Schlussart, mode of argument, mode of inference, mode of reasoning ⟨MS⟩, syllogistic figure ⟨K⟩. Cf. **Art, Schlussfigur, Schlussweise.**

Schlussergebnis, final result ⟨MS 1⟩, upshot ⟨WH 1, MS 2⟩.

(Schlussfehler), fallacy ⟨Bn⟩. Cf. **Fehlschluss.**

(Schlussfigur), syllogistic figure ⟨Bn⟩. Cf. **Schlussart.**

Schlussfolge, train (*or* course) of reasoning ⟨MS 1⟩; argument ⟨WH 1,

MS 2⟩, inference ⟨WH, MS⟩, conclusion ⟨WH, MS⟩. Cf. **Folge 1, Folgerung, Schlusskette, Schlussweise.**

Schlussfolgerung, Equivalent to Schlussfolge ⟨q.v.⟩.

Schlussform, argument-form, form of inference, (*forme de déduction* ⟨B⟩), form of conclusion, syllogistic form. Cf. **Beweisform.**

schluss(ge)recht, (formally) valid (in the logical sense), logical ⟨MS 2⟩, (consistent ⟨MS⟩), (conclusive ⟨MS 1⟩). Cf. **folgerecht, konsequent, recht.**

Schlusskette, chain of reasoning. Cf. **Schlussfolge(rung).**

(Schlussmodus), mode of inference ⟨Bn⟩, syllogistic mode (*or* mood) ⟨Bn⟩. Cf. **Schlussweise.**

Schlussprinzip, principle of inference.

Schlusspunkt, point of (its own) conclusion, (*point final* ⟨B⟩).

Schlussreihe, Equivalent to "Schlussfolge" ⟨MS⟩ ⟨q.v.⟩.

schlussrichtig, Equivalent to "schluss(ge)recht ⟨MS⟩ ⟨q.v.⟩. Cf. **richtig.**

Schlusssatz, (logic): conclusion, (*conclusio* ⟨K, Pf⟩), (conclusion-proposition), (*proposition-conclusion* ⟨B⟩). (grammar:) concluding (*or* closing) sentence. Cf. **Folgesatz, Schluss 2, Schlussurteil.**

Schlussurteil, conclusion, (*jugement déductif* ⟨B⟩). Cf. **Folgesatz, Folgeurteil, Schluss, Schlusssatz.**

Schlussverfahren, deductive procedure.

Schlussweise, mode of argument, mode of inference, (*mode de déduction* ⟨B⟩), inference, (*inférence* ⟨PL⟩). Cf. **Folgerung, Schlussart, Schlussfolge, Schlussfolgerung, Schlussmodus, Weise.**

schlusswidrig, inconsistent ⟨MS 1⟩, (logically) invalid ⟨MS 2⟩. Cf. **folgewidrig, inkonsequent.**

Schriftzeichen, written mark. Cf. **Zeichen.** | **hingeschriebenes** —, written mark.

Schwankung, vacillation ⟨WH, MS⟩, fluctuation ⟨Bn, WH, MS⟩.

Seele, psyche, (mind ⟨Bn, MS⟩), (soul ⟨WH 1, MS 1⟩), (*âme* ⟨R, B⟩). Cf. **Geist.**

Seelenleben, psychic life, (mental life ⟨WH 1⟩), (*vie de l'âme* ⟨B⟩).

seelenlos, inanimate ⟨WH, MS⟩ (in the proper sense), mindless.

seelisch, psychic ⟨WH 1, MS 1⟩, (mental). Not "psychological" ⟨WH⟩. Cf. **geistig, psychisch.**

Sehding, sight thing, thing that is an object of sight, visual thing. Cf. **Ding, Sinnending, Tastding.**

sehen, to see ⟨WH 1, MS 1, BG⟩, (*voir* ⟨R, B⟩), to behold ⟨WH, MS⟩. Cf. **absehen, einsehen, erschauen, schauen.**

Sehen, seeing ⟨MS 1, BG⟩, (*voir* ⟨B⟩). Save "vision" ⟨BG⟩ for "Gesicht" and "Einsicht" ⟨q.v.⟩. Cf. **Einsehen, Erschauung, Schauung.**

(Sehgrösse), apparent size ⟨Boring, 1942⟩.

seiend, existing, existent, (*existant* ⟨B⟩). Cf. **an sich seiend, daseiend, soseiend.** | **alles S∼e,** all (*or* everything) that exists; every existent, (*tout* (*être*) *existant* ⟨B⟩), everything existing. | **das S∼e,** what exists, the existent, (*l'existant* ⟨B⟩), (something existing), (*l'étant* ⟨B⟩), (*l'être* ⟨B⟩). Cf. **Zusammenseiendes.** | **ein S∼es,** something that exists, an existent. Cf. **ein Daseiendes** (*sub* **daseiend**). | **identisch S∼es,** (an) identical existent, (*existant identique* ⟨B⟩). | **S∼es,** something existent, an existent, (*un existant* ⟨B⟩), what is existent, what exists, (*l'existant* ⟨B⟩), (*un être* ⟨B⟩). Cf. **Zusammenseiendes.** | **weltlich S∼es,** a worldly existent, (*l'existant* "*mondain*" ⟨B⟩). | **weltlich S∼es überhaupt,** whatever exists as worldly, (*l'existant* "*mondain*" *en général* ⟨B⟩). Cf. **überhaupt.**

seiend-geltend, accepted as existing, (*dont l'existence est valable* ⟨B⟩). Cf. **geltend.**

sein, to be ⟨MS 1, WH 2⟩, (*être* ⟨R, B⟩), to have being, to exist ⟨MS⟩, (*exister* ⟨R, B⟩). Cf. **ausmachen, bestehen, gewesen.**

Sein, being ⟨Bn, MS 1, BG⟩, (*être* ⟨R, B, de M⟩), existence ⟨MS 2⟩, (existent ⟨?⟩ ⟨BG⟩). Cf. **An-sich-sein, Bestehen, Dasein, Eigensein, Existenz, Gewesenheit, Ich-sein, Mitsein, Sichtigsein, Sosein, Wesen, Wirklichsein.**

Seinsall, All of being, (*totalité de l'être* ⟨B⟩). Cf. **All.**

Seinsanspruch, something that claims being. Cf. **Anspruch.**

Seinsart, mode of being, (*manière d'être* ⟨B⟩), mode of existence. Cf. **Seinsweise.**

Seinsboden, field (*or* realm) of being; existing basis. Cf. **Boden.**

Seinscharakter, characteristic of being, (*caractère d'être* ⟨R⟩), being-characteristic. Not "character of Being" ⟨BG⟩; not "ontical character" ⟨BG⟩. Cf. **Charakter.**

Seinserkenntnis, cognition of being, (*connaissance de l'être* ⟨B⟩), ontological cognition. Cf. **Erkenntnis, Wesenserkenntnis.**

Seinsgeltung, acceptance of being (*or* existence), acceptance as being (*or* as existing), acceptance; existence-status, existential status, status; (existential positedness); existential validity; being-value, existence-value, (*valeur d'existence* ⟨B⟩). Cf. **Geltung, Wirklichkeitsgeltung.** | **in — bleiben,** to remain accepted as existent. Cf. **in Geltung bleiben** (*sub* **Geltung**). | **in — haben,** to accept as existent, (*accorder valeur d'existence* ⟨B⟩). Cf. **in Geltung haben** (*sub* **Geltung**). | **in — setzen,** to give acceptance to as existent, (*poser en accordant valeur d'existence* ⟨B⟩). Cf. **in Geltung setzen** (*sub* **Geltung**).

Seinsgenesis, genesis of (its) being, (*genèse d'être* ⟨B⟩).

Seinsgewissheit, certainty of (its) being, (*certitude de l'être* ⟨R⟩), certain existence (*or* being), existential certainty. Not "ontical certainty" ⟨BG⟩. Cf. **Gewissheit.**

Seinsglaube(n) ⟨masc.⟩, belief in existence (*or* being), (*croyance à l'être* ⟨B⟩). Cf. **Glaube(n)** ⟨masc.⟩.

Seinsglauben ⟨neut.⟩, believing (in existence *or* in being). Cf. **Glauben** ⟨neut.⟩. | **im** —, believingly, (*tandis qu'on croit en leur être* ⟨B⟩). Cf. **im Glauben** (*sub* **Glauben** ⟨neut.⟩).

Seinskonstitution, constitution of something existent, (*constitution de l'être* ⟨R⟩).

seinsmässig ⟨adv.⟩, as existent, (*du point de vue de l'être* ⟨B⟩).

Seinsmaterie, material of being, (*matière d'être* ⟨R⟩).

Seinsmeinung, something meant as being. Cf. **Meinung.**

Seinsmodalität, modality of being ⟨BG⟩, (*modalité d'être* ⟨R⟩). Not "ontical modality" ⟨BG⟩.

Seinsmöglichkeit, possibility of being, possible being. Cf. **Seinswirklichkeit.**

Seinsnotwendigkeit des A, necessity of the being (of something), (*nécessité d'être que possède l'A* ⟨R⟩).

Seinsobjekt, Object posited as existent, (*objet d'être* ⟨R⟩). Not "ontical object" ⟨BG⟩, not "object that is" ⟨BG⟩.

Seinsollen, should-be. Cf. **Sollen.**

Seinsordnung, order of being ⟨BG⟩, (*ordre d'êtres* (ou *des êtres*) ⟨R⟩). Not "ordered being" ⟨BG⟩. Cf. **Ordnung.**

Seinsphänomen, phenomenon of being.

seins-setzend, that posits being ⟨BG⟩, (*qui pose de l'être* ⟨R⟩).

Seinssetzung, positing of being (*or* existence), positing (of something) as being, existence-positing. Cf. **Daseinssetzung, Setzung.**

Seinssinn, being-sense, (*sens(-)d'être* ⟨B⟩), existence-sense, existential sense. Cf. **Wahrheitssinn.**

Seinssphäre, | transzendentale —, sphere of transcentental being.

Seinsstellungnahme, taking a position as to being, existential position. Cf. **Stellungnahme.**

Seinsverhalt, predicatively formed being-complex. Cf. **Verhalt.**

Seinsvorzug, precedence in respect of (its) being, (*privilège d'existence*).

Seinswahrheit, trueness of being, (*vérité de l'être* ⟨B⟩). Cf. **Urteilswahrheit, Wahrheit.**

Seinsweise, mode of being, (*mode d'être* ⟨R⟩), mode of existence. Cf. **Seinsart, Weise.**

Seinswirklichkeit, actuality of being, actual being. Cf. **Seinsmöglichkeit.** | transzendentale ∼en, actualities of transcental being.

Seite, side ⟨WH 1, MS 1, BG⟩, (*côté* ⟨B⟩), aspect ⟨WH⟩, direction, (of a solid:) face, standpoint, (*point de vue* ⟨R⟩). Cf. **Richtung, Rückseite, Vorderseite.** | stoffliche —, stuff-aspect, (*côté matériel* ⟨B⟩).

Selbigkeit, self-identity, (*identité* ⟨B⟩), self-sameness.

selbst, | "es —", "it itself", ("*cela lui-même*" ⟨B⟩). | "—", ((*la chose*) "*elle-même*" ⟨B⟩), (*en personne* ⟨B⟩). | **S** ∼, self ⟨WH 1, MS, BG⟩, (*ipséité* ⟨R, de M⟩), It-Itself, (*soi-même* ⟨R, B⟩), affair (*or* objectivity) itself.

Selbstabwandlung, self-variation. Cf. **Abwandlung.**

selbständig, selfsufficient, (*indépendant* ⟨R, B⟩). Not "independent" ⟨WH 1⟩. Cf. **eigenständig** ⟨adj.⟩, **für sich, unabhängig, unselbständig, verselbständigen.**

Selbstaufhebung, self-annulment.

Selbstbeobachtung, self-observation, (*introspection* ⟨R⟩). Not "introspection" ⟨WH 1, L⟩. Cf. **Beobachtung.**

Selbstbesinnung, (meditative) self-examination, investigation of its own sense, reflective sense-investigation, self-investigation, reflective meditation, (self-clarification), (clarification of its own sense), (*retour sur soi-même* ⟨PL⟩), (*prise de conscience de soi-même* ⟨B⟩). Cf. **Besinnung.**

Selbstbildung, shaping of something itself, (*autoformation* ⟨B⟩). Cf. **Bildung.**

Selbst-da, itself-there.

Selbstdarstellung, self-presentation, self-exhibition. Cf. **Auftreten, Darstellung, Selbstgebung, Sich-selbstdarstellen.**

selbsteigen, very own, own ⟨WH 1⟩- (*qui lui est propre* ⟨B⟩), (*le plus in,*

time ⟨R⟩). Cf. **eigen.** | **mir** —, (peculiarly) my own. Cf. **Mir-Eigenes.**
Selbsteigenes, what is peculiarly my (*or* his) own, what is peculiar to my own self. Cf. **Eigenes.**
Selbsteigenheit, (peculiar) ownness. Cf. **Eigenheit.**
Selbsterfahrung, self-experience; experience of something itself. | **die transzendentale** —, my experiencing of my transcendental self.
selbsterfasst, itself(-)grasped; itself seized upon, (*saisi "lui-même"* ⟨B⟩).
Selbsterfassung, grasping (of) something itself; seizing upon something itself, (*saisie de la chose "elle-même"* ⟨B⟩). Cf. **Erfassung.** | **absolute** —, seizing upon my absolute self.
Selbsterscheinung, self-appearance. Cf. **Erscheinung.**
Selbst-Erscheinung eines Etwas, appearance of a Something itself, (*apparition phénoménale d'un quelque chose "lui-même"* ⟨B⟩).
selbstgebend ⟨attrib. adj.⟩, that gives (us) something(-)itself (*or* the object itself *or* it itself *or* them themselves), (*qui donne quelque chose "elle-même"* (ou *les choses elles-mêmes* ou *les choses mêmes* ⟨B⟩), (*qui la donne "elle-même"* ⟨B⟩). Cf. **selbst gebend** (*sub* **gebend**).
selbstgebend ⟨pred. adj.⟩, a giving of something(-)itself. Cf. **gebend.**
Selbstgebung, 1. (noetic:) giving of something-itself (*or* of it-itself, *or* of the thing itself, *or* of the object itself).
2. (noematic:) something that is itself given, something's giving of itself, something giving itself.
3. (noetic or noematic:) (*donation de la chose "elle-même"* (ou *des choses elles-mêmes* ou *des choses mêmes* ou *des objectités mêmes*) ⟨B⟩). Cf. **gebend, Selbstdarstellung, Sich-selbstgeben.**
selbst(-)gegeben, itself(-)given, (*donné lui-même* ⟨B⟩), (*donné en personne* ⟨R⟩).
Selbstgegebenheit, itself-givenness, givenness of something itself, (givenness originaliter); something itself-given. Cf. **Gegebenheit.** | **zur** — **kommen,** to become itself-given, (*venir se donner en personne* ⟨R⟩), (*venir à être donné en personne* ⟨B⟩).
Selbstgegenwart, one's own (*or* the ego's) present; own presence.
selbstgegenwärtig, itself present, (*présent "lui-même"* ⟨B⟩).
Selbsthabe(n), having (of) something itself (*or* it itself *or* them themselves), (*possession de la chose "elle-même"* (ou *des choses "elles-mêmes"*) ⟨B⟩). Cf. **Habe.**
Selbstheit, selfhood ⟨BG⟩, (*ipséité* ⟨R, de M⟩).
Selbstimmigkeit, self-consistency, self-correctness. Cf. **Konsequenz, Unstimmigkeit.**
selbstverantwortlich, self-responsible. Cf. **verantwortlich 1.**
Selbstverantwortlichkeit, self-responsibility, (*responsabilité* ⟨PL⟩).
Selbstverantwortung, self-responsability, (*responsabilité de soi* ⟨B⟩).
Selbstvergangenheit, one's own (*or* the ego's) past.
Selbstverständigung, self-understanding.
selbstverständlich ⟨adj.⟩, unquestioned, without question, (unquestionable); (apparently) truistic, understandable of itself, self-understandable, self-understood ⟨MS 1⟩, a matter of course ⟨MS 3, WH 4⟩, matter-of-course, obvious. Cf. **fraglos.**
selbstverständlich ⟨adv.⟩, without question, self-understandably, of course ⟨WH 1, MS 1⟩ undoubtedly, (*bien évidemment* ⟨B⟩).
Selbstverständlichkeit, matter of course, (*chose* (ou *proposition*) *qui va de soi* ⟨B⟩), (apparent) truism, something understandable of itself, matter-of-course conviction; unquestionedness, unquestioned obviousness, (*évidence naturelle* ⟨B⟩).
sensuell, sensual, (*sensuel* ⟨R⟩), sensuous. Cf. **Empfingungs-, sinnlich.**
setzbar, positable.
setzen, to posit ⟨Bn⟩, to put ⟨WH⟩, (*poser* ⟨R, B⟩). Cf. **ansetzen, ver-**

meinen. | **ausser Geltung** —, to deprive of acceptance, (to render inoperative). Cf. **Geltung.** | **ausser Spiel** —, to put out of action, (*mettre hors jeu* ⟨B⟩); to leave out of account, (*ne pas tenir compte de* ⟨PL⟩), (*ne pas accepter comme donné* ⟨PL⟩). | **Energie an etwas** —, to put energy into something. | **in Geltung** —, to give acceptance to, to posit, (*poser comme valable* ⟨B⟩). Cf. **Geltung.** | **in Idee** —, to put into an idea, (*poser en ideé* ⟨R⟩). | **in Seinsgeltung** —, to give acceptance to as existent, (*poser en accordant valeur d'existence* ⟨B⟩). Cf. **Seinsgeltung.**

Setzen, positing, (*poser* ⟨B⟩), (*acte de position* ⟨B⟩), setting. Cf. **Darauf hinsetzen, Position, Thesis, Zwecksetzen.**

setzend, positing, (ponent ⟨in OED⟩), (*qui pose* ⟨B⟩).

Setzung, 1. position, (*position* ⟨R, B, de M⟩).
2. (noetic, usually:) positing, (setting ⟨MS 1⟩), (willing).
3. (noematic, sometimes:) (*être posé* ⟨B⟩).
Cf. **Ansetzung, Daseinssetzung, Hinsetzung, Mittelsetzung, Position, Seinssetzung, Stellung, Stellungnahme, Thesis, Urteilssetzung, Voraussetzung, Zwecksetzung.** | **zur — kommen,** to become posited, (*venir à être posé* ⟨B⟩).

Setzungscharakter, 1. positional character(istic).
2. (noetic, sometimes:) positing-character(istic), character of the positing. Cf. **Charakter.**

Setzungsmaterial, position-material. Not "positing-material" ⟨BG⟩.

Setzungsmodalität, modality of positing, (positional modality ⟨BG⟩).

Setzungsmodus, | **doxischer** —, mode of doxic positing, (*mode doxique de position* ⟨B⟩).

Sich-abwandeln, (process of) becoming modified, undergoing of modification. | **kontinuierlich retentionales** —, undergoing of continuous retentional modification.

Sich-denken, thinking of; phantasying. Cf. **Denken, sich denken** (*sub* **denken**), **Umdenken.**

Sicherheit, assurance ⟨WH⟩, (*confiance* ⟨B⟩), (*certitude* ⟨R⟩).

Sichfreuen, (ant. Betrübtsein:) being glad, (*joie* ⟨R⟩). Save "joy" ⟨BG⟩ for "Freude" ⟨q.v.⟩.

Sichhineindenken, Cf. **hineindenken.** | **— in ein Erfahren,** clearly phantasied possible experiencing, (*acte par lequel on se transporte par la pensée dans un acte d'expérience* ⟨B⟩).

Sich-selbst-darstellen, self-presentation, self-exhibiting. Cf. **Auftreten, Selbstdarstellung, sich darstellen** (*sub* darstellen).

Sich-selbst-geben, self-presenting, self-giving. Cf. **Auftreten, Selbstgebung, sich geben** (*sub* geben).

sichtbar machen, to bring to light, (*rendre visible* ⟨B⟩). Cf. **herausstellen, klarlegen.**

sichtig, sighted. | **das S ~ e,** what is sighted. | **— haben,** to sight, (*avoir un aperçu* ⟨R⟩).

Sichtighaben, sighting.

Sichtigkeit, Cf. **Phantasiesichtigkeit.**

Sichtigsein, being sighted, sightedness, (*aperçu* ⟨R⟩).

sichtlich ⟨adj.⟩, visible ⟨WH 1, MS 1⟩, (*visible* ⟨B⟩), (*évident* ⟨B⟩), obvious ⟨MS⟩, plain, apparent. ⟨MS⟩. Cf. **erschaubar.**

sichtlich ⟨adv.⟩, visibly ⟨WH 1, MS 1⟩, obviously ⟨MS⟩, plainly, apparently, (*d'une manière manifeste* ⟨B⟩).

Sichverhalten, self-comportment ⟨?⟩. Cf. **Gebaren, Gehaben, Verhalten, Verhaltung.**

Signifikation, (equivalent to "Bedeutung" and contrasted with "Intuition" ⟨LU, VI. Unters., *33 n.*⟩) Signification (capitalized), Signifying (capitalized); intending to something that is symbolized. Cf. **Bedeuten, Bedeutung.** | **Akt der** —, (contrasted with "Akt der Intuition" (loc. cit.)), act of Signifying.

signifikativ ⟨adj.⟩, (Equivalent to "signitiv" ⟨LU, VI. Unters., *33 n.*⟩:) significative, significational. Cf. **bedeutend, bedeutungsmässig.** | ∼er **Akt,** significative act. Cf. **signitiver Akt** (*sub* **signitiv** ⟨adj.⟩). **signitiv** ⟨adj.⟩, (Equivalent to "signifikativ" and opposed to "intuitiv" ⟨LU, VI. Unters., *33 n.*⟩:) significative, (*signifiant* ⟨B⟩), significational, (signitive ⟨not in OED⟩). Save "symbolic" ⟨L⟩ and "symbolical" (despite loc. cit.) for "symbolisch", because this word expresses a broader sense in Ideen I, § *43, 3. Absatz.* Cf. **bedeutend, bedeutungsmässig.** | ∼er **Akt,** (Equivalent to "signifikativer Akt", "Akt der Bedeutungsintention", and "Akt des Bedeutens":) significative act, (signifying act). | **S**∼**es,** something significational, something signified. **signitiv** ⟨adv.⟩, significatively, significationally; as represented by signs, (*au moyen des signes* ⟨B⟩), in terms of signs. Not "in symbols" ⟨L⟩, for the reason given *sub* signitiv ⟨adj.⟩. **singulär,** single; (Urteil:) singular, (*singulier* ⟨R, B⟩). Save "certain" ⟨BG⟩ for "gewiss". So far as possible save "individual" ⟨BG⟩ for "individuell". Cf. **einzeln.** | **das S**∼**e,** the single example, (the single individual).

Singularität, singularity, singleness, singular; single example. Cf. **Besonderung, Einzelheit, Vereinzelung, Wahrnehmungssingularität.**

Sinn, sense ⟨WH 1, MS 1⟩, (*sens* ⟨R, B, de M⟩); (rarely:) scope. Save "meaning" ⟨Ueberweg trln of Berkeley, quoted in LU, II. Unters.; WH; MS; F; BG⟩ for "Meinen" ⟨q.v.⟩, "Meinung" ⟨q.v.⟩, and "Vermeinen" ⟨q.v.⟩. Cf. **Bereich, Erinnerungssinn, Erkenntnissinn, Einheitssinn, Seinssinn, Tragweite, Umfang, Unsinn, Wahrheitssinn, Wahrnehmungssinn, Wertungssinn, Widersinn, Zwecksinn.** | **etwas im** ∼**e haben,** to intend ⟨WH 1⟩ something. | **Ganzes des** ∼**es,** whole that is a sense, (*totalité du sens* ⟨B⟩). | **im erfassenden —,** in the sense of a seizing-upon. Cf.

erfassend. | **im physischen** ∼**e,** physically. | **im realen** ∼**e,** really; in the sense of realities. | **im** ∼**e der Formenlehre,** according to the theory of forms, (*au sens de la morphologie* ⟨B⟩). | **im** ∼**e der Deutlichkeitsevidenz,** in the sense proper to distinct evidence. | **im** ∼**e der Gegebenheiten,** like the data, (*au sens des données* ⟨B⟩). Cf. **Gegebenheit.** | **im** ∼**e der Logik,** in the sense proper to logic, (*au sens de la logique* ⟨B⟩); in logic's sense of the word; as logic intends it. | **im** ∼**e des Positivismus,** in accordance with positivism. | **im** ∼**e der Psychologie,** in the psychological sense, (*au sens de la psychologie* ⟨R, B⟩), as meant in psychology; for psychology. | **im** ∼**e der Tradition,** according to the tradition, (*au sens de la tradition* ⟨B⟩). | **im** ∼**e der traditionellen Auffassung,** as traditionally conceived. | **im** ∼**e der Über- und Unterordnungen,** in conformity with the superordinations and subordinations, (*au sens des ordinations et sous-ordinations* ⟨B⟩). | **im** ∼**e des Apriori,** in conformity with the Apriori, (*au sens de l'apriori* ⟨B⟩). | **im** ∼**e einer Schwächung wirken,** to tend to weaken. | **im** ∼**e positiver Evidenz,** in a positive evidence. | **im** ∼**e strenger Wissenschaft,** as strict science. | **in Berkeleys** ∼**e,** in the Berkeleian manner. | **in diesem** ∼**e,** accordingly, (*en ce sens* ⟨B⟩). | **in echtem** ∼**e,** genuine, genuinely, (*au sens authentique* ⟨R⟩). | **in positivem** ∼**e,** positively, (*dans le sens positif* ⟨B⟩). | **Umfang im** ∼**e der** (*oder* von) **Wahrheit,** true extension.

sinnbelebt, animated with sense. Not "animated with a meaning" ⟨F⟩.

Sinnbeziehung, sense-relation, (*relation de sens* ⟨B⟩), (*rapport que le sens a* ⟨B⟩). Cf. **Beziehung.**

Sinnbildung, sense-fashioning, (*formation du sens* ⟨B⟩). Cf. **Bildung.**

Sinndaten, Data of the senses, (*data sensuels* ⟨R⟩). Cf. **Datum.**

Sinnending, thing pertaining to the senses, thing that is an object of the senses, (sensible thing), (*chose sensible* ⟨R⟩). Not "sensory thing" ⟨BG⟩, not "thing of sense" ⟨BG⟩. Cf. **Ding, Sehding, Tastding.** | sonstige ∼**e,** things pertaining to the other senses.

Sinnenschein, illusion of the senses. Cf. **Schein.**

sinnerfüllt, sense-filled, (*rempli par un* (ou *le*) *sens* ⟨B⟩). Cf. **erfüllt.**

Sinnesaufstufung, superaddition of sense. Cf. **Aufstufung.**

Sinnesauslegung, explication of sense, (*explication du sens* ⟨B⟩). Cf. **besinnliche Auslegung** (*sub* **Auslegung**). | **noematische** —, explication of the noematic sense, (*explicitation noématique du sens* ⟨R⟩).

Sinnesbestand, sense-composition, (*fonds de sens* ⟨R⟩). Cf. **Bestand.**

Sinnesboden, basis of sense. Cf. **Boden.**

Sinneseinheit, unity of sense, (*unité de sens* ⟨B⟩). Cf. **Einheit.**

Sinnesempfindung, sensation ⟨Gomperz trln of Mill, quoted in LU, II. Unters.⟩, (sensuous feeling ⟨?⟩). Cf. **Empfindung.**

Sinnesform, sense-form, (*forme du sens* ⟨B⟩).

Sinnesgenesis, genesis of (its) sense, (*genèse de sens* ⟨B⟩). Cf. **Genesis.**

Sinneshorizont, sense-horizon, (*horizon du sens* ⟨B⟩). Cf. **Horizont.**

sinnesidentisch, as having its identical sense, (*dont le sens reste identique* ⟨B⟩).

Sinneskern, sense-core, core of sense, (*noyau de* (ou *du*) *sens* ⟨R⟩), (sense nucleus), (nucleus of sense). Not "meaning-nucleus" ⟨BG⟩, not "kernel of meaning" ⟨BG⟩. Cf. **Kern.**

Sinneslehre, theory of senses, sense-theory, (*doctrine du sens* ⟨B⟩).

Sinnesmodifikation, modification of sense, (*modification de sens* ⟨B⟩).

Sinnesmoment, sense-moment.

Sinnesorgan, (with reference to Hume:) organ of sensation.

Sinnesquelle, sense-giving source.

Sinnesreflexion, reflective focusing on senses, (*réflexion* ⟨B⟩).

Sinnesregion, region of senses, (*région du sens* ⟨B⟩).

Sinnessphäre, sphere of senses, (*sphère du sens* ⟨B⟩). | **reine** —, sphere of pure senses. (*pure sphère du sens* ⟨B⟩).

Sinnesurteil, judgment about a sense, (*or* about senses), (*jugement en tant que sens* ⟨B⟩). Cf. **Urteil.**

sinngebend, sense-bestowing, (*donateur de sens* ⟨B⟩). Not "sensegiving". Cf. **bedeutungsgebend, gebend, sinnverleihend.**

Sinngebilde, (produced) sense-formation. Cf. **Gebilde.**

Sinngebung, sense-bestowing, (*donation de sens* ⟨R, B⟩). Not "sensegiving".

Sinngehalt, sense-content(s), (*teneur de sens* ⟨B⟩). Cf. **Gehalt.**

Sinngestalt, sense-formation, (*forme de sens* ⟨B⟩). Cf. **Gestalt.**

sinnhaft, senseful. Cf. **sinnvoll.**

sinnhaftig ⟨adj.⟩, senseful. Cf. **sinnvoll** ⟨adj.⟩.

sinnhaftig ⟨adv.⟩, sensefully. Cf. **sinnvoll** ⟨adv.⟩.

Sinnhaftigkeit, sensefulness, (*capacité de sens* ⟨B⟩), (*sens* ⟨B⟩).

sinnleistend, sense-producing. Cf. **leistend.**

sinnlich ⟨adj.⟩, sensuous ⟨WH 2, MS⟩, (sensible ⟨L, BG⟩), (*sensible* ⟨PL, R, B⟩), (physiology:) sensory ⟨BG⟩. Cf. **Empfindungs-, sensuell.** | ∼**e Erscheinungsweise,** mode of sensuous appearance (or appearing), (*manière d'apparaître sensible* ⟨R⟩), (sensuous manner of appearing). Not "sensory way of appearing" ⟨BG⟩. Cf. **Erscheinungsweise.**

sinnlich ⟨adv.⟩, sensuously, (*de façon sensible* ⟨R⟩), (*d'une manière sensible* ⟨B⟩). Not "sensorily" ⟨BG⟩.

Sinnlichkeit, sensuousness ⟨WH 1, MS 1⟩, (*sensibilité* ⟨R, B⟩), (*sensualitas* ⟨K⟩). "Sensuality" ⟨WH 3, MS⟩ obs. in this sense. Save "sensibility" for "Empfindlichkeit".

sinnlich-leibhaft ⟨adv.⟩, sensuously "in person", (*corporellement aux sens*

⟨R⟩). Not "in a sensory body" ⟨BG⟩. Cf. **leibhaft(ig)** ⟨adv.⟩.

sinnverleihend, sense-conferring. Cf. **bedeutungsverleihend, sinngebend, verleihend.**

Sinnverweisung, reference to sense, (*renvoi au sens* ⟨B⟩). Cf. **verweisen.**

sinnvoll ⟨adj.⟩, senseful, (*plein de sens* ⟨B⟩). Cf. **sinnhaft** ⟨adj.⟩, **sinnhaftig** ⟨adj.⟩.

sinnvoll ⟨adv.⟩, sensefully. Cf. **sinnhaftig** ⟨adv.⟩.

Situation, Cf. **Erlebnissituation.**

skeptisch, skeptical ⟨L⟩, of skepticism.

soeben (gegangen), just ⟨WH 2, MS 3⟩ (gone), just now ⟨WH 3⟩, ((*qui vient*) *justement* (*d'exister*) ⟨R⟩).

sofern, if ⟨WH 1⟩; since, because, (inasmuch as); as far as, (*dans la mesure où* ⟨R⟩). Cf. **insofern als.**

solch, | **als** ~**es,** (sometimes:) as such. Almost always repeat the antecedent. | **das reine Bewusstsein als** ~**es,** pure consciousness in its purity.

Sollen, should, (ought ⟨Bn⟩), (oughtness ⟨Bn⟩). Cf. **Nichtsollen, Seinsollen.** | **Aussage des** ~**s,** should-statement. Cf. **Aussage.** | **die Rede von** —, should-statements. Cf. **Rede.**

Sonderanschauung, particular intuition. Cf. **Anschauung, Einzelanschauung.**

Sondercogitatum, particular cogitatum.

Sondererscheinung, separate appearance. Cf. **Erscheinung.**

Sonderfassung, | **in** —, taken separately. Cf. **Fassung 5.**

Sonderform, part-form, partial form; (particular form), (*forme particulière* ⟨B⟩).

Sondergebiet, particular province, (*domaine particulier* ⟨B⟩). Cf. **Gebiet.**

Sondergebilde, particular formation, (*formation particulière* ⟨B⟩). Cf. **Gebilde.**

Sondergestalt, particular formation, (*ramification* ⟨R⟩). Not "special pattern" ⟨BG⟩. Cf. **Gestalt.**

Sondergestaltung, particular formation. Cf. **Gestaltung.**

Sonderglaube, particular belief, component belief, (*croyance partielle* ⟨B⟩). Cf. **Glaube(n)** ⟨masc.⟩.

Sonderkategorie, particular category.

Sonderung, separation ⟨WH 1⟩, (*distinction* ⟨R⟩), difference.

Sondervorstellung, separate objectivation. Cf. **Vorstellung.**

Sonderwissenschaft, separate science; particular science, (*science particulière* ⟨B⟩). Cf. **Fachwissenschaft.**

soseiend, being thus and so, thus and so determined, thus determined, (*existant de telle manière* ⟨B⟩). Cf. **bestimmt.**

Sosein, being thus, (*être-tel* ⟨R⟩), thusness ("colloquial" — OED), *quale,* nature. Cf. **Art, Artung, Natur.**

(Sparsamkeit), parsimony ⟨Bn, WH 2, MS⟩.

spezialisierend, | ~**es Meinen,** act of meaning a species.

Spezialisierung, specialization ⟨MS 1, WH 2⟩; division (into species). Cf. **Besonderung.** | — **in Fachwissenschaften,** division into special sciences.

Spezialität, specificity, (*spécification* ⟨R⟩), speciality. Save "specialization" ⟨L⟩ for "Spezialisierung" ⟨q.v.⟩.

speziell ⟨adv.⟩, specifically ⟨BG⟩; especially, (*spécialement* ⟨R, B⟩), (*d'une manière spéciale* ⟨B⟩). Not "as a special case" ⟨BG⟩.

Spezies, Cf. **Farbenspezies, Formspezies.**

spezifisch, | ~**es Meinen,** meaning (of) something specific. Cf. **Meinen.** | ~**es Vorstellen,** objectivating of species. Cf. **Vorstellen.**

Sphäre, sphere, (*sphère* ⟨B⟩), (*cycle* ⟨R⟩). Cf. **Bereich, Bewusstseinssphäre, Eigenheitssphäre, Eigensphäre, Geltungssphäre, Kreis, Natursphäre, Problemsphäre, Sachsphäre, Sinnessphäre, Umfang, Urteilssphäre.**

Spiegelung, mirroring. Save "reflection" ⟨WH 1, MS 1⟩ for "Reflexion".

Spiel, | **aus dem — lassen,** to leave out of account. | **ausser — setzen,** to put out of action, (*mettre hors de jeu* ⟨B⟩); to leave out of account; (*ne pas tenir compte de* ⟨PL⟩), (*ne pas accepter comme donné* ⟨PL⟩). | **in —,** active, (*en jeu* ⟨B⟩). | **ins — setzen,** to bring into play, (*mettre en jeu* ⟨B⟩).

Spielraum, open range; scope ⟨WH, MS⟩.

Spielregel, rule of the game ⟨WH 1, MS 1⟩, (*règle du jeu* ⟨B⟩).

Sprache, language ⟨WH 2, MS 2⟩, (*langage* ⟨B, de M⟩), (speech ⟨WH 1, MS 1⟩).

Sprachbestand, Cf. **Bestand.** | **nach dem —,** as composed of language.

sprachlich ⟨adj.⟩, verbal, (*verbal* ⟨B⟩), lingual, language-, (*du discours* ⟨B⟩). Cf. **grammatisch.** | **das S~e,** language. | **~e Form,** verbal form, lingual form, (*expression verbale* ⟨B⟩). | **~er Ausdruck,** verbal expression, (*langage* ⟨B⟩). | **~er Leib,** verbal body. Cf. **Leib.** | **~er Satz,** sentence. Cf. **Satz 2.** | **~es Denken,** verbal thinking, (*pensée qui s'exprime dans le langage* ⟨B⟩). | **~es Gebilde,** verbal formation, (*formation de langage* ⟨B⟩). Cf. **Gebilde.**

sprachlich ⟨adv.⟩, in language, (*dans le langage* ⟨B⟩), lingually, (*considéré sous le point de vue du langage* ⟨B⟩), (*au niveau du langage* ⟨B⟩).

stammen, (particularly with reference to Locke:) to originate ⟨WH, MS⟩, to be derived ⟨WH⟩ (from), (*remonter (à)* ⟨B⟩). Not "to stem" ⟨L⟩. Cf. **entspringen.**

ständig, constant ⟨MS⟩. Cf. **beständig, stet, stetig.**

Standpunkt, standpoint ⟨WH 1⟩; respect. Cf. **Gesichtspunkt, Hinsicht.**

Steigerung, heightening, enhancement ⟨WH 4, MS 4⟩, increase ⟨MS 2, WH 3, F, BG⟩, (*accroissement* ⟨R⟩), (*augmentation* ⟨B⟩), (intensification).

Steigerungsreihe, ascending series ⟨F⟩.

Stelle, place ⟨WH 1, MS 1⟩, (*place* ⟨B⟩), locus. Save "position" ⟨WH, MS⟩

for "Position", "Stellung", etc. Cf. **Zeitstelle.**

stellen, Cf. **ausstellen, darstellen, einstellen, herausstellen, vorstellen.** | **ein Problem —,** to set (*or* to propound) a problem, (*poser un problème* ⟨B⟩). Cf. **Problemstellung.** | **eine Frage —,** to put (*or* to raise *or* to ask) a question. | **etwas auf ein Ziel —,** to aim something. | **in Frage —,** to question ⟨MS 1, WH 2⟩, to call in question ⟨WH 1⟩, (*mettre en question* ⟨B⟩).

Stellung, position ⟨WH, MS⟩, (*position* ⟨B⟩), (*place* ⟨B⟩), situation, (*situation* ⟨R, B⟩), setting. Not "view" ⟨F⟩. Cf. **Einstellung, Position, Problemstellung, Setzung, Zielstellung.**

Stellungnahme, taking (of) a position, (*prise de position* ⟨R, B⟩), position-taking, decision, position. Not "mental attitude" ⟨BG⟩: save "attitude" ⟨WH 1⟩ for "Einstellung" ⟨q.v.⟩ and "Haltung" ⟨q.v.⟩. Not "position assumed" ⟨BG⟩. Cf. **Denkstellungnahme, Position, Seinsstellungnahme, Setzung.** | **— zu,** position taken respecting (*or* toward(s)).

stellungnehmend, | **— zu,** in which a position is taken respecting, (*qui prend position à l'égard de* ⟨B⟩). | **~er Akt,** position-taking act, (*acte prenant position* ⟨B⟩), act in which a position is taken, (*acte de prise de position* ⟨B⟩). Not "attitude-expressing act" ⟨BG⟩.

Stellvertreter, proxy ⟨WH, MS⟩.

Stellvertretung, proxyship. Save "representation" ⟨WH 1, MS 1⟩ for "Repräsentation" and "Darstellung" ⟨q.v.⟩.

stet, steady ⟨WH 1, MS 1⟩, constant ⟨WH 2⟩, (*constant* ⟨B⟩); continuous ⟨MS 3⟩. Cf. **beständig, ständig, stetig.**

stetig ⟨adj.⟩, continuous, (*continuus* ⟨Wolff⟩), (*continuel* ⟨B⟩). Cf. **beständig, ständig, stet.**

stetig ⟨adv.⟩, continuously, perpetually.

Stetigkeit, continuity ⟨WH 1⟩, (*constance* ⟨B⟩).

stets, always ⟨MS 1, WH⟩, (*toujours*

⟨B⟩), (*constamment* ⟨B⟩). Cf. **beständig** ⟨adv.⟩.
stiften, to institute ⟨WH, MS⟩, to set up, (to originate ⟨WH, MS⟩), (*fonder* ⟨B⟩). Save "to found" ⟨MS 1, WH⟩ for "fundieren".
Stiftung, institution ⟨WH, MS⟩, instituting, something instituted, origination, (*fondation* ⟨B⟩). Save "foundation" for "Fundament", "Grund" "Grundlage", "Grundlegung" ⟨qq. vv.⟩. Cf. **Urstiftung.**
Stilform, stylistic form, style, (*structure* ⟨PL⟩).
stimmen mit, to accord with ⟨WH 1⟩. Cf. **einstimmig, Übereinstimmung.**
(Stimmung), mood ⟨Bn, WH, MS⟩.
Stoff, stuff ⟨WH, MS⟩, material ⟨WH, MS⟩, (*matériau* ⟨B⟩), (matter ⟨WH, MS⟩), (*matière* ⟨R, de M⟩), (*hylé* ⟨R⟩). Save "hyle" ⟨Ideen I, *209*; WH⟩ for "Hyle". Not "substance" ⟨WH, MS, F⟩. Cf. **Kernstoff, Materie, Verhältnis.**
stofflich, stuff-, material ⟨MS 1⟩, (*matériel* ⟨R, B⟩). Cf. **sachlich.** | ~**er Gehalt,** stuff-content. Cf. **Gehalt.** | ~**es Moment,** stuff-moment, (*moment matériel* ⟨B⟩).
Strahl, ray ⟨MS 1, WH 2, BG⟩, (*rayon* ⟨R, B⟩). Cf. **Blickstrahl, Ichstrahl.**
streben, to endeavor ⟨WH⟩, to strive ⟨WH 1, MS 1⟩, (*tendre* ⟨B⟩). Cf. **hinstreben, zustreben.** | (— **nach),** (math:) to approach ⟨Bn⟩.
Streben, endeavor ⟨WH, MS⟩, conation ⟨Bn⟩, striving ⟨WH 1, MS 1⟩, (*effort* ⟨B⟩), (*tâche* ⟨B⟩). Cf. **Erkenntnisstreben, Tendenz.**
strebend, endeavoring, conative.
Strebung, aiming, (*effort* ⟨B⟩). Cf. **Absehen, Abzielung, Zielung.**
Strecke, extent ⟨WH 1, MS 2⟩, (stretch ⟨WH 2⟩), (while), (sequence). Cf. **Dauerstrecke, Erstreckung, Tonstrecke, Zeitstrecke.**
streng ⟨adj.⟩, strict ⟨WH 2, MS, L⟩, (*strict* ⟨B⟩), (rigorous ⟨MS 2, WH 3, L⟩), (*rigoureux* ⟨R, B⟩), (*exact* ⟨B⟩). Cf. **eigentlich** ⟨adj.⟩.
streng ⟨adv.⟩, strictly ⟨WH 1, MS⟩, (*strictement* ⟨R, B⟩), (*stricte* ⟨K⟩),

(rigorously). Cf. **eigentlich** ⟨adv.⟩.
Strom, stream ⟨WH, L⟩, flow ⟨WH⟩. Cf. **Erlebnisstrom, Fluss, Inhaltsstrom.**
strömend-stehend, flowing but fixed ⟨?⟩, flowingly stagnant ⟨?⟩.
Struktureinsicht, Cf. **Einsicht.** | **prinzipielle** ~**en,** insights by which the essential structure is seen, (*évidences structurelles principielles* ⟨B⟩). Cf. **prinzipiell** ⟨adj.⟩.
strukturell, structural ⟨L⟩, in structure.
Strukturtypik, set of structural types. Cf. **Typik.**
Stück, piece ⟨WH 1, MS 1⟩, bit ⟨WH 2, MS 3⟩, (*fragment* ⟨B⟩), concrete part, portion ⟨WH 4, MS 5⟩, (*élément* ⟨R, B⟩); (loose sense:) part ⟨WH 3, MS 4⟩. Cf. **Abstückung, Bestandstück, Bestimmungsstück, zerstücken.**
Stufe, level ⟨WH, MS, BG⟩, (*niveau* ⟨R, B⟩), step ⟨WH 1, MS 1⟩, stage ⟨WH, MS, BG⟩, degree ⟨WH, MS⟩, (*degré* ⟨R, B⟩), grade ⟨WH, MS, BG⟩, gradation, (graded level), (plane). Cf. **abgestuft, Abstufung, Gradualität, Erkenntnisstufe, Mass, Schachtelungsstufe, Unterstufe, Urteilsstufe, Vorstufe.** | (**formale** —), (in method:) formal step ⟨Bn⟩. | **zweite** —, second degree.
stufenartig, hierarchical(ly).
Stufenbau, hierarchical structure, (*hiérarchie* ⟨B⟩); storied edifice. Cf. **Bau.**
Stufenbildung, hierarchical formation, (*hiérarchie* ⟨R⟩), level, layer. Cf. **Bildung.**
Stufenfolge, sequence of levels (or of steps), (*succession* ⟨B⟩), hierarchical series, hierarchical sequence, (*suite hiérarchisée* ⟨B⟩), hierarchical structure, hierarchy, (*hiérarchie* ⟨R⟩). Cf. **Folge 3.**
Stufengestalt, structure appropriate to a level. Cf. **Gestalt.**
Stufenordnung, hierarchical order; order, (*ordre* ⟨B⟩); Cf. **Ordnung.**
Stufenreihe, series of levels; hierarchical series, graded series.
Stufensystem, system of levels.

Subjektglied, subject-member, (*membre-sujet* ⟨B⟩).

subjektiv ⟨adj.⟩, | das S ~e, the subjective, the subjective moment. | **in** ~**er Hinsicht,** in its subjective aspect, with respect to the subjective (*or* to subjectivity), (*dans la perspective subjective* ⟨B⟩). Cf. **Hinsicht.** | ~**e Einstellung,** focusing on what is subjective, subjective focus, (*attitude subjective* ⟨B⟩). Cf. **Einstellung.** | ~**e Forschung,** investigation of the subjective. Cf. **Forschung.** | ~**e Reflexion auf Einsicht,** reflection on subjective insight, (*réflexion subjective sur l'évidence rationelle* ⟨B⟩). Cf. **Einsicht, Reflexion.** | ~**e Wendung,** turning toward the subjective, (*conversion subjective* ⟨B⟩); subjective location, (*tournure subjective* ⟨B⟩). Cf. **Wendung.** | ~**es Gebilde,** subjectively produced formation, (*formation subjective* ⟨B⟩). Cf. **Gebilde.**

subjektiv ⟨adv.⟩, subjective ⟨L⟩, on the subjective side, (*dans la perspective subjective* ⟨B⟩). | — **erlebt,** really immanent in subjective life. Cf. **erlebt.** | — **gerichtet,** directed to the subjective, (*dirigé vers le subjectif* (ou *vers la subjectivité* ou *du côté subjectif* ou *du côté de la subjectivité*) ⟨B⟩; relating to (*or* concerning) the subjective. | — **gerichtete Thematik,** thematizing of the subjective, thematizing activity directed to the subjective, (*thématique dirigée vers la subjectivité* ⟨B⟩). Cf. **Thematik.** | — **gewendet,** turned toward(s) the subject (himself), (*orienté vers le sujet* ⟨PL⟩), turned toward(s) the subjective. | — **gewendete logische Arbeit,** efforts that logic devotes to the subjective, (*travail logique dans son orientation subjective* ⟨B⟩).

subjektivieren, to subjectivize ⟨in OED⟩, to subjectivate ⟨not in OED⟩.

Subjektivierung, subjectivizing, (*subjectivisation* ⟨B⟩).

Subjektivität, subjectivity ⟨WH 1⟩, (*subjectivité* ⟨R⟩); subjectiveness.

subjektiv-phänomenologisch ⟨adv.⟩, | — **gerichtet,** directed phenomenologically to the subjective, (*dirigé vers la subjectivité dans la perspective phénoménologique* ⟨B⟩).

Substantivität, substantivity ⟨not in OED⟩, (*substantivité* ⟨B, de M⟩); (concretum:) substantive.

Substrat, substrate, (*substrat* ⟨R, B⟩). Save "substratum" ⟨MS 1⟩ for "Untergrund", "Unterlage", and "Unterschicht" ⟨qq. vv.⟩. Save "basis" ⟨WH 1, MS 2, BG⟩ for "Boden" and "Unterlage" ⟨qq. vv.⟩. Save "foundation" ⟨WH 2⟩ for "Fundament", "Grundlage" etc. Cf. **Bestimmungssubstrat, Ursubstrat.**

Substratglied, substrate-member, (*membre-substrat* ⟨B⟩).

substruieren, (to substruct ⟨in OED⟩), to hypothesize. Cf. **mitsubstruieren.**

Substruktion, hypothesizing; (substruction ⟨in OED⟩), basis ⟨BG⟩ for inferring, (*base* ⟨R⟩).

Syllogistik, syllogistics ("rare" — OED), (*syllogistique* ⟨B, de M⟩).

syllogistisch, syllogistic ⟨WH 1, MS 1⟩, (*syllogistique* ⟨B⟩), comprised in syllogistics.

symbolisch, symbolic, symbolical. | ~**e Bedeutung,** symbolical signification. Cf. **Bedeutung.**

Synkategorematika, syncategorems, (*syncategorématiques* ⟨R⟩).

synthetisch ⟨adj.⟩, synthetic, (*synthétique* ⟨B⟩), synthetical, to a synthesis. | ~**er Übergang,** synthetical transition, (*passage synthétique* ⟨B⟩), transition to a synthesis. Cf. **Übergang.**

synthetisch ⟨adv.⟩, synthetically, (*synthétiquement* ⟨B⟩), by the synthesis. | — **hervortreten,** to be brought out by the synthesis. Cf. **hervortreten.**

Tastding, touch thing, thing that is an object of touch, tactual thing. Cf. Ding, Sehding, Sinnending.
Tat, deed ⟨WH 3, MS 3, BG⟩, (oeuvre ⟨R⟩), (fact). Save "act" ⟨WH 1, MS 2⟩ for "Akt". Save "action" ⟨MS 1, WH 2⟩ for "Handlung" ⟨q.v.⟩, "Tätigkeit" ⟨q.v.⟩, etc.
tätig ⟨adj.⟩, doing ⟨MS 2⟩, in action, active ⟨WH 1, MS 1, BG⟩, (actif ⟨R, B⟩), (ayant une activité ⟨B⟩), operative. Cf. aktuell, betätigen, Bewusstseinstätiges, handelnd, zwecktätig.
tätig ⟨adv.⟩, | frei —, by free action, (dans une libre activité ⟨B⟩).
Tatsache, matter of fact ⟨Ideen I, 5; WH, MS⟩, factual matter, fact ⟨WH, MS, BG⟩, (fait ⟨R⟩). Save "reality" ⟨MS⟩ for "Reales", "Realität", and "Wirklichkeit" ⟨q.v.⟩. So far as possible save "fact" for "Faktum". Cf. Sache, Sachverhalt, Wesenstatsache.
Tatsachen-Aussagen, predicating that concerns matters of fact, (énoncé relatif à des faits ⟨R⟩). Not "to express a fact" ⟨BG⟩.
Tatsachen-Denken, thinking that concerns matters of fact, (pensée relative à des faits ⟨R⟩). Not "to think a fact" ⟨BG⟩.
Tatsachenerkenntnis, cognition of matters of fact. Cf. Erkenntnis, matter-of-fact-Erkenntnis.
Tatsachenwahrheit, matter-of-fact truth, (vérité portant sur des faits ⟨R⟩).
Tatsachenzusammenhang, Cf. Zusammenhang. | intersubjektiver —, connexion between intersubjective facts. Not "intersubjective connexion of facts" ⟨L⟩.
Tatsächlichkeit, factualness, (facticité ⟨R⟩).
täuschend, deceptive ⟨MS 1, WH 3⟩, (trompeux ⟨B⟩). Cf. enttäuschend.
Täuschung, deception ⟨WH 2, MS⟩, (illusion ⟨Bn, WH, MS⟩), (illusion ⟨B⟩). So far as possible save "il-

lusion" for "Schein" ⟨q.v.⟩. Cf. Enttäuschung, Trug.
tautologisch, tautological ⟨WH 1, MS 1⟩; ⟨in LU:⟩ strictly equivalent. Cf. gleichbedeutend.
Technik, technique ⟨WH, MS⟩, (technique ⟨B⟩), (where contrasted with "schöne Kunst":) mechanical art. Cf. Kunst.
technisieren, to reduce to a technique.
Technisierung, reduction to a technique, (technisation ⟨B, de M⟩).
Teilbedeutung, partial signification, (signification partielle ⟨B⟩). Cf. Bedeutung.
Teilbegriff, component concept. Cf. Begriff, Totalbegriff.
Teilmeinung, partial meaning-process. Cf. Meinung.
Teilung, partition ⟨WH 3, MS 4⟩, (division ⟨B⟩). So far as possible save "division" ⟨WH 1, MS 1⟩ for "Einteilung" and "Scheidung"; so far as possible save "separation" for "Scheidung". Cf. Zerstückung.
Tendenz, tendency ⟨WH 1, MS 1⟩, (striving). Cf. Intention, Streben. | — auf, (sometimes:) striving toward(s).
tendentiös, tendential.
Terminus, term ⟨WH 1, MS 1⟩, (terme ⟨R, B⟩). Save "expression" ⟨MS 2⟩ for "Ausdruck". Cf. Name, Rede 2.
Thema, theme ⟨WH 1, MS 1⟩, (thème ⟨B⟩), (rarely:) object. Cf. Gegenstand.
Thematik, themes, theme; thematizing, thematizing activity; (thématique ⟨B⟩). Cf. Reflexionsthematik. | doppelseitige —, two-sided themes. | gerade —, straightforward thematizing activity. Cf. gerade. | in konkreter —, when taken as a concrete theme. | korrelative —, perfectly correlated themes, (thématiques corrélatives ⟨B⟩). | logische —, themes of logic; logical thematizing. | mathematische —, themes of mathematics. | objektive —, Objective theme(s). | praktische —, practical thematizing. | psychologische —,

psychological thematizing. | **Richtung einer** —, direction of a thematizing activity. Cf. **Richtung.** | **subjektiv gerichtete** —, thematizing activity directed to the subjective, (*thématique dirigée vers la subjectivité* ⟨B⟩). | **subjektive** —, thematizing of the subjective. | — **der Denkhandlung,** thematizing of actions of thinking. | **theoretische** —, theoretical thematizing. | **Zwitterhaftigkeit der** —, hybridism of theme. **thematisch** ⟨adj.⟩, thematic, (*thématique* ⟨B⟩); of themes, of the theme; as a theme; on a theme; thematical; in respect of theme. Cf. **ausserthematisch.** | ∼**er Begriff,** concept of (its) theme(s); (*concept thématique* ⟨B⟩). | ∼**e Beschränkung,** restriction of the theme, (*limitation thématique* ⟨B⟩). | ∼**er Blick,** thematizing regard, (*regard* (ou *vue*) *thématique* ⟨B⟩). Cf. **Blick.** | in ∼**em Blick,** as an object of thematizing regard, (as a thema within one's field of regard (*or* of vision)). Cf. **Blick.** | ∼**e Einstellung,** focusing on a theme, thematizing focus, (*orientation thématique* ⟨B⟩). Cf. **Einstellung.** | ∼**e Einheit,** unity in respect of theme. | ∼**es Feld,** thematic field, (*champ thématique* ⟨B⟩). | ∼**es Gebilde,** thematic formation. Cf. **Gebilde.** | in ∼**er Richtung auf etwas,** when one directs oneself to something as one's theme. | ∼**e Tendenz,** thematizing tendency. Cf. **Tendenz.** | ∼**e Umstellung,** change of thematizing focus, (*déplacement thématique* ⟨B⟩). Cf. **Umstellung.** | ∼**e Unterschiedenheit,** diversity of themes. | ∼**e Wendung,** shift of thematizing interest, (*revirement thématique* ⟨B⟩). Cf. **Umstellung, Wendung.** | — **werden,** to be made thematic. **thematisch** ⟨adv.⟩, thematically, (*thématiquement* ⟨B⟩). | **uns auf etwas** — **hinlenkend,** leading us to make something our theme. **Thematisierung,** (*thématisation* ⟨B⟩). | **in einer doxischen** —, as the theme of a doxic act.

Theoretik, of theory; theoretics ⟨in OED⟩. **Theoretiker,** theorizer, (*théoricien* ⟨B⟩). Not "theorist" ⟨WH 1, MS 1⟩. **theoretisch** ⟨adj.⟩, theoretical ⟨MS 1, WH, BG⟩, of theory, for a theory, theoretic, (*théorique* ⟨B⟩). **theoretisch** ⟨adv.⟩, theoretically, (*d'une manière théorique* ⟨B⟩), (*dans la* (ou *une*) *perspective théorique* ⟨B⟩), (*du point de vue théorique* ⟨B⟩); in a theory. **theoretisch-technisch,** in the manner characteristic of a theoretical technique, (*dans une technique théorique* ⟨B⟩). **theoretisierbar,** theorizable, (*susceptible de théorétisation* ⟨B⟩). **theoretisieren,** (transitive) to treat theoretically, ((*en*) *faire la théorie* ⟨B⟩), to theorize ⟨BG⟩ (about), to judge about. **Theoretisieren,** theorizing, (*activité de théorisation* ⟨B⟩), theorization, (*théorisation* ⟨B⟩), (*passage au stade théorique*⟨R⟩). Not "theoretization". **theoretisierend,** | ∼**es Bewusstsein,** theorizing consciousness, (*conscience au stade théorique* ⟨R⟩). **These** ⟨f.⟩, thesis ⟨WH 1, MS 1⟩. Cf. **Satz 1.** **Thesis** ⟨f.⟩, (active) positing, thesis ⟨WH 1, MS 1, BG⟩, (*thèse* ⟨R, B⟩). Cf. **Daseinsthesis, Gegenthesis, Generalthesis, Glaubensthesis, Position, Satz, Setzen, Setzung.** **thetisch,** posited; positional; (thetic ⟨L, BG⟩), (*thétique* ⟨R⟩). Cf. **monothetisch, polythetisch.** **Tier,** brute ⟨WH, MS⟩, brute animal, (*animal* ⟨B⟩). Not simply "animal" ⟨Bn, WH 1, MS 1⟩, not "beast" ⟨WH, MS, BG⟩. Cf. **Animalia, Animalien.** **tierisch,** brute-animal. Not simply "animal" ⟨WH 1, MS 1⟩. **Tinktion,** tincture. **Titel,** title ⟨WH 1, MS 1, L, BG⟩, (*titre* ⟨R⟩), name, (*dénomination* ⟨B⟩); heading, (*rubrique* ⟨B⟩). Cf. **Gesamttitel.** | **unter einem** — **erfassen,** to designate by a name. Cf. **erfassen.**

τόδε τί, τόδε τί, this-here. Cf. **Dies-da.**
Ton, tone ⟨MS 1, WH 2⟩, sound ⟨WH 1, MS 2⟩, (*son* ⟨B⟩), note ⟨WH 3⟩. Cf. **Laut.**
Tondauer, tone-duration.
Tonempfindung, tone-sensation, (sensation of sound ⟨Gomperz trln of Mill, quoted in LU, II. Unters.⟩).
(Tonfarbe), tone tint ⟨?⟩ ⟨Bn⟩.
Tonphase, note-phase.
Tonpunkt, tone-point.
Tonstrecke, tone-extent. Cf. **Strecke.**
Totalanschauung, intuition of a totality.
Totalform, | **prädikative** —, total predicational form, (*forme prédicative totale* ⟨B⟩).
Totalbegriff, Cf. **Begriff, Teilbegriff.** | **gegenständlicher** —, concept of a totality of objects, (*concept total d'objet* ⟨B⟩).
tradierend, transmissive.
Traditionalität, traditionariness. "Traditionality" not in OED.
Tragfähigkeit, competence.
Tragweite, range ⟨WH 1, MS 1⟩, (*portée* ⟨B⟩), scope. Cf. **Bereich, Sinn, Umfang.**
transzendent ⟨adj.⟩, | ∼**e Wahrnehmung,** perception of something transcendent, (transcendent perception ⟨BG⟩), (*perception transcendante* ⟨R⟩). Cf. **immanente Wahrnehmung** (*sub* **immanent** ⟨adj.⟩).
transzendent ⟨adv.⟩, | — **bezogen,** related to something transcendent, (*rapporté de façon transcendante* ⟨R⟩). Not "transcendently related" ⟨BG⟩. Cf. **immanent b.** (*sub* **immanent** ⟨adv.⟩). | — **gerichtet,** directed to something transcendent, (*dirigé de façon transcendante* ⟨R⟩). Not "transcendently directed" ⟨BG⟩.
Transzendenz, 1. (the action of transcending, the condition or quality of being transcendent:) transcendence ⟨BG⟩. Cf. **Hinausreichen über.** 2. (the fact of transcending, an instance of this:) transcendency, something transcendent. 3. (Fr.:) (*transcendance* ⟨R, B, de M⟩).

transzendierend, that goes beyond, (*qui transgresserait* ⟨R⟩).
Trauer, sorrow ⟨WH⟩, (*tristesse* ⟨R⟩).
treffen, to reach, (*atteindre* ⟨R⟩); to have an effect on. Not "to contact" ⟨L⟩. Cf. **betreffen, betroffen.**
Trieb, drive, impulse ⟨Bn, James, WH, MS⟩, (*impulsion* ⟨R⟩), impetus ⟨WH, MS⟩. Not "instinct" ⟨WH, MS⟩.
triftig, (*valide* ⟨R⟩).
Triftigkeit, well-foundedness, reaching (of) the (*or* their) target, target-reaching, (*validité* ⟨R⟩).
Trug, deception ⟨WH 1, MS 1⟩, Cf. **Schein, Täuschung.**
Trugschluss, fallacy ⟨WH 2, MS 2⟩, (*fallacia* ⟨K⟩), paralogism ⟨WH 3, MS 3⟩, (sophism ⟨Bn, WH 4⟩). Cf. **Fehlschluss, Schluss.**
tun, to do ⟨WH 1, MS 1⟩, (*faire* ⟨R⟩), (*agir* ⟨R⟩), to accomplish, (*effectuer* ⟨B⟩). Cf. **leisten.**
Tun, doing ⟨WH 1, MS 1⟩, doings ⟨MS 2, WH⟩, (*action* ⟨B⟩), (*activité* ⟨B⟩), what something does, dealing with. Cf. **Handeln, Tat.** | **das urteilende** —, the judicative doing. | **das wissenschaftliche** —, what science does, (*l'action scientifique* ⟨B⟩). | **leistendes** —, productive doing, (*activité d'effectuation* ⟨B⟩). Cf. **leistend.**
Typik, (*typique* ⟨B⟩), set of types, differentiation into (*or* according to) types, grouping according to types, types, typicality ⟨in OED⟩, conformity to type, description of types, (*typologie* ⟨R⟩). Cf. **Formtypik, Formtypus, Strukturtypik, Urteilstypik.** | — **haben,** to fall under types.
typisch ⟨adj.⟩, typical, in type, characteristic. | ∼**e Unterschiede,** differences in type.
typisieren, to reduce to type(s).
Typisierung, constitution of types, reduction to types.
Typus, type ⟨MS 1, BG⟩, (*type* ⟨B⟩), (*genre* ⟨R⟩), stamp, character. Cf. **Charakter, Formtypus, Gestalt, Wesenstypus.** | — **haben,** to have a stamp (*or* character).

U

Überdeckung, overlaying. Cf. Deckung, übergreifen, Überkreuzung, Überschiebung.

übereinanderbauen, to build one over another. Cf. bauen.

Übereinstimmung, accord ⟨WH 1⟩, agreement ⟨MS 1, WH 2⟩, (consistency ⟨Bn, MS 4⟩. Cf. Einstimmigkeit, Konsequenz, stimmen mit.

überführen, to convert, (*transposer* ⟨R⟩), (*transformer* ⟨B⟩), to translate; to lead (over), (*mener* ⟨B⟩), (*amener* ⟨B⟩), (*faire passer* ⟨R⟩); to take over. Not "to carry over" ⟨WH⟩; not "to transform"; not "to transfer" ⟨MS⟩; not "to differentiate" ⟨BG⟩.

Überführung in, conversion into.

Übergang, change ⟨WH⟩, transition ⟨WH, MS, L, BG⟩, (*passage* ⟨R, B⟩), going over ⟨WH, MS⟩, shift, shifting. Cf. Verschiebung, Wendung, Wechsel. | qualitativer —, transition from one quality to another. | synthetischer —, synthetical transition, (*passage synthétique* ⟨B⟩); transition to a synthesis.

übergehen (trans.), to pass over ⟨WH 1, MS 2⟩, (*négliger* ⟨R⟩). Not "to pass by" ⟨WH, MS, BG⟩.

übergehen (intrans.), | — auf, to be passed on to. | — in, to change into ⟨MS 1⟩, to turn into ⟨WH 1, MS 2⟩, (*se convertir dans* ⟨R⟩), (*se transformer en* ⟨B⟩), to pass over into. Cf. sich in etwas verwandeln (*sub* verwandeln). | — in einander, to blend ⟨WH 1⟩. | — zu, to go (on) to, (*passer à* ⟨B⟩), (*arriver à* ⟨B⟩), to shift to.

Übergehen, transition, passing on.

übergreifen, overreaching, (overlapping). Cf. Deckung, Überdeckung, Überkreuzung, Überschiebung.

übergreifend, overlapping, that overlap; (more) comprehensive; (*qui empiètent sur* ⟨B⟩).

überhaupt, 1. universally, (*en général* ⟨R, B⟩), without exception; taken (*or* conceived) universally (*or* ge-

nerically *or* in specie), (*pris en général* ⟨B⟩); as a universal.
2. whatever, of whatever (*or* every *or* any) sort, of all sorts.
3. somehow, by just any A.
4. altogether ⟨WH, MS⟩, (*de toute façon* ⟨B⟩), entirely, through out, as a whole; at all.
5. as such, (*comme tel* ⟨R⟩).
Not "in general" ⟨WH 1, BG⟩; not "generally" ⟨WH 2, MS 2, BG⟩. Cf. allgemein, als solches (*sub* solch), ganz. | alle A —, all A's of whatever sort, all A's without exception, (*tous les A, pris en général* ⟨B⟩). | (das) A —, 1. A of every (*or* any *or* whatever) sort, any A whatever.
2. (the) A (taken *or* conceived) universally (*or* generically *or* in specie), (*A en général* ⟨R⟩), A as a universal, the universal A.
3. (the) A as such, (*l'A comme tel* ⟨R⟩).
4. (the) A as a whole, the whole (of) A, all (the) A.
Not "A in general" ⟨BG⟩. Cf. Etwas(-)überhaupt, Gegenstandüberhaupt. | (die) A —, 1. (the) A's universally, (*les A en général* ⟨R, B⟩), (the) A's without exception, all A's, (the) A's of all sorts, A's of whatever sort, any A's whatever. Not "A's generally" ⟨BG⟩. | ein A —, 1. an A universally, an A of whatever sort, any A whatever, some A or other.
2. a universal A, (*un A pris en général* ⟨B⟩).
3. an A as such (*or* as exemplifying the universal A), (*un A en général* ⟨B⟩).
4. a whole A.
| Individuelles —, an individual something or other, (*l'individuel en général* ⟨B⟩). | irgend ein A —, 1. any A whatever.
2. any A as such (*or* as exemplifying the universal A).
| — durch ein A, by just any A. | — ist das wahr, universally that is true.

| — **nicht,** not at all ⟨WH 1, MS 1⟩. |
— **seine Intention,** its whole intention. | — **wahr,** altogether (*or* entirely) true. | — **zu klären,** at all clarifiable. | **weltlich Seiendes** —, whatever exists as worldly (*l'existent "mondain" en général* ⟨B⟩).
Überhaupt, | **das** —, the Whatever, (the) Any-Whatever, the universal, (*"en général"* ⟨B⟩). | **der Modus des** —, the mode Any, (*le mode du: "en général"* ⟨R⟩).
Überhaupt-Urteil, all-or-none judgment, universal judgment, (*jugement qui contient "en général"* ⟨B⟩). Cf. **allgemeines Urteil** (*sub* **allgemein**), **Urteil.**
Überkreuzung, intersection (with partial identity). Cf. **Überdeckung, Überschiebung.**
überlegen, to think over ⟨WH⟩, to consider ⟨WH⟩. Not "to examine" ⟨L⟩.
Überlegung, deliberation ⟨MS 3⟩, consideration ⟨WH 1, MS 1⟩, (*considération* ⟨B⟩), (analysis), (reflection ⟨MS 2, WH 3, BG⟩), (*réflexion* ⟨R, B⟩), (*reflexio* ⟨K⟩). So far as possible save "reflection" for "Reflexion". Cf. **Besinnung, Betrachtung, Erwägung.**
Überlieferung, transmission ⟨Bn, WH, MS⟩, tradition ⟨Bn, WH, MS⟩.
Überschiebung, overlapping, (*glissement* ⟨B⟩), partial coincidence. Cf. **Ähnlichkeitsüberschiebung, Dekkung, Überdeckung, übergreifen, Überkreuzung.**
überschreiten, to go beyond ⟨WH, MS⟩, (*dépasser* ⟨B⟩), to step outside, to transgress ⟨WH⟩, (*enfreindre* ⟨B⟩).
Überschreitung, going beyond, (*dépassement* ⟨B⟩); crossing ⟨MS 1⟩, (*franchissement* ⟨B⟩).
Überschwänglichkeit, excess ⟨WH 1⟩.
Übertragung auf, (sometimes:) extension to, (*extension à* ⟨R⟩).
Überzeugung, conviction ⟨WH 1, MS 2, BG⟩, (*conviction* ⟨PL, B⟩), (settled belief), (*présupposition* ⟨B⟩), persuasion ⟨MS 1, WH 3⟩.
Umbilden, transforming. Cf. **Bilden.**
Umbildung, transformation ⟨WH 1,

MS 1⟩, (*transformation* ⟨R⟩), recasting ⟨WH, MS⟩. Cf. **Bildung.**
Umdenken, phantasying otherwise, (*re-penser* ⟨B⟩). Cf. **Denken, Sichdenken.**
Umdeutung, reinterpretation (*fausse interprétation* ⟨B⟩). Cf. **Deutung.** | — **in,** interpretation that converts into, (*interprétation qui transforme en* ⟨B⟩).
Umfang, 1. (of an eidos, a concept, a science:) sphere ⟨WH, MS⟩, range ⟨Bn, WH, MS⟩, (*étendue* ⟨B⟩), (*champ* ⟨B⟩), (*domaine* ⟨B⟩), (*ressort* ⟨B⟩), (*multiplicité* ⟨B⟩). 2. (of an eidos, a concept, a term:) extension, (*extension* ⟨R, B⟩). 3. (of a reduction:) scope, (extent ⟨?⟩), (*extension* ⟨R⟩). Not "extension" ⟨BG⟩. 4. (of a physical reality, in transferred senses:) extent ⟨WH, MS, L⟩, extensiveness. Cf. **Bereich, Geltungsbereich, Kreis, Rahmen, Sinn, Sphäre, Tragweite.** | **ein** — **von Dingen,** many things. | **im** —, extensionally.
Umfangsallgemeinheit, extensional universality. Cf. **Allgemeinheit.**
umfangslogisch, in terms of an extensional logic, (*dans la perspective de la logique de l'extension* ⟨B⟩). Cf. **logisch.**
Umfangssinn, | **individueller** —, extensional sense as embracing individuals.
umfingieren, to phantasy as different. Cf. **fingieren.**
Umgebung, surroundings ⟨MS 1, WH 2, BG⟩, those around someone, environment ⟨WH⟩, (*environnement* ⟨R⟩). Cf. **Zeitumgebung.**
Umgeltung, revaluing ⟨?⟩. Cf. **Geltung.** | — **von Geltungen,** revaluing of values ⟨?⟩.
umgestalten, to reshape, (*transformer* ⟨B⟩). Cf. **gestalten, neugestaltet.** | **sich** —, to become reshaped. Not "to transform itself" ⟨L⟩. Cf. **sich gestalten** (*sub* **gestalten**).
umgreifen, to envelop, (*cerner* ⟨B⟩), to embrace, to take in, to comprehend, (*saisir* ⟨B⟩). Cf. **befassen, begreifen,**

fassen, greifen, mitbegreifen, Unverständnis.

umgrenzen, to ascertain the limits (*or* the boundaries) of, to delimit, to set the limits for, to bound ⟨WH 2⟩, (*circonscrire* ⟨B⟩), to define ⟨WH⟩, (*embrasser* ⟨R⟩).

Umgrenzung, ascertaining the limits (*or* the boundaries); delimitation, (*délimitation* ⟨B⟩). Cf. **Abgrenzung, abschliessen, Begrenzung, Grenze, Wesensumgrenzung.**

umschreiben, to delimit. Cf. **abschliessen.**

umschreibend, roundabout.

Umschreibung, delimitation. Cf. **Abgrenzung, Begrenzung.**

Umstand, circumstance ⟨WH 1⟩; circumstantiality. Not "refinement" ⟨L⟩.

Umstellung, change of focus, (*changement d'attitude* ⟨B⟩), redirection, (*déplacement* ⟨B⟩). Cf. **Einstellung.** | **thematische —,** change of thematical focus, (*déplacement thématique* ⟨B⟩). Cf. **thematische Einstellung** (*sub* **thematisch**).

Umsturz, overthrow ⟨MS 1, WH 2⟩, (*renversement* ⟨R⟩), (*eversio* ⟨Descartes⟩), (*révolution* ⟨PL⟩).

umwandeln, Cf. **sich wandeln.** | **sich —,** to change ⟨WH 1⟩. Cf. **sich wandeln** (*sub* **wandeln**). | **— in,** to transmute into, (*convertir en* ⟨B⟩).

Umwandlung, transmutation, change ⟨WH 1, MS 1⟩, (transfiguration), (*transformation* ⟨R, B⟩). Save "transformation" ⟨WH 2, MS 3⟩ for "Umformung", "conversion" ⟨MS 2⟩ for "Verwandlung", "Umwendung", etc. Cf. **Abwandlung, Wandel, Wandlung, Wechsel.**

Umwelt, surrounding world, (world about one ⟨BG⟩), (*monde environnant* ⟨R, B⟩), (*environnement* ⟨R⟩). Not "environment" ⟨Bn, WH 1⟩ and not "milieu" ⟨WH 2⟩, because the express reference to world should be preserved.

Umweltlichkeit, belonging to the surrounding world.

Umwendung, turn(ing) ⟨MS 1⟩, reversal ⟨MS⟩, (*changement d'orientation* ⟨B⟩), conversion. Cf. **Verwandlung, Wendung.**

umwerten, to change the value of, (*déformer la valeur de* ⟨B⟩); to reinterpret.

Umwertung, changing of value, (*conversion de valeur* ⟨R⟩), revaluation, (*renversement des valeurs* ⟨B⟩). Cf. **Wertung.**

Unabgehobenheit, lack of outstandingness, lack of prominentness, *etc.*; undifferentiatedness, lack of contrast, inconspicuousness. See Abgehobenheit. | **Untergrund der —,** inconspicuous substratum, (*tréfonds où se trouve ce qui n'est pas détaché* ⟨B⟩). Cf. **Untergrund.**

unabhängig, independent ⟨WH 1, MS 1⟩. Cf. **eigenständig, für sich, selbständig.**

unangenehm, disagreeable ⟨WH 2, MS 2⟩, (*désagréable* ⟨R⟩). Save "unpleasant" ⟨WH 1, MS, L, BG⟩ for "missfällig". Cf. **angenehm.**

unanschaulich ⟨adj.⟩, not intuitable ⟨BG⟩, (*dépourvu d'intuitivité* ⟨R⟩). Cf. **anschaubar, anschaulich.** | **das sinnlich U ~e,** that which is not sensuously intuitable, (what is not intuitable by sense ⟨BG⟩), (*l'élément dépourvu d'intuitivité sensible* ⟨R⟩).

unanschaulich ⟨adv.⟩, non-intuitionally, (*d'une manière non-intuitive* ⟨R⟩). | **— vorstellig haben,** to have as non-intuitionally objective, (*se représenter d'une manière non-intuitive* ⟨R⟩). Cf. **vorstellig haben** (*sub* **vorstellig**).

Unanschaulichkeit, Cf. **Anschaulichkeit.** | **sinnliche —,** absence of sensuous intuitability, (*manque d'intuitivité sensible* ⟨R⟩). Not "sensory unintuitability" ⟨BG⟩. Cf. **Anschaulichkeit 3, sinnlich** ⟨adj.⟩.

unaufhebbar, indefeasible, (*irrécusable* ⟨R⟩), which cannot be annulled ⟨BG⟩. Cf. **aufheben.**

unaufheblich, See aufheblich.

Unaufmerksamkeit, inattention ⟨WH 1⟩, (*inattention* ⟨R⟩). Cf. **Aufmerksamkeit.**

unbedenklich, Cf. bedenklich. | nicht —, not unquestionably correct.

unbegrenzt, (math:) without limit, unlimited ⟨MS 1, WH 2⟩, undelimited. Cf. begrenzt.

unbekannt, unacquainted, unknown ⟨WH 1, MS 1, BG⟩, (inconnu ⟨R⟩). Cf. bekannt.

unberechtigt, illegitimate ⟨MS 2⟩, (illégitime ⟨R⟩), unwarranted ⟨WH 1⟩, unjustified ⟨BG⟩. Cf. berechtigt, vollberechtigt.

unbestimmbar, | das U ⁓e, the indeterminable (what of). Not "indeterminable element" ⟨L⟩.

unbestimmt-beliebig, indeterminately optional, (indéterminé quelconque ⟨B⟩). Cf. bestimmt.

Unbestimmtheit, (logico-grammatical:) indefiniteness. Cf. Bestimmtheit.

undenkbar, inconceivable ⟨WH, MS⟩. Cf. denkbar.

undeutlich, indistinct ⟨WH 1, MS 1⟩. Save "confused" ⟨MS 2⟩ for "verworren". Cf. deutlich.

Undurchstreichbarkeit, uncancellableness. Cf. durchstreichen.

unecht, not genuine ⟨WH 1, MS 1⟩, spurious ⟨MS 2, WH⟩. Save "false" ⟨WH 2⟩ for "falsch". Cf. echt.

Unechtheit, spuriousness ⟨MS 1⟩, (inauthenticité ⟨B⟩).

uneigentlich ⟨adj.⟩, improper ⟨WH 1⟩, (impropre ⟨B⟩), not proper, metonymical, loose, figurative ⟨WH 2, MS⟩, imprecise; non-presentive; unreal ⟨F⟩. Cf. darstellend, eigentlich ⟨adj.⟩, irreal. | eine ⁓e Einheit, no proper unity. Cf. Einheit. | im ⁓en Sinn, (sometimes:) in a metonymical sense, by metonymy.

uneigentlich ⟨adv.⟩, improperly, not properly, metonymically, etc. See uneigentlich ⟨adj.⟩. Cf. eigentlich ⟨adv.⟩.

uneinsichtig, without insight, insightless, not a matter (or an object) of insight, lacking the quality of insight; intellectually obscure; not apodictically evident; non-evident, (non-évident ⟨B⟩). Cf. einsichtig ⟨adj.⟩.

Uneinsichtigkeit, absence of insight; (intellectual) unseenness; lack of apodictic evidentness; non-evidentness. Cf. Einsichtigkeit.

unendlich, infinite ⟨MS 1, WH 2⟩, (infini ⟨B⟩). Save "endless" ⟨WH 1, MS 2⟩ for "endlos". Cf. endlich.

unerschlossen, undiscovered. Cf. erschliessen 2.

universal, all-inclusive, all-embracing, all-pervasive, universal ⟨WH 1, MS 1⟩, (universel ⟨PL, B⟩). Cf. allgemein durchgehend, universell. | ⁓e Wissenschaftsidee, idea of an all-embracing science, (idée universelle de la science ⟨B⟩).

Universalgebiet, all-inclusive province, (domaine universel ⟨B⟩). Cf. Gebiet.

universal-objektivierend, universally objectivating, (objectivant universel ⟨B⟩).

Universalregion, all-inclusive region, (région universelle ⟨B⟩).

Universalvorstellung, all-inclusive idea. Cf. Vorstellung 4 & 5.

universell, universal ⟨WH 1, MS 1⟩, (universel ⟨B⟩). Cf. allgemein, universal.

unlebendig, lifeless, (privé de vie ⟨R⟩). Cf. lebendig.

unmerklich, unnoticeable. Not "imperceptible" ⟨WH 1, MS 1, Bn⟩. Cf. merken.

Unrecht, wrongness, wrong ⟨MS 1, WH 2⟩, injustice ⟨WH 1, MS 2⟩, (non-droit ⟨B⟩). Cf. Recht, verkehrt.

unrechtmässig, illegitimate ⟨WH, MS⟩, (illegitimus ⟨K⟩). Cf. rechtmässig.

unreflektiert, not reflected on (or upon) ⟨BG⟩, (irréfléchi ⟨R⟩), not modified reflectionally (see Ideen I, §78); non-reflective. Cf. reflektiert.

unrichtig, incorrect ⟨WH 2, MS 3⟩, wrong ⟨WH 1, MS 2⟩. Cf. richtig, verfehlt, verkehrt.

Unrichtigkeit, incorrectness ⟨MS 1, WH 2⟩. Cf. Richtigkeit.

unselbständig ⟨adj.⟩, non-selfsufficient, not selfsufficient, (non-indépendant ⟨B⟩), (non-autonome ⟨B⟩), (dépourvu d'autonomie ⟨R⟩), (dépendant ⟨R⟩). Save "dependent" ⟨WH 1, MS 1,

BG⟩ for "abhängig". Cf. **selbständig.**
unselbständig ⟨adv.⟩, non-selfsufficiently, (*d'une manière non-indépendante* ⟨B⟩); interdependently.
Unsinn, nonsense ⟨WH 1, MS 1⟩, (*nonsens* ⟨B, de M⟩), absence of sense. Save "absurdity" ⟨WH 2, MS 3⟩ for "Absurdität" and "Widersinn" ⟨q.v.⟩.
Unstimmigkeit, discordancy, (*discordance* ⟨B⟩), inconsistency ⟨WH 1⟩. Cf. **Inkonsequenz, Konsequenzlosigkeit, Selbstimmigkeit, zusammenstimmend.**
(Unterbegriff), minor term ⟨Bn⟩, (*terminus minor* ⟨K⟩). Cf. **Oberbegriff.**
Untergrund, substratum ⟨WH 1⟩, (*tréfonds* ⟨B⟩), underlying basis, basis ⟨BG⟩, (subsoil ⟨MS 1, WH 2⟩), (*arrière-fond* ⟨B⟩). Cf. **Aktuntergrund, Boden, Grund, Hintergrund, Substrat, Unterlage, Unterschicht.** | — **der Unabgehobenheit,** inconspicuous substratum, (*tréfonds où se trouve ce qui n'est pas détaché* ⟨B⟩). Cf. **Unabgehobenheit.**
Unterlage, foundation ⟨WH 1, L⟩, substratum ⟨WH, MS⟩, (*soubassement* ⟨R, B⟩), (*infrastructure* ⟨R⟩), support, basis, ⟨BG⟩; (theoretical basis). Cf. **Boden, Fundament, Grund, Grundlage, Substrat, Untergrund, Unterschicht, Unterstufe.**
unterlegen, (governing dative:) to attach to, (*attribuer à* ⟨B⟩), (to give to), (to supply to ⟨BG⟩); (to put in the place of); (*soutenir* ⟨R⟩).
(Untersatz), minor premise ⟨Bn⟩, (*propositio minor* ⟨K⟩). Cf. **(Obersatz), Satz 1.**
unterscheiden, to distinguish ⟨MS 1, WH 2, BG⟩), (*distinguer* ⟨B⟩), to discriminate, ⟨Bn, WH 3, MS 3⟩, to differentiate ⟨WH 4, MS 4⟩, (*séparer* ⟨B⟩). Cf. **abheben, kennzeichnen, scheiden.** | **sich** —, to be distinguished (from one another), (*se distinguer* ⟨B⟩), to be differentiated.
unterscheidend, distinctive ⟨Gomperz trln of Mill, quoted in LU, I. Unters.; WH 1; MS 1⟩. Cf. **ausgezeichnet.**
Unterscheidung, distinction ⟨WH 1,

MS 1⟩, (*distinction* ⟨R, B⟩), differentiation ⟨WH, MS⟩. Cf. **Scheidung, Unterschied, unterschiedslos, Urteilsunterscheidung.**
Unterschicht, lower stratum ⟨WH 1, MS 2⟩, substratum ⟨WH 2, MS 3⟩, (*infrastructure* ⟨R⟩). Cf. **Oberschicht, Substrat, Untergrund, Unterlage.**
unterschieben, to ascribe, to attach.
Unterschied, difference ⟨WH 1, MS 1⟩, (rarely:) differentia; contrast, distinction ⟨WH 2, MS 2, L, BG⟩, (*distinction* ⟨B⟩). So far as possible save "distinction" for "Unterscheidung" ⟨q.v.⟩. Cf. **Bewusstseinsunterschied, Differenz, Verschiedenheit.**
unterschieden, different ⟨WH 1⟩, differentiated. Cf. **verschieden.**
Unterschiedenheit, differentness, diversity, differentiatedness. Cf. **Verschiedenheit.**
unterschiedslos ⟨adv.⟩, without differentiation ⟨L⟩. Cf. **Unterscheidung.**
unterstehen, to come under ⟨WH, MS⟩, (*être soumis à* ⟨B⟩), (einer Kritik:) to be subject to ⟨WH⟩, (einer Spezies:) to be subsumed under.
Unterstufe, 1. lower level, (*soubassement* ⟨R⟩). Save "basis" ⟨BG⟩ for "Boden", "Grund", "Untergrund", "Unterlage", ⟨qq. vv.⟩.
2. preliminary stage, (*stade préliminaire* ⟨R⟩). Cf. **Stufe, Vorstufe.**
untersuchen, to investigate ⟨WH 2, MS⟩. Cf. **sich besinnen** (*sub* **besinnen**), **forschen, nachgehen.**
Untersuchung, investigation ⟨WH 1, MS, BG⟩, (*étude* ⟨R, B⟩). Save "study" ⟨BG⟩ for "Studium", particularly because *Logische Studien* was Husserl's earlier title for *Erfahrung und Urteil*. Cf. **Ursprungsuntersuchung.**
unverändert, (at least sometimes:) unchanging. Cf. **Veränderung.**
unvereinbar, non-unifiable. Save "incompatible" ⟨WH 1, MS 1⟩ for "unverträglich" and "inconsistent" ⟨WH 2, MS⟩ for "inkonsequent" ⟨q.v.⟩ and "unstimmig".
Unvereinbarkeit, non-unifiability. Save "incompatibility" ⟨WH 1, MS 1⟩ for

"Unverträglichkeit" and "inconsistency" ⟨Bn, WH 2, MS 2, L⟩ for "Inkonsequenz" and "Unstimmigkeit" ⟨q.v.⟩.

unverständlich, unintelligible, (*incompréhensible* ⟨R, B⟩), enigmatic ⟨WH 3⟩. Cf. **Rätsel.**

Unverständnis, incomprehension, (*noncompréhension* ⟨B⟩).

Unverträglichkeit, incompatibility ⟨MS⟩, (*incompatibilité* ⟨R⟩). Cf. **Verträglichkeit.**

unwert, negatively valuable. Cf. **Wert.** | **ein U~es,** something negatively valuable.

Unwert, disvalue, (*non-valeur* ⟨B⟩), concrete disvalue, evil. Cf. **Wert.**

Unwirklichkeit, non-actuality. Cf. **Inaktualität 2, Wirklichkeit.**

unzweifelhaft ⟨adj.⟩, doubtless, not doubtful, undoubted. Cf. **zweifelhaft, zweifellos.**

unzweifelhaft ⟨adv.⟩, doubtlessly.

Ur-, primal ⟨MS⟩, proto-, (*proto-* ⟨R⟩), primitive ⟨WH, MS⟩, originary, original ⟨WH 1, MS⟩. Save "primordial" for "primordi(n)al". Cf. **original, originär, ursprünglich, urtümlich.**

Urabwandlung, primitive variant, (*variante primitive* ⟨B⟩). Cf. **Abwandlung.**

Ur-Arche, original ark.

Urauffassung, primitive apprehension. Cf. **Auffassung.**

Urbegriff, primitive concept, (*concept primitif* ⟨B⟩). Cf. **Begriff.**

Urbild, prototype ⟨WH 1, MS 2⟩, (*prototypon* ⟨K⟩), (archetype ⟨Bn, MS 3⟩). Cf. **Bild, Vorbild.**

Urboden, primitive basis, (*base primitive* ⟨B⟩); primal realm. Cf. **Boden, Urgrund.** | **auf dem —,** within the primal realm, (*sur la base primitive* ⟨B⟩).

Urdoxa, protodoxa.

Urform, primitive form ⟨WH 1⟩, (*forme primitive* ⟨B⟩), (primal form), (*forme originaire* ⟨de M⟩), (*formemère* ⟨R⟩). Not "root-form" ⟨BG⟩.

Urgegenständlichkeit, primitive objectivity.

Urgrund, primitive basis, (*fondement primitif* ⟨B⟩). Cf. **Grund, Urboden.**

Urimpression, originary impression.

Urjetzt, primal Now.

Urlogos, primal logos, (*logos primitif* ⟨B⟩).

Urmodalität, primitive modality, (*modalité fondamentale* ⟨B⟩).

Urmodus, primitive mode, (*mode primitif* ⟨B⟩).

Urmoment, Ur-Moment, originary moment. Cf. **Ursprungsmoment.**

Urphantasma, originary phantasm.

Urquelle, primal source, (*source* ⟨R⟩). Cf. **Quelle, Ursprung.**

urquellend, originarily arising.

Ursache, cause ⟨WH 1, MS 1, BG⟩, (*cause* ⟨R⟩), (rarely:) reason ⟨WH 2, MS 2⟩. Cf. **Grund.**

Ursache-Meinung, cause-meaning. Cf. **Meinung.**

Ursachrealität, causative reality, (*réalité causale* ⟨R⟩), (causal reality ⟨?⟩ ⟨BG⟩).

Ursprung, origin ⟨WH, MS, BG⟩, (*origine* ⟨R, B⟩), (source ⟨WH 1⟩), (non-technical sense, sometimes:) inception. Cf. **Entstehung, Quelle, Urquelle.** | **des ~s,** original, (*originel* ⟨B⟩). | **seinen — haben in,** to originate in ⟨WH 1⟩. Cf. **entspringen in.**

ursprünglich ⟨adj.⟩, original ⟨WH 1, MS 1, BG⟩, (*originel* ⟨R, B⟩), originary ("now rare" — OED), (*originaire* ⟨de M⟩), (*originarius* ⟨K⟩), primitive, (*primitif* ⟨R⟩), (*primitivus* ⟨Leibniz⟩). Cf. **original, originär** ⟨adj.⟩, **Ur-, urtümlich.**

ursprünglich ⟨adv.⟩, originally ⟨MS⟩, (*originellement* ⟨B⟩), in an original (or originary) manner, (*d'une manière originelle* ⟨B⟩), originaliter, (originarily ⟨not in OED⟩). Cf. **originär** ⟨adv.⟩. | **— anschaulich,** in a manner that characterizes original (or originary) intuition.

ursprünglich-genetisch ⟨adv.⟩, by a process of original genesis, (*d'une manière génétiquement originelle* ⟨B⟩).

Ursprünglichkeit, originality ⟨MS 1, WS 2, BG⟩, (*originalité* ⟨B⟩), origin-

ariness, originalness, (*originel* ⟨B⟩).
Cf. **Originalität, Originarität.**
ursprungsecht, authentic, (*originel*
⟨B⟩). Cf. **echt.**
Ursprungsechtheit, originary genuineness, authenticity, (*authenticité originelle* ⟨B⟩). Cf. **Echtheit.**
Ursprungsforschung, (scientific) inquiry into origins, (*recherche sur
l'originel* ⟨B⟩). Cf. **Forschung.**
Ursprungsklärung, originary clarification, (*clarification de l'origine*
⟨B⟩). Cf. **Klärung.**
ursprungsmässig ⟨adv.⟩, according to
their origins, (*d'une manière originelle* ⟨B⟩).
Ursprungsmoment, original moment.
Cf. **Urmoment.**
Ursprungssinn, originary sense, (*sens
originel* ⟨B⟩).
Ursprungsuntersuchung, investigation
of origins. Cf. **Untersuchung.** | **die
~en der Logik,** those investigations
of origins which pertain to logic,
(*études sur l'origine de la logique* ⟨B⟩).
Urstiftung, primal instituting, primal
institution, (*fondation primitive* ⟨B⟩)
Cf. **Stiftung.**
Ursubstrat, primitive substrate, (*substrat primitif* ⟨B⟩). Cf. **Substrat.**
Urteil, judgment ⟨WH 1, MS 1⟩, (*jugement* ⟨R, B, de M⟩), (*judicium* ⟨K⟩),
(rarely:) judging. When trltd "judging" the original should be given.
Cf. **Aussageurteil, Erfahrungsurteil,
Gesetzurteil, Gewissheitsurteil, Sinnesurteil, Urteilen, Wahrnehmungsurteil.**
urteilen, to judge ⟨WH 1, MS, BG⟩,
(*juger* ⟨R, B⟩), (*produire un jugement* ⟨B⟩). Cf. **beurteilen.**
Urteilen, judging, (*juger* ⟨B⟩), (*activité
de jugement* ⟨B⟩), (*judication* ⟨de
M⟩). Cf. **Urteil.**
urteilend ⟨adj.⟩, judging ⟨BG⟩, (*jugeant* ⟨R, B⟩), who is doing the
judging, (*qui juge* ⟨B⟩), judicative,
(*judicatoire* ⟨B⟩), (*opéré par le juge-
ment* ⟨B⟩). Cf. **urteilsmässig.** ⟨adj.⟩. |
~e Aktivität, judicative activity,
(*activité judicatoire* ⟨B⟩). | **~e Mei-
nung,** judging process of meaning,

judicative meaning, (*jugement en
tant qu'opinion* ⟨B⟩). Cf. **Meinung,**
urteilendes Meinen (*sub* urteilend
⟨adj.⟩), **Urteilsmeinung.** | **~e Ver-
nunft,** judicative reason, (*raison dans
l'ordre du jugement* ⟨B⟩). | **~es Lei-
sten,** judicative producing, (*effectuation de jugement* ⟨B⟩). Cf. **Leisten,
Urteilsleisten.** | **~es Meinen,** judging
process of meaning, (*intention du jugement* ⟨B⟩), (*activité d'opinion qui
juge* ⟨B⟩). Cf. **Meinen,** urteilende
Meinung (*sub* urteilend ⟨adj.⟩).
urteilend ⟨adv.⟩, in judging, (*en jugeant* ⟨B⟩), judgingly, judicatively.
Cf. **urteilsmässig** ⟨adv.⟩.
urteilend-erkennend ⟨adj.⟩, judicatively cognizing, (*jugeant et connaissant*
⟨B⟩). Cf. **erkennend.**
Urteilsakt, act of judgment, (*acte de
jugement* ⟨B⟩), judgment-act.
Urteilsaktion, action of judgment, (*action de jugement* ⟨B⟩), action involved in judging, judicial action,
(judging).
Urteilsarbeit, work of judging, (*travail
dans la sphère du jugement* ⟨B⟩). Cf.
Arbeit, Erkenntnisarbeit.
Urteilsausdruck, judgment-expression,
expression of the judgment, (*jugement exprimé* ⟨B⟩). Cf. **Wunschausdruck.**
Urteilsaussage, statement of a (or the)
judgment, (*énoncé d'un jugement*
⟨B⟩), judicial statement, judicial
predication. Cf. **Aussage, Wunschaussage.**
Urteilsbedeutung, judicial signification, judgment-signification, (*signification du jugement* ⟨B⟩), signified
judgment, (*jugement en tant que
signification* ⟨B⟩). Cf. **Bedeutung 1.**
Urteilsbegriff, concept of (the) judgment, (*concept de jugement* ⟨B⟩),
judgment-concept. Cf. **Begriff.**
Urteilsbestandstück, judgment-com-
ponent, (*élément constitutif dans le
jugement* ⟨B⟩). Cf. **Bestandstück.**
Urteilsbewusstsein, judging consciousness, (*conscience de jugement* ⟨R⟩).
Urteilsbildung, judgment-formation,
(*organisation du jugement* ⟨B⟩). Cf.

Bildung, Urteilsgebilde, Urteilsgestalt.

Urteilsboden, basis for judgment(s). Cf. **Boden.**

Urteilseinheit, judgment-unity of (the) judgment, (*unité de* (ou *du*) *jugement* ⟨B⟩). Cf. **Einheit.**

Urteilseinstellung, judicative attitude, (*orientation du jugement* ⟨B⟩). Cf. **Einstellung.**

Urteilsenthaltung, abstention from judgment, (*suspension de jugement* ⟨R⟩). Cf. **Enthaltung.**

Urteilsentscheidung, judicial decision. Cf. **Willensentscheidung.**

Urteilsergebnis, judgment-result, resultant judgment, (*jugement résultant* ⟨B⟩), (*résultant de la sphère du jugement* ⟨B⟩).

Urteilserlebnis, mental judgment-process, mental process of judgment, (*vécu du jugement* ⟨B⟩). Cf. **Erlebnis, Urteilsprozess, Vorstellungserlebnis.**

Urteilsevidenz, judicative evidence, (*évidence de jugement* ⟨B⟩), (*évidence relative au jugement* ⟨B⟩).

Urteilsform, judgment-form, (pl:) judgment-forms (*or* forms of judgments), (*forme de* (ou *du*) *jugement* ⟨B⟩). Cf. **Formenlehre der Urteile** (*sub* **Formenlehre**), **Urteilsgestalt.**

Urteilsgebiet, judgment-province. Cf. **Gebiet.**

Urteilsgebilde, (produced) judgment-formation, (formation produced by judging), (*formation de jugement* ⟨B⟩), (*formation (de la sphère) du jugement* ⟨B⟩). Cf. **Gebilde, Gegenstandsgebilde, Urteilsform, Urteilsbildung, Urteilsgestalt.**

Urteilsgegenstand, judgment-object, (*objet du jugement* ⟨B⟩).

Urteilsgegenständlichkeit, judgment-objectivity, (*objectité du jugement* ⟨B⟩), (*objet intervenant dans le jugement* ⟨B⟩).

Urteilsgemeinschaft, judgment-community, (*communauté qui se forme sur le plan du jugement* ⟨B⟩). Cf. **Gemeinschaft.**

Urteilsgestalt, judgment-formation, judgment-configuration, judgment-

form, (*forme de jugement* ⟨B⟩). Cf. **Erkenntnisgestalt,Erfahrungsgestalt, Gestalt, Urteilsbildung, Urteilsform, Urteilsgebilde.**

Urteilsgewissheit, judgment-certainty, (*certitude* ⟨B⟩). Cf. **Gewissheitsurteil, Urteilsmodalität.**

Urteilsinhalt, judgment-content, (*contenu du jugement* ⟨B⟩). Cf. **Inhalt.**

Urteilsintentionalität, judicative intentionality, (*intentionnalité de jugement* ⟨B⟩).

Urteilskomplexion, judgment-combination. Cf. **Komplexion.**

Urteilskonsequenz, judgment-consequence, consequence-relationship of judgments, (*conséquence des jugements* ⟨B⟩), (*suite conséquente de jugements* ⟨B⟩), (*jugement conséquent* ⟨B⟩).

Urteilslehre, judgment-theory, (*doctrine du jugement* ⟨B⟩).

Urteilsleistung, judicative performance, (*effectuation de* (ou *du*) *jugement* ⟨B⟩). Cf. **Leistung, urteilende Leistung** (*sub* **Leistung**) **urteilendes Leisten** (*sub* **Leisten**).

Urteilslogik, logic of judgments, (*logique du jugement* ⟨B⟩).

urteilsmässig ⟨adj.⟩, judicial, (*de la nature du jugement* ⟨B⟩), judgment-, (*des jugements* ⟨B⟩), judging, as objects of judgments.

urteilsmässig ⟨adv.⟩, judicially, judgingly, by judgment(s), (*dans les jugements* ⟨B⟩), (*dans le jugement* ⟨B⟩), in consequence of judgments, at the level of judgments, to make judgments about. | — **eingehen,** to enter in consequence of judgments. | — **für uns da,** there for us to make judgments about. | — **gemeint,** meant judgingly, (*visé dans le jugement* ⟨B⟩). | — **konstituieren,** to constitute at the level of judgments, (*constituer dans les jugements* ⟨B⟩).

urteilsmässig-mittelbar, as mediated by judgments, (*médiatement par l'intermédiaire du jugement* ⟨B⟩).

Urteilsmaterie, judgment-material, (*matière du jugement* ⟨B⟩). Cf. **Materie.**

Urteilsmeinung, judicial meaning, judicial opinion, (*jugement-opinion* ⟨B⟩), (*opinion qui se spécifie en jugement* ⟨B⟩), judicial meaning or opinion. Cf. **urteilende Meinung** (*sub* Meinung), **urteilendes Meinen** (*sub* Meinen), **Willensmeinung, Wunschmeinung.**
Urteilsmodalität, judgment-modality, modality of judgment, (*modalité du jugement* ⟨B⟩).
Urteilsproblem, problem concerning judgment (*or* judging), (*problème du jugement* ⟨B⟩).
Urteilsprozess, judgment-process, process of judgment, (*processus de jugement* ⟨B⟩). Cf. **Urteilserlebnis.**
Urteilsrichtigkeit, correctness of a judgment, (*justesse du jugement* ⟨B⟩). Cf. **Richtigkeit.**
Urteilssatz, proposition, judged proposition, (judicial positum), (*jugement-proposition* ⟨B⟩). Cf. **Satz.**
Urteilsschritt, judgment-step, (*démarche du jugement* ⟨B⟩).
Urteilssetzung, judgment-positing, judicial positing, (*position de jugement* ⟨B⟩). Cf. **Setzung.**
Urteilssinn, judgment-sense, (*sens du jugement* ⟨B⟩), (*jugement considéré en tant que sens* ⟨B⟩).
Urteilssphäre, judgment-sphere, sphere comprising judgments, (*sphère du jugement* ⟨B⟩). | apophantische —, sphere comprising apophantic judgments, (*sphère apophantique du jugement* ⟨B⟩).
Urteilsstufe, level of judging, (*niveau de base du jugement* ⟨B⟩).
Urteilssynthesis, judgment-synthesis, (synthesis of judgment ⟨BG⟩).

Urteilstätigkeit, activity of judgment, (*activité de jugement* ⟨B⟩), judicial activity, (judging activity). Cf. **Tätigkeit.**
Urteilstheorie, judgment-theory, (*théorie du jugement* ⟨B⟩).
Urteilstypik, grouping of judgments according to types, (*typique du jugement* ⟨B⟩). Cf. **Typik.**
Urteilsunterscheidung, distinction pertaining to judgments, (*distinction de jugements* ⟨B⟩).
Urteilsverhalt, (predicatively formed) judgment-complex, (*état* (-*des-choses*) *du jugement* ⟨B⟩). Cf. **Sachverhalt, Verhalt.**
Urteilsvollzug, judgment-performing, judgment-performance, (*effectuation de jugement* ⟨B⟩). Cf. **Aktvollzug, Vollzug.**
Urteilswahrheit, judicial truth, (*vérité du jugement* ⟨B⟩). Cf. **Seinswahrheit, Wahrheit.**
Urteilsweise, manner of judging, (*mode de jugement* ⟨B⟩). Cf. **Weise.**
Urteilszusammenhang, judgment-complex; judgment-continuity, (*enchaînement de jugements* ⟨B⟩).
Urteilszusammensetzung, judgment-compound, (*assemblage de jugements* ⟨B⟩). Cf. **Zusammensetzung.**
urtemporal ⟨adj.⟩, original-temporal.
urtümlich, primal, (*original* ⟨B⟩). Save "original" ⟨WH 1, MS 1⟩ for "originär" ⟨q.v.⟩, "originär" ⟨q.v.⟩, and "ursprünglich" ⟨q.v.⟩.
urwüchsig, natural ⟨MS⟩. Not "inborn" ⟨L⟩. Cf. **naheliegend, natürlich.**

V

Variation, variation ⟨WH 1⟩, varying. | freie —, free variation, varying free.
variieren, to vary ⟨WH 1, MS 1⟩, to change (into). Cf. **ändern, verwandeln.**

verabscheuen, (ant. begehren:) to shrink from.
Verallgemeinerung, universalization; (generalization ⟨WH 1, MS 1, L⟩, (*généralisation* ⟨B⟩). So far as possible save "generalization" for "Ge-

neralisierung". Cf. **allgemein** ⟨adj.⟩, **Wesensverallgemeinerung.** | **empirische** —, empirical generalization ⟨L⟩. | **in der** —, (at least sometimes:) in referring to universalizations.

Veränderlichkeit, alterableness, mutability ⟨Bn, MS⟩, (math:) variability ⟨MS 1, WH⟩. Cf. **abwandelbar, ändern.**

verändern, | **sich** —, to change ⟨WH 2⟩.

Veränderung, alteration ⟨MS 2, WH 3⟩, (*altération* ⟨R⟩), change ⟨WH 1, MS 1, L⟩, mutation, (math:) variation. Cf. **Abänderung, ändern, unverändert, Wandel, Wandlung, Wechsel, Wendung.**

veranschaulichen, to illustrate ⟨WH 1⟩ intuitionally; to make intuitable; (*donner la richesse de l'intuition* ⟨R⟩). Cf. **anschaulich, anschaulich machen** (*sub* **anschaulich**).

Veranschaulichung, intuitional illustration, illustration ⟨WH 1, MS 1⟩, illustrative intuition; making intuited (*or* intuitable); actualizing an intuition (*or* intuitions). Cf. **anschaulich, nachveranschaulichend, vorveranschaulichend.** | **analogisierende** —, intuitional by analogy. | **einheitliche** —, unitary intuitional illustration.

verantwortlich, 1. (persons:) responsible ⟨WH 1, MS 2⟩. Not "accountable" ⟨Bn, WH 3, MS 3⟩. 2. (things:) justifiable ⟨WH 1, MS 1⟩. Cf. **selbstverantwortlich.**

Verband, combine ⟨not in OED⟩, combination, association ⟨?⟩ ⟨WH, MS⟩, (*assemblage* ⟨B⟩). Cf. **Kombination, Komplexion, Verbindung, Verflechtung.**

verbildlichen, to pictorialize. Cf. **bildlich, vorverbildlichen.**

verbildlichend, pictorializing. Not "imaginative" ⟨BG⟩.

verbinden, to combine ⟨MS 2⟩, to connect ⟨WH, MS⟩, (*lier* ⟨B⟩). Not "to conjoin". Cf. **kombinieren, verflechten, verknüpfen.**

verbindend, combining, combinative, connective, (*liant* ⟨B⟩), that con-

nects. | **~e Rede,** speech that connects (minds).

Verbindung, combination ⟨Kemp Smith trln of Kant, WH, MS⟩, connexion ⟨Bn, WH 2, MS, BG⟩, (*liaison* ⟨B⟩), (*composition* ⟨B⟩), (*union* ⟨B⟩), (chem:) compound, (*conjunctio* ⟨K⟩). Not "conjunction" ⟨WH, MS⟩; cf. Logik, *263*. Cf. **Anknüpfung, Beziehung, Kombination, Komplexion, Verband, Verflechtung, Verknüpfung, Verwebung, Zusammenhang, Zusammensetzung.** | **in** — **mit,** combinated with. | **kontinuierliche** —, continuous connexion. | **(** — **und Einteilung),** (fallacies:) composition and division ⟨Bn⟩.

Verbindungsform combination-form, form of combination, (*forme de liaison* ⟨B⟩).

Verbindungsweise, mode of combination, (*mode de liaison* ⟨B⟩). Cf. **Weise.**

verborgen, hidden, ⟨WH 2, MS 2⟩, (*caché* ⟨R⟩), (*occultus* ⟨K⟩).

verbunden, combined ⟨WH 1⟩, (inter-) connected, (*lié* ⟨R, B⟩). Not "bound" ⟨BG⟩. Cf. **gebunden, komplex, verbinden.**

Verbundenheit, combinedness, connectedness, (*liaison* ⟨B⟩). | **kontinuierliche** —, continuous connectedness.

verdeutlichen, to make distinct, (*rendre distinct* ⟨B⟩). Cf. **deutlich.** | **sich** —, to become distinct, (*devenir distinct* ⟨B⟩).

Verdeutlichung, 1. (process:) making distinct, (*procès qui rend distinct* ⟨B⟩), becoming distinct. 2. (result:) distinct explicate. Cf. **Explikat.**

verdinglichen, to physicalize, (*objectiver* ⟨B⟩). Not "to hypostatize" ⟨WH 1, K⟩. Cf. **dinglich.** Not "to reify" ⟨L⟩.

vereigentlichend, "properizing". Cf. **eigentlich.**

Vereigentlichung, "properization".

Vereinbarkeit, unifiability, (*compatibilité* ⟨B⟩), (*association* ⟨B⟩). Cf. **Verträglichkeit.**

vereinen, | sich miteinander —, to unite. (Vereinigung der Kräfte), composition of forces ⟨Bn⟩.
vereinzelt, isolated ⟨WH 2, MS, L⟩.
Vereinzelung, singularization, (individuation ⟨R, B⟩), (ramification ⟨R⟩); isolation ⟨MS 1⟩. Save "individuation" ⟨BG⟩ for "Individuation" and "particularization" for "Besonderung" ⟨q.v.⟩. Cf. Einzelheit, Singularität.
Verfassung, Cf. Grundverfassung, Lebensverfassung.
verfehlen, to miss ⟨WH 1, MS 1⟩.
verfehlt, wrong ⟨MS⟩. Cf. unrichtig, verkehrt.
verflechten, to combine, (composer ⟨R⟩), to involve ⟨WH⟩; to interweave ⟨MS 2, WH⟩, (to intertwine ⟨MS 3⟩), (entremêler ⟨B⟩). Cf. kombinieren, mitverflochten, verbinden. | sich — mit, to combine with; to become involved in, (s'entremêler avec ⟨B⟩), (s'entrelacer avec ⟨B⟩).
Verflechtung, combination ⟨MS, L⟩, (combinaison ⟨R⟩), involvement; (entrelacement ⟨R⟩), tissue, complex. Cf. Assoziationsverflechtung, Kombination, Komplexion, Verbindung, Verwebung.
verfliessen, to flow away ⟨WH 2, MS 2⟩, to pass ⟨WH⟩, (se dissiper ⟨B⟩).
Verflossenheit, fusedness. Cf. Verschmelzung, Verworrenheit.
Vergangenheitsmoment, pastness-moment.
vergegenständlichen, to objectify ⟨WH 1, BG⟩, (objectiver ⟨R⟩). Cf. vorstellen, vorstellig machen (sub vorstellig).
Vergegenständlichung, objectification, (objectivation ⟨R⟩). Save "Objectivation" (capitalized) for "Objektivation" and "Objektivierung"; save "objectivation" (not capitalized) for "Vorstellung" ⟨q.v.⟩.
vergegenwärtigen, 1. (technical senses:) to presentiate ⟨in OED⟩, (présentifier ⟨R, B⟩), to make present in non-original intuition, to make present in phantasy.

2. (non-technical senses:) to recall; (to represent ⟨WH 1, MS 1⟩); (to reproduce); (to envisage). Cf. darstellen, Gegenwärtigen, vorstellen. | sich —, to presentiate to oneself, (se présentifier ⟨B⟩), to make present to oneself in phantasy, (évoquer ⟨R⟩). Not "to rehearse to oneself" ⟨BG⟩.
vergegenwärtigend ⟨adv.⟩, presentiatively. Not "by presentifying" ⟨L⟩. Cf. gegenwärtigend.
Vergegenwärtigung, presentation, (présentification ⟨R⟩), presentiating, non-original presentation (or intuition), making present (in non-original intuition), something made present, re-presentation⟨Zeitv.,400⟩, (representation ⟨BG⟩), (reproduction⟨see Ideen I, §111; E. u. U., 237⟩). Cf. Darstellung, Erinnerungsvergegenwärtigung, Gegenwärtigung, Vorstellung 3, Wiedervergegenwärtigung. | bildliche —, making present as something depicted, (présentification du type portrait ⟨R⟩). Cf. bildlich.
vergeistern, to inspirit, (spiritualiser ⟨B⟩).
vergemeinschaften, to make common, (mettre en commun ⟨B⟩), to communalize, to make communal, to pool; to effect a communion; to establish (a) community; (to socialize ⟨Sch⟩). So far as possible save "to socialize" for "vergesellschaften".
Vergemeinschaftung, communalization, making common, (mise en commun ⟨B⟩), pooling; effecting of communion; establishing of (a) community; (communauté ⟨B⟩); (socialization).
Vergesellschaftung, association ⟨MS 1⟩.
Verhalt, predicatively formed complex, (state of affairs ⟨WH 1, MS 1⟩ (hyphenated, if desirable to prevent ambiguity)), (état de chose ⟨R⟩), (relationship), (rapport ⟨PL⟩). Cf. Komplexion, Relation, Sachverhalt, Seinsverhalt, Urteilsverhalt, Verhältnis, Wertsachverhalt, Wertverhalt,

Wesensverhalt, Wirklichkeitsverhalt.

verhalten, | **sich so und so** —, to comport oneself ⟨WH⟩ thus and so, *(se comporter de telle et telle façon* ⟨R, B⟩*)*; to stand ⟨WH, MS⟩ thus and so, to be the case ⟨WH, MS⟩. Cf. **Sichverhalten.** | **sich zu etwas** —, to bear a relationship to something. **Verhalten,** behaviour ⟨WH⟩, *(comportement* ⟨B⟩*)*; *(conduite* ⟨B⟩*)*; procedure ⟨WH, MS⟩. Cf. **Gebaren, Gehaben, Sichverhalten, Verhaltung.**

Verhältnis, 1. relationship ⟨MS 2, WH⟩, relation ⟨MS 1, WH⟩, *(relatio* ⟨K⟩*)*, *(rapport* ⟨R, B⟩*)*, (of quantities:) ratio ⟨Bn, WH, MS⟩, *(proportio* ⟨Wolff⟩*)*. 2. (pl., sometimes:) circumstances ⟨WH⟩, matters ⟨WH⟩, the situation, *(situation* ⟨B⟩*)*. Cf. **Beziehung, Bezug, Materie, Relation, Rückbezogenheit, Sache, Stoff, Verhalt.** | — **der Konsequenz,** consequence-relationship, *(relation de conséquence* ⟨B⟩*)*. Cf. **Konsequenzverhältnis.** **(Verhaltung),** behavior ⟨MS; Aster 1935, discussing behaviorism⟩. Cf. **Gebaren, Gehaben, Sichverhalten, Verhaltungsweise.**

Verhaltungsweise, | **kausale** —, mode of causal behavior, *(comportement causal* ⟨R⟩*)*. Cf. **Weise.**

verharren, to persist ⟨WH, MS⟩, *(persister* ⟨B⟩*)*, *(demeurer* ⟨B⟩*)*.

verhüllt, veiled from sight, *(caché* ⟨B⟩*)*.

verkehrt, wrong ⟨WH, MS⟩, false, *(faux* ⟨B⟩*)*, *(absurde* ⟨B⟩*)*. Not "perverse" ⟨BG⟩. Cf. **Unrecht, unrichtig, verfehlt.**

Verkehrtheit, wrong opinion; wrongness, error, absurdity ⟨WH 1, L⟩, *(absurdité* ⟨R⟩*)*. Not "perversity" ⟨MS 1, WH, BG⟩. Cf. **Widersinn.**

verknüpfen, to connect ⟨Gomperz trln of Mill, quoted in LU, I. Unters.; WH; MS; BG⟩, *(lier* ⟨B⟩*)*, *(rattacher* ⟨R, B⟩*)*, (to annex ⟨Ueberweg trln of Berkeley, Lipps trln of Hume, both quoted in LU, II. Unters.⟩*)*, *(associer* ⟨B⟩*)*, *(coordonner* ⟨B⟩*)*. Cf. **verbinden.**

Verknüpfung, connexion ⟨MS 1, WH

2, L, BG⟩, *(liaison* ⟨R, B⟩*)*, connecting, nexus ⟨L⟩, *(unification* ⟨B⟩*)*, *(union* ⟨B⟩*)*, *(réunion* ⟨B⟩*)*. Cf. **Anknüpfung, Beziehung, Bezug, Formenverknüpfung, Verbindung, Zusammenhang.**

Verlauf, course ⟨WH 3, MS 3⟩, *(cours* ⟨B⟩*)*, flow ⟨BG⟩, *(déroulement* ⟨B⟩*)*, process ⟨WH, MS⟩, (sequence), *(suite* ⟨B⟩*)*. Cf. **Ablauf, Belauf, Bewusstseinslauf, Fluss, Fortgang, Wortverlauf.**

verlaufen, to flow away ⟨MS⟩, to flow, *(se dérouler* ⟨B⟩*)*, *(s'écouler* ⟨B⟩*)*, to go on, to proceed, to occur, *(se développer* ⟨B⟩*)*.

verleihen, to confer ⟨WH, MS⟩, *(fournir* ⟨B⟩*)*, *(procurer* ⟨B⟩*)*. Cf. **geben.**

verleihend, conferring. Cf. **bedeutungverleihend, gebend, sinnverleihend.**

vermeinen, to suppose ⟨WH 1, MS 2⟩, to presume ⟨WH⟩, *(présumer* ⟨R, B⟩*)*, to mean, *(viser* ⟨R⟩*)*, (to intend to), (to posit); to believe ⟨MS 1, WH⟩. Cf. **LU, I.** Unters. *40*; Ideen I, *357*; CM *51*. Not "to pretend" ⟨L⟩. Cf. **bedeuten, denken, meinen, setzen, vermeint, vermuten.**

Vermeinen, supposing, (mental) process *(or* act) of meaning, believing, (intending); *(visée* ⟨R⟩*)*. Not "intention" ⟨L⟩. Cf. **Meinen.**

vermeinend, suppositive, *(présumant* ⟨B⟩*)*.

vermeint, supposed, *(présumé* ⟨B⟩*)*, *(prétendu* ⟨B⟩*)*, meant ⟨BG⟩, supposed or meant, intended, *(intentionné* ⟨B⟩*)*, *(visé* ⟨R⟩*)*; believed-in. Not "conjectural" ⟨L⟩. Cf. **gemeint, vermeinen.** | **das V∼e,** the supposed, the meant, the supposed or meant, the intended, *(le visé* ⟨R⟩*)*, *(ce qui est intentionné* (ou *présumé)* ⟨B⟩*)*. | **das A-V∼e,** A-that-is-meant. | **V∼es,** a meant, something intended.

Vermeintheit, supposition, supposedness, something supposed, supposed objectivity, (meantness), (what is meant), *(entité intentionnée* ⟨B⟩*)*. Cf. **Meinung.** | **die blosse** —, merely what is meant, *(ce qui est purement visé* ⟨R⟩*)*. | **kategoriale** —, supposed

(*or* meant) categorial objectivity, (*entité catégoriale* (*intentionnée*) ⟨B⟩), categorial supposition.
vermeintlich ⟨adj.⟩, supposed ⟨WH 1, MS⟩, suppositive, (*présumé* ⟨B⟩).
vermeintlich ⟨adv.⟩, supposedly, suppositively; as meant ⟨?⟩.
Vermeinung, supposition, (*présomption* ⟨B⟩). Cf. **Vermutung, Voraussetzung.**
vermengen, to confound ⟨WH⟩, (*confondre* ⟨R⟩), (to confuse ⟨WH, MS, BG⟩).
vermengt, confounded. So far as possible, save "confused" for "verworren".
vermischen, to confound.
vermischt, confounded; (*hybridus* ⟨K⟩).
vermitteln, | **die beiden** —, to intermediate the two, (to mediate between the two ⟨BG⟩), (*médiatiser les deux* ⟨R⟩).
(vermittelnd), (*intermedius* ⟨K⟩).
vermögen, to be able ⟨WH 1, MS 1⟩, (*être capable de* ⟨R⟩).
Vermögen, ability, (faculty ⟨Br⟩), (*faculté* ⟨B⟩), (*facultas* ⟨Wolff⟩), (*capacité* ⟨B⟩). Cf. **Fähigkeit.** | — **des Redens,** ability to speak. Cf. **Reden.**
vermöglich, lying within one's ability (*or* power), that lies within one's ability (*or* power).
Vermöglichkeit, facultative possibility, ability, power.
vermuten, to presume ⟨MS 2, WH⟩ (uncertainly), to deem likely, (*conjecturer* ⟨B⟩). Cf. **vermeinen.**
Vermuten, uncertain presuming, deeming likely, (*conjecturer* ⟨B⟩), (*conjecture* ⟨R⟩).
vermutet, presumed uncertainly, deemed likely, presumed as likely. Not "opined" ⟨L⟩.
vermutlich ⟨adj.⟩, presumable ⟨MS 2, WH 3⟩ (as likely), (*présumable* ⟨B⟩), presumptive ⟨WH⟩, likely ⟨WH 1, MS 4⟩, (*conjecturé* ⟨R, B⟩). Save "probable" ⟨WH 2, MS 3, BG⟩ for "wahrscheinlich". Cf. **naheliegend, wahrscheinlich.**
vermutlich ⟨adv.⟩, presumably.

Vermutlichkeit, likelihood, (presumption ⟨BG⟩ ⟨?⟩), (*conjecture* ⟨R⟩). Save "probability" for "Wahrscheinlichkeit".
Vermutung, 1. (subjective or objective:) uncertain presumption, (*conjecture* ⟨R, B⟩).
2. (subjective only:) deeming likely, presumption ⟨BG⟩ of likelihood, (consideration as likely), (considering as likely).
3. (objective only:) presumed likelihood, something deemed likely. Cf. **Vermeinung, Voraussetzung.**
verneinen, to answer (a question) negatively; to deny ⟨WH, MS⟩. Cf. **negieren.**
verneinend, negative ⟨WH 1, MS 1⟩, (*négateur* ⟨B⟩), denying.
Verneinung, denial ⟨WH 2, MS 2⟩, negation ⟨WH 1, MS 1⟩, (*négation* ⟨R⟩). So far as possible save "negation" for "Negation".
Vernichtung, annihilation ⟨MS 1, WH 2⟩, (*anéantissement* ⟨R⟩). Cf. **Aufhebung, Durchstreichung, Zunichtemachen.**
Vernunftbewusstsein, rational consciousness ⟨BG⟩.
Vernunftcharakter, rational character, character of rationality ⟨BG⟩.
Vernunftgebilde, rational product, (*formation rationnelle* ⟨B⟩). Cf. **Gebilde.**
Vernunftgegebenheit, datum of reason, (*donnée rationnelle* ⟨R⟩). Cf. **Gegebenheit.**
vernünftig ⟨adj.⟩, rational ⟨MS 1, WH 2⟩, (*rationnel* ⟨R, B⟩). Not "reasonable" ⟨WH 1, MS 3, BG⟩.
vernünftig ⟨adv.⟩, | — **gefordert,** demanded by reason, (*exigé par la raison* ⟨R⟩).
Vernünftigkeit, rationality ⟨MS 1, WH 2⟩, (*rationalité* ⟨R, B⟩).
Vernunftleistung, rational production, (*effectuation de la raison* ⟨B⟩). Cf. **Leistung.**
Vernunftnorm, | **reine** —, norm of pure reason. Not "pure rational norm" ⟨L⟩.

(Vernunftschluss), (*ratiocinatio* ⟨K⟩). Cf. **Schluss.**
Vernunftvorzug, | **einen — haben gegenüber,** to be rationally superior to. Cf. **Vorzug.**
Vernunftwert, rational value.
Verrechnen, misreckoning. Cf. **Rechnen.**
Verrichtung, | **eine — vollziehen,** to perform an operation ⟨Gomperz trln of Mill, quoted in LU, I. Unters.⟩. Cf. **Vollziehen.**
Versachlichung, materializing. Cf. **sachlich, verdinglichen.**
Verschiebbarkeit, lability, (*possibilité de subir des déplacements* ⟨B⟩).
verschieben, to shift ⟨MS 1, WH 2⟩, to displace ⟨WH 3, MS⟩.
Verschiebung, shift, shifting ⟨MS 1, WH 2⟩, displacement, (*déplacement* ⟨B⟩), dislocation ⟨WH⟩, (*translation* ⟨de M⟩). Cf. **Übergang, Wendung.**
verschieden, different ⟨WH 1, MS 1, BG⟩, (*différent* ⟨R, B⟩), (differing ⟨WH 2, MS 2, BG⟩), diverse ⟨MS⟩, divers ⟨WH⟩, (various ⟨trln of Mill in LU II/1, Einl.; WH⟩). Cf. **mannigfaltig, vielfältig.** | **— von,** (math:) not equal to.
verschiedenartig, different in sort, disparate. Cf. **gleichartig.**
Verschiedenheit, differentness, difference ⟨Arith, 52, WH 1, MS 1⟩, diversity, (*diversité* ⟨B⟩), (concrete:) different. Cf. **Differenz, Unterschied, Unterschiedenheit.**
Verschmelzung, fusion ⟨Bn, MS 2, WH 3⟩, (*fusion* ⟨B⟩), blending ⟨Bn, WH 2, MS 3 "von Farben usw.", F⟩. Cf. **Verflossenheit, Verworrenheit.**
verschossen, fascinated.
verschwommen, blurred ⟨WH 2⟩.
Verschwommenheit, blurriness.
verselbständigen, to make selfsufficent, to make independent ⟨WH 1⟩, to emancipate. Cf. **selbständig.**
Versenkung in, penetration of, (*exploration en profondeur dans* ⟨B⟩).
Verstand, 1. understanding ⟨WH 1, MS 1⟩, (*entendement* ⟨B⟩), (intellect ⟨Bn, WH 2, MS⟩), (intelligence ⟨Bn, WH 3, MS⟩).
2. signification, sense ⟨WH, MS, BG⟩, (*acceptation* ⟨R⟩). Cf. **Bedeutung, Sinn.** | (gemeiner (Menschen-) —), (*sensus communis* ⟨K⟩).
verstanden, understood ⟨BG⟩, (*entendu* ⟨R⟩), conceived, (*compris* ⟨B⟩); taken.
Verständigung, Cf. **Selbstverständigung.**
verständnismässig, in the manner pecular to the understanding.
verstehen, to understand ⟨WH 1, MS 1, BG⟩, (*comprendre* ⟨R, B⟩), (*intellegere* ⟨K⟩), to mean ⟨WH⟩. Cf. **befassen, Einverstehen, meinen, Nachverstehen, Unverständnis.**
Versuch, experiment ⟨WH 1, MS 2, Bn⟩, trial ⟨MS 1, WH 3⟩, (*essai* ⟨B⟩), attempt ⟨WH 4, MS 5⟩, (*tentative* ⟨B⟩), effort ⟨WH 5, MS 6⟩.
versuchsweise, tentatively ⟨WH⟩; by way of a trial (*or* an experiment ⟨WH⟩) ⟨MS⟩.
verteilen, | **sich — auf,** to be distributed among.
vertauschen, | **Einstellungen —,** to shift back and forth between attidudes.
Verteilung, distribution ⟨WH 1, MS 1, Bn⟩, (*distribution* ⟨R⟩).
vertiefen, | **sich in die Phänomene —,** to pore into the phenomena.
Vertiefung, poring.
Verträglichkeit, compatibility ⟨WH 2, MS⟩, (*compatibilité* ⟨B⟩). Cf. **Unverträglichkeit, Vereinbarkeit.**
Vertrautheit, familiarity ⟨WH 2, MS 2⟩. Cf. **Bekanntheit.**
Vervielfältigungszahlen, (*numeralia multiplicativa* (Arith, 3)).
verwandelbar, convertible ⟨MS 3⟩, changeable ⟨MS 4⟩, commutable ⟨MS 2⟩, (math:) transformable ⟨MS 1⟩. Cf. **abwandelbar, Veränderlichkeit.**
verwandeln, to convert ⟨WH 3, MS 4⟩, to change ⟨WH 1, MS 2⟩, (math. only:) to transform ⟨MS 1, WH 4⟩. Cf. **ändern, variieren, wandeln.** | **in etwas —,** to convert (*or* turn ⟨WH⟩)

into something ⟨MS⟩, (*convertir en quelque chose* ⟨R⟩), (*changer en quelque chose* ⟨B⟩). | **sich** —, to change ⟨MS 1, WH 2⟩, (*se changer* ⟨B⟩). | **sich in etwas** —, to become (*or* be) converted into something, (*se convertir dans quelque chose* ⟨R⟩), to change into something ⟨MS 2⟩, (*se changer en quelque chose* ⟨B⟩). Cf. **übergehen in.**

Verwandlung, conversion ⟨WH 2, MS 3⟩, converting, change ⟨WH 4, MS 5⟩, (*changement* ⟨B⟩); (math:) transformation ⟨WH 1, MS 1⟩. Cf. **Abwandlung, Formenverwandlung, Rückverwandlung, Umwandlung, Umwendung, Wandel, Wechsel, Wendung.** | **synthetische** —, syntactical change.

Verwandschaft, kinship ⟨Bn, MS 1⟩, affinity ⟨WH 3, MS⟩, (*affinitas* ⟨K⟩).

Verwebung, combining. Cf. **Komplexion, Verbindung, Verflechtung.**

verweisen, to refer (one to something) ⟨WH 1, MS 1, BG⟩, (*renvoyer* ⟨B⟩), (*amener* ⟨R⟩). Cf. **sich auf etwas beziehen** (*sub* **beziehen**), **hinweisen, Sinnverweisung, weisen.**

Verwendung, application ⟨Schultze trln of Hume, quoted; WH 2; MS 2⟩.

Verwertung, utilization ⟨WH 1, MS 1⟩. Not "evaluation" ⟨L⟩.

verwirklichen, to actualize, to make actual, (to effect), (to "realize"), (*réaliser* ⟨PL, R, B⟩). Not "to show" ⟨BG⟩. Cf. **verdinglichen, wirklich.**

Verwirklichung, actualization. Save "realization" ⟨WH 1, MS 1⟩ for "Realisierung" ⟨q.v.⟩. Cf. **Aktualisierung.** | **ideale** —, actualization of the ideal.

verworren ⟨adj.⟩, confused ⟨WH 3⟩, (*confus* ⟨B⟩). Cf. **undeutlich, vermengt.**

verworren ⟨adv.⟩, confusedly, (*d'une manière confuse* ⟨B⟩).

Verworrenheit, confusion ⟨WH 1⟩, (*confusion* ⟨R, B⟩). Cf. **Verflossenheit, Verschmelzung.** | **in der** —, as confused, (*dans l'état confus* ⟨B⟩), confusedly, (*dans la confusion* ⟨B⟩).

Modus der —, confused mode, (*mode de la confusion* ⟨B⟩).

Vieldeutigkeit, multisignificance, (*multivocité* ⟨B⟩), equivocalness, ambiguity ⟨WH 1, MS 1⟩. Cf. **Äquivokation, Eindeutigkeit.**

vielfach ⟨adv.⟩, | — **gegliedert,** highly articulated. Cf. **gegliedert.**

Vielfachheit, multiplexity. Cf. **Mannigfaltigkeit, Menge.**

vielfältig, multifarious ⟨WH 2, MS 3⟩, many different, (*divers* ⟨B⟩). Cf. **mannigfaltig, verschieden.**

vielgestaltig, complex, (*de forme complexe* ⟨R⟩).

Vielgliedrigkeit, | **synthetische** —, many-membered synthesis.

Vielheit, plurality ⟨Bn, MS 2, WH 3, F⟩, (*pluralité* ⟨B⟩), (particularly where it is desirable to indicate the etymological relation to "viel":) manyness, multitude ⟨WH 1, MS, Bn⟩, (math:) multiplicity ⟨Bn, MS 1, WH 4⟩. Cf. **Mannigfaltigkeit, Mehrheit, Menge, Vielfachheit.**

vollberechtigt, fully qualified ⟨WH 1, MS⟩. Cf. **berechtigt.**

vollendet, completed, consummate, (*consummatus* ⟨K⟩), (perfect ⟨WH 1⟩). So far as possible, save "perfect" for "vollkommen". Cf. **vollständig.**

vollkommen ⟨adj.⟩, perfect ⟨WH 1, MS 1⟩, (*parfait* ⟨B⟩), (*perfectus* ⟨Br⟩), (complete), (*entier* ⟨R⟩). Not "plenary" ⟨Bn⟩. Cf. **vollständig.**

vollkommen ⟨adv.⟩, perfectly ⟨BG⟩, (*parfaitement* ⟨R, B⟩), thoroughly.

Vollkommenheit, perfection ⟨WH 1, MS 1⟩, (*perfection* ⟨B⟩), (*perfectio* ⟨K⟩).

vollständig, complete ⟨WH 1, MS 1⟩, (*complet* ⟨B⟩), (*intégral* ⟨R⟩), (*saturé* ⟨B⟩). Cf. **abgeschlossen, durchgängig, vollkommen** ⟨adj.⟩.

Vollständigkeit, completeness ⟨MS 1⟩, (*complétude* ⟨B⟩), (*completudo* ⟨K⟩), (*saturation* ⟨B⟩). Cf. **Ausführlichkeit.**

vollziehbar, producible, that can be effected, (*que l'on peut effectuer* ⟨B⟩).

Vollziehbarkeit, effectibility, possible effectuation, (*possibilité d'effectuation* ⟨B⟩).

vollziehen, 1. to make ⟨BG⟩, (*faire* ⟨R⟩), to frame, to bring about, to produce, to effect, (*effectuer* ⟨B⟩), (*opérer* ⟨R⟩).
2. to carry on, (*poursuivre* ⟨R⟩), to perform ⟨WH 3, MS 7⟩, to do ⟨MS 9⟩.
3. to carry out ⟨WH 2, MS 4, BG⟩, to put into effect ⟨MS⟩, (*réaliser* ⟨R⟩), to execute ⟨WH 1, MS 6⟩, to accomplish ⟨MS 1⟩, (*accomplir* ⟨B⟩), to achieve ⟨MS 2⟩. Not "to rehearse to ourselves" ⟨BG⟩, not "to realize" ⟨L⟩. Cf. **Ausführung, ergeben, erzeugen, herstellen, leisten, nachvollzogen, schaffen, wirken, zustandebringen. | die Denkschritte** —, to make the steps of thinking. | **einen Akt** —, to perform an act. | **ein Gebilde** —, to produce a formation, (*effectuer une formation* ⟨B⟩). Cf. **Gebilde. | ein Urteil** —, to make (*or* perform) a judgment. Not "to carry out a judgment" ⟨BG⟩. Cf. **ein Urteil fällen** (*sub* **fällen**). | **eine Aktivität** —, to carry on an activity. | **eine Analyse** —, to carry on an analysis. | **eine Apperzeption** —, to perform an apperception. | **eine Aussage** —, to make a statement. | **eine Durchstreichung** —, to make a cancellation. | **eine Erfüllung** —, to perform a fulfilling. | **eine Leistung** —, to bring about a performance, (*accomplir une effectuation* ⟨B⟩). Cf. **vollzogene Leistung** (*sub* **Leistung**). | **eine Reduktion** —, to make a reduction, (*opérer une réduction* ⟨R⟩). | **eine Urteilskonsequenz** —, to bring about (*or* effect) a consequence-relationship of judgments, (*effectuer une suite conséquente de jugements* ⟨B⟩). Cf. **Urteilskonsequenz. | eine Verallgemeinerung** —, to bring about a universalization, (*effectuer une généralisation* ⟨B⟩). | **eine Verrichtung** —, to perform an operation ⟨Gomperz trln of Mill, quoted in LU, I. Unters.⟩. | **einen Aussagesatz** —, to frame a statement, (*effectuer un énoncé* ⟨B⟩). Cf. **Aussagesatz. | Formalisierung** —, to carry out formalisation, (*accomplir la formalisation* ⟨B⟩). | **indem es vollzogen wird,** while it is going on. | **Konstruktionen** —, to construct, to make constructions, (*effectuer des constructions* ⟨B⟩). | **sich** —, 1. to be made, to be brought about, to be effected, (*s'effectuer* ⟨B⟩), (*s'opérer* ⟨R⟩).
2. to be carried on, to be performed, to be done.
3. to come to pass, to take place, (*avoir lieu* ⟨B⟩), to go on.
4. to be carried out, to be put into effect, to be executed, to be accomplished, (*s'accomplir* ⟨B⟩), to be achieved. | **Sinngebungen** —, to bring about sense-bestowings.

vollziehend, 1. performing. 2. executant.

Vollziehung, 1. performance. 2. execution ⟨WH 1, MS 2⟩, accomplishment. Cf. **Ausführung, Leistung.**

Vollzug, 1. making, bringing about, producing, effecting, (*opération* ⟨R⟩).
2. carrying on, performing, performance, doing, taking.
3. execution ⟨WH 1, MS 2⟩, effectuation, (*effectuation* ⟨B⟩), (*accomplissement* ⟨B⟩). Save "fulfilment" ⟨BG⟩ for "Erfüllung" ⟨q.v.⟩. Not "adoption" ⟨BG⟩. Cf. **Aktvollzug, Ausführung, Leistung, Tun, Urteilsvollzug. | in** — **halten,** to keep in effect. | — **einer Ablehnung,** making of a refusal. Cf. **Ablehnung. | — einer Aussage,** making a statement. | — **einer Bedeutung,** producting of a signification. | — **einer Einstellung,** taking an attitude. | — **einer Ideation,** bringing about an ideation. | — **einer Subjektsetzung und ...,** carrying on of a subject-positing and... | — **einer Wahl,** making of a choice. | — **einer Wertung,** making of a valuation. | — **einer Zweifelsentscheidung,** bringing about the settlement of a doubt, settling a

doubt. | — **eines Satzes,** making of a proposition.

Vollzugsform, form pertaining to the performing, (*forme d'effectuation* ⟨B⟩). | ~**en der Deutlichkeit,** forms of distinct judgings, (*formes de l'effectuation de la "distinction"* ⟨B⟩).

Vollzugsmodus, mode of performing (*or* performance), (*mode d'accomplissement* ⟨B⟩).

Voraussetzung, presupposition ⟨Bn, WH⟩, (*présupposition* ⟨R, B⟩), (*présupposé* ⟨de M⟩). Cf. **Annahme, präjudizieren, Setzung, Vermeinung, Vermutung.**

Vorbedingung für, prerequisite to ⟨WH 1⟩.

Vorbild, pattern ⟨WH 1, MS 2⟩, model ⟨WH 1⟩, archetype, prefiguration. Save "preconception" ⟨L⟩ for "Vormeinung" ⟨q.v.⟩. Cf. **Urbild, Vor-Bild, Vorzeichnung.**

Vor-Bild, prefiguration, (*pré-figuration* ⟨B⟩). Cf. **Bild, Vorbild, vor-ver-bildlichen.**

Vordergrundbewussthaben, foreground consciousness-of. Cf. **Bewussthaben, Hintergrundbewussthaben.**

Vordersatz, 1. (grammar or logic:) antecedent ⟨WH 3⟩, (*proposition antécédente* ⟨B⟩), (*antecedens* ⟨K⟩). 2. (grammar only:) antecedent clause, protasis ⟨MS 1, WH, K⟩. 3. (logic only:) premise ⟨Bn, WH 2⟩, antecedent proposition. Cf. **Nachsatz, Satz.**

Vorderseite, front ⟨WH 1, MS 1⟩, front aspect. Cf. **Rückseite, Seite.**

vordeuten, to indicate in advance; to point ahead. Cf. **andeuten, anzeigen, hinweisen auf, hinzeigen.**

Vordeutung, preliminary indication, (*indication préparatoire* ⟨B⟩).

Vorerinnerung, anticipation, (*pro-souvenir* ⟨B⟩). Cf. **Erinnerung, Erwartung, Rückerinnerung.**

Vorerwartung, (*prosouvenir* ⟨de M⟩). Cf. **Erwartung.**

Vorerwägung, | **eidetische —,** preliminary eidetical deliberation, (*ré-flexion eidétique préliminaire* ⟨R⟩). Cf. **Erwägung.**

Vorform, preliminary form, (*première forme* ⟨B⟩).

vorgangsmässig, | — **sich aufbauend,** in process of construction, (*en se construisant à la manière d'événements* ⟨B⟩).

vorgeben, to give beforehand (*or* in advance), (to pre-give), (to give), (*livrer* ⟨B⟩). Cf. **vorzugeben.**

vorgebend, that gives beforehand, (*qui donne au préalable* ⟨B⟩).

vorgegeben, (that is) given beforehand (*or* in advance), (*donné au préalable* (ou *préalablement*) ⟨B⟩), already given ⟨BG⟩, (*déjà donné* ⟨B⟩), (pre-given), (*donné* ⟨B⟩), (ready-made), (*qui existe déjà* ⟨B⟩), ((*déjà*) *existant* ⟨B⟩). | — **vor,** (already) given prior to (*or* before).

Vorgegebenheit, prior givenness, givenness beforehand (*or* in advance), (pre-givenness); something (*or* thing *or* affair) (that is) given beforehand, (*prédonné* ⟨B⟩). Cf. **Gegebenheit.** | **passive —,** something (*or* things) given beforehand and accepted passively, (*prédonnée passive* ⟨B⟩).

vorgegenwärtig, Cf. **gegenwärtig.** | **V ~es,** something formerly present. Not "pre-present" ⟨L⟩.

Vorgestalt, prior formation. Cf. **Gestalt, Nachgestalt.**

vorgestellt, 1. (directly, broad sense:) objectivated, (made present). 2. (directly, narrower sense, sometimes:) (clearly) phantasied (objectivatingly), objectivated in (clear) phantasy, (*représenté* ⟨R, B⟩). Not "represented" ⟨L, BG⟩. 3. (indirectly:) represented. Cf. **dargestellt, vergegenwärtigt, vorstellig.** | **bildlich —,** represented pictorially ⟨L⟩. Cf. **bildlich, Bildvorstellung.** | **V ~es,** something objectivated, (something made present). **vorgreifen,** to fore-seize, to anticipate ⟨MS 1, WH 2⟩. Cf. **greifen.**

Vorhabe, proposal, anticipation, purpose ⟨?⟩, prepossession ⟨?⟩, prospect ⟨?⟩.

Vorhaben, intent ⟨WH 1⟩, purpose. Cf. **Absehen, Absicht.**

Vor-Haben, prospective having.

vorhanden, on hand ⟨WH, MS⟩, (*présent devant nous* ⟨B⟩), (*présent* ⟨R⟩), there, extant ⟨WH, MS⟩. Save "at hand" ⟨WH 1, MS 1⟩ for "zuhanden", "present" for "gegenwärtig", "jetzig" ⟨q.v.⟩ and "aktuell" ⟨q.v.⟩. Cf. **daseiend.**

Vorhandensein, being on hand, presence ⟨WH 2, MS 2⟩. Cf. **Aktualität 1, Dasein, gegenwärtig, Präsenz.**

vorhin, just now ⟨WH⟩, (*il y a un instant* ⟨B⟩), a little while ago ⟨MS 2, WH 3⟩, (*plus haut* ⟨R⟩). Not "previously" ⟨BG⟩.

Vorintention, expectant intention, (*intention préalable* ⟨B⟩). Cf. **Intention.**

Vorkenntnis, previous knowledge. Cf. **Erkenntnis, Kenntnis, Wissen.**

vorkommen, to occur ⟨WH⟩, to be found, (*se présenter* ⟨R⟩), (*intervenir* ⟨B⟩). Cf. **Bewusstseinsvorkommnis.**

vorkonstituiert, preconstitued.

vorläufig ⟨adj.⟩, provisional ⟨Bn, WH 1, MS⟩, (*provisoire* ⟨PL, B⟩); precursory ⟨MS 1⟩.

vorliegen, to present itself ⟨WH 1⟩, (*se présenter* ⟨R⟩). Cf. **auftreten, sich darstellen** (*sub* **darstellen**), **sich geben** (*sub* **geben**).

vorliegend, present ⟨WH 2⟩. Cf. **aktuell** ⟨adj.⟩ 1, **gegenwärtig, jetzig.**

vormeinen, to fore-mean ⟨in OED⟩; to mean expectantly, (to expect); to preconceive; to have a preconceived opinion. So far as possible save "to expect" for "erwarten".

vormeinend, fore-meaning, (expectantly), (with expectation).

Vormeinung, fore-meaning, expectant meaning, something meant expectantly; preconception, (*préconception* ⟨R⟩), preconceived opinion, (*pré-opinion* ⟨B⟩). Cf. **Erwartung, Meinung, Mitmeinung.**

vornherein, | von —, from the start, (*dès le début* ⟨B⟩), (*dès le commencement* ⟨B⟩), from the very beginning ⟨MS 1, L⟩, at the outset ⟨MS 2⟩, from the first ⟨WH 1, MS 3⟩, (*de*

prime abord ⟨B⟩), (*dès l'abord* ⟨R⟩), as a matter of course ⟨MS 4⟩. Cf. **vorweg.**

(Vorschluss), prosyllogism ⟨Bn⟩. Cf. **Schluss 1.**

vorschweben, Cf. **Leervorschweben. | uns** —, to hover before us, (*flotter devant nous* ⟨R⟩). Not "to float past us" ⟨BG⟩. **| — haben,** to have within view. Cf. **vor Augen stehen** (*sub* **Auge**).

Vorschweben, quasi-presentedness, hovering (before one), (*acte de l'évocation flottante* ⟨R⟩).

vorschwebend, quasi-presented in imagination. **| das V⁓e,** that which is quasi-presented, what hovers before one, (*ce qui flotte en suspens devant l'esprit* ⟨R⟩).

vorstellbar, (clearly) phantasiable, that can be (clearly) phantasied, (loosely:) imaginable (cf. vorstellen 3), (strictly:) that can be objectivated in clear phantasy (cf. vorstellen 2).

Vorstellbarkeit, 1. (abstract:) phantasiableness, imaginableness. 2. (concrete:) phantasiable, imaginable. Cf. **Fingierbarkeit.**

vorstellen, 1. (broadest phenomenological senses:) to objectivate ⟨see LU II/1, Unters., *140*⟩ (mentally), to intend to (objectivatingly). Cf. **vergegenständlichen, vorstellig machen** (*sub* **vorstellig**).

2. (narrower phenomenological senses, sometimes:)

a. to recall or phantasy (objectivatingly), to objectivate recollectively or in phantasy, (*se représenter* ⟨R⟩). Save "to represent" ⟨BG⟩ for "darstellen" ⟨q.v.⟩ and "vergegenwärtigen" ⟨q.v.⟩. Save "to presentiate" and "to make present to oneself" for "vergegenwärtigen" ⟨q.v.⟩.

b. to phantasy (objectivatingly), to objectivate in phantasy. Cf. **sich denken** (*sub* **denken**), **fingieren, phantasieren, vorstellbar.**

3. (loosely:) to have an idea (of), to conceive, to think of, to imagine. Cf. **denken, einbilden, fassen, sich denken** (*sub* **denken**), **vorstellbar.**

4. (loosely:) to be an idea of. Save "to sense" ⟨BG⟩ for "empfinden". | **mit** —, to intend also to, (*mettre en avant* ⟨B⟩). | **sich** —, (governing dative:) to phantasy.
Vorstellen, 1. (broadest sense:) (mental) objectivating, (*représentation* ⟨R⟩).
2. (narrower senses, sometimes:) recalling or phantasying (in an objectivating manner), (objectivating recollectively or in phantasy); phantasying (in an objectivating manner), objectivating in phantasy. Cf. **Sachvorstellen.** | **allgemeines** —, (mental) objectivating of the universal (*or* of universals). Cf. **allgemein** ⟨adj.⟩. | **spezifisches** —, (mental) objectivating of species.
vorstellend, 1. objectivating. 2. phantasying (in an objectivating manner), objectivating in phantasy, (*formant des représentations* ⟨R⟩), (loosely:) imagining ⟨BG⟩.
vorstellig, 1. objective (cf. LU, V. Unters., *410*: "gegenständlich bzw. vorstellig").
2. recalled or phantasied (objectivatingly), objective recollectively or in phantasy, (*représenté* ⟨R⟩); phantasied (objectivatingly), objective in phantasy.
3. presented, (*représenté* ⟨R⟩). Cf. **gegenständlich, leer vorstellig, objektiv, sachlich, vorgestellt.** | unanschaulich — **haben,** to have as nonintuitionally objective, (*se représenter d'une manière non-intuitive* ⟨R⟩). | — **haben,** to have as objective. | — **in der Phantasie,** objective in phantasy, (*représenté dans l'imagination* ⟨B⟩). Cf. **Phantasievorstellung.** | — **machen,** to make objective. Cf. **vergegenständlichen, vorstellen 1.**
Vorstellung, 1. (broadest Husserlian sense:) (mental) objectivation, (mental) objectivating, objectivating intention, (*présentation* ⟨B⟩), (*représentation* ⟨R⟩). Cf. **Intention, Objektivation, Objektivierung, Vergegenständlichung.**
2. (narrower Husserlian senses:) *a.*

(objectivating *or* objective) phantasy; objectivation in memory or in phantasy; (*représentation* ⟨R, B⟩). Cf. **Phantasie.** *b.* presentation ⟨Bn, F, BG⟩.
3. (Cartesian-Lockean sense:) idea ⟨Gomperz trln of Mill, quoted in LU, I. Unters.⟩, representation.
4. (with reference to Hume:) perception ⟨Br trln⟩, (*perceptio* ⟨K⟩), (*représentation* ⟨B⟩). Cf. **Wahrnehmung.**
5. (Kantian sense:) presentation ⟨Bn, OED⟩, (representation ⟨?⟩ ⟨Kemp Smith⟩), (*repraesentatio* ⟨K⟩).
6. (with reference to Mill:) conception ⟨Gomperz trln, quoted in LU, II. Unters.⟩.
7. (loosely or in non-philosophic sense:) idea ⟨WH 1, MS⟩, conception ⟨WH 2, MS, L⟩, imagination, thought, (pl:) imagery. Cf. **Auffassung, Gedanke.** So far as possible save "presentation" for "Darstellung" ⟨q.v.⟩ and "Gegenwärtigung" ⟨q.v.⟩. Save "representation" (Husserl's suggestion in conversation) for "Darstellung" and "Vergegenwärtigung" ⟨q.v.⟩. Cf. **Abbildung, Bedeutungsvorstellung, Bildvorstellung, Einzelvorstellung, Gesamtvorstellung, Leervorstellung, Phantasievorstellung, Sondervorstellung, Universalvorstellung, "Weltvorstellung", Zeichenvorstellung.** | **abstrakte** —, (mental) objectivation of an abstraction. | **allgemeine** —, 1. (Husserlian senses:) (mental) objectivation of a (*or* the) universal. 2. (non-Husserlian senses:) general presentation, general idea. Cf. **allgemein** ⟨adj.⟩, **Allgemeinvorstellung.** | **begriffliche** —, conceptual objectivation. | **gegenständliche** —, (mental) objectivation having an existent object. Cf. **gegenständlich** ⟨adj.⟩. | **gegenstandslose** —, (mental) objectivation having no existent object. Cf. **gegenstandslos** ⟨adj.⟩. | **in der** —, in idea. | **individuelle** —, (mental) objectivation of something individu-

al. | **logische** —, idea with which logic is concerned. | **nominale** —, naming objectivation; (mental) objectivation of something as named. Cf. **nominal, Wortvorstellung.** | **zur** — **kommen,** to become (mentally) objectivated.
Vorstellungserlebnis, (mental) objectivation-process, (mental) objectivational process. Cf. **Erlebnis, Urteilserlebnis.**
Vorstellungsgestalt, | **in ursprünglicher** —, conformably to the original idea of it.
Vorstellungsgrundlage, objectivational foundation. Cf. **Grundlage.**
Vorstellungsintention, objectivational intention, objectivating intention ⟨?⟩. Cf. **Intention.**
Vorstellungsobjekt, Object of a (or the) mental objectivation. Not "object of presentation" ⟨BG⟩. Cf. **Objekt.**
Vorstellungstätigkeit, objectivational activity. Cf. **Tätigkeit.**
Vorstufe, preliminary stage, (premier degré ⟨B⟩), preliminary (to), something preliminary. Cf. **Stufe, Unterstufe.** | **propädeutische** —, propaedeutic.
vorveranschaulichend, making (something) intuited beforehand. Cf. **nachveranschaulichend, veranschaulichen.**
vor-verbildlichen, to prefigure, (préfigurer ⟨B⟩). Cf. **verbildlichen, Vor-Bild.**

vorweg, beforehand ⟨WH 2, MS 2⟩, preliminary, in advance ⟨MS⟩, (à l'avance ⟨B⟩), to begin with, (de prime abord ⟨B⟩). Cf. **von vornherein** (sub **vornherein**).
Vorweis, pointing ahead.
vorweisen, to exhibit, to show, to point ahead, (indiquer ⟨B⟩). Cf. **ausstellen, darstellen, herausstellen, weisen, zeigen.**
Vorzeichen, (math:) sign ⟨MS 1⟩, (signe ⟨R⟩).
Vorzeichenänderung, change of sign, (changement de signe ⟨R⟩). Not "change of signature" ⟨BG⟩. Cf. **ändern.**
vorzeichnen, to predelineate ⟨not in OED⟩; to mark out ⟨MS⟩ (apriori); (to delineate ⟨MS⟩), (tracer ⟨R, B⟩), (ébaucher ⟨B⟩); to prescribe ⟨WH⟩; (to predesignate). Not "to fore token" ⟨BG⟩. Cf. **zeichnen.**
Vorzeichnung, predelineation, (préfiguration ⟨B⟩), (pré-scription ⟨de M⟩), delineation, (indication ⟨B⟩). Cf. **Vorbild.**
Vorzug, primacy, precedence; superiority ⟨WH, MS⟩, (supériorité ⟨B⟩); advantage ⟨WH, MS⟩; preference ⟨MS⟩; (privilège ⟨B⟩); merit ⟨WH, MS⟩. Not "prerogative" ⟨BG⟩. Cf. **Seinsvorzug, Vernunftvorzug.**
vorzugeben, given. Not "alleged" ⟨L⟩. Cf. **vorgeben.**
vorzüglich ⟨adv.⟩, pre-eminently ⟨MS 2⟩, (de préférence ⟨B⟩).

W

wach, waking ⟨BG⟩, (vigilant ⟨R⟩), (dans l'état de vigilance ⟨R⟩). Not "wakeful" ⟨BG⟩. Cf. **geweckt, Weckung.**
wahrgenommen, | **das W ~e,** the perceived, (le perçu ⟨R⟩), that which is being perceived, the percept. | **immanent W ~es,** immanent percept, (perçu immanent ⟨B⟩). | **W ~es,** something perceived ⟨BG⟩, perceived ⟨BG⟩, (perçu ⟨R⟩), percept. Cf. **Baumwahrgenommenes.**

wahrhaft ⟨adv.⟩, truly ⟨BG⟩, (vraiment ⟨B⟩), (d'une manière véritable ⟨B⟩), (avec vérité ⟨B⟩).
Wahrhaftigkeit, veracity ⟨Bn, WH 1, MS 2⟩.
Wahrheit, truth ⟨WH 1, MS 1⟩, (sometimes better:) trueness, (vérité ⟨R, B, de M⟩). Cf. **Seinswahrheit, Urteilswahrheit, Wesenswahrheit.**
Wahrheitslogik, truth-logic, (logique de la vérité ⟨B⟩). Cf. **Gewissheitslogik.**
Wahrheitsprinzip, truth-principle,

(*principe qui concerne la vérité* ⟨B⟩).
Wahrheitssinn, truth-sense, (*sens de vérité* ⟨B⟩). Cf. **Seinssinn.**
wahrnehmbar, perceivable ⟨MS 1⟩, (*perceptible* ⟨R⟩).
wahrnehmen, to perceive ⟨WH 1, MS 1, BG⟩, (*percevoir* ⟨R⟩), (*percipere* ⟨K⟩), (*apercevoir* ⟨B⟩). Cf. **gewahren, wahrgenommen.**
Wahrnehmender, percipient (subject), (*être percevant* ⟨B⟩).
Wahrnehmung, perception ⟨WH 1, MS 1, BG⟩, (*perception* ⟨R, de M⟩), (perceiving). Cf. **Dingwahrnehmung, Vorstellung.**
Wahrnehmungsauffassung, perceptual apprehension. Cf. **Auffassung.**
Wahrnehmungsaussage, perceptional (*or* perceptual) statement. Cf. **Aussage.**
Wahrnehmungsausweisung, perceptual demonstration. Cf. **Ausweisung.**
Wahrnehmungsbereitschaft, readiness to be perceived.
Wahrnehmungserlebnis, mental process of perception, (*vécu de perception* ⟨R⟩). Not "perceptual experience" ⟨BG⟩. Cf. **Erlebnis.**
Wahrnehmungserscheinung, perceptual appearance. Cf. **Erscheinung.**
Wahrnehmungsfeld, field of perception. | aktuelles —, field of actual perception, (*champ actuel de la perception* ⟨R⟩).
Wahrnehmungsgegenstand, object of perception, perceptual object.
Wahrnehmungsglaube, perceptual belief ⟨BG⟩, (*croyance perceptive* ⟨R⟩). Cf. **Glaube.**
Wahrnehmungsinhalt, content of (the *or* a) perception. Cf. **Inhalt.**
wahrnehmungsmässig ⟨adj.⟩, perceptual. Cf. **perzeptiv** ⟨adj.⟩.
wahrnehmungsmässig ⟨adv.⟩, perceptually ⟨BG⟩, (*de façon perceptive* ⟨R⟩), (*dans la perception* ⟨R⟩), (*par voie de perception* ⟨R⟩). Not "by way of perception ⟨BG⟩. Cf. **perzeptiv** ⟨adv.⟩.
Wahrnehmungsnoema, perception-noema, (*noème de perception* ⟨R⟩).

Wahrnehmungsnoesis, perception-noesis, (*noèse de perception* ⟨R⟩). Cf. **Erinnerungsnoesis.**
Wahrnehmungsqualität, perceptual quality ⟨BG⟩, (*qualité de perception* ⟨R⟩).
Wahrnehmungssingularität, single example of perception. Cf. **Singularität.**
Wahrnehmungssinn, sense of the perception, (*sens de la perception* ⟨R⟩); perceptual sense, (*sens de perception* ⟨R⟩). Cf. **Erinnerungssinn, Phantasiesinn.**
Wahrnehmungsurteil, perceptual judgment, (*jugement de perception* ⟨R⟩). Cf. **Erfahrungsurteil.**
Wahrnehmungszusammenhang, nexus of perceptions, (*enchaînement de perceptions* ⟨R⟩). Cf. **Erfahrungszusammenhang, Zusammenhang.**
wahrscheinlich, probable ⟨WH 2, MS 2⟩, (*vraisemblable* ⟨R⟩). Save "likely" ⟨WH 1, MS 1⟩ for "vermutlich" ⟨q.v.⟩.
Wahrscheinlichkeit, probability, (*probabilitas* ⟨K⟩). Save "likelihood" ⟨WH 1, MS 1⟩ for "Vermutlichkeit".
Wahrscheinlichkeitsgrund, ground of probability, basis of probability, (probability-ground). Cf. **Grund 1&3.**
Wahrscheinlichkeitslehre, theory of probability, (*théorie des probabilités* ⟨R⟩).
Wahrscheinlichkeitsschluss, probability inference ⟨Bn⟩, (*raisonnement de probabilité* ⟨B⟩). Cf. **Schluss 3.**
Wahrscheinlichkeitszusammenhang, nexus of probability. Cf. **Zusammenhang.**
walten, to govern ⟨WH 2, MS 2⟩, to hold sway ⟨BG⟩, (*dominer* ⟨R⟩). Cf. **beherrschen, regeln, schalten.**
Walten, governing, governance, functioning, action ⟨?⟩, governable action ⟨?⟩. Cf. **Funktion.**
waltend, governing, (*qui règne* ⟨B⟩), functioning.
Wandel, change ⟨MS 1, WH 2⟩, (*changement* ⟨B⟩), alteration ⟨MS 2⟩, mutation ⟨WH 1⟩, (*variation* ⟨B⟩), changing flow. Cf. **ändern, Funk-**

tionswandel, Verwandlung, Wandlung, Wechsel, Wendung.
wandeln, to change, to alter, (transformer ⟨B⟩). Cf. ändern, verwandeln. | sich —, to change ⟨WH 1, MS 1⟩, to become changed, (se changer ⟨B⟩). Cf. sich umwandeln (sub umwandeln).
Wandlung, change ⟨WH 1⟩, (thorough) change ⟨MS 2⟩, (changement ⟨B⟩), (mutation ⟨R, B⟩). Cf. Abwandlung, ändern, Bewusstseinswandlung, Umwandlung, Veränderung, Verwandlung, Wandel, Wechsel.
Was, What, (quid ⟨R⟩), (contenu ⟨B⟩). Cf. das Unbestimmbare (sub unbestimmbar), wie.
Wasgehalt, what-contents, (contenu qualitatif ⟨B⟩). Cf. Gehalt.
Washeit, whatness, quiddity.
Wechsel, change ⟨WH 1, MS 1⟩, changes, (vicissitudes ⟨B⟩), alteration, variation, (modification ⟨B⟩); exchange ⟨WH, MS⟩, interchange ⟨WH⟩, interchanging, alternation ⟨WH, MS⟩, (succession ⟨B⟩); fluctuation ⟨MS⟩; transition ⟨MS⟩. Cf. Abwandlung, Beleuchtungswechsel, ändern, in Gleichheit (sub Gleichheit), Übergang, Umwandlung, variieren, Veränderung, Verwandlung, Wandel, Wandlung, Wendung.
Wechselgemeinschaft, intercommunion. Cf. Gemeinschaft.
wechselnd, changing, varying ⟨L⟩, (variable ⟨R⟩), (mouvant ⟨R⟩), shifting ⟨Bn, BG⟩; (successif ⟨B⟩); alternative.
Wechselrede, colloquy, conversation ⟨F⟩. Cf. Rede 1, Wechselverkehr.
Wechselverkehr, conversation. Cf. Rede 1, Wechselrede.
(Wechselwirkung), reciprocal action ⟨Bn, MS⟩, (reciprocity ⟨Bn⟩). Cf. Wirkung.
Weckung, awakening, (évocation ⟨B⟩). Cf. Erweckung, geweckt, wach. | in der —, when it becomes awakened, (dans l'évocation ⟨B⟩).
Weise, manner ⟨MS 1, WH 2⟩, (manière ⟨B⟩), mode ⟨WH 1⟩, (mode ⟨R,

B⟩), fashion ⟨WH, MS⟩, (façon ⟨R, B⟩), way ⟨WH 3, MS, BG⟩; type. Cf. Anschauungsweise, Art, Auffassungsweise, Betrachtungsweise, Bewusstseinsweise, Erlebnisweise, Erscheinungsweise, Gegebenheitsweise, Gemeintheitsweise, Modus, Schlussweise, Seinsweise, Typus, Verbindungsweise. | Art und —, manner, (mode ⟨Gomperz trln of Mill, quoted in LU, II. Unters.⟩).
weisen, Cf. aufweisen, ausweisen, beweisen, erweisen, hinweisen, nachweisen, rückweisen auf, verweisen, zeigen, zurückweisen auf. | einem etwas —, to show one something ⟨MS 1, WH⟩. | — auf, to point to (or out) ⟨WH, MS⟩.
Weiser, pointer ⟨MS 2⟩, indicator ⟨MS 3, WH⟩. Cf. Anzeiger, Zeiger.
Weiss, white ⟨MS 1, BG⟩, (blanc ⟨R⟩). Save "whiteness" ⟨WH 2, BG⟩ for "Weisse".
Weisse, whiteness ⟨Gomperz trln of Mill, cited in LU, I. Unters.; WH 1; MS 1; BG⟩, (blancheur ⟨R⟩).
Weisung, showing ⟨MS 1⟩, indicating, direction ⟨WH 2, MS 3⟩. Cf. Anweisung auf, Aufweisung, Ausweisung, Rückweisung.
Welt, world, (omnitudo ⟨Ideen I, 6⟩).
Weltall, all the world, mundane universe. Not just "universe" ⟨Bn, WH 1, MS 1⟩. Cf. All.
Weltanschauung, world view ⟨Bn⟩. Cf. Anschauung, Raumanschauung, Zeitanschauung.
weltbezogen, related to the world. Cf. bezogen sein auf etwas (sub bezogen).
Weltboden, | auf dem —, on the basis of the world; in the mundane realm. Cf. Boden.
Welterfahrung, world-experience, (expérience du monde ⟨B⟩), world-experiencing, experiencing the world. Cf. Erfahrung.
(Weltgrund), world ground ⟨Bn⟩. Cf. Grund.
weltlich ⟨adj.⟩, worldly ⟨WH 2⟩, (mondain ⟨B⟩), belonging to the world, of something worldly, presupposing

the world. So far as possible save "mundane" ⟨WH 1, MS 2⟩ for "mundane". | äusseres W ~es, what belongs to the external world. Cf. äussere.

weltlich ⟨adv.⟩, as worldly, in the world, mundanely.

Weltlichkeit, worldliness ⟨WH 1, MS 1⟩, (world-acceptance). | Einstellung der —, world-accepting attitude. Cf. Einstellung.

Weltobjekt, world Object. Cf. Objekt.

"Weltvorstellung", "idea of the world". Cf. Vorstellung 4 & 7.

wenden, Cf. gewendet. | sich —, to turn ⟨WH 1, L⟩.

Wendung, turning ⟨MS 1, WH 2, BG⟩, (tournure ⟨B⟩), (conversion ⟨B⟩), (when equivalent to "Zuwendung" ⟨q.v.⟩:) advertence, turn ⟨WH 1, MS 2⟩, shift, shifting, (transposition ⟨B⟩), (passage ⟨B⟩), change ⟨WH, MS⟩, (revirement ⟨B⟩); version, variant; locution ⟨WH⟩. Not "turn of thought" ⟨BG⟩. Cf. Abwandlung, Abwendung, Blickwendung, gewendet, Prägung, Rede 2, Umwendung, Veränderung, Verschiebung, Verwandlung, Wandel, Wechsel, Zuwendung. | subjektive —, turning toward the subjective, (conversion subjective ⟨B⟩); subjective locution, (tournure subjective ⟨B⟩). | thematische —, shift of thematizing interest, (revirement thématique ⟨B⟩). | — auf, turning toward(s) (or to).

werden, to become ⟨WH 1, MS 1⟩, to come into being, to be generated, to be made, (se faire ⟨B⟩), (se former ⟨B⟩), (être formé ⟨B⟩), (to develop). Cf. fortwerdend, geworden, zustande kommen (sub zustande). | thematisch —, to be made thematic.

Werden, (origination) and development, (développement ⟨B⟩), genesis ⟨WH, MS⟩, (devenir ⟨de M⟩).

Werk, | im ~e sein, to be under way.

Werkleistung, product of work. Cf. Leistung.

wert, valuable ⟨MS, BG⟩, (valable ⟨R⟩), (valued ⟨?⟩ ⟨WH, BG⟩), (éva-

lué ⟨R⟩). Cf. unwert. | ein W ~es, something valuable.

Wert, value ⟨MS 1, WH 2, BG⟩, (valeur ⟨R, B⟩), (worth ⟨Bn, WH 1, MS 2⟩); valuable object, object with value, concrete value, good. Cf. das Gute (sub gut), Erkenntniswert, Geltung, Geltungswert, Güte, Güter, Unwert, Wertewelt. | den — eines A haben, to be equivalent to an A.

(wertachten), to esteem ⟨WH 1, MS 1⟩, to respect ⟨WH 2, MS 3⟩, to appreciate ⟨MS 2⟩, to have a (great) regard for. Cf. (werthalten), (wertschätzen).

(Wertachtung), esteem ⟨MS 1⟩, appreciation ⟨MS 2⟩, respect ⟨MS 3⟩, regard ⟨MS 4⟩.

Wertcharakter, value-characteristic, (caractère de valeur ⟨R⟩). Not "value-character" ⟨BG⟩. Save "value" ⟨BG⟩ for "Wert" ⟨q.v.⟩. Cf. Charakter.

werten, to value ⟨WH 1, MS 1⟩, (évaluer ⟨R, B⟩). Not "to evaluate". Cf. bewerten, Umwerten.

Werten, valuing, (évaluation ⟨R⟩). Not "evaluating"; not "appreciating" ⟨BG⟩. Cf. Werthaltung.

wertend ⟨adj.⟩, valuing, axiological, (axiologique ⟨R⟩). Not "of appreciation" ⟨BG⟩.

wertend ⟨adv.⟩, valuingly, (in valuing ⟨?⟩ ⟨BG⟩), (pour évaluer ⟨R⟩). Not "in appreciation" ⟨BG⟩.

Wertewelt, world of objects with values, (world of values ⟨?⟩ ⟨BG⟩), (monde des valeurs ⟨B⟩). Cf. Güterwelt.

(werthalten), to value ⟨WH 1⟩, to appreciate ⟨MS 2⟩. Cf. (wertachten), werten.

Werthaltung, valuation, valuing, appreciation. Cf. (Wertachtung), Werten.

Wertheit, value-quality, (qualité de valeur ⟨R⟩), value. Not "quality of value" ⟨BG⟩.

wertlich, value-.

Wertobjektivität, Object with value, (objectivité qui porte la valeur ⟨R⟩).

Not "objectified value". Cf. **Objektivität**.

Wertsachverhalt, (*état de valeur* ⟨R⟩). Cf. **Sachverhalt, Wertverhalt**.

wertschätzend ⟨adj.⟩, | ∼es Interesse, interest in estimating values.

wertschätzend ⟨adv.⟩, by valuing.

Wertschätzung, estimation of value, valuation. Cf. **Bewertung, Schätzung, Werthaltung, Wertung**.

Wertung, valuation ⟨WH 1⟩, (*évaluation* ⟨R⟩), holding valuable, (*appréciation* ⟨R⟩). Not "evaluation"; not "appreciation". Cf. **Bewertung, Entwertung, Gefühlswertung, Umwertung, Werthaltung, Wertschätzung**.

Wertungssinn, valuational sense. Cf. **Wahrnehmungssinn**.

Werturteil, value-judgment, (*jugement de valeur* ⟨R⟩).

Wertverhalt, predicatively formed value-complex, (*état de valeur* ⟨R⟩). Cf. **Sachverhalt, Verhalt, Wertsachverhalt**.

Wesen, essence ⟨WH, MS, BG⟩, (*essence* ⟨R, B, de M⟩), (*esse* ⟨K⟩); (when designating a concrete individual:) being ⟨WH 1, MS⟩, (*être* ⟨R, de M⟩). Not "essential nature" ⟨BG⟩. Cf. **Art, Eigenwesen, Gegenwesen, Sein**.

Wesenhaftigkeit, (of a concept:) correspondence to an essence, corresponding to a possibly exemplified essence. Cf. **Wesenlosigkeit**.

Wesenheit, essentiality, (*essence* ⟨B⟩), (*nature eidétique* ⟨R⟩).

Wesenlosigkeit, (of a concept:) correspondence to no (possibly exemplified) essence. Cf. **Wesenshaftigkeit**.

Wesensabwandlung, essential variant. Cf. **Abwandlung**.

wesensallgemein, | ein W ∼es, an essentially universal moment.

Wesensallgemeinheit, eidetic universality, (*généralité eidétique* ⟨R⟩), (*généralité essentielle* ⟨B⟩). Cf. **Allgemeinheit**. | reine —, purely eidetic universality, (*pure généralité eidétique* ⟨R⟩).

Wesensanalyse, eidetic analysis, (*analyse (d'ordre) eidétique* ⟨R⟩), analysis of something in respect of its essence,

(essence-analysis). Not "analysis of essence" ⟨L, BG⟩, not "essential analysis" ⟨L⟩. Cf. **Wesenserforschung, Wesenserkenntnis, Wesensstudium**.

Wesensanschauung, intuition of an essence, essence-intuition, eidetic intuition, (*intuition eidétique* ⟨R⟩). Cf. **Anschauung, Wesenserschauung, Wesensschau, Wesensschauung**.

Wesensart, essential sort, (*type essentiel* ⟨B⟩). Cf. **Art**.

Wesensaussage, Cf. **Aussage**. | gesetzliche —, statement of an eidetical law.

Wesensbedingung, essential condition, (*condition d'essence* ⟨B⟩).

Wesensbegriff, eidetic(al) concept, concept of an essence, (*concept essentiel* ⟨B⟩).

Wesensbestand, essential composition, essential make-up, (*fonds eidétique* ⟨R⟩); (pl., at least sometimes:) essential facts, (*ensemble des essences* ⟨B⟩). Not "state of essential being" ⟨BG⟩. Cf. **Bestand**.

Wesensbeziehung, essential relation, essential interrelation, (*relation eidétique* ⟨R⟩). Cf. **Beziehung**.

Wesenseigenheit, essential peculiarity (*or* property), (*propriété essentielle* ⟨B⟩), (*caractère propre d'essence* ⟨B⟩). Cf. **Eigenheit**.

Wesenseigenschaft, essential property ⟨BG⟩, (*propriété essentielle* ⟨B⟩), (*propriété eidétique* ⟨R⟩). Cf. **Eigenschaft**.

Wesenseinsicht, eidetic insight, (*évidence essentielle* ⟨B⟩). Cf. **Einsicht**.

Wesenserfassung, grasping of essences, (*saisie des essences* ⟨R⟩), grasping of the essence. Not "apprehension of the essence" ⟨BG⟩, not "grasp of essence" ⟨L⟩. Cf. **Erfassung, Wesensfassung**.

Wesenserforschung, exploration of essences, exploration of something in respect of its essence. Not "essential investigation" ⟨L⟩, not "investigations into essences" ⟨L⟩. Cf. **Erforschung, Wesensanalyse, Wesens-**

erkenntnis, Wesensforschung, Wesensstudium.

Wesenserkenntnis, eidetic cognition, cognition of essences, (*connaissance de l'essence* ⟨R⟩), cognition of something in respect of its essence. Not "essential knowledge" ⟨L⟩. Cf. **Erkenntnis, Wesensanalyse, Wesenserforschung, Wesensstudium.**

Wesenserschauung, seeing an essence, seeing essences, (*intuition de l'essence* ⟨R⟩). Not "vision of Essential Being" ⟨BG⟩. Cf. **Erschauung, Wesensanschauung, Wesensschau, Wesensschauung.** | **originärgebende** —, the seeing that gives an essence originally.

Wesensfassung, apprehension of essences, (*traitement eidétique* ⟨R⟩). Not "grasp of the essential" ⟨BG⟩. Cf. **Fassung 1, Wesenserfassung.**

Wesensform, essential form, (*forme essentielle* ⟨B⟩).

Wesensforschung, (scientific) inquiry into essences. Not "essential investigation" ⟨L⟩. Cf. **Forschung, Wesenserforschung.**

Wesensgattung, essential genus, (*genre essentiel* ⟨B⟩). Not "generic essence" ⟨BG⟩. Cf. **Gattung.**

Wesensgegebenheit, eidetic datum, (*donnée eidétique* ⟨R⟩); givenness of the essence, (the essence's givenness). Not "the essence in its givenness" ⟨L⟩. Cf. **Gegebenheit.** | **zur — kommen,** to become given essentially, (*accéder au rang de donnée eidétique* ⟨R⟩).

Wesensgehalt, essential content ⟨BG⟩, (*contenu essentiel* ⟨B⟩), essential contents, (*statut eidétique* ⟨R⟩). Cf. **Gehalt, Inhalt.** | **eigener —,** essential contents proper. Cf. **eigen** ⟨adj.⟩.

Wesensgemeinschaft, community of essence, (*communauté d'essence* ⟨R⟩). Cf. **Gemeinschaft.**

Wesensgesetz, eidetic law, (*loi d'essence* ⟨R, B⟩), (*loi essentielle* ⟨B⟩).

wesensgesetzlich ⟨adj.⟩, according to an eidetic law, (*en terme de lois eidétiques* ⟨R⟩), as an eidetic law, (*relevant de lois essentielles* ⟨B⟩).

wesensgesetzlich ⟨adv.⟩, by an eidetic law.

Wesensgesetzlichkeit, set of eidetic laws, (*légalité essentielle* ⟨B⟩). Cf. **Gesetzlichkeit.**

Wesensgesetzmässigkeit, system (*or* set) of eidetic laws, eidetic law, (*légalité essentielle* ⟨B⟩), (*sphère des lois essentielles* ⟨B⟩). Cf. **Gesetzmässigkeit.**

Wesensgestalt, (of a genesis:) essential structure, (*forme essentielle* ⟨B⟩). Cf. **Gestalt.**

wesensgleich ⟨adj.⟩, essentially quite alike. Cf. **gleich.**

Wesensgrund, essential ground ⟨BG⟩, (*principe essentiel* ⟨B⟩); eidetic reason, (*raison eidétique* ⟨R⟩), (*raison d'essence* ⟨B⟩). Cf. **Grund.** | **aus W ~en notwendig,** essentially necessary.

Wesenslage, essential situation, (*situation essentielle* ⟨B⟩). Cf. **Sachlage.**

Wesenslehre, eidetic doctrine, doctrine of essences, (*doctrine des essences* ⟨R⟩).

wesensmässig ⟨adj.⟩, befitting its essence, consonant with (its) essence, (*conforme à l'essence* ⟨B⟩), essentially determined, prescribed by its essence, essentially necessary, by (virtue of) its essence, in its essence, essential, (*essentiel* ⟨B⟩), (*relatif aux essences* ⟨B⟩), eidetic. Cf. **wesentlich** ⟨adj.⟩.

wesensmässig ⟨adv.⟩, as essential, (as a matter) of essential necessity, (*conformément à l'essence* ⟨B⟩), (*du point de vue eidétique* ⟨R⟩), (*par essence* ⟨R, B⟩), essentially, (*d'une manière essentielle* ⟨B⟩), (necessarily). Cf. **mit Wesensnotwendigkeit** (*sub* **Wesensnotwendigkeit**), **wesentlich** ⟨adv.⟩.

Wesensmöglichkeit, eidetic possibility, (*possibilité eidétique* ⟨R⟩), (*possibilité sur le plan des essences* ⟨R⟩), essential possibility ⟨BG⟩.

Wesensnotwendigkeit, eidetic necessity, (*nécessité eidétique* ⟨R⟩), essential necessity ⟨BG⟩, (*nécessité essentielle* ⟨B⟩). | **mit —,** as a matter of eidetic (*or* essential) necessity.

Wesenssachverhalt, (*état* (*de chose*) *eidétique* ⟨R⟩). Cf. **Sachverhalt, Wesensverhalt.**

Wesensschau, seeing (of) an essence (*or* essences), (*vision des essences* ⟨B⟩). Cf. **Schau, Wesensanschauung, Wesenserschauung, Wesensschauung.**

Wesensschauen, seeing (of) essences. Not "essential intuition" ⟨L⟩. Cf. **Schauen.**

Wesensschauung, seeing (of) an essence (*or* essences), (*vision de l'essence* ⟨R⟩), eidetic seeing. Not "intuiting essences" ⟨L⟩, not "essential intuition" ⟨L⟩. Cf. **Schauung, Wesensanschauung, Wesenserschauung, Wesensschau, Wesensschauen.**

Wesenssein, eidetic being, essential being, (being as essence ⟨L⟩).

Wesenssphäre, sphere of essences, (*sphère essentielle* ⟨B⟩). | **hyletischsachhaltige** —, sphere of hyletic materially determinate essences.

Wesensstruktur, essential structure, (*structure essentielle* ⟨B⟩); eidetic structure.

Wesensstudium, study of something in respect of its essence. Not "essential study" ⟨L⟩. Cf. **Wesensanalyse, Wesenserforschung, Wesenserkenntnis.**

Wesenstatsache, Cf. **Tatsache.** | **intentionale** —, fact pertaining to the intentional essence, (*fait intentionnel imposé par l'essence* ⟨B⟩).

Wesenstypus, essential type, (*type essentiel* ⟨B⟩); essential character. Cf. **Typus.**

Wesensumgrenzung, ascertaining the essential limits; essential delimitation, (*délimitation essentielle* ⟨B⟩). Cf. **Umgrenzung.**

Wesensurteil, eidetic judgment, judgment concerning what is essential, (*jugement qui porte sur des essences* ⟨R⟩), judgement concerning (the) essences. Not "essential judgment" ⟨L⟩. | **reines** —, purely eidetic judgment, judgment concerning what is purely essential, (*jugement relatif aux essences* ⟨R⟩).

Wesensverallgemeinerung, eidetic uni-

versalization, (*généralisation essentielle* ⟨B⟩). Cf. **Verallgemeinerung.**

Wesensverhalt, eidetic relationship, essential relationship, (*relation essentielle* ⟨B⟩), relationship among essences; (predicatively) formed eidetic (*or* essence-) complex, (eidetic state-of-affairs), (*état de choses eidétique* ⟨R⟩), (*état d'essence* ⟨R⟩). Cf. **Sachverhalt, Verhalt, Wesensverhalt, Wirklichkeitsverhalt.**

Wesenswahrheit, eidetic truth, (*vérité essentielle* ⟨B⟩), (*vérité d'essence* ⟨R⟩), (*vérité concernant les essences* ⟨R⟩). Cf. **Wahrheit.**

Wesenszusammenhang, essential inter. connexion, (*liaison essentielle* ⟨B⟩)- Cf. **Zusammenhang.**

wesentlich ⟨adj.⟩, essential ⟨WH 1, MS 1, BG⟩, (*essentiel* ⟨R, B⟩); essential necessary, substantial ⟨WH 2, MS 2⟩; (loose sense:) principal. Cf. **eigenwesentlich** ⟨adj.⟩, **prinzipiell** ⟨adj.⟩, **wesensmässig** ⟨adj.⟩.

wesentlich ⟨adv.⟩, essentially, (*essentiellement* ⟨B⟩), (*pour l'essentiel* ⟨B⟩); (loose sense:) importantly, appreciably. Cf. **eigenwesentlich** ⟨adv.⟩, **prinzipiell** ⟨adv.⟩, **wesensmässig** ⟨adv.⟩.

Widerfolge, anti-consequence, (*contreconséquence* ⟨B⟩). Cf. **Folge 1, Inkonsequenz, Widerspruch.**

Widersinn, countersense, (*contre-sens* ⟨B, de M⟩), (absurdity ⟨WH 2, MS 3, L, BG⟩), (*absurdité* ⟨R⟩), (contrariety of sense). Save "nonsense" ⟨WH 1, MS 2⟩ for "Unsinn" ⟨q.v.⟩. So far as possible, save "absurdity" for "Absurdität" and "Verkehrtheit" ⟨q.v.⟩.

widersinnig ⟨adj.⟩, countersensical ⟨not in OED but justified by analogy with "nonsensical"⟩, countersenseful, (absurd ⟨WH 2, MS, L, BG⟩), (*absurde* ⟨R, B⟩). Save "nonsensical" ⟨WH 1, MS 1⟩ for "unsinnig". | **~er Kreis,** vicious circle ⟨L⟩.

widersinnig ⟨adv.⟩, in contravention of their sense, in a manner that contravenes their sense.

Widersinnigkeit, countersensefulness, (*contre-sens* ⟨B⟩).
(Widerspiel), (reciprocity ⟨?⟩ ⟨Bn⟩).
Widerspruch, contradiction ⟨WH 1, MS 1⟩, (*contradiction* ⟨B⟩), (*contradictio* ⟨K⟩). Cf. **Kontradiktion.**
Widerspruchsgesetz, | analytisches —, law of analytic contradiction, (*loi analytique de la contradiction* ⟨B⟩).
widerspruchslos ⟨adj.⟩, non-contradictory, (*non-contradictoire* ⟨B⟩), (contradictionless).
widerspruchslos ⟨adv.⟩, without contradiction, (*de façon non-contradictoire* ⟨B⟩).
Widerspruchslosigkeit, non-contradiction, (*non-contradiction* ⟨B⟩), (non-contradictoriness), (absence of contradiction).
Widerstand, resistance ⟨WH 1, MS 1⟩; opposition ⟨WH 2, MS 2⟩.
Widerstreit, conflict ⟨WH 3, MS⟩, (*conflit* ⟨R, B⟩), antagonism ⟨MS 1⟩, (*lutte* ⟨B⟩).
widerstreitend, conflicting ⟨WH 1, MS 1⟩, antagonistic ⟨MS 1, WH 2⟩, (*ce qui apporte une contradiction* ⟨B⟩).
Widerwollen, willing against, (*contre-vouloir* ⟨R⟩). Not "voluntary aversion" ⟨BG⟩. Cf. **Wollen.**
Wie, How, (*quomodo* ⟨de M⟩), (*comment* ⟨de M⟩), (*manière* ⟨B⟩). Cf. **Was.**
Wiedererinnerung, recollection ⟨WH 1, WH 2⟩, (*re-souvenir* ⟨R⟩), (*ressouvenir* ⟨B⟩), (*souvenir* ⟨de M⟩). Cf. **Erinnerung, Rückerinnerung, Vorerinnerung.** | **Evidenz der —,** recollective evidence, (*évidence du ressouvenir* ⟨B⟩).
wiedererinnerungsmässig ⟨adj.⟩, recollective. Cf. **erinnerungsmässig.**
wiedererinnerungsmässig ⟨adv.⟩, recollectively, (*en tant que souvenir* ⟨B⟩). Cf. **erinnerungsmässig.**
Wiederholung, reiteration ⟨MS 2⟩, repetition ⟨WH 1, MS 1⟩, (*répétition* ⟨B⟩), recapitulation ⟨MS 3⟩, iteration; renewal. Cf. **Iteration.**
Wiederholungszahlen, (*numeralia iterativa* ⟨Arith, 3⟩.
Wiedervergegenwärtigung, re-presen-

tiating, (*présentification* ⟨R⟩). Not "repeated presentation" ⟨BG⟩. Cf. **Vergegenwärtigung.**
Wille(n), will ⟨WH 1, MS 1, L⟩, volition ⟨MS 2, WH 3⟩, (*vouloir* ⟨B⟩). Cf. **Erkenntniswillen, Willkür, Wollen.**
Willens-, volitional, of volition, voluntary ⟨Bn⟩, (*volitif* ⟨R⟩). Save "volitive" for "wollend" ⟨q.v.⟩. Cf. **willentlich, Willkür-, willkürlich.**
Willensakt, act of volition ⟨WH 1, MS 1⟩, act of will ⟨BG⟩.
Willensentscheidung, volitional decision. Cf. **Urteilsentscheidung.**
Willensmeinung, (*visée volontaire* ⟨R⟩). Cf. **Meinung, Urteilsmeinung, Wunschmeinung.**
Willensrichtung, volitional bent. Cf. **Richtung.**
Willenstätigkeit, volitional activity. Cf. **Tätigkeit.**
Willenstheorie, theory of volition.
willentlich, by volition, (*à dessein* ⟨B⟩). Cf. **mit Absicht** (*sub* **Absicht**).
Willkür, free choice, (*libre-choix* ⟨B⟩), (*libertas* ⟨Heidegger⟩), will, power to decide or choose, (*arbitrium* ⟨K⟩); (*phantaisie* ⟨B⟩). Cf. **Belieben, Willen, Wollen.**
Willkür-, volitional ⟨Bn⟩.
willkürlich ⟨adj.⟩, voluntary; arbitrary ⟨WH 1, MS 1⟩. Cf. **Willens-, willentlich, wollend.**
wirken, to operate ⟨WH, MS⟩, to effect ⟨WH 3, MS 3⟩, to work ⟨WH 1, MS 1⟩. Cf. **auswirken, herstellen, leisten, vollziehen, zustandebringen.**
wirklich ⟨adj.⟩, actual ⟨Bn, WH 2, MS 2⟩, effective ⟨WH, MS⟩, (*effectif* ⟨B⟩), true ⟨Ideen I, § 22, WH 3, MS⟩, (*véritable* ⟨B⟩), genuine ⟨WH 4, MS⟩, real ⟨WH 1, MS 1, L, BG⟩, (*réel* ⟨R, B⟩). So far as possible save "true" for "wahr" and "wahrhaft", "genuine" for "echt" ⟨q.v.⟩ and "reell" ⟨q.v.⟩, "real" for "real" and "reell". Cf. **aktuell** ⟨adj.⟩, **eigentlich** ⟨adj.⟩, **daseiend, faktisch** ⟨adj.⟩, **reell.** | **das W ∼e,** the actual (thing), (*la réalité* ⟨R⟩). Not "the reality" ⟨BG⟩.
wirklich ⟨adv.⟩, actually ⟨WH 2⟩,

(*effectivement* ⟨B⟩), (indeed ⟨WH⟩), (*véritablement* ⟨R⟩), (*vraiment* ⟨B⟩), (*réellement* ⟨R, B⟩). Not "really" ⟨WH 1, MS 1, BG⟩. Cf. **aktuell** ⟨adv.⟩, **eigentlich** ⟨adv.⟩, **faktisch** ⟨adv.⟩.

Wirklichkeit, actuality ⟨WH, MS⟩, (effectiveness), (loosely:) reality ⟨WH 1, MS 1, BG⟩, (*réalité* ⟨R, B⟩), (*réalité effective* ⟨B⟩). Save "fact" ⟨WH, MS, BG⟩ for "Faktum" ⟨q.v.⟩ and "Tatsache" ⟨q.v.⟩. So far as possible save "reality" for "Reales" ⟨q.v. *sub* real⟩ and "Realität". Cf. **Aktualität, Dasein, Faktizität, Seinswirklichkeit, Unwirklichkeit, Wirklichsein.**

Wirklichkeit-als-ob, as-if actuality.

Wirklichkeitsaussage, statement about actuality, (*énoncé concernant la réalité* ⟨R⟩). Cf. **Aussage.**

Wirklichkeitsgeltung, actuality-status. Cf. **Geltung, Seinsgeltung.**

Wirklichkeitsverhalt, actuality-relationship ⟨?⟩, (predicatively formed) actuality-complex, (state of actual affairs), (*état de choses propre à la réalité* ⟨R⟩). Cf. **Sachverhalt, Verhalt, Wesensverhalt.**

Wirklichsein, actualness, (actual being), (*être réel* ⟨R⟩). Cf. **Dasein, Faktizität, Wirklichkeit.**

Wirkung, effect ⟨WH 1, MS⟩, (*effet* ⟨B⟩), action ⟨WH⟩. Cf. **Auswirkung, (Einwirkung), Folge 4, (Gegenwirkung), Leistung, Tätigkeit, (Wechselwirkung).**

wissen, to know ⟨WH 1, MS 1⟩. Cf. **erkennen, kennen.** | — **von,** to know of ⟨WH 1, MS 1⟩.

Wissen, knowledge ⟨Bn, WH 1, MS 1, BG⟩, (*savoir* ⟨PL, R, B⟩), knowing (of), ken. Cf. **Erkenntnis, Kenntnis, Kunde, (Nichtwissen).**

Wissenschaftlichkeit, being scientific, scientific(al)ness, (*scientificité* ⟨B⟩), scientific character ⟨MS 1⟩ (*or* status). | **echte** —, being genuinely scientific, genuine scientificalness, genuinely scientific character.

Wissenschaftsform, science-form, (*for-*

me de science ⟨B⟩). Cf. **Form der Wissenschaft** (*sub* **Form**).

Wissenschaftsidee, idea of science. | **universale** —, idea of an all-embracing science, (*idée universelle de science* ⟨B⟩). Cf. **universal.**

Wissenschaftslehre, theory of science, (*doctrine de la science* ⟨B⟩). | **objektive** —, theory of Objective science, (*doctrine objective de la science* ⟨B⟩). Cf. **objektiv.**

wissenschaftstheoretisch, of theory of science, belonging to the theory of science, that belongs to a theory of science, in the theory of science, as theory of science, for (the) theory of science, (*épistémologique* ⟨B⟩).

Wissenschaftstheorie, theory of science, (*théorie* (ou *doctrine*) *de la science* ⟨B⟩).

Wissensgebilde, knowledge-formation, (*formation du savoir* ⟨B⟩). Cf. **Erkenntnisgebilde, Gebilde.**

Wohlgefallen, liking ⟨MS 1⟩, ((*sentiment de*) *plaisir* ⟨R⟩). Cf. **Gefallen, Missfallen.**

wollen, to will ⟨Ueberweg's trln of Berkeley, quoted in LU, II. Unters.; WH 1; MS 3; BG⟩, (*vouloir* ⟨R, B⟩), to intend ⟨WH, MS⟩, to mean ⟨WH⟩. Cf. **hinauswollen auf.**

Wollen, willing, (will ⟨WH 1, MS 2, BG⟩), (*vouloir* ⟨R⟩). Cf. **Widerwollen, Willen, Willkür.**

wollend, willing ⟨MS 1, BG⟩, (*voulant* ⟨R⟩); volitive, (*de la volonté* ⟨B⟩). Cf. **Willens-, willentlich, Willkür-, willkürlich.**

wonach, (at least sometimes:) whereby.

Wortbedeutung, 1. (noematic:) signification of the word (*or* of words), (*signification du mot* ⟨B⟩), (*signification des mots* ⟨R⟩), word-signification, verbal signification. Not "word-meaning" ⟨L⟩. 2. (noetic:) verbal signifying. Not "meaning of the word" ⟨BG⟩. Cf. **Bedeutung 1 & 2.**

Wortbegriff, verbal concept. Not "word-concept" ⟨L⟩. Cf. **Begriff.**

Wortgebilde, word-formation, (*formation des mots* ⟨B⟩), (*formation du langage* ⟨B⟩). Cf. **Gebilde.**

Wortlaut, sound of words, (*son du langage* ⟨B⟩), verbal sound, (*mot prononcé* ⟨B⟩).
Wortmeinung, verbal opinion, (*intention verbale* ⟨R⟩). Cf. **Meinung.**
Wortverlauf, word-sequence, (*déroulement des mots* ⟨B⟩). Cf. **Verlauf.**
Wortvorstellung, word-objectivation. Cf. **nominale Vorstellung** (*sub* **Vorstellung**).
Wortzeichen, verbal sign, (pl:) (*signes des mots* ⟨B⟩). Cf. **Zeichen.**

Wunschausdruck, wish-expression, (*expression du souhait* ⟨B⟩). Cf. **Urteilsausdruck.**
Wunschaussage, wish-statement, (*énoncé de souhait* ⟨B⟩), optative statement. Cf. **Aussage.**
Wunschmeinung, wish-meaning or wish-sense, (*opinion qui se spécifie en souhait* ⟨B⟩). Cf. **Meinung, Urteilsmeinung, Willensmeinung.**
Wunschrede, optative locution. Cf. **Rede 2.**

Z

Zahl-, numerical ⟨Bn⟩.
Zahlenbildung, numerical formation, (*assemblage de nombres* ⟨B⟩). Cf. **Bildung.**
Zahlengebilde, numerical formation, (*formation de nombres* ⟨B⟩), (numerical structure), (*construction numérique* ⟨R⟩). Not "construction of a numerical kind" ⟨BG⟩. Cf. **Gebilde.**
Zeichen, sign ⟨Ueberweg trln of Berkeley, quoted in Arith and LU, II. Unters.; Bn; WH1; MS 2; F; BG⟩, (*signe* ⟨R, B, de M⟩), (mark ⟨Gomperz trln of Mill, quoted in LU, I. Unters.; WH; MS⟩); (algebraic, sometimes:) symbol; ((etymological sense:) token ⟨MS 1, WH⟩. Cf. **Anzeichen, Beschaffenheit, Bezeichnen, Bezeichnung, Erinnerungszeichen, Kennzeichen, Merkmal, Merkzeichen, Schriftzeichen, Vorzeichen, Wortzeichen.**
Zeichensein, being a sign, signhood. Cf. **Anzeichensein.**
Zeichenvorstellung, sign-objectivation. Not "sign-furnishing presentation" ⟨BG⟩. Cf. **Bildvorstellung, Vorstellung 1.**
zeichnen, to mark ⟨WH, MS⟩, (to brand ⟨WH, MS⟩), (to sign ⟨WH, MS⟩), to mark out, to draw ⟨WH 1⟩, (*tracer* ⟨B⟩). Cf. **anzeichnen, bezeichnen, kennzeichnen, vorzeichnen.**
zeigen, to indicate ⟨WH 2, MS 3⟩, to

show ⟨WH 1, MS 1⟩, (*montrer* ⟨B⟩), to point out ⟨WH, MS 2⟩. Save "to demonstrate" ⟨Ueberweg trln of Berkeley, quoted in LU, II. Unters.; WH⟩ for "beweisen", "ausweisen", "nachweisen"⟨qq.vv.⟩. Cf. **andeuten, anzeigen, bedeuten, hindeuten, hinweisen auf, hinzeigen, vorweisen, weisen.** | sich —, to show itself ⟨WH 1, MS 1⟩, (*se manifester* ⟨B⟩), to become apparent ⟨WH⟩, (*apparaître* ⟨R, B⟩). Cf. **auftreten, erscheinen, sich anzeigen** (*sub* **anzeigen**), **sich herausstellen** (*sub* **herausstellen**), **zur Erscheinung kommen** (*sub* **Erscheinung**).
Zeiger, indicator ⟨WH 3, MS⟩, pointer ⟨WH 1⟩, (*index* ⟨B⟩). Cf. **Anzeichen, Anzeiger, Weiser.**
Zeitanschauung, intuition of time; (natural-scientific:) view of time. Cf. **Anschauung.**
Zeitbewusstsein, consciousness of time, (*conscience de temps* ⟨R⟩), (*conscience du temps* ⟨B⟩), time-consciousness. | inneres —, consciousness of internal time. Not "internal (*nor* inner) consciousness of time"; not "internal (*nor* inner) time-consciousness". Cf. **inner.** | primäres —, primary consciousness of time. | subjektives —, subjective consciousness of time. Not "consciousness of subjective time".
Zeitbeziehung, time-relation. Cf. **Beziehung.**

Zeitbezogenheit, relatedness to time, (*référence au temps* ⟨B⟩). Cf. **Bezogenheit**.
Zeitdatum, | **immanentes** —, Datum occurring in immanent time, (*datum immanent temporel* ⟨B⟩).
Zeitdauer, time-duration. Cf. **Dauer**.
Zeiterlebnis, time-consciousness, (lived) consciousness of time. Cf. **Erlebnis**.
Zeithof, temporal fringe. Cf. **Hof**.
Zeithorizont, temporal horizon. Cf. **Horizont**.
zeitigen, to constitute as temporal ⟨?⟩, to temporalize ⟨?⟩ ⟨not in OED⟩.
Zeitkontinuum, time-continuum.
Zeitlang, | **eine** —, for a time ⟨WH⟩.
zeitlich, temporal ⟨WH 1, MS 1⟩, in time. Cf. **objektiv-zeitlich**.
Zeitlichkeit, temporality, (*temporalité* ⟨B⟩), temporalness ("rare" ⟨OED⟩). Cf. **Erlebniszeitlichkeit**.
Zeitobjekt, temporal Object. | **immanentes** —, Object in immanent time.
Zeitphase, time-phase, temporal phase.
Zeitpunkt, point of time, time-point.
Zeitsphäre, | **immanente** —, sphere of immanent time, (*sphère temporelle immanente* ⟨B⟩).
Zeitstelle, temporal locus, (*place temporelle* ⟨B⟩), (*place dans le temps* ⟨R⟩), (*situation temporelle* ⟨B⟩). Cf. **Stelle**.
Zeitumgebung, contemporaries. Cf. **Umgebung**. | **in einer** —, among contemporaries. Not "in an epoch" ⟨L⟩.
Zeitstrecke, temporal extent. Cf. **Strecke**.
zergliedern, to dismember ⟨WH 1, MS 1⟩, (*démembrer* ⟨R⟩), (*décomposer* ⟨B⟩), to analyze (*or* divide) into members, to dissect ⟨WH 2, MS 2⟩. Cf. **gliedern**.
(Zerstreuung), dispersion ⟨Bn, WH 1⟩.
zerstückbar, that can be divided into "pieces", (*que l'on peut morceler* ⟨B⟩).
zerstücken, to divide ⟨MS⟩, (into pieces), (*morceler* ⟨B⟩), to fragment. Cf. **Stück**.

Zerstückung, division ⟨MS⟩ into pieces (*or* parts), fragmentation. Cf. **Abstückung, Einteilung, Teilung**.
ziehen, | **Urteile** —, to derive judgments ⟨L⟩. | **nach sich** —, to entail ⟨WH 3, MS 3⟩, (*entraîner* ⟨B⟩). Cf. **beschliessen, einschliessen, in sich schliessen** (*sub* **schliessen**).
Ziel, aim ⟨Bn, WH 1, MS⟩, (*but* ⟨PL, R, B⟩), target ⟨WH 3, MS⟩, goal ⟨WH, MS⟩; (broad sense:) end ⟨Bn, WH, MS⟩, (*fin* ⟨PL⟩). Cf. **Absicht, Abzielen, Abzielung, Erkenntnisziel, Erzielung, Zweck**. | **etwas auf ein** — **stellen**, to aim something. | **prinzipielle** ~**e**, essential goals. Cf. **prinzipiell** ⟨adj.⟩.
Zielidee, goal-idea, (*idée-fin* ⟨B⟩). Cf. **Zweckidee**.
Zielpunkt, target, (*point de mire* ⟨R⟩).
Zielstellung, goal-setting, (*position du but* ⟨B⟩), (*détermination du but* ⟨PL⟩), aim. Cf. **Absehen, Abzielen, Abzielung, etwas auf ein Ziel stellen** (*sub* **Ziel**), **Stellung**.
Zielung, aiming, (*visée* ⟨B⟩), pointing. Cf. **Absehen, Abzielung, Strebung**.
zudeuten, to assign.
Zufall, accident ⟨WH 2, MS⟩.
zufällig, adventitious ⟨WH⟩, accidental ⟨Bn, WH 1, MS 1⟩, contingent ⟨MS⟩, (*contingent* ⟨R, B⟩), (chance ⟨WH, L⟩).
Zufälligkeit, contingency, (*contingence* ⟨R⟩); accidental (feature).
Zug, (sometimes:) trait. Cf. **Grundzug**.
zugänglich, accessible ⟨WH 1⟩, within reach.
Zugangsform, form giving access, form that gives access.
zugehören, (sometimes:) to be a member of.
zugehörig, belonging to ⟨MS 1, WH 2⟩, (*afférent* ⟨B⟩), that belongs to, appertinent, (*relevant de* ⟨B⟩), attendant, (*qui s'y rattache* ⟨R⟩), pertaining to, pertinent ⟨MS⟩; that belongs with, corresponding, (*correspondant* ⟨B⟩), that correspond(s) to, (*qui lui correspond* ⟨B⟩), requisite ⟨WH 3, MS⟩, (*dont il dépend* ⟨B⟩). Cf. **anhaftend, eigen, gehörig**. | **ein**

notwendig Z~es, a necessary appertinent. | ein Z~es, an appertinent. Cf. ein Gehöriges (sub gehörig).

Zugehörigkeit, (appartenance ⟨R, B⟩). Cf. Ichzugehörigkeit, Zusammengehörigkeit. | — haben, to be appertinent.

zugeordnet, (sometimes:) attaching (or attached) to.

zugestaltend, Cf. gestaltend. | etwas Form —, imposing form on something, conferring form upon something.

Zugewendetsein, advertedness, ((state of) being turned towards ⟨B⟩), (fait d'être tourné vers ⟨R⟩). Cf. Zuwendung.

zugrunde, Cf. Grund, Grundlage, Grundlegung. | — legen, to take as one's basis, (prendre pour base ⟨B⟩). | — liegen, to be at the basis of ⟨F⟩, (être à la base de ⟨B⟩), to underlie. | ~ liegend, at the basis of ⟨F⟩, (qui est à la base ⟨B⟩), (de base ⟨B⟩), underlying, foundational, (qui est le fondement ⟨B⟩). Cf. Grund 3.

zumeinen, to attribute to.

zumessen, to ascribe to. Cf. zurechnen, zuschreiben.

zumuten, to attribute.

Zumutung, demand, something claimed, (prétention ⟨R⟩).

Zunichtemachung, annihilation, undoing; (anéantissement ⟨B⟩). Cf. Aufhebung, Durchstreichung, Nichtigkeit, Vernichtung.

zurechnen, to include in, to take to be an intrinsic part of. Cf. einlegen, zumessen, zuschreiben.

zurückbezogen, | — auf sich, reflexively related to itself, bearing reflexively on itself, (renvoyé à lui-même ⟨B⟩). | — sein auf etwas, to relate (or refer ⟨BG⟩) back to something, (être rapporté à quelque chose ⟨R, B⟩). Cf. bezogen sein (sub bezogen).

Zurückbezogenheit auf sich, reflexive bearing upon itself, (référence à soi-même ⟨B⟩). Cf. Bezogenheit.

zurückfragen, to inquire back, to inquire regressively (or retrogressively), to ask back, to go back and ask (about). Cf. Rückfrage.

zurückführen auf, trace back to ⟨WH⟩. (Zurückführung), (logic:) reduction ⟨Bn, WH 1, MS⟩.

zurückgehen, | — auf, to go back to ⟨WH 1, MS 1⟩, (revenir à ⟨B⟩), to turn back to ⟨WH 2⟩, to recur to. | — zu, to return ⟨MS 2, WH 3⟩ to, (revenir à ⟨B⟩).

zurückgreifen auf, to reach back and seize, (ressaisir ⟨B⟩). Cf. greifen.

zurücksinken, (temporally:) to sink backward.

Zurückverweisung, referring (one) back (to). Cf. verweisen.

zurückweisen auf, to point back to, to point back at, (of a clue:) to lead back to, to refer (one) back to ⟨MS 1⟩, (renvoyer à ⟨R, B⟩). Cf. rückweisen auf.

Züruckwendung, reversion. Cf. Umwendung, Wendung.

Zusammen, ensemble, gathering.

Zusammenbruch, collapse ⟨WH 2⟩, (breakdown ⟨WH 1⟩).

zusammenfassen, to take together, (rassembler ⟨R⟩), to comprise ⟨WH⟩, (in words:) to summarize ⟨WH, MS⟩, (résumer ⟨B⟩). Cf. fassen 5.

zusammengehören, to belong together, (avoir entre eux une solidarité ⟨R⟩), (être en connexion ⟨B⟩), (avoir une parenté ⟨B⟩).

zusammengehörig, belonging together ⟨MS 1⟩, that (or which) belongs together, (having parts that belong together), intimately related, (apparenté ⟨B⟩), (parenté ⟨B⟩), (qui ont une parenté ⟨B⟩), interrelated, (connexe ⟨B⟩), (solidaire ⟨R⟩), homogeneous, congruous, germane. Not "mutually attached" ⟨BG⟩. Cf. gehörig, zugehörig.

Zusammengehörigkeit, belongingness together, (relationship of) belonging together, correlation, correspondence, intimate relatedness, (parenté ⟨B⟩), homogeneity, congruity, (convenance ⟨B⟩), (commune appartenance ⟨B⟩), (appartenance ⟨R⟩), (solida-

rité ⟨B⟩). Cf. **Korrelation, Zugehörigkeit.**

Zusammengeltung, conjoint acceptance, co-positedness, (con-positio ⟨Logik, *143*⟩), (joint validity), (*co-validité* ⟨B⟩), (*valoir ensemble* ⟨B⟩). Cf. **Geltung, Mitgeltung.**

Zusammengerücktheit, compressedness.

zusammengesetzt, composite ⟨Bn, MS 1, WH 2⟩, (*composé* ⟨B⟩), (*compositum* ⟨K, Br⟩). Cf. **Zusammensetzung.**

Zusammengreifen, gripping (objects) together, (*appréhension globale* ⟨R⟩). Cf. **greifen.**

Zusammenhang, 1. connexion ⟨MS 1, WH⟩, (*connexion* ⟨R, B⟩, (*liaison* ⟨B⟩), (*lieu* ⟨B⟩); interconnexion, (*enchaînement* ⟨R, B⟩); coherence ⟨WH⟩, coherency; continuity ⟨Gomperz trln of Mill, quoted in LU, II. Unters.; MS⟩, (*suite* ⟨B⟩); (physical:) cohesion ⟨WH 1, MS⟩; (*rapport* ⟨R⟩). If possible, save "relation" ⟨WH⟩ for "Beziehung" ⟨q.v.⟩, "Bezug", "Relation" ⟨q.v.⟩, and "Verhältnis" ⟨q.v.⟩.
2. nexus ⟨K⟩, (coherent) complex, configuration, coherent whole, (*ensemble* ⟨B⟩), (*groupe de questions* ⟨B⟩), (*système* ⟨R⟩); (chiefly literary:) context, (*contexte* ⟨R⟩), (*cadre* ⟨B⟩). Not "ensemble" ⟨L⟩ and not "totality" ⟨L⟩. Save "system" ⟨BG⟩ for "System". Cf. **Begründungszusammenhang, Bewusstseinszusammenhang, Beziehung, Bezug, Einfühlungszusammenhang, Einheitszusammenhang, Einordnung, Erfahrungszusammenhang, Erfüllungszusammenhang, Erlebniszusammenhang, Erscheinungszusammenhang, Gestalt, Ineinander, Komplexion, Motivationszusammenhang, Motivierungszusammenhang, Notwendigkeitszusammenhang, Redezusammenhang, Satzzusammenhang, Tatsachenzusammenhang, Urteilszusammenhang, Verbindung, Verknüpfung, Wahrnehmungszusammenhang, Wahrscheinlichkeits-**

zusammenhang, Wesenszusammenhang, Zweckzusammenhang. | ausser —, not connected. Not "disconnected" ⟨BG⟩. | logische ∼e, logical interconnexions. | sachlicher —, (objective) connexion between (*or* among) affairs (*or* affair-complexes), materially coherent whole, (*ensemble cohérent de choses* ⟨B⟩). Cf. **sachlich, Sachverhalt.** | ∼e der Erfahrung, coherencies of experience, (*enchaînements de l'expérience* ⟨R⟩). Not "connexions of experience" ⟨BG⟩.

zusammenhängen, to be connected ⟨WH, MS, L⟩, (*être en connexion* ⟨B⟩); to hang together ⟨WH 1, MS 1⟩, to cohere ⟨WH, MS⟩. | gegenständlich —, to hang together by virtue of their objects, (*être en connexion objective* ⟨B⟩). | mit etwas —, to be connected with something ⟨L⟩, (*se trouver en liaison avec quelque chose* ⟨B⟩).

zusammenhängend, connected, (*connexe* ⟨B⟩), (*en liaison* ⟨B⟩); interconnected, (*qui s'enchaîne* ⟨B⟩); coherent, (*cohérent* ⟨R⟩), cohering, cohesive, (*qui a une cohésion* ⟨B⟩); (related). | — mit, connected with, tied up with.

zusammenhangslos, unconnected, (*incohérent* ⟨B⟩).

zusammenschliessen, | sich — zu, to join together (*or* to combine) to make (up), (*s'enchaîner ensemble pour former* ⟨B⟩), (*s'agréger* ⟨R⟩), (*se résumer dans* ⟨R⟩), (*se rattacher à* ⟨B⟩).

Zusammenseiendes, what exists together. Cf. **Seiendes** (*sub* seiend).

Zusammensetzung, composition ⟨WH 1, MS⟩, (*composition* ⟨B⟩), (*compositio* ⟨K⟩); compound ⟨WH, MS⟩, (*assemblage* ⟨B⟩); compositeness. Cf. **Urteilszusammensetzung, zusammengesetzt.**

zusammenstimmend, concordant, (*harmonique* ⟨B⟩). Cf. **Unstimmigkeit.**

Zuschauer, onlooker. | unbeteiligter —, non-participant onlooker.

zuschreiben, to ascribe ⟨WH, MS⟩, (*at-*

tribuer ⟨B⟩); to take to be an intrinsic part of. Cf. **zumessen, zurechnen**.
zusprechen, to affirm, to predicate, to award. Cf. **absprechen, Bejahung, prädizieren**.
Zustand, state ⟨MS 1, WH 2, BG⟩, (*état* ⟨R⟩), state or condition, (*habitus* ⟨K⟩). Cf. **Beschaffenheit, Erlebnissituation, Habitualität, Habitus, Sachlage, Zuständlichkeit**.
zustande, | — kommen, to come about ⟨WH 1, MS 1⟩, to come into being, (*se réaliser* ⟨B⟩). Cf. **werden**. **| ~- bringen**, to bring about ⟨WH, MS⟩, to effect, (*réaliser* ⟨B⟩). Cf. **herstellen, leisten, vollziehen, wirken**.
Zuständlichkeit, set (*or* sequence) of states. Cf. **Zustand**.
Zustimmung, assent ⟨WH 1, MS⟩, (*assentiment* ⟨R, B⟩).
zustreben, | der Idee —, to approach the idea, (*tendre vers l'idée* ⟨B⟩). Cf. (**streben nach**) (*sub* **streben**).
zuwachsen, to accrue ⟨WH, MS, BG⟩, (*échoir* ⟨R, B⟩), (*faire apparition* ⟨B⟩). Cf. **erwachsen**.
zuwenden, | sich —, to turn to (*or* towards ⟨WH 1, MS 1⟩), (*se tourner* ⟨R, B⟩), to address oneself (to), (*s'occuper* (*de*) ⟨R⟩).
Zuwendung, advertence, turning towards ⟨BG⟩; (*conversion* ⟨R⟩). Not "bestowing" ⟨BG⟩; and not "tendencies to turn toward" ⟨BG⟩, not "orientation" ⟨BG⟩. Cf. **Anwendung, Wendung, Zugewendetsein**.
zwar, (sometimes:) more particularly.
Zweck, end ⟨Bn, WH, MS⟩, (*fin* ⟨B⟩), (*finis* ⟨Baumgarten⟩), (*but* ⟨B⟩), purpose ⟨WH, MS⟩, (*dessein* ⟨B⟩), (pl:) (*propos* ⟨R⟩). Not "design" ⟨Bn, WH, MS⟩; not "interest" ⟨BG⟩. Save "aim" ⟨WH 1, MS, L⟩ for "Absicht" ⟨q.v.⟩.
Zweckidee, final idea, (*idée-fin* ⟨PL⟩),

goal idea, (*idée téléologique* ⟨B⟩). Cf. **Zielidee**.
zwecklos, pointless, (*gratuit* ⟨B⟩).
Zweckmässigkeit, fitness ⟨Bn, WH, MS⟩ to an end (*or* a purpose); expediency ⟨WH, MS⟩. Cf. **Angemessenheit**.
Zwecksetzen, purposing, setting an end. Cf. **Absehen, Setzen**.
Zwecksetzung, (process of) setting an end. Cf. **Mittelsetzung, Setzung**.
Zwecksinn, final sense, (*sens final* ⟨PL⟩), (*sens téléologique* ⟨B⟩).
zwecktätig ⟨adj.⟩, purposefully active. Cf. **tätig**.
zwecktätig ⟨adv.⟩, by purposeful action, (*dans une activité téléologique* ⟨B⟩).
Zweckzusammenhang, complex of ends. Cf. **Zusammenhang**.
Zweifältigkeit, duality, (*caractère double* ⟨B⟩).
zweifelhaft, doubtful ⟨WH 1, MS 1, BG⟩, dubious ⟨WH 2, MS 2⟩, (*douteux* ⟨R⟩), uncertain ⟨WH, MS⟩, suspicious ⟨WH⟩. Save "questionable" ⟨WH 3, MS 3⟩ for "fraglich" ⟨q.v.⟩. Cf. **unzweifelhaft**.
Zweifelhaftigkeit, (abstract:) doubtfulness ⟨MS 1⟩, (concrete:) dubiosity.
zweifellos ⟨adj.⟩, doubtless ⟨WH 1, MS 1⟩.
zweifellos ⟨adv.⟩, without doubt, indubitably, (*indubitablement* ⟨B⟩).
Zweifelsentscheidung, settlement (*or* settling) of a doubt. Cf. **Entscheidbarkeit**.
zweiseitig ⟨adj.⟩, two-sided ⟨WH 1, MS 1⟩, (*à double face* ⟨B⟩), dual.
zweiseitig ⟨adv.⟩, two-sidedly, bilaterally, (in both directions ⟨BG⟩), (*dans les deux sens* ⟨R⟩).
zweiseitig-einheitlich ⟨adj.⟩, bilateral-unitary, (*unitaire mais à double face* ⟨B⟩). Cf. **einheitlich**.
Zweiseitigkeit, (*bilatéralité* ⟨de M⟩).

NOTES

NOTES

NOTES

NOTES

NOTES